# ARCO'S COMPLETE
# WOOD-WORKING
## HANDBOOK

# ARCO'S COMPLETE
# WOOD-WORKING
## HANDBOOK

## J. T. ADAMS

**ARCO PUBLISHING, INC.**
219 PARK AVENUE SOUTH, NEW YORK, N.Y. 10003

Published by Arco Publishing, Inc.
219 Park Avenue South, New York, N.Y. 10003

Copyright ©1981 by Arco Publishing, Inc.

**Library of Congress Cataloging in Publication Data**

Adams, Jeannette T
  Arco's complete woodworking handbook.

  Published in 1975 under title: Arco's new
complete woodworking handbook.
  Includes index.
  1. Woodwork.  I. Title.  II. Title:
Complete woodworking handbook.
TT180.A17    1980    684'.08  80-18786
ISBN 0-668-04829-8

Printed in the United States of America

# Table of Contents

# Section IV—Exterior Projects

# Section V—Interior Projects

# Section VI—Paints and Painting

# Section VII—Home Improvements

# Acknowledgments

THE AUTHOR desires to acknowledge, with thanks, the assistance of the following national organizations and branches of the government that have co-operated in the production of this book:

American Brush Co., American Institute of Timber Construction, American Plywood Association, American Society for Testing Materials, American Steel & Wire Co., Armstrong Cork Co., Atlas Press Co., Black & Decker Mfg. Co., California Redwood Association, Carborundum Co., Cleveland Twist Drill Co., Delta Power Tool Division—Rockwell Manufacturing Co., DeVilbiss Co., Devoe & Raynolds Co., DeWalt Division—American Machine and Foundry Co., Douglas Fir Plywood Association, E.I. duPont de Nemours & Co., Franklin Glue Co., Henry Disston & Sons, Hilti Fastening Systems, Insulation Board Institute, Keuffel and Esser Co., Mall, National Bureau of Standards, National Lumber Manufacturers Association, National Paint, Varnish and Lacquer Association, National Retail Lumber Dealers Association, Nicholson File Co., Northern Hemlock & Hardwood Manufacturers Association, Northern Pine Manufacturers Association, Oliver Machine Co., Pittsburgh Plate Glass Co.—Brush Division, Porter-Cable, S.C. Johnson & Son, Sherwin-Williams Co., South Bend Lathe Works, Southern Pine Association, Stanley Works, United States Department of Agriculture, United States Department of the Army, United States Department of Commerce, U.S. Forest Service—Forest Products Laboratory, United States Department of the Navy, United States Plywood Corp., United States Steel Corp., University of Wisconsin, Western Pine Association, and Yale & Towne Manufacturing Co.

# Preface to the
# Revised Edition

CRAFTSMANSHIP IN WOODWORKING is a combination of knowledge on how to use tools and of hand-skill in the use of these tools. Unfortunately there is no magic shortcut to craftsmanship. No book could possibly give you all the tricks of the trade or the skill of the old master craftsman. These must be learned from practice, familiarity with the tools themselves, and through the sort of trial and error that will teach you the best way of handling any particular task.

On the other hand, the COMPLETE WOODWORKING HANDBOOK can supply the all-important source of knowledge for the mastery of basic principles and later on for the broadening of the skills, techniques, and procedures upon which master craftsmanship is built. It is offered as a guide and source of basic information for the beginner, apprentice, homeowner, builder, carpenter, and all others working with wood.

In addition to the chapters on woodworking hand tools and how to use them; power tools; floor framing; exterior wood coverings; porches and garages; exterior frames, windows, and doors; construction of stairs; basement rooms; interior wall and ceiling finish; floor coverings; thermal insulation, vapor barriers, and sound absorption; and ventilation; you will find new chapters covering the following:

Equipment for holding work; methods of fastening; lumber; woodworking joints and splices; methods of frame construction;

methods of reducing building costs; building layout, tools and materials; foundation construction; wall framing; framing layout and erection; wall sheathing; forms for concrete; roofing; reroofing; window and door screens, and hood or canopy; interior doors and trim; fundamental purposes of painting, paints, and equipment; surface preparation for painting; paint mixing and conditioning, methods of applying paint, and colors; deterioration of paint, painting safety, and wood preservatives; and protection against decay and termites.

The following appendices have been added to the book—a glossary of terms; standard lumber abbreviations; woodworking symbols; and the metric system. You will also find a comprehensive index.

If the COMPLETE WOODWORKING HANDBOOK succeeds in clearing up some of the problems which seem confusing to the woodworker; if it instills in him or her some of the spirit and pride of accomplishment of the old master craftsman; if it creates a desire to expand the worker's knowledge of woodworking to the broad horizons available; then it will have accomplished its purpose.

J.T.A.

# ARCO'S COMPLETE
# WOOD-
# WORKING
# HANDBOOK

# Woodworking Tools and Equipment

Hand tools, equipment for holding work, power tools, and fasteners; their proper uses and proper safety methods.

## CHAPTER 1

# Woodworking Hand Tools and How To Use Them

## WOODWORKING HAMMERS

The essential parts of a *claw* hammer, the most commonly used woodworking hammer, are shown in Fig. 1. Other types illustrated are the *ripping, upholsterer's,* and *tack* hammers. Hammer sizes are determined by the weight of the head, which ranges from 5 to 28 oz. The heavier hammers are for driving larger nails into soft material or ordinary nails into harder wood. For general use, a 16-oz. hammer is recommended.

Smooth-face hammers are either plain or bell-face. The *bell-face* type is slightly more convex than the *plain.* While the novice cannot drive a nail as straight and as easily with a bell-face hammer, this type is more frequently used because, with a little experience, a nail can be driven flush and sometimes even below the surface of the work without leaving any hammer marks.

**Correct method of using a hammer.** *Driving nails*—The effectiveness of a hammer is dependent on its weight and the manner in which the blow is struck. To use a hammer correctly, grip it firmly in the right hand, close to the end of handle (Fig. 1). Always strike with a free arm movement. Grasp the nail with the thumb and forefinger of the other hand and place it exactly at the point where it is to be driven. Unless the nail is to be driven at an angle, it should be held perpendicular to the surface of the work. To set the nail, center the face of the hammer on the head of the nail and give it several light taps before removing the fingers. Then drive the nail in as far as desired with a few firm

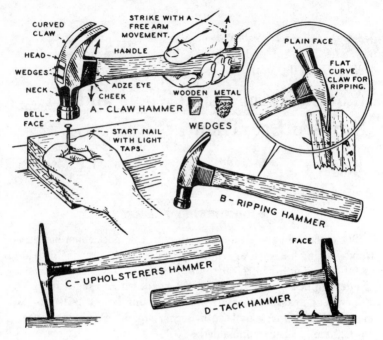

**Fig. 1.**

blows, using the center of the hammer face. Nails that do not go in straight or bend shoould be drawn out and thrown away. If, after several attempts, the nail continues to bend or go in crooked, the work should be investigated. If there is a knot or some other obstruction, drill a small hole through the obstruction and then drive the nail through.

*Pulling out nails*—When nails are pulled out with the claw end of a hammer, the head of the nail should clear the surface of the work sufficiently to permit the claws to grip it. To prevent marring the work and to secure extra and safe leverage, place a small block of wood under the head of the hammer as shown in Fig. 2. Be careful to place the block of wood in the correct position, that is, against the nail, to avoid enlarging the hole from which the nail is pulled.

*Clinching nails*—For added holding power, nails are sometimes *clinched.* The nails used for clinching must be long enough to penetrate the wood so that at least an inch and a half of the point protrudes from the underside. The protruding point is then bent over in direct line with the grain of the wood and hammered flat. When clinching nails, rest the work on a solid surface and be careful to avoid splitting the wood (Fig. 2).

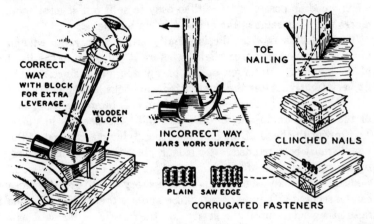

CORRECT WAY WITH BLOCK FOR EXTRA LEVERAGE.

WOODEN BLOCK

INCORRECT WAY MARS WORK SURFACE.

TOE NAILING

CLINCHED NAILS

PLAIN   SAW EDGE

CORRUGATED FASTENERS

**Fig. 2.**

*Toenailing*—Driving nails obliquely is called *toenailing*. This type of nailing is employed when the end of one piece of wood is fastened to the side of another, as shown in Fig. 2.

*Driving corrugated fasteners*—Corrugated fasteners, as shown in Fig. 2, are often called *wiggle nails*. They are used to a large extent in the making of screens and picture frames and for similar purposes. They are procurable with either a plain or saw edge. The *plain-edged* fastener is used for hard wood; the *saw-edged* type for soft wood. When driving corrugated fasteners, use a medium-weight hammer. Strike evenly distributed light blows. It is important that the lumber being fastened together rest on a solid surface while the work is being done.

*Ripping*—To rip woodwork apart, insert the claw part of a *ripping* hammer into a crack as near to a nail as possible. Use a quick, jolting movement to loosen each nail. Pull out the nails as previously described. Then rip out the boards or woodwork as required (Fig. 1).

*Replacing a broken hammer handle*—Machine-made hickory handles in various sizes can be secured at most hardware stores. The portion of the broken handle that remains in the hammer head must be removed. The simplest and most effective method of doing this is to drill through it with a twist drill to remove as much wood as possible. It is then easy to split out several small pieces and thus remove the old wedged-in handle.

The end of a new handle is usually larger than required and must be scraped or pared slightly before it will fit into the head of the hammer. However, do not pare it too much, since it must fit very tightly. After the small fitted end of the handle is inserted into the opening in the head of the hammer, tamp the other end of the handle against a solid surface until the head is in place. To prevent the head of the hammer from flying off, the end of the handle must be expanded, after it is in place in the hammer head, by inserting several wooden or metal wedges (Fig. 1). Wooden wedges can be made of either maple or hickory wood. Metal wedges can be secured at any hardware store and are preferable. Do not insert the wedges until the head is on the handle as far as it can go. When using wooden wedges, make a saw cut about as long as the wedge in the end of the handle before inserting it into the head of the hammer. Saw cuts are not necessary when using metal wedges.

## HANDSAWS

The essential parts of a handsaw are shown in Fig. 3.

There are many types and sizes of handsaws. The ripsaw and the crosscut saw are most commonly used.

The *ripsaw* is designed specifically for cutting with the grain (Fig. 3). The teeth of the ripsaw are set alternately, that is, one tooth is bent slightly to the left and the next one to the right for the entire length of the saw to give the proper clearance when cutting through the work. A good ripsaw usually has five and one-half points to every inch, with each tooth acting like a vertical chisel, chipping out a small portion of the wood from the *kerf*, or cut.

*Crosscut* saws are designed to cut against, or across, the grain of the wood. The teeth of a crosscut saw are ground to a *true taper* for the additional clearance required when cutting across the grain. The front faces of the teeth have an angle of 15°, and the backs have an angle of 45°. The upper halves of the teeth are set alternately to the right and to the left to insure proper clearance. The teeth of a crosscut saw have an action similar to that of a chisel (Fig. 3).

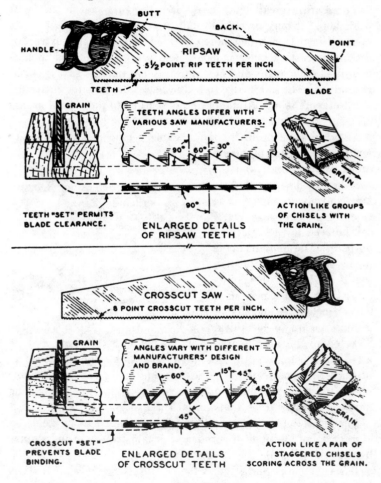

Fig. 3.

The *backsaw* is useful for all types of cabinetwork. Its fine teeth and stiff back make possible the smooth, accurate cutting necessary for making joints. It is the ideal saw to use for cutting light stock, such as moldings and screen and picture frames. Backsaws are available in 8″, 10″, 12″, 14″, and 16″ lengths, with from 12 to 16 points to the inch. The 12″ length, with 14 points to the inch, is the most popular size (Fig. 4).

There are a great many uses for a *compass saw* in the home workshop. It may be used for cutting curves and circles and for starting a cut from a hole bored in wood (Fig. 5). It is extremely useful for cutting holes in board and plaster walls and in floor boards to receive gas or water pipes. The compass saw is taper-ground from the tooth edge to a thin back, allowing for clearance. It also tapers to a sharp point and is toothed to the point for easy access to holes and for cutting sharp curves.

An ideal type is an interchangeable compass saw. Different lengths and types of blades are available for it and the handle can be adjusted to any convenient angle. The three blades shown in Fig. 5 can be used for a variety of purposes. The *compass* blade in the center of the illustration is 14″ long, with 8 points to the inch, and can be used for cutting curves and shapes in material up to ⅜″ thick.

**Fig. 4.** Backsaw.

**Fig. 5.** Compass saw.

The top blade, known as a *pruning* blade, is 16″ long and, in addition to being used for pruning trees, can also be employed as a general-purpose saw. The other blade in the set is a *keyhole* blade, 10″ long, 10 points to the inch. It can be used for cutting keyholes, sharp curves, and similar small work.

The *keyhole saw* is a special-purpose saw for cutting keyholes and for doing all kinds of cutout pattern, or fretwork, and similar light work. (Fig. 6).

The *coping* saw is designed for cutting curves (Fig. 7). It is also used for shaping the ends of molding, for scrollwork, and

**Fig. 6.** Keyhole saw.

similar light work on thin wood or plastic. It has very narrow blades, only ⅛″ wide, fitted at each end with a pin that is inserted in a stretcher at each end of the frame. A square nut forced into the handle engages the threaded end of the stretcher. By turning the handle, the blade is tautened. The blade, when stretched tight in the frame, may be turned as required for cutting sharp angles. The frame of a coping saw should be made of good steel. It is usually ⅜″ wide, ³⁄₁₆″ thick, and 4½″ deep from the tooth edge to the inside of the back. The blades of a coping saw should be made of good spring steel ⅛″ wide, 17 points to the inch, and 6⁷⁄₁₆″ in length from pin to pin.

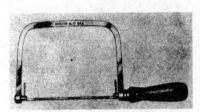

**Fig. 7.** Coping saw.

**Using a handsaw.** Each type of saw is designed for a specific purpose and should be used for that purpose only. If you value your tools and the material on which you are working, never use a crosscut saw for work that requires a ripsaw, or vice versa. Ripsaws are specifically designed to cut with the grain of the wood. This is called *ripping*. Crosscut saws are designed for *crosscutting* (sawing against the grain).

To hold a saw properly, grasp the handle firmly with the right hand, with the thumb and index finger touching the sides of the handle (Fig. 8). This grip makes it easy to guide the direction of the saw cut. Always start a saw cut with an upward stroke, using the thumb of the left hand to guide the saw. Never under any circumstances start a saw cut with a downstroke. Draw the saw slowly upward several times at the point where the cut is to be made (Fig. 8). Do this very slowly or your saw will jump; instead of a well-cut piece of lumber you will have a badly cut thumb. When the line of cut has been started properly, proceed to cut on the downstroke.

For ripping, use a ripsaw to permit long, easy strokes. Cutting with just a few inches of blade in the middle of the saw usually makes it difficult to keep the line of cut straight. When ripping lumber, support the work on sawhorses, and start the cut by using the finer teeth at the end of the blade. If the work cannot be supported on sawhorses, place it in a vise. A cutting angle of 60°

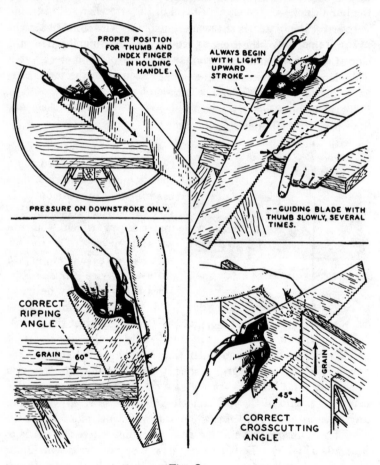

Fig. 8.

between the edge of the saw and the face of the work gives best results (Fig. 8).

To begin a crosscut, rest the blade on the waste side of the line of cut, support the side of the blade with the thumb, and draw the saw upward a few times until a slight groove appears (Fig. 8).

When either crosscutting or ripping, it is good practice to cut on the outer, or waste, side of a line; do not attempt to saw directly on the line.

In crosscutting, 45° is the proper angle to maintain between the saw and the face of the work. Extending the forefinger along the side of the handle aids considerably in guiding the blade (Fig. 8). Take long, easy strokes to utilize a maximum of the saw's cutting edge. Always keep saw square with surface of wood (Fig. 9).

When the cut is nearly completed, support the piece to prevent the wood from splintering on the underside. Never twist the piece off with the saw blade or in any other way; cut right through to the end, using light final strokes to avoid splitting.

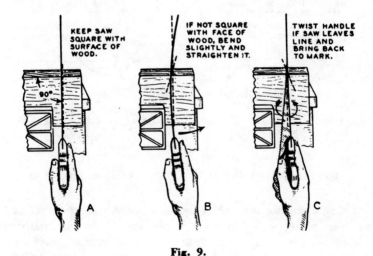

Fig. 9.

**Using a backsaw.** When using a backsaw in a miter box, be sure that the work lines up with the slots in the box. Hold the

**Fig. 10.**  Using a backsaw in a miter box.

work against the back of the box (Fig. 10). Start the cut carefully with a backstroke, holding the handle of the saw slightly upward. As the cutting proceeds, level the saw gradually and continue cutting with the blade horizontal. Hold the saw firmly for clean, straight, accurate cutting.

If a miter box is not used, it is advisable to support the work with a bench hook. For long material, two bench hooks are necessary. A bench hook and its use is shown in Figs. 11 and 12.

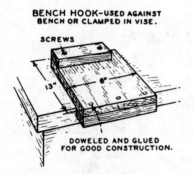

**Fig. 11.**  Bench hook.

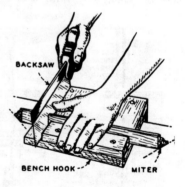

**Fig. 12.**  Using bench hook.

**Using a coping saw.**  A *coping* saw is used to cut curves and intricate patterns in thin wood or plastic. The correct position for use is shown in Fig. 13. A coping saw is generally used with a saddle to support the work. The *saddle* consists of a board cut with a V-notch, about 3″ wide and 3½″ deep, attached to a support. Hold the blade so that it moves vertically. Cutting strokes should be as long as possible to avoid overheating the blade. In cutting scrollwork, furniture overlay, and similar articles, the piece marked with the design to be cut out is held on the saddle and shifted so that the saw can cut along the curves as it progresses. To avoid breakage of blades, change the angle of the blade in the frame when making sharp turns.

**Setting and sharpening a handsaw.** A good saw is a fine tool and will give a lifetime of service if properly handled. The saw teeth will require setting and

**Fig. 13.** Coping saw.

sharpening from time to time. This may seem to be an involved operation, but if directions are followed carefully, it is not difficult.

A special *saw clamp* (Fig. 14) and several files are all the equipment needed. The following table indicates the file to be used.

SAW CLAMP FOR FILING AND TEETH "SET"

FIRST "SET" OR BEND EVERY OTHER TOOTH ON ONE SIDE, THEN REVERSING SAW IN SAW CLAMP REPEAT "SET" FOR OPPOSITE SIDE.

HAND SAWSET

**Fig. 14.**

| Points to the Inch | File to Be Used |
|---|---|
| 4½, 5, 6 | 7″ slim taper |
| 7, 8 | 6″ slim taper |
| 9, 10 | 5″ to 5½″ slim taper |
| 11, 12, 13, 14, 15 | 4½″ slim taper |
| 16 or more | 4½″ or 5″ superfine, No. 2 cut |
| For jointing teeth | 8″ or 10″ mill bastard |

Examine the teeth of the saw to see if they are uniform in size and shape and are properly set. A good saw will not need resetting of the teeth every time it is sharpened. If the teeth are touched up occasionally with a file of the proper size, they will cut longer and better and retain sufficient set to enable the saw to clear itself. The proper amount of set is shown in Fig. 15.

Before proceeding to set and sharpen a handsaw, study the shape of the teeth. The teeth of saws for crosscutting and for ripping should be similar to those shown at *A* and *B* in Fig. 15. A saw cannot do a good cutting job unless the teeth are even and properly shaped. If the teeth are found to be uneven, it is necessary to joint and file them, using the following procedure.

**Jointing handsaw teeth.** *Jointing*, or filing, the teeth to the same shape and height is necessary when they are uneven or incorrectly shaped or when the tooth edges are not straight, or slightly breasted. Unless the teeth are regular in size and shape it is wasted effort to set and file a saw.

To joint a saw, place it in a saw clamp, with the handle of the saw to the right (*C* and *G*, Fig. 15). Lay a mill file, of the proper size, flat lengthwise on the teeth. Pass it lightly back and forth across the tips of all the teeth, for the full length of the blade. If the teeth are very uneven, it is better not to make all of them the same height the first time they are jointed. Joint only the highest teeth first, then shape the teeth that have been jointed. Proceed by jointing the teeth a second time, passing the file along the tops of all the teeth until every tooth is touched by the file. Never allow the file to tip to one side or the other—always file flat. The use of a handsaw jointer is shown at *E*, Fig. 15.

**Shaping handsaw teeth.** After jointing, proceed with *shaping* the teeth. All the teeth must be filed to the correct shape, with all the gullets of equal depth (Fig. 15). The fronts and backs must have the proper shape and angle. The teeth must be uniform in size, disregarding the bevel, which will be taken care of later. To bring the gullets down to equal depth, place the file well into each gullet and file straight across the saw at right angles to the blade (*D*, Fig. 15). Never hold the file at any other angle during this operation. If the teeth are of unequal size, file in turn the ones with the largest tops until the file reaches the center of the

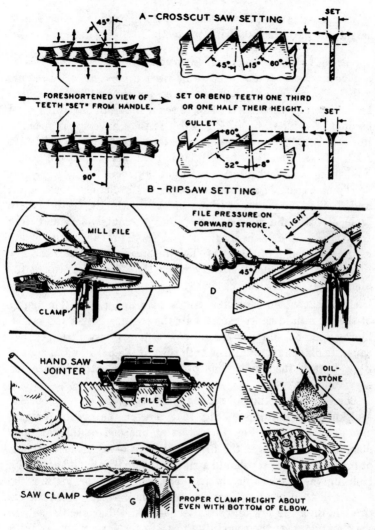

**A - CROSSCUT SAW SETTING**

45°

SET

t

FORESHORTENED VIEW OF TEETH "SET" FROM HANDLE.

45° 15° 60°

SET OR BEND TEETH ONE THIRD OR ONE HALF THEIR HEIGHT.

90°

GULLET

60°

SET

52° 8°

**B - RIPSAW SETTING**

MILL FILE

FILE PRESSURE ON FORWARD STROKE.

LIGHT

45°

CLAMP    C

D

HAND SAW JOINTER

E

FILE

OIL-STONE

F

SAW CLAMP

G

PROPER CLAMP HEIGHT ABOUT EVEN WITH BOTTOM OF ELBOW.

**Fig. 15.**

flat top made by jointing; then move the file to the next gullet. File until the rest of the top disappears and the tooth has been brought up to a point. Do not attempt to bevel any of the teeth at this time.

After all the teeth have been properly shaped and are even in height, the next step is setting the teeth.

**Setting handsaw teeth.** As mentioned previously, the teeth of a good handsaw do not need to be reset every time they require a little sharpening. If it is not necessary to joint and shape the teeth, carefully examine the saw to see if the teeth have the proper amount of *set* (*A* and *B*, Fig. 15). If they have the proper set, the saw is ready for filing; if not, they should be set. Always set the teeth after they have been jointed and shaped but before final filing, to avoid injury to the cutting edges.

The operation of setting saw teeth has a distinct purpose. *A* and *B*, Fig. 15, show end views of saw teeth; the teeth of both crosscut saws and ripsaws are sprung alternately left and right (not more than half the length of each tooth) for the entire length of the tooth edge of the saw. This arrangement enables the saw to cut a kerf, or path, slightly wider than the thickness of the blade itself, giving the necessary clearance and preventing any friction that would cause the saw to bind in the cut. The depth of the set should never exceed half the tooth, whether the saw is fine or coarse. A taper-ground saw requires very little set, because its blade tapers thinner both toward the back and along the back toward the point, thus providing sufficient clearance for easy running.

The simplest method of setting a saw is by the use of a special tool known as a *saw set* (Fig. 16). Fasten the saw in the saw clamp, as shown in Fig. 14. Start at one end of the saw and place the saw set over the first tooth bent away from you. The plunger in the saw set should strike the tooth firmly and squarely. Holding the saw set firmly in place, compress the handle: the tooth will then bend against the saw clamp. Work across the entire length of the saw and set alternate teeth. Reverse the saw in the clamp and set the remaining teeth in the same manner. With the saw still in the clamp, joint the teeth by lightly rubbing a file lengthwise over them until they all have flat tops, which will provide a proper guide for filing.

Extreme care must be taken to see that the set is even and regular. It must be the same width from end to end of the blade and the same width on both sides of the blade, otherwise the saw will run out of line and cuts made with it will not be true. After the saw has been properly set, the next step is to file the teeth.

**Filing handsaw teeth.** The type of file to use for filing the teeth is determined by the number of tooth points to the inch. For a crosscut saw, measure one inch from the point of any tooth. For a ripsaw

**Fig. 16.** Saw set.

having 5½ or fewer points to the inch, the teeth near the point of the blade are finer than the rest; therefore measure the regular-size teeth at the butt of the blade. For the best working position, align the top of the clamp with the elbow. Place the saw in the clamp with its handle at the right. Allow the bottom gullets to protrude ⅛″ above the jaws of the clamp, otherwise the file will chatter or screech.

**Filing a crosscut saw.** To file a crosscut saw, stand at the first position shown in Fig. 17. Start at the point and pick out the first tooth that is set toward you. Hold the file in the position shown in the illustration. Place the file in the gullet to the left of the tooth, holding it directly across the blade. Swing the file handle left to the correct angle, as shown in Fig. 17. Hold the file level and maintain this angle; never allow it to tip either upward or downward. Be certain at all times that the file is set well down into the gullet. Let it find its own bearing against the teeth it touches. For guidance in filing, study and duplicate the shape and bevel of some of the least-used teeth, those near the handle end.

File on the push stroke only: the back of the left tooth and the front of the right tooth are thus filed simultaneously. File the teeth until half of the flat tops previously made on them are cut away; then lift the file from the gullet. Skip the next gullet to the right and place the file in the second gullet toward the handle.

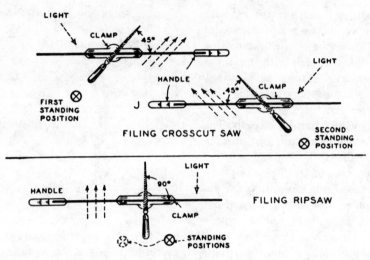

**Fig. 17.**

Repeat the filing operation as previously described, filing at the same angle as for the first set of two teeth. Proceed by placing the file in every second gullet until the handle end of the saw has been reached.

For the second position, turn the saw around in the clamp with the handle to the left. Take the position shown in Fig. 17 and place the file in the gullet to the right of the first tooth set toward you. This is the first of the gullets skipped when the reverse side of the saw was filed. Now turn the file handle to the desired angle toward the right. Proceed to file until the other half of the flat top made on each tooth as a guide has been cut away and the tooth is sharpened to a point. Continue by placing the file in every second gullet until the handle of the saw is reached.

Be sure that in the final sharpening all the teeth are of the same size and height, otherwise the saw will not cut satisfactorily. When teeth are of uneven sizes, stress is placed on the larger or higher teeth, thus causing the saw to jump or bind in the kerf.

**Filing a ripsaw.** The procedure for filing ripsaws is similar to that for crosscut saws, with a single exception (Fig. 17). Ripsaws are filed with the file held straight across the saw at a right angle to the blade. Place the file in the gullet so as to give the front of each tooth an angle of 8° and the back an angle of 52°. Place the saw in the clamp with the handle toward the right. Place the file in the gullet to the left of the first tooth set toward you. Continue by placing the file in every second gullet and filing straight across. When the handle of the saw is reached, turn the saw around in the clamp. Start at the point again, placing the file in the first gullet that was previously skipped when filing from the other side. Continue to file in every second gullet to the handle end of the saw.

One final precaution: never try to avoid reversing the saw in the clamp or attempt to file all the teeth from the same side of the blade. This procedure is certain to make the saw run to one side.

**Angle and bevel of teeth.** The angle of the teeth in crosscut saws is of great importance. Imagine that Fig. 18 is a board, across which a deep mark with the point of a knife is to be made. If the knife is held nearly perpendicular, as at *B*, it will pull harder and will not cut so smoothly as when it is inclined

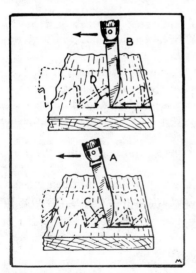

**Fig. 18.** Shapes and angles of saw teeth.

forward, as at *A*. It follows, then, that the cutting edge of the crosscut saw should be at an acute angle, as at *C*, rather than perpendicular, as at *D*.

The angles of 15° front and 15° back for crosscut saws, and 8° front and 52° back for ripsaws, as set at the factory, prove most satisfactory for general use. When a saw has less angle at the front of the teeth than specified above, it is said to have more *hook* or *pitch*. If too much hook is given to the teeth, the saw often takes hold too keenly, causing it to "hand up" or stick suddenly in the cut, thus kinking the blade. When there is too much set, the teeth may be broken, as the resulting strain is out of proportion to the strength of the blade.

In filing saws for crosscutting, the file is held at an angle; therefore the teeth are given an angle. This angle on the front and back of the teeth is called *bevel.*

**How to bevel teeth.** The proper amount of bevel to give the teeth is important. If there is too much bevel, the points of the teeth will score so deeply that the wood fibers severed from the stock will not clear and will have to be removed with a file or rasp. In Fig. 19, *B* shows a tooth (enlarged) of a crosscut saw with the same amount of bevel front and back; suitable for softwoods where rapid work is required.

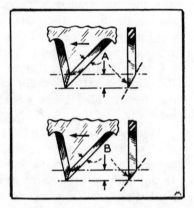

**Fig. 19.** Bevel of teeth.

*A*, in Fig. 19, shows a tooth (enlarged) of a saw suitable for medium hardwoods. It has less bevel on the back, which gives a shorter bevel to the point, as at *B*.

These illustrations show that the bevel on the front of the teeth is about the same, but the bevel of the point (looking lengthwise along the blade) is quite different, depending on the difference in the angles of the backs of the teeth. Experience will indicate what bevel is best.

For the beginner, the instructions given under Filing the Teeth should be followed carefully.

**Side-dressing saws.** After jointing, setting, and filing the saw, side-dress it by laying it on a flat surface and lightly rubbing the sides of the teeth with an oilstone as shown in *F*, Fig. 15.

## SCREWDRIVERS

**Types of screwdrivers.** There are many sizes and several types of screwdrivers. The size is always given by the length of the blade: a 6″ screwdriver has a 6″ blade, and so on. Narrow-tipped blades are designed for small screws, and blades with larger tips for heavier screws. The following types are in general use: common screwdriver, ratchet, spiral ratchet, offset, Phillips.

*Common screwdriver*—The common screwdriver is available in many sizes, each for a specific size of screw. The various parts of a common screwdriver are shown in Fig. 20.

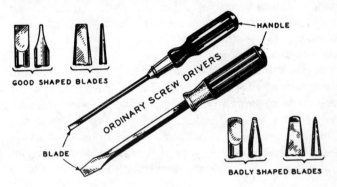

Fig. 20.

*Ratchet and spiral ratchet screwdrivers*—Two variations of the common screwdriver are shown in Fig. 21. They are the ratchet

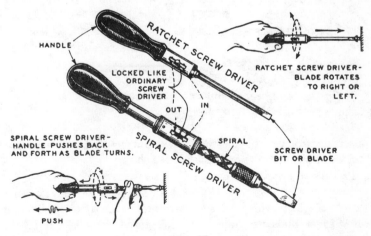

Fig. 21.

and the spiral ratchet types. Similar in operation to the common screwdriver, the ratchet type drives screws in much faster and works semiautomatically. Blades of various sizes can be secured for both types of ratchet screwdriver, and both types can be set for driving screws in or extracting them. The handle of the ratchet screwdriver turns back and forth in the direction set.

The spiral ratchet screwdriver operates even faster than the ratchet. It can be set for either in or out. To drive the screw, set the blade in the screw slot and push on the handle, steadying the blade with the other hand. The blade makes several turns for each push.

*Offset screwdriver*—Offset screwdrivers are designed for driving screws located where there is insufficient space to use the conventional type of screwdriver (Fig. 22). The offset screwdriver is made from a piece of either round or octagonal steel with two blades at right angles to one another and to the shaft at opposite ends. When screws have to be driven in or extracted in inaccessible places, it is sometimes necessary to use both ends of the

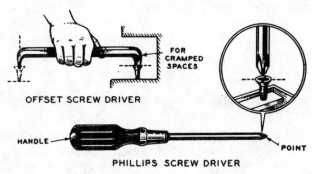

FOR CRAMPED SPACES

OFFSET SCREW DRIVER

HANDLE

POINT

PHILLIPS SCREW DRIVER

**Fig. 22.**

offset screwdriver, turning the screw a short distance with one end and then with the other.

*Phillips screwdriver*—The Phillips screwdriver is used only for driving the Phillips screw (Fig. 22). Phillips screws have a head with two V-slots which cross at the center. The tip of the Phillips screwdriver blade is shaped like a pointed or beveled cross to fit into these slots. To keep the blade in the cross slots of the screw more downward pressure is used. Phillips screws are used to a great extent in radio sets, on moldings, the trim of automobiles, and furniture and cabinetwork. This type of screwdriver cannot slip out of the slot or otherwise damage expensive finishes.

**Correct method of using a screwdriver.** Choose the right size of screw and screwdriver, and be sure to use the longest screwdriver that is available and convenient for the particular job. The blade of the screwdriver must fit the screw slots. It must be neither too small nor too large. If it is too small, the blade may break. If it is too large, it may slip out and mar the surface of the wood.

The quickest way to ruin any screwdriver is to use it as a can opener, a putty- or paint-mixer, or as a lever.

The tip of a screwdriver must be square. A round-tipped screwdriver is dangerous: it is apt to slip when driving a screw, causing serious injury.

When driving screws with a common screwdriver, grasp the handle with the thumb side of the hand toward the blade. Use automatic screwdrivers according to directions given by the manufacturer of each type. Place the screw in the pilot hole, hold it straight with the left hand, set the blade in the slot, and start turning the screwdriver, exerting pressure with the right hand. As soon as the screw has taken hold of the wood, remove the left hand, and continue driving the screw in. Hold the screwdriver steady, with the blade in a direct, straight line with the screw.

Before screws are driven, pilot holes should be bored. Locate the exact positions for the screws, and with a small *brad awl* mark the places. For small screws, the holes can be bored with the awl. For large screws, bits or twist drills should be used. The pilot holes should be slightly smaller in diameter than the screw. For softwoods, such as spruce, pine, and similar types, the pilot holes should be bored only about half as deep as the threaded part of the screw. For hardwoods, such as maple, birch, oak, and mahogany, they must be drilled almost as deep as the screw itself. In hardwood, if the screw is large or if you happen to be using brass screws, the pilot holes must first be bored slightly smaller than the threaded part of the screw, then enlarged at the top with a second drill of the same diameter as the unthreaded portion of the screw.

When two pieces of wood are to be fastened together with screws, two sets of holes must be drilled. The top piece is clamped to the lower piece only by the pressure of the screw head, and for this reason the holes are drilled so that the threaded portion of the screw takes hold of only the under piece of the wood. Locate the positions for the screws and mark each with a brad awl. Bore the pilot hole of smaller diameter than the threaded portion of the screw. This pilot hole must be bored all the way through the upper piece of the wood and for about half the length of the threaded part of the screw into the lower piece. Enlarge the pilot hole in the upper piece of wood to the same diameter as the unthreaded portion of the screw. Countersink the clearance hole in the upper piece of wood. Drive all of the screws firmly into place; then tighten each consecutively.

Where flathead or oval-head screws are used, the upper end of the pilot hole should be bored out or countersunk to match in size the diameter of the heads of the screws that are used. Countersinking is a simple operation, and the tool used is called a *countersink* (Fig. 23), its size depending on the size of the screw. It fits into a brace (Fig. 23).

**Driving screws into hardware, hinges, and handles.** While steel screws are used generally in woodworking, brass screws also are used to some extent for fastening small hinges and hardware on cabinets and furniture. General directions for the use of brass screws are approximately the same as for steel screws.

Directions for fastening hinges and other types of hardware, where a recess must be made before the fixtures can be mounted, are described in Chaps. 20 and 26, devoted to hanging doors and the like.

When the work does not need to be recessed, place the hardware in the required position

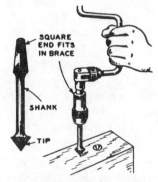

SQUARE
END FITS
IN BRACE

SHANK

TIP

COUNTERSINK

**Fig. 23.**

and mark the screw holes with a brad awl. Bore the pilot holes, following the directions given in the previous paragraphs on the Correct Method of Using a Screwdriver. Where screws are short, only a pilot hole is needed, but long screws require a clearance hole of the same diameter and length as the unthreaded part of the screw.

Use the largest size of screw that will slip easily through the holes in the hardware. If the holes in the hardware are countersunk, oval-head or flathead screws to fit the countersink should be used; if they are not countersunk, use round-head screws. Do not tighten the screws until all of them have been driven in.

**Concealing screws with plugs.** It is sometimes necessary to set screws below the surface of the wood and to conceal them with a plug of the same type of wood. For instance, the planking on boats is usually fastened to the frames in this manner. Wooden plugs of various diameters, made from mahogany, oak, pine, cedar, and cypress, can be bought from dealers in boat supplies for this purpose.

To conceal screws with wooden plugs, bore a hole with the bit and brace to fit the plug, then bore the pilot and clearance holes for the screws, and drive the screws into place. To insure a tight fit, put glue or wood filler in the plug hole and drive in the plug with a hammer. When the glue or filler is set, pare off the top of the plugs with a chisel, and sandpaper it even with the surface of the work.

**Removing tight screws.** To remove a tight screw, use a screwdriver that has a blade with parallel sides, and fits the screw slot perfectly. If the right size and shape of screwdriver is not used, the screw becomes "chewed," making the job more difficult. A tight screw sometimes can be started by giving it a slight twist in a clockwise direction, that is, the same direction which drives it in. If this does not help, twist the screw both ways, backing it out as far as it will go easily, and then turning it part way back in again. Each time this is repeated, the screw usually will back out a little farther until it is all the way out. In some cases, a screw with a damaged slot can be backed partly out, and then turned the rest of the way with a pair of pliers.

**Dressing screwdriver blades.** A screwdriver is not a cutting tool and for that reason does not have to be sharpened, but it must be dressed or kept in condition. This is done by occasionally grinding it on an emery wheel or by filing the blade with a flat file. Correct and incorrect shapes for a screwdriver are shown in Fig. 20.

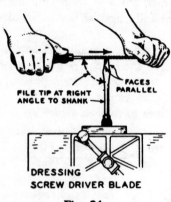

FILE TIP AT RIGHT
ANGLE TO SHANK

FACES
PARALLEL

DRESSING
SCREW DRIVER BLADE

**Fig. 24.**

When dressing a screwdriver with a file, hold the screwdriver in a vise and file the tip absolutely straight across both ends, at right angles to the shank and the sides, with the faces near the tip as parallel as possible to each other (Fig. 24). Never bevel or round the tip of a screwdriver.

When using an emery wheel for dressing a screwdriver, do not hold the blade against the wheel too long, or the friction wheel will heat the steel and draw the temper or soften the blade. When dressing a screwdriver, dip the blade in water at frequent intervals.

## PLANES

Planes are used for roughing down the surface of lumber and as finishing tools. They are classified as either *bench* or *block*. The bench plane is always used with the grain of the wood; the block plane for cutting across the grain. Bench planes are made in several types, each of which has outstanding features.

The bench planes in common use are the *smoothing, jack, fore,* and *jointer types* (Fig. 25). The smoothing plane, the shortest of these, is used for finishing or leveling flat surfaces after the rough surface and unevenness has been removed with a jack plane. It is handy to use where only small areas are to be leveled off, as its short length makes it simple to locate and remedy these uneven spots.

The smoothing plane is smaller than a jack plane, but considerably larger than the block plane. It does not cut the end

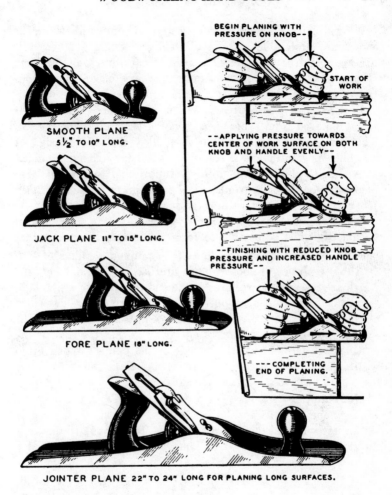

SMOOTH PLANE
5½" TO 10" LONG.

JACK PLANE 11" TO 15" LONG.

FORE PLANE 18" LONG.

JOINTER PLANE 22" TO 24" LONG FOR PLANING LONG SURFACES.

BEGIN PLANING WITH PRESSURE ON KNOB--

START OF WORK

--APPLYING PRESSURE TOWARDS CENTER OF WORK SURFACE ON BOTH KNOB AND HANDLE EVENLY--

--FINISHING WITH REDUCED KNOB PRESSURE AND INCREASED HANDLE PRESSURE--

---COMPLETING END OF PLANING.

**Fig. 25.**

grain of lumber as well as a block plane. It ranges in size from 5½" to 10" in length and is made like a jack plane, but has a shorter sole or bottom. A plane-iron cap to coil and break the shavings is attached to the plane iron. The cutting edge on the blade of a smoothing plane must be set rather close to make a fairly fine shaving.

A fore plane is merely a shorter type of jointer plane, and is sometimes preferable because of its light weight. When it is necessary to true up edges of boards preparatory to fitting them closely or jointing them, the jointer plane is used. These four types of planes are shown in Fig. 25.

**Roughing or scrub plane.** When more than ¼″ of waste is to be removed from a board, a *roughing* or *scrub* plane is used. This plane is available in two sizes, 9½″ and 10½″ long. A roughing or scrub plane is equipped with heavy rounded blades. It is used to clean up rough, dirty timber and to true up large pieces of wood to approximate size, preliminary to doing a finish job with either the smoothing or jack plane.

**Circular plane.** This special-type plane has a flexible steel bottom which is adjustable to form a curve for planing either concave or convex surfaces down to a minimum radius of 20″.

**Rabbet plane.** Rabbet planes are used to cut out *rabbets,* which are rectangular recesses at the ends or edges of a plank, to form what is known as a *rabbet joint.* Rabbet joints are described more fully in Chap. 6, Woodworking Joints and Splices. The sole, or bottom, of this plane is cut away so that the edge of the cutting iron is in line with the side of the plane. When fitted with a special iron called a *spur,* the rabbet plane can be used also for planing across the grain (Fig. 26).

**Modelmaker's plane.** The *modelmaker's* plane, also called a *violin* plane, is only 3″ to 4″ in length. The sole is curved in both directions and the blade is rounded, conforming to the same curvature. It can be used to remove excess wood from a flat, convex, or concave surface of any radius down to a minimum of 12″. It is used by patternmakers, violin- and other instrument-makers, and professional modelbuilders. It can be bought only on special order.

**Spokeshave.** While a spokeshave is not strictly a plane, it sometimes is used for the same purpose and in the same manner. It is an excellent tool for shaping curved pieces.

**Adjustment of plane irons.** A plane is a cutting tool set in a block of metal or wood which serves to act as a guide to regulate the depth of the cut. The plane iron, a chisel-like tool, does the actual cutting. Like all cutting tools, it must have a keen,

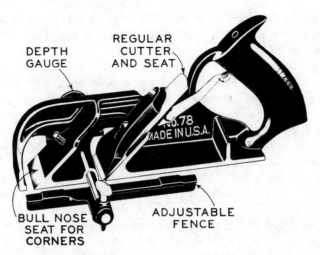

DEPTH GAUGE

REGULAR CUTTER AND SEAT

NO. 78
MADE IN U.S.A.

BULL NOSE SEAT FOR CORNERS

ADJUSTABLE FENCE

**Fig. 26.** Parts of a rabbet plane.

sharp edge and be adjusted correctly.

Bench planes, that is, the smoothing, fore, jointer, and jack planes, have a plane-iron cap clamped to the cutting blade to stiffen the iron and break and curve the shavings as they come up through the throat of the tool. The position of the cap in relation to the plane iron is adjustable by loosening the clamping screw. In general, the edge of the cap should be about $\frac{1}{16}''$ back of the cutting edge of the iron. To regulate the thickness of shavings, turn the plane upside down, holding the knob in the left hand and the handle in the right. Look along the bottom of the plane, and with the right hand begin turning the adjusting screw until the blade projects about the thickness of a hair. Then turn the adjusting lever left or right to straighten the blade: the blade should never be at an angle.

In block planes, the blade is locked in position by a lever cap or by a cam lever, which differ slightly in planes produced by different companies. Moving the lever-cap screw, or the lever, in one direction locks the plane iron; moving it in the opposite direction unlocks the iron when it is necessary to remove it from the plane. By means of an adjusting screw, the sharpened lower edge of the plane iron can be moved in and out of the mouth of the plane. A block-plane iron is beveled on only one side of the sharpened edge, and it is set in the frame of the plane with the bevel up.

To adjust a block plane, hold it up with the toe, or front, of the plane facing forward, and the bottom level with the eye. To regulate the thickness of shavings, turn the adjusting screw until the sharp edge of the iron projects slightly through the sole. This is called a vertical adjustment. To produce even shavings, a lateral adjustment is made by loosening slightly the lever-cap screw or the lever cam. Sight along the bottom of the plane. Press the upper end of the blade near the adjustment screw either to the right or left to bring the cutting edge of the blade parallel to the bottom of the plane. Never set one corner of the blade farther out of the throat of the plane than the other. Do not set the blade too far out of the throat; it should project just enough for the edge to be visible and to be felt with the fingertips (Figs. 27 and 28).

**Correct method of using a plane.** Grasp the handle of the plane with the right hand, holding the knob firmly between the thumb and forefinger of the left hand, with the finger joints of the left hand protruding slightly over the edge of the plane. At the beginning of each stroke, the pressure and driving force is exerted by the left hand. As the stroke progresses, the pressure of the left hand is gradually lessened, and that of the right hand correspondingly increased until the pressure from both of the hands is approximately equal. Continue increasing the pressure from the right hand. At the end of the cut, the right hand will be exerting the power and driving the plane, while the left hand will be guiding the tool (Fig. 26).

When planing, always hold the plane level. If the plane is tilted, it will produce uneven, thick shavings and ruin the trueness of the work. To avoid dulling the cutter unnecessarily, lift the plane above the work on all return strokes. When working on long surfaces, begin at the right-hand side of the board, taking a few strokes; then step forward and take the same number of strokes, repeating until the entire surface of the board has been planed, always *with* the grain. As the work progresses, use a try square and level to determine the accuracy. For the first cuts

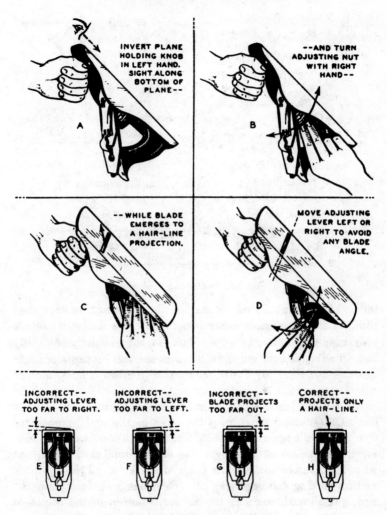

**Fig. 27.** Adjusting a plane.

on any wide surface, a jack plane should be used. Its long face rides over the low spots and dresses down the higher ones. The cutter on a jack plane is ground in a slightly convex form, which facilitates the removal of thick shavings, and at the same time avoids a rectangular shaving that would tend to choke up the

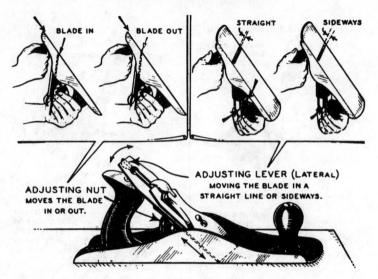

**Fig. 28.** Adjusting a plane.

throat of the plane. Thus all parts of the blade coming in contact with the work cut smooth, even shavings. This important fact is also true of the cutter on a fore plane, except convexity is slightly less. The convex cutters of both planes will leave a series of slight grooves, but these are easily removed with either a smoothing or a jointer plane.

For cutting against the grain, the block plane is used. Only one hand is employed; grasp the sides of the tool between the thumb and the second and third fingers, with the forefinger resting in the hollow of the finger rest at the front of the tool, and with the lever cap under the palm of the hand. Pressing down and forward at the beginning of each stroke and maintaining an even pressure throughout the forward motion is the secret of properly using a block plane. To avoid splitting, plane the end grain halfway, alternately from each edge. If the plane is pushed all the way across an end grain, the corners and the edge of the work are apt to split off.

**Sharpening a plane iron.** Sharpening a plane iron involves two operations: *grinding* and *whetting*. As a rule, the cutting edge can be whetted several times before grinding is necessary.

A plane iron requires grinding only when its bevel has become short or when the edges have been nicked. Because whetting is done after grinding, the process of grinding is described here first.

While the grinding of a plane iron is similar to grinding a chisel or gouge, two important points must be considered: avoiding burning the cutting edge and maintaining the correct bevel. If a motor-driven grinder is not available, use a small hand-driven grinder equipped with a carborundum wheel of the right type for chisels and plane irons. Either type of grinding wheel must be provided with an adjustable tool rest, which is set to a grinding angle of 25°-30° to produce the desired bevel (Fig. 29).

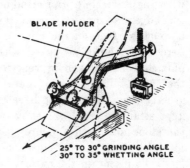

Grinding a plane iron on a dry emery or carborundum wheel requires considerable care and some experience. Burring can be avoided by grinding

**Fig. 29.** Grinding a plane iron.

very lightly and by dripping either kerosene or water onto the wheel to keep it from getting too dry, and by frequently dipping the plane iron in water. If these precautions are not taken the edge will overheat or burn, turning a blue-black color, and will lose its temper. Steel that has lost its temper is softened and can never be resharpened.

The edge of a grinding wheel must always be dressed smooth. If it becomes grooved or out of true, dress it with a carborundum stick especially made for the purpose. Hold the carborundum stick against the revolving wheel until the wheel has been smoothed out.

Preparatory to grinding, the plane iron must be removed from the plane. If it is a double plane-iron type, the iron must be separated from the cap by loosening the screw and sliding it along to the end of the slot, where its head will pass through the hole.

The right bevel or grinding angle for plane irons is 25° to 30°. Maintaining it throughout is a simple matter if the adjustable tool rest is used. Turn the wheel toward the tool, at the same time moving the tool from side to side against the wheel. Exert only a slight pressure against the wheel, as too much will cause overheating, thus spoiling the tool. Grind the plane iron until a fine bevel or wire edge appears.

**Whetting a plane iron.** A plane iron must be whetted after grinding to remove the burr or wire edge and to produce a clean cutting edge. When a plane iron has become only slightly dull, whetting it without prior grinding will usually restore a keen cutting edge. A common oilstone with a fine surface on one side and a rough surface on the other is used, with a light oil, such as kerosene or kerosene mixed with a light motor oil, to float the particles of steel and prevent them from filling up the pores of the stone. The whetting bevel is usually 30° to 35°, slightly greater than the grinding bevel. The bevel must at all times be kept straight. With a steady motion, move the tool parallel to the stone and with a figure-eight movement make certain that all parts of the cutting edge come in contact with the stone (Fig. 30). To maintain the correct bend, use the toolholder shown in the same illustration. After this bevel is cut, or if the blade has been ground, the back of the blade will have a wire edge. Remove this edge by reversing the plane iron and taking several strokes with the blade flat on the stone (Fig. 30). Then complete the whetting by drawing the edge over a small wooden block or a leather strap. Hold the blade up to the light to determine its sharpness. A sharp edge does not reflect light. A dull edge will show as a fine white line; if this occurs, repeat both operations.

**Reassembling a plane iron.** Reassemble a newly sharpened plane iron with extreme care to avoid nicking its keen edge. Lay the plane-iron cap across the flat side of the iron with the screw in the slot. Pull it down and away from the cutting edge, and turn the cap parallel to the iron when it is almost at the end of the slot. Hold the cap and iron together and slide the cap forward until its edge is about $\frac{1}{16}''$ back of the cutting edge of the iron. To avoid nicking or dulling the blade, do not move the cap or drag it across the cutting edge. When the cap is in proper position, hold the cap and iron firmly together and tighten the screw that will hold the two parts of the double plane iron together. When not in use, lay the plane down on its side to protect the blade, and set the blade far in so that it cannot be damaged by other tools falling against it (Figs. 31 and 32).

## CHISELS AND GOUGES

There are many kinds of woodworking chisels and gouges: paring, firmer, framing, packet, slikh, gouge, butt, and mill chisels (Fig. 33). Those most generally used in the home workshop are the framing, butt, and packet types, each of which is available with either a straight or a bevel edge, according to its intended use. All chisels and gouges come in two types known as the tang and the socket (Fig. 34). For general use the socket type is preferable be-

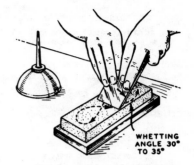

WHETTING ANGLE 30° TO 35°

WHETTING A PLANE IRON ON THE OIL-STONE TO OBTAIN THE PROPER CUTTING EDGE AND ANGLE.

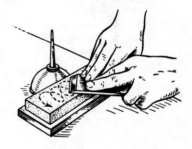

KEEP IRON FLAT IN REMOVING BURR OR WIRE EDGE IN FINAL SHARPENING.

**Fig. 30.** Whetting a plane iron.

cause it is more durable. One end of the steel blade of the socket chisel is formed into a funnel-shaped socket that fits over the tapered end of either a wood or plastic handle. The lighter chisels range from ⅛″ to 1″ in width in gradations of ⅛″. The heavier type range from 1″ to 2″ in width in gradations of ¼″.

While each type of chisel is designed for a specific job, a set of nine or ten, which includes four or five of each of the firmer and framing type, is considered sufficient for general work. The firmer chisel is sturdier than the paring chisel, is capable of doing fairly heavy work, and is used for paring and light mortising work. The framing chisel is a heavy-duty tool that cuts deeply, and it will stand considerable hard handling.

The keen cutting edge of a good chisel demands constant care.

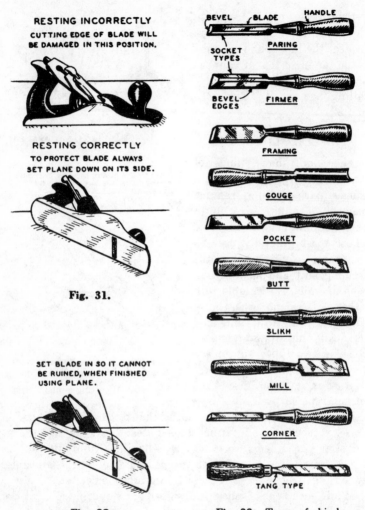

RESTING INCORRECTLY
CUTTING EDGE OF BLADE WILL
BE DAMAGED IN THIS POSITION.

RESTING CORRECTLY
TO PROTECT BLADE ALWAYS
SET PLANE DOWN ON ITS SIDE.

**Fig. 31.**

SET BLADE IN SO IT CANNOT
BE RUINED, WHEN FINISHED
USING PLANE.

**Fig. 32.**

BEVEL   BLADE   HANDLE
SOCKET TYPES
PARING

BEVEL EDGES
FIRMER

FRAMING

GOUGE

POCKET

BUTT

SLIKH

MILL

CORNER

TANG TYPE

**Fig. 33.**  Types of chisels.

A chisel never should be used as a can opener, wedge, putty knife, nail remover or screwdriver. When a chisel is not in use, protect its cutting edge from rust with a coat of oil and hang it up to prevent damage.

Gouges are chisels with rounded edges.  There are two main

classes of gouges: firmer and paring. The firmer gouge is either outside- or inside-ground. The paring gouge is ground on the inside only. Firmer gouges are used for cutting hollows or grooves. Paring gouges are used to cut surfaces or ends in irregular forms, and are used by pattern-makers almost exclusively for the shaping of core boxes and patterns. Both

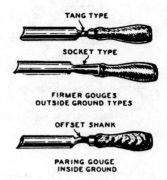

**Fig. 34.** Types of gouge.

types are available with either socket or tang handles, and the sizes range from ⅛″ to 2″ in gradations of ⅛″.

**Wood-carving chisels and gouges.** Wood-carving chisels and gouges differ considerably from the ordinary types. The sides, instead of being parallel, taper toward the shoulder, and they are beveled. For general wood-carving, gouges are available in eleven different curves, graduating from almost flat to a deep U-curve. They are classified according to their shape (Figs. **35** and **36**).

The small, deep U-shaped gouges are called veiners. Fluters are the larger ones that have quick turns. Flats are those that have a slight curve and are almost flat. In addition to these, there are three V-shaped gouges also known as parting tools, further classified as being acute, medium, and obtuse.

Wood-carving chisels are classified as firmers and skew firmers, and are either square or oblique on the ends (Fig. 37). Skew firmers with bent shanks are also available for either right- or left-hand use. Wood-carving chisels are available in eighteen different sizes, from 1/32″ to 1″ in 1/16″ gradations. They are fitted with either straight or bent shanks. The firmers range from 1/64″ to 1″ in 1/16″ gradations. The other wood-carving chisels are available in six sizes from 1″ to 2″ in ¼″ gradations. All the smaller sizes are available with either spade- or fishtail-shaped blades. These specially shaped blades afford greater clearance back of the cutting edge and are used only when carving intricate

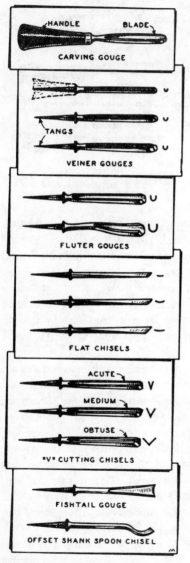

**Fig. 35.** Wood-carving chisels and gouges.

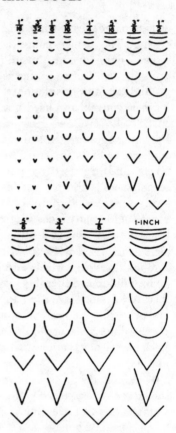

**Fig. 36.** Chart of sizes and cutting edges of wood-carving chisels and gouges.

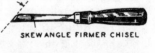

SKEW ANGLE FIRMER CHISEL

SQUARE FIRMER CHISEL

**Fig. 37.**

designs (Fig. 35).

**Using a chisel.** To preserve the fine cutting edge of a chisel or a gouge, use another tool, such as a saw, auger, or plane, to remove as much of the waste part of the wood as possible. A chisel should be used only for the finishing cuts.

Grasp the handle of the chisel firmly with the right hand, which supplies the driving power. Hold the blade with the left hand to control the direction of the cut. Secure the work in a vise, and keep hands away from the cutting edge of tool to avoid injury. Do not start to cut directly on the guideline, but slightly away from it, so that any accidental splitting will occur in the waste portion rather than in the finished work. Shavings made with a chisel should always be thin, especially when making the finishing cut. Always cut with the grain as much as possible, for cutting against the grain splits the fibers of the wood, leaving it rough. Cutting with the grain leaves the wood fairly smooth. Make chiseling cuts either horizontally or vertically. Vertical chiseling cuts are usually made across the grain.

When using a chisel, hold it at a slight angle to the cut instead of straight. This produces a clean shearing cut that is smooth when made with the grain and on end grains (Fig. 38). On cross-grained wood, work from both directions (Fig. 39).

To cut curves on corners or edges, first remove as much waste as possible with the saw. To cut a concave curve, hold the chisel with the bevel on the work, and make the cut by pushing down and then pulling back on the handle (Fig. 40). For a convex cut, hold the chisel with the flat side of the tool on the work and the beveled side up, with the left hand holding the tool and applying the necessary pressure, while the right hand guides it and acts as a brake at the same time. To secure a clean shearing cut, hold the chisel tangent to the curve and move from side to side.

When paring on corners and ends, observe the direction of the grain and begin the cut at the edge of the work (*A*, Fig. 41). This prevents the work from splitting. Round corners are pared in the same manner (*B*, Fig. 41). When making a shearing cut, bring the chisel from a straight to a slanting position, sliding it from side to side as you press it down on the work, as shown in *C* and *D*, Fig. 41.

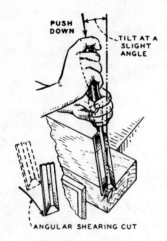

**Fig. 38.**

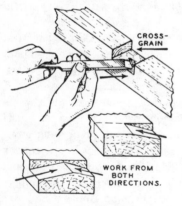

**Fig. 39.** Cross-grain paring.

When paring a shoulder of a joint or cleaning out a corner, first hold the chisel vertically, then tipped to get a shearing cut when you draw it toward you, as shown at *A* in Fig. **42**. The position of the chisel for flat or horizontal paring is shown at *B*. When making a shearing cut in a recess or other close place, take half the cut, as in *C*. When it is necessary to work across the grain, the position of the tool for vertical paring is shown at *D*.

**Using a gouge.** Gouges are used for cutting hollows and grooves, and are handled in the same manner as chisels, with the following exceptions. Gouge cuts are always started at the edge of a cut and driven toward the center. When gouging out a large hollow, cut across grain. Gouges with inside bevels are used in the same manner as chisels with the bevel up, those with outside bevels as chisels with the bevel down.

**Using a wood-carving gouge or chisel.** Wood-carving chisels and gouges are used in carving designs in low relief. Sketch or trace an outline of the required design on the wood (*A*, Fig. 43). Use a small-sized gouge, or what is known as a pattern tool, to go over the entire outline of the design, cutting on the background side of the outline (*B*, Fig. 43). When doing this, be very careful to note the direction of the grain in the raised part of the design. Observe the curves of the design and cut out the outline with the proper curved chisel or gouge, tapping the tool with a mallet (*C*, Fig. 43). Use a gouge to cut out the background. The final step in carving is to model the face of the design by putting in the details with the veiners. Then clean out the edges and background of the work and even it off (*D*, Fig. 43). To have a really effective piece of wood carving, be careful to avoid cutting under the outline of the design, making the edges too sharp, or even giving too smooth a finish to the carved-out background.

Many beautiful designs can be executed by merely outlining with one of the small gouges or veiners. Work can

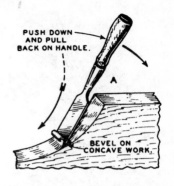

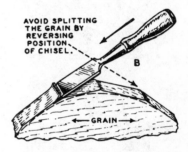

**Fig. 40.** Cutting concave and convex curves.

be improved further by cutting or stamping down the background and by slightly modeling the raised part of the design. The skew chisel is used for chip carving, which is very simple and, when not overdone, very effective (Fig. 44). Trace or draw the design on the work. Make the necessary vertical first cuts with the carving tool to the required depth (*A*, Fig. 44). Then make the second or tapering cut toward the bottom of the first cut. If properly cut, the portion to be removed will come out in one chip (*B*, Fig. 44). Another method used for chip carvings is shown at *C*, Fig. 44.

**Sharpening a chisel or gouge.** When the cutting edge of a chisel or gouge becomes dull, whetting will restore its keeness. While the procedure for whetting and grinding a chisel is the same as for a plane iron, the following must be considered. The

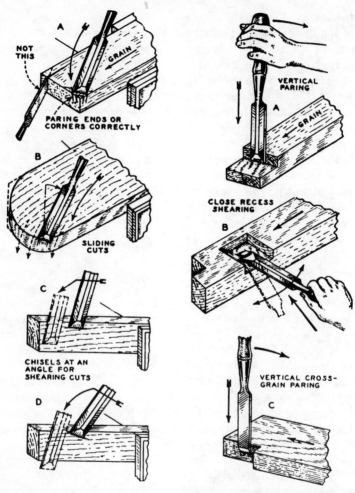

**Fig. 41.** Paring corners and end sections.

**Fig. 42.** Cleaning corners and paring shoulders of joints.

large bevel of 25° to 30° must be whetted on the coarse side of the oilstone and the small bevel on the fine side. Remove the burr or wire edge on the fine side of the stone. When the cutting edge has become badly nicked or when the tool has lost its original bevel, grinding is necessary. To sharpen a chisel by either whetting or

SKETCH OR TRACE OUTLINE OF DESIGN ON WOODEN SURFACE.

PARTING OR GOUGING OUT BACK-GROUND.

LIGHTLY TAPPING CHISEL WITH MALLET.

CLEAN-UP EDGES AND BACK-GROUND.

**Fig. 43.** Wood-carving procedures.

grinding, see the directions for Sharpening a Plane Iron, just a few paragraphs back (Fig. 45).

**Whetting and grinding a gouge.** Directions for sharpening a gouge are to a large extent the same as for a plane iron or a chisel, with the exception that a gouge is curved and must be sharpened by being turned from side to side as it is pushed forward on the oilstone (*D*, Fig. 46). A slipstone must be used for removing the burr wire edge or a gouge with an outside bevel and for whetting a gouge with an inside bevel (*A, B,* and *C,* Fig. 46). When holding the slipstone in the hand, be careful to keep the cutting edge of the gouge true. The wire edge of the gouge with an inside bevel is removed by holding the unbeveled side flat to the stone (Fig. 46).

### BRACES AND BITS

The three types of braces are the plain, the ratchet, and the corner brace (Fig. 47). The brace and bit are used for boring holes in wood. The bit bores the holes, while the brace holds the bit in the chuck and turns it. The chuck is adjustable and can hold any type or size of auger bit. A brace can also be utilized as a screwdriver by inserting a screwdriver bit in the chuck.

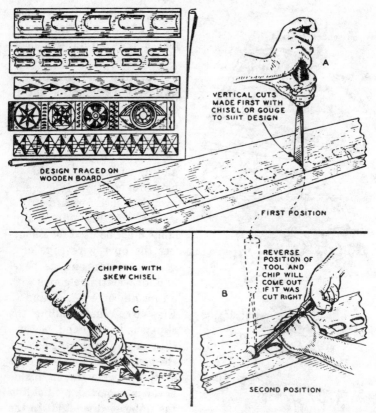

DESIGN TRACED ON WOODEN BOARD

VERTICAL CUTS MADE FIRST WITH CHISEL OR GOUGE TO SUIT DESIGN

A

FIRST POSITION

CHIPPING WITH SKEW CHISEL

C

REVERSE POSITION OF TOOL AND CHIP WILL COME OUT IF IT WAS CUT RIGHT

B

SECOND POSITION

**Fig. 44.** Chip carving procedures and suggested border designs.

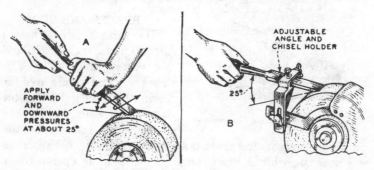

A

APPLY FORWARD AND DOWNWARD PRESSURES AT ABOUT 25°

ADJUSTABLE ANGLE AND CHISEL HOLDER

25°

B

**Fig. 45.** Sharpening a chisel.

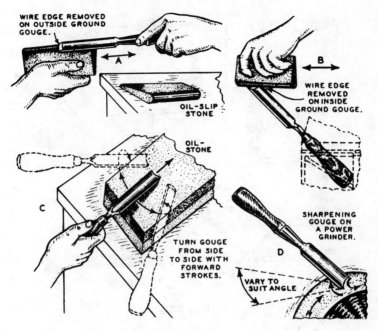

**Fig. 46.** Whetting and sharpening a gouge.

The most practical type of brace for general use is the one with the ratchet control. This has a ball-bearing handle which makes it easy to turn, and the ratchet can be locked or made to operate in either direction. This brace can be used in places where it is impossible to make a full turn of 360°. In corners or other inaccessible places, the corner brace is used.

**Types and sizes of auger bits.** Auger bits are available in sizes from ¼″ to 1″ in diameter, graduated by ¹⁄₁₆″. For boring holes smaller than ¼″ in diameter, drills, gimlet bits, and even awls are used. For boring holes larger than 1″, expansive or Forstner bits are used. Sizes of auger bits are indicated by a number stamped on the shank of the bit which gives the diameter of the hole it will bore, in sixteenths of an inch. A No. 8 auger bit bores a hole ½″ in diameter and a ⁵⁄₁₆″ auger is marked No. 5, and so on.

An auger bit is essentially a cutting tool. The working parts

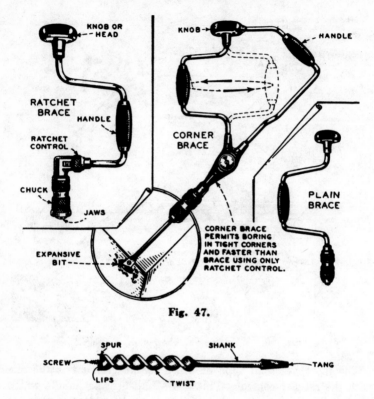

**Fig. 47.**

**Fig. 48.** Parts of the auger bit.

of the bit are the screw, the spurs or nibs, and the lips (Fig. 48).
The spurs or nibs score the circumference of the hole, the lips cut
the shavings, and the twist or thread of the bit pulls the shavings
out of the hole. The three types of auger bits are the single-twist,
double-twist, and straight-core or solid-center.

The single-twist and the straight-core types are more generally
used in woodworking. These are fast borers, and they clear
themselves of chips more readily and quickly than the double-
twist type. They are generally used for hard and gummy woods.
While the double-twist type works slower than the single-twist,
it makes a more accurate and smoother hole. It is generally used
for working with softwoods.

**Dowel bits.** The dowel bit is a shorter bit, averaging about one half the length of the auger bit. As the name indicates, it is used principally for drilling holes for the insertion of dowels (Fig. 49).

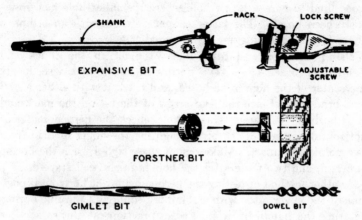

**Fig. 49.** Types of bits.

**Gimlet bits.** Considerably longer than any of the other bits, gimlet bits are from 18″ to 24″ in length (Fig. 49). They are used to bore holes through very thick timbers and planks in heavy construction work. Some gimlet bits have neither screw nor spur.

**Forstner bits.** The Forstner bit has neither screw, spurs, nor twist (Fig. 49). The lack of a guiding screw makes this bit more difficult to center than the conventional type. Cutting is accomplished by the two lips and a circular steel rim, with the rim centering the bit and scoring the circumference of the hole. These are very accurate bits and are made in sizes up to 2″ in diameter, with the size indicated in sixteenths of an inch on the tang of the tool.

Centering a Forstner bit is a little tricky, but it can be simplified by drawing a circle on the work equal in diameter to the size of the hole that is to be bored. Then start the bit so that the rim cuts into the circumference of the circle. Although more difficult to use than the ordinary type, the Forstner bit has certain advantages. It is used in end wood, where an auger bit does not bore so well, and to bore holes near an end in very thin wood, where the screw on an auger bit would split the stock. A Forstner bit is used to bore holes straight through cross-grained and knotty wood, and to bore a larger hole where a smaller hole has previously been bored. The latter cannot be done with an ordinary auger bit without plugging up the smaller hole.

**Using a brace and bit.** Insert the bit in the chuck and tighten the brace (Fig. 47). Secure the work in a vise, locate the center of the hole to be bored, and mark it with either a nail or a brad awl. Place the lead screw of the bit on the mark and start boring. To bore a straight hole, check the perpendicular or horizontal position of the bit by sighting the auger or drill from two points 90° apart. Make one of these sights when the boring is begun, and two more after the hole is fairly well started.

Another method of testing the perpendicular or horizontal position of the auger bit is with a small try square. Continue boring, rotating the handle in a clockwise direction, at the same time exerting pressure on the head of the brace with the other hand. The harder the wood, the more pressure has to be applied. Avoid splintering the wood by stopping when the bottom of the lead screw appears on the underside of the work. Remove the work from the vise, reverse it, replace it in the vise, and complete the boring from the reverse side (Fig. 50).

Boring a hole at an angle is just as simple as boring a perpendicular hole. The only difference is in the sighting. A simple

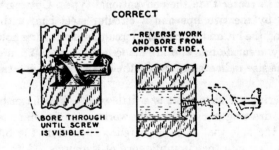

CORRECT

--REVERSE WORK AND BORE FROM OPPOSITE SIDE.

BORE THROUGH UNTIL SCREW IS VISIBLE---

**Fig. 50.** Correct method of boring.

method is to lay out the required angle on a piece of cardboard or thin wood and use this angle in sighting the direction of the auger bit. If the bit is kept parallel to this template, it will bore the hole at the desired angle.

**Depth Gauge.** A depth gauge is used to bore a hole to a desired depth (Fig. 51). While ready-made gauges are available, a wooden gauge can be made from a small block of wood. Bore a hole in a block, slightly larger in diameter than the bit. The height of the block will vary inversely according to the depth of the hole that is to be bored. The depth gauge is slipped over the bit prior to boring.

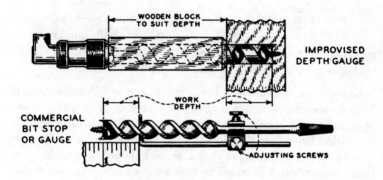

**Fig. 51.** Using depth gauges.

**Twist drills.** Twist drills from $\frac{1}{16}''$ to $\frac{3}{4}''$ in diameter are available with tapered shanks to fit in a ratchet brace. Morse twist drills (Fig. 52) are made with a straight shank to fit in the chuck of either a hand, automatic push, electric, or breast drill (Fig. 53). The three-jaw chuck in a hand or electric drill will take drills up to $\frac{1}{4}''$ in diameter. For a larger size, use a breast drill. The chuck on a breast drill takes drills up to $\frac{1}{2}''$ in diameter. Twist drills are available in over fifty sizes.

**Using a twist drill.** A twist drill must be held steady and driven at moderate speed in a straight direction. The shank of a proper twist drill is made of soft steel and will bend if too much

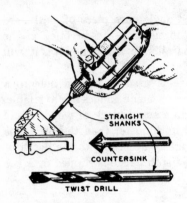

**Fig. 52.** Morse twist drill and countersink bit.

pressure is exerted on it. The body of the drill is of tempered steel and if strained or twisted it will snap off. When driven at excessive speed, a twist drill bites rapidly into the wood and the chips do not clear out of the flutes of the drill. The drill then becomes hot, at times hot enough to char the wood and spoil the temper of the drill, ruining its keen cutting edge. When the flutes of a twist drill become jammed with chips, the drill squeaks as it revolves. To clear the chips from the flutes, the drill should be withdrawn from the hole several times during the drilling.

**Expansion or extension bits.** *Expansion* or *extension* bits are used to bore holes larger than 1″ in diameter (Fig. 49). These bits fit into the chuck of a brace. Two sizes are available: one for boring holes from ½″ to 1½″ in diameter, the other for boring holes from ⅞″ to 3″ in diameter. They have adjustable cutting blades which can be set to bore holes of any diameter within their range. Loosening the screw that fastens the spur and the cutting lip to the shank makes it possible to move the spur and adjust the bit to the required diameter. Before using, tighten this screw so that the spur will not slip. The accuracy of the adjustment that has been made should be tested by boring a sample hole through a piece of waste wood. Expansion bits are secured in the chuck of the brace and used in the same manner as other types of bits.

**Countersink bits.** *Countersink* bits are available in two types: one with a tapered shank fitting into the chuck of a brace, the other with a straight round shank fitting into the chuck of a drill. Countersinks are used to shape the upper portion of a hole so that the head of a flathead screw can be driven flush with or slightly below the surface of the work.

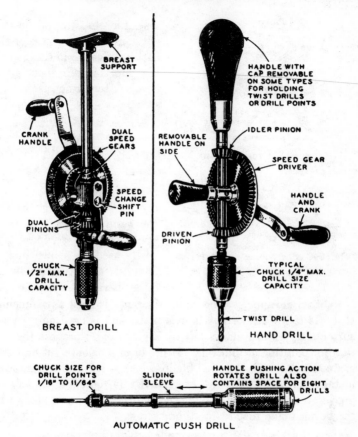

**Fig. 53.** Types of hand drills.

**Sharpening an auger bit.** An auger-bit file and a slipstone are used to sharpen an auger bit. The specially designed file is small, double-ended, and tapered so that the narrow portion can be used on small-diameter bits and the wider portion on larger bits (Fig. 54). One end is made with the sides "safe" or uncut, while the other end has cut edges. In sharpening an auger bit, file both the lips and the nibs of the spurs. The safe section of an auger-bit file makes it easy to file either the lips or the nibs without damaging any of the adjacent surfaces. To keep the original diameter of the bit, file the nibs only on the inside. To maintain the proper clear-

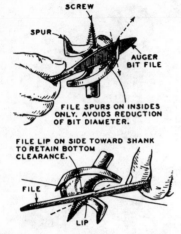

**Fig. 54.**   Sharpening an auger bit.

ance file the lips of the bit only on the top surface of the cutting edge. Hold the bit in a vise and maintain its original bevel. After filing, use a slip-stone.

## SCRAPERS

The two types of scrapers used in woodworking are the *cabinet* scraper (Fig. 55) and the *hand* scraper. The three styles of hand scrapers generally used are shown in Fig. 56. All are available with either bevel or straight edges.

**Cabinet scraper.**   The cabinet scraper is used as a finishing tool.   It takes a finer cut than a plane and is used only on flat surfaces to remove marks left by a plane or to prepare the surface for painting or finishing.   It produces a smooth cut on cross-grained wood.   The beveled blade, which is set in a two-handled metal frame (Fig. 55), can be removed by loosening the adjusting screw and the clamp thumbscrew.   Insert the new blade with the beveled side toward the thumbscrew.

**Using a cabinet scraper.**   Before using a cabinet scraper, place it on a flat wooden surface and adjust the blade so that it is even with the bottom of the scraper by pressing it down lightly against the wood.   Tighten both the clamp screw and the adjusting screw and make a test cut on some waste wood.   Continue to tighten the adjusting screw between test cuts until the blade projects far enough to produce a thin shaving.

The work should be secured in a vise.   Hold the tool in both hands and either push or pull it over the surface of the work. As a rule, it is pushed rather than pulled (Fig. 55).

**Hand scrapers.**   The two types of one-hand scrapers generally used are the hand scraper, which is rectangular, and the molding

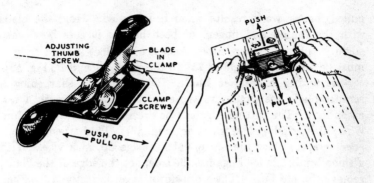

**Fig. 55.** Cabinet scraper.

scraper, which is curved (Fig. 56). They are made of high-tempered steel in various sizes and can be used on both flat and curved surfaces. They are available with both square and beveled edges. The square-edge type produces a smoother and flatter surface, but is not so fast as the bevel-edge type, and becomes dull sooner. Square-edge scrapers are used for furniture, moldings, and cabinetwork. Bevel-edge scrapers are used for scraping floors and other large areas.

**Using a hand scraper.** A hand scraper produces finer shavings than a cabinet scraper. While it may be either pushed or

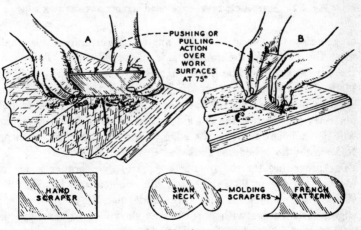

**Fig. 56.** Hand scrapers.

pulled, better work results when it is pulled. Hold the blade
with the thumb and fingers of both hands; it cuts best when
slightly curved. When either pushed or pulled, a hand scraper
must be held at an angle of 75° to the work (*A* and *B*, Fig. 56).

**Sharpening a scraper blade.** Directions for sharpening a
scraper blade are similar to those for a plane iron, with a few
exceptions. The cutting edge can be dressed several times before
it requires grinding and whetting (Fig. 57). To sharpen a bevel-
edge scraper, place the blade, cutting edge up, in a vise. With
a smooth mill file held against the side, not the edge of the blade,
remove the old burr. The worn-down bevel is restored by filing

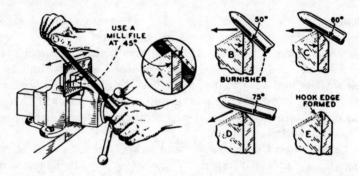

**Fig. 57.** Sharpening bevel-edge hand scraper and drawing edge.

or grinding the blade to a 45° angle. Maintaining this angle,
whet the bevel on the smooth side of an oilstone. To remove
the wire edge, whet the blade face-down on the stone. Lay the
blade, bevel side down, on the work, with the edge projecting
slightly over the edge of the bench. With the burnisher held
perfectly flat against the flat side of the blade, a few firm strokes
will be sufficient to draw the edge to the required 50°. Proceed
to form the hook edge as shown at *C, D* and *E*, Fig. 57.

The procedure for sharpening a square-edge scraper is as follows: Hold file at 90° angle and file edge square (*A*, Fig. 57).
Whet edge on oilstone and turn blade on side to remove wire
edges. Draw edge with burnisher as shown at *B;* then proceed
with steps *C, D* and *E*, Fig. 58.

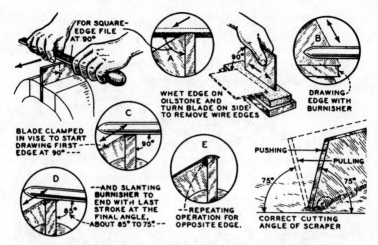

**Fig. 58.** Methods of sharpening square-edge hand scraper.

## MEASURING AND LAYING-OUT TOOLS

Prior to cutting lumber to any required size or shape, guiding lines must be accurately measured and laid out. The measuring and laying-out tools are *rules, straightedges, squares,* and *gauges.*

**Rules.** Rules are used for measuring material to exact dimensions. Those most generally used in woodworking are made of wood and are called *zigzag* and *boxwood.* Both the zigzag and boxwood types fold into 6″ lengths. Boxwood is the smaller of the two, can be opened to either 2′ or 3′, and is marked in inches and graduations to ⅛″. The zigzag rule opens to a length of 6′ and is marked in inches and graduations to 1/16″ (Fig. 59).

Steel tape rules are used to measure the diameter of dowels and drills, the thickness of boards and for inside direct measurements. They are more accurate than other rules for these specific purposes (Fig. 60). They are available in several sizes, ranging from 2′ to 8′ in length, and are graduated in feet, inches, and fractions of inches on both sides.

Where absolute accuracy to 1/32″ is necessary, the caliper rule shown in Fig. 61 is used for both inside and outside measurements. The boxwood caliper rule is used to measure outside diameters or

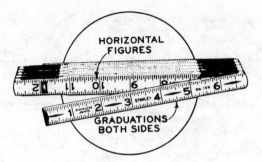

**Fig. 59.** Zigzag rule.

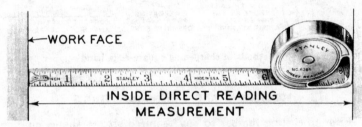

**Fig. 60.** Steel tape rule.

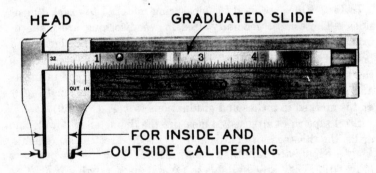

**Fig. 61.** Inside and outside caliper rule.

thicknesses (Fig. 62).

**Steel straightedges.** Steel straightedges are strips of hardened tempered steel that have been accurately ground. They are available in lengths ranging from 1' to 6'. Unlike rules, they are not graduated in inches or fractions of an inch. They are used as guides for scribing working lines with a knife or pencil when extreme accuracy is required. Straightedges are also used for testing flatness of surfaces.

**Squares.** The several types of squares used in woodworking are the *carpenter's* or *framing* square, the *try square* with fixed blade, and the adjustable *miter and try square* with sliding blade and spirit level.

**Carpenter's or framing squares.** The carpenter's or framing square is made of flat steel. It is available in two standard sizes, 24" by 16" and 24" by 18". The 24" side is called the body, and the shorter dimension at right angles is called the tongue. Both are marked not only in inches and fractions of an inch, but with several essential tables and scales. They can be used both as rules and as straightedges (Fig. 63).

**Try squares.** Try squares are constantly used in woodworking for testing the trueness of edges and ends with adjoining edges and with the

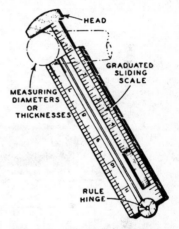

**Fig. 62.** Boxwood caliper rule.

face of the work after the work has been cut or planed. The common or fixed type is constructed of two parts, a thick wood or iron stock, and a thin steel blade, fixed at 90° to each other; the blade is graduated in inches and fractions of an inch. The sizes of the blades vary from 2" to 12" (Fig. 64).

The adjustable miter and try square is similar in every respect to the fixed-blade type with the exception that it can be used for both 45° and 90° work (Fig. 65). Its blade can be locked at any point along its length. The stock is fitted with a spirit level.

**Using a square.** In using a square, a guideline must always be marked across the surface of the work. When it is necessary

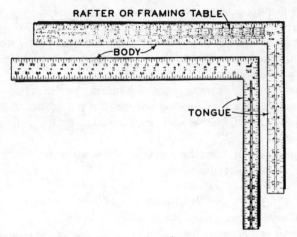

**Fig. 63.** Carpenter's or framing squares.

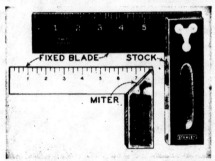

**Fig. 64.** Try and miter squares with fixed blade.

to cut, plane, or chisel a board square, either a try square or a carpenter's square is used to lay out the work or to mark the necessary guideline. A pencil is quite satisfactory for marking guidelines for roughing out woodwork, but where accuracy is necessary, guidelines should preferably be laid out with the blade of a pocketknife or a bench knife. The tip of the blade should be used to get a clean, accurate line. A guideline must be exactly located

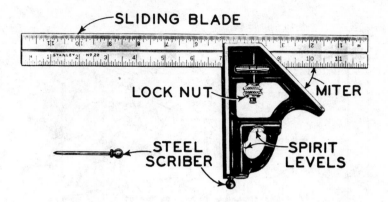

**SLIDING BLADE**

**LOCK NUT**   **MITER**

**STEEL SCRIBER**   **SPIRIT LEVELS**

**Fig. 65.** Adjustable try and miter square.

and must always be square with the edges of the work. If a board is wide, that is, if it averages wider than the blade of a try square, a carpenter's square must be used. To square a line with a try square, press the stock of the try square firmly against the edge of the board, and mark the guideline along the blade with the point of the pencil or the knife blade (*A*, Fig. 66).

In squaring a line across a board, one edge and one face of the board should be marked with X's so that they can be distinguished as the working edge and face. Then square a line from the working edge across the working face (*B*, Fig. 66). Be certain that the working edge is perfectly flat so that the square does not rock. Always square lines from the working face across both edges. Then, holding the stock of the square up against the working edge, square a line across the face on the side of the board opposite the working edge.

**Testing for squareness.** To test a board for squareness, place the inside edge of the stock of the square in contact with one surface. Face the light so that it will shine on the work. Slide the square downward and observe where the blade first comes in contact with the surface of the work. If the angle is square and the surface of the work is true, no light will be visible. If the angle does not happen to be square, or if the surface of the work is not absolutely true, light will shine through between the blade and the

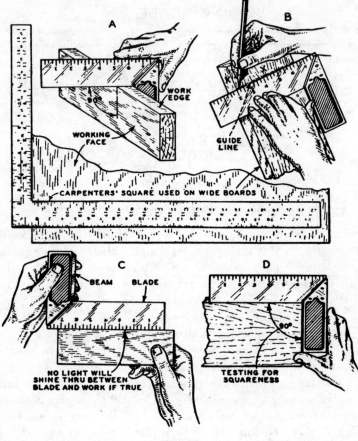

Fig. 66.

work (*C* and *D*, Fig. 66).

**Gauges.** Two types of gauges are used by the woodworker: the *marking* gauge and the *mortise* gauge. The marking gauge is the one more commonly used when absolute accuracy is required. Constructed of either wood or metal, the marking gauge consists of an 8" bar on which the head of the gauge slides. The head can be secured at any desired point on the bar by means of a thumbscrew (Fig. 67). A sharpened pin or spur affixed near the end of

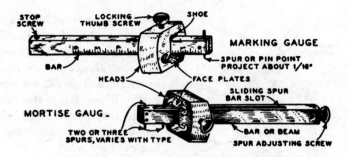

**Fig. 67.** Two types of woodworking gauges.

the bar scores the gauged line on the work. The bar of the marking gauge is graduated in inches and fractions of an inch.

The mortise gauge is a marking gauge with two spurs instead of one and is used for laying out mortises and tenons. The two spurs, one of which can be set independently, are used to score parallel lines.

**Using marking gauges.** Set the head of the gauge the required distance from the spur or pin, and secure it in place with the locking screw. Grasp the gauge with the palm and the fingers of the right hand. Press the head firmly against the edge of the work to be marked, and with a motion of the wrist, tip the head forward slightly until the point of the spur just touches the wood. Score the line by pushing the gauge away from you, keeping the head firmly against the edge of the work (Fig. 68). Note that the point of the spur must always be filed sharp and project approximately ¹⁄₁₆″.

The mortise gauge is used in approximately the same manner as the marking gauge, the only difference being that the two spurs are set the required distance apart by securing the movable one with the thumbscrew in the end of the beam, before the head is adjusted (Fig. 68).

## LEVELS

A level is a simple tool that indicates true vertical and true level positions. It will usually have either an aluminum or a

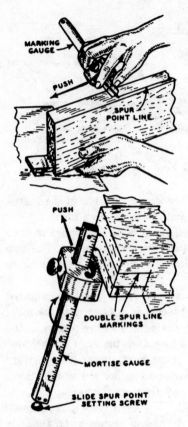

wooden frame in which two or four glass liquid-and-bubble tubes are mounted. Levels made of aluminum are light in weight and do not warp or rust. When there are four tubes, they are mounted in sets of two, each set at right angles to the other.

**Using a level.** The use of a level on either a flat or a vertical surface is shown in Fig. 69. In either position, when the bubble in one of the tubes is absolutely in the center— that is, between indicated lines on the tube—the work is level or plumb. When the bubble is off center, the work is not level.

## GLASS CUTTER

The procedures for the use of all types and sizes of glass cutters are identical. When cutting glass with this simple tool, a steel ruler or straight edge must be used to guide the

**Fig. 68.** Marking gauges.

tool. Set rule where cut is desired. Exert an even pressure of the

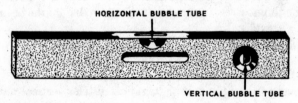

HORIZONTAL BUBBLE TUBE

VERTICAL BUBBLE TUBE

**Fig. 69.** Carpenter's level.

wheel of the tool on both the glass and the edge of the ruler or straight edge to score a line at required place on glass. After line has been scored, grip the waste part of the glass in the groove of the cutter and snap gently to break the glass along the scored line.

### SCRATCH AWL

Lines for cuts may be drawn on stock with a sharp pencil, tilted to bring the pencil point close to the straightedge. However, a more accurate location of the line will be obtained if you scribe the stock with a *scratch awl* (Fig. 70).

**Fig. 70.** Scratch awl.

### CHALK LINE

Long straight lines between distant points on surfaces are marked by snapping a *chalk line* as shown in Fig. 71. The line is first chalked by holding the chalk in the hand and drawing the line across it several times. It is then stretched between the points and snapped as shown. For an accurate snap, never snap the chalk line over a 20′ distance.

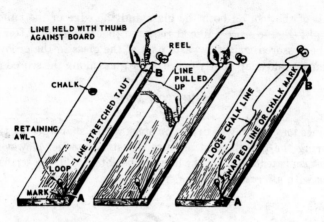

**Fig. 71.** Snapping a chalk line.

## FORSTNER BIT

The *forstner bit* does not have a feed screw but must be fed by pushing while turning. The rim projects slightly and prevents the bit from creeping when used. There is no tendency to split the wood as is often the case with screw-feed bits. Forstner bits, because of the absence of a feed screw, will bore holes almost through a board without defacing the opposite side of the board. The size markings are the same as auger bits.

## DRAWKNIFE

The *drawknife* (Fig. 72) is a two-hand cutter like the spokeshave; it is also pulled toward the operator in cutting. The blade has a single-bevel edge, like that of a plane iron, chisel, or spokeshave. The drawknife is used principally for rough-shaping cylindrical timbers, but it is also useful for removing a heavy edge-cut prior to finish planing. Grinding and whetting procedures are about the same as they are for a plane iron, chisel, or spokeshave. The width of the bevel should be about twice the thickness of the blade.

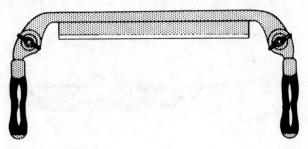

**Fig. 72.** Drawknife.

## NAIL SET

A *nail set* (Fig. 73) is used to *set* (meaning to countersink slightly below the surface) the heads of nails in finish carpentry. The purpose of setting is to improve the appearance of the work by concealing the nail heads. A nail is set by placing the tip of the nail set on the head of the nail and striking the set a blow or two with the hammer. The small surface hole above the head is usually plugged with putty.

**Fig. 73.** Nail set.

## PLASTIC FACED HAMMER

The *plastic faced hammer* (Fig. 74) has a metal head on a wooden handle, with replaceable plastic faces which can be screwed onto the ends of the head.

**Fig. 74.** Plastic faced hammer.

The plastic faces, being of a soft material, may be easily damaged in use. The faces may be restored by rasping off the damaged surface with a wood rasp, then smoothing with a file and sandpaper. Care should be taken to remove the same amount from each end of the head in order to maintain the proper balance of the hammer. When the faces are too badly scarred for repair, they should be unscrewed from the head and new ones inserted.

### WOOD MALLET

The *wood mallet* (Fig. 75) has a head 5″ long and 3″ in diameter, with two flat, circular faces reinforced by iron bands. It is set on a wooden handle.

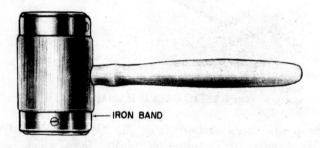

←IRON BAND

**Fig. 75.** Wood mallet

**Uses.** The mallet is used for driving wooden stakes, for smoothing out dents in sheet metal, or for turning thin metal edges without cutting the metal surface. It is also used for driving the framing chisel, in place of the plastic-faced hammer.

**Maintenance and care.** The mallet is never used to drive spikes or any other sharp-headed metallic object.

Mallets should be stored out of direct sunlight or away from heating pipes, since excessive drying will cause cracking and splitting.

When the edges of the faces become mushroomed, the iron band should be removed and the faces restored by sawing off a thin section. The edges are then dressed with a wood rasp, and the iron bands replaced.

Handles are replaced in the same manner as described previously.

## KNIVES

Most knives are used to cut, pare, and trim wood, leather, rubber, and other similar materials. The types most frequently used are the shop knife, pocket knife, and the putty knife (Fig. 76).

Multipurpose knives have an assortment of blades designed for forcing holes, driving screws, and opening cans, as well as cutting.

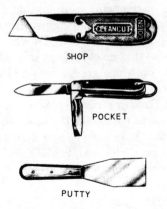

SHOP

POCKET

PUTTY

**Fig. 76.** Knives.

A putty knife is used for applying putty to a window sash when setting in panes of glass. The blade has a wide, square tip available in different lengths and widths.

(*See* Chap. 2, Equipment for Holding Work; *see also* Chap. 6, Power Tools; and Chap. 4, Methods of Fastening.)

## TOOL STORAGE AND RUST PREVENTION

Every tool in the workshop should have its proper place. Tools that are most often in use should be kept at hand on a tool rack specially designed for that purpose.

Tools that are not used frequently should be stored in a tool chest or in the individual boxes in which they were originally packed. During the damp spring and summer months, each tool should be coated with a film of oil or grease to prevent rust. When tools are to be stored for any length of time, it is good practice, in addition to coating, to wrap them in paper for protection from moisture and dust.

The cutting edges of tools must be protected at all times. In addition to the tool rack, a well-designed tool chest or a sturdy workbench in which each tool has its own place is desirable.

**Removing rust from tools.** When rust forms on hammers, chisels, saws, and screwdrivers, it can be easily removed. While there are several rust-removing solutions that work fairly well, the most satisfactory method of removing rust from these tools is with No. 240 emery paper or emery cloth. To remove a heavy coating of rust from surfaces that must be kept true, like the bottom of a plane, or a surface on which graduations and scales are marked, place this fine emery cloth on a flat surface and rub the tool on it.

This method of removing rust serves a double purpose, for it helps to retain the true surface of the tool and also removes any high or low spots that have been caused by the formation of rust. After the rust has been removed, rub the tool clean with a dry cloth and coat it with a film of oil or grease.

## CHAPTER 2

# Equipment for Holding Work

## BENCH VISE

A woodworking *bench vise*, designed for holding work for planing, sawing, or chiseling on the bench is shown in Fig. 1. Turning the *screw* by means of the *handle* causes the *movable jaw* on the vise to move in or out on the *slide bars* (sometimes called the *guide bars*). On a vise with a *continuous screw*, the movable jaw must be threaded all the way. On a vise with an *interrupted screw* (which is called a *quick-acting* vise), the movable jaw can be moved rapidly in or out when the screw is in a certain position. When the jaw is in the desired position against the work, the quick-acting vise can be tightened by a partial turn of the handle.

Most woodworking vises are equipped with a *dog* as shown in Fig. 1. The dog, which can be raised as shown or lowered flush with the top of the vise, is used in conjunction with a *bench stop* to hold work that is too wide for the maximum span of the vise.

Sometimes a bench is equipped with two vises, so that long work can be held at both ends. When this is the case, the principal vise is called the *side vise* and the auxiliary vise the *tail vise*.

A *bench hook* (Fig. 2) is a device for holding work for backsawing.

## SAWHORSE

The *sawhorse* might be called the carpenter's portable work bench and scaffold. If you do not already have a good sawhorse you will have to make one, and the layout part of the job will give you an idea of the practical use you can make of the framing

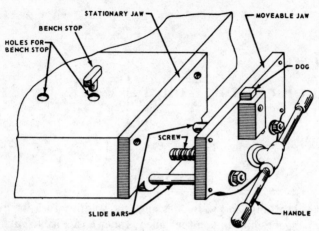

**Fig. 1.** Woodworking bench vise.

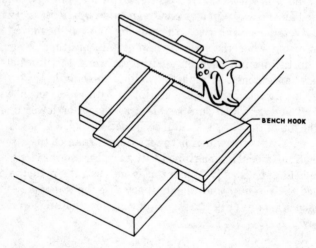

**Fig. 2.** Bench hook.

square. A working drawing for a good, sturdy sawhorse is shown in Fig. 3. A few pointers on the layout part of the job are as follows.

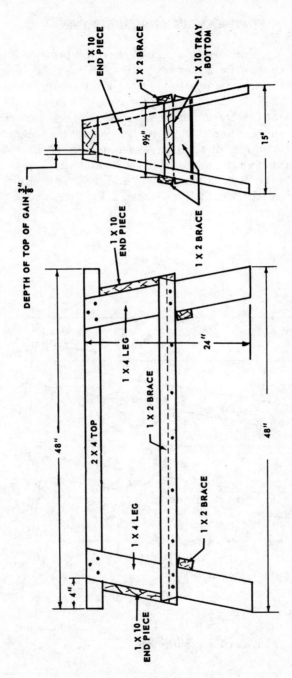

Fig. 3. Sawhorse.

The first layout problem is laying off the end cuts for the legs. If you think about it for a moment while examining the drawing, you will see that there is a right triangle involved here, with a total rise of 24″ (vertical height of the sawhorse) and a total run of 4″ (amount that the top of the leg is set away from the end of the top). To get the correct end cuts, then, you set the square to 4″ on the tongue and 24″ on the blade, as shown in Fig. 4. How long a piece will you need to start with? If you measure the hypotenuse, as shown in the illustration, you will find that the length of the finished piece will be a little more than 24¼″. Start with a piece about 26″ long.

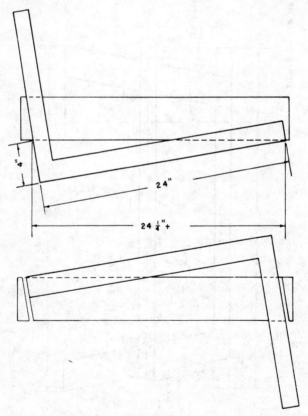

**Fig. 4.** Laying off end cuts for legs.

Mark the left-hand end cut along the tongue and mark the point where the end of the blade contacts the edge of the piece at the opposite end. Then turn the square over end-for-end and mark the opposite end cut as shown. Saw off the ends and use the piece as a pattern for laying out the end cuts on the other three legs.

The next problem is to lay off the *side cuts* on the legs. Once again there is a right triangle involved, and once again the total rise is 24″ (vertical height of the sawhorse). The total run is a little harder to figure. If you study Fig. 3 closely, you will see that the total run must amount to half the span of the legs (15″ divided by two, or 7½″) minus the horizontal thickness of the leg (you can call that ¾″), and minus half the *actual* width of the top (a 2 × 4 is usually only about 3¾″ wide, and half of that is 1⅞″) less the depth of the top of the gain, which is shown in the illustration to be ⅜″.

If you cannot quite see why this is so, study the simplified drawing in Fig. 5 where the basic triangle you are solving is shaded in. If you work out the arithmetic in the previous paragraph, you will find that the total run is 5¼″. To lay off the side cuts for the legs, then, you set the square to 5¼″ on the tongue and 24″ on the blade, against the edge of a leg, as shown in Fig. 6. Mark a line along the tongue, carry the line across the face of the piece, parallel to the line of the end cut, and bevel the end down to the line with a plane.

To lay out the gain on the side of the top, first set the top of a leg in place against the side, 4″ from the end, as shown in Fig. 7, top view, and draw the lines for the sides of the gain. Then use the marking gage to score a line ⅜″ from the edge of the top and chisel out the gain as indicated in the lower view.

The set of the framing square for the edges of the 1 × 10 end piece is the same as the set for the side cuts of the legs; a study of Fig. 5 will show you why. Select a piece that is *actually* 10″ wide, and lay off the line for one of the edges as shown in Fig. 8. Since you will not be able to end-for-end the square to get the line for the other edge in this case, the best way to lay that line off is to set the T-bevel to the other line, measure off the prescribed 9½″ along the bottom, reverse the T-bevel, set it to the mark, and lay off the line as indicated in Fig. 8.

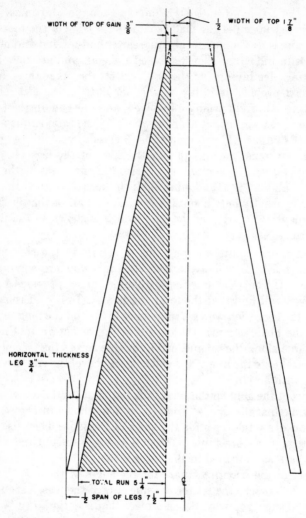

**Fig. 5.** Basic triangle for end cuts for legs.

The set of the framing square for the edge cuts for the 1 × 10 tray is also 5½″ on the tongue and 24″ on the blade, but the best way to fit the tray is to set it in place and mark it after the top,

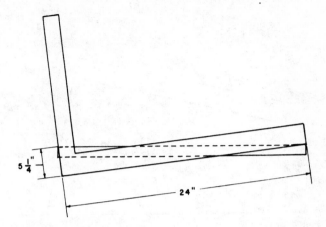

**Fig. 6.** Laying off side cuts for legs.

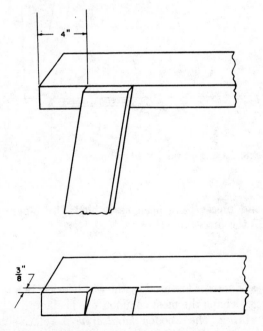

**Fig. 7.** Laying out the gains for the legs.

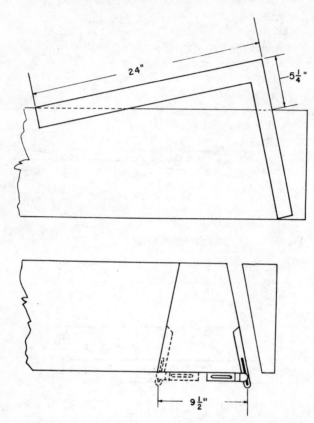

**Fig. 8.** Laying off the 1 × 10 end piece.

legs, and end pieces have been assembled. Use 8-penny coated nails to nail the pieces together.

## CLAMPS

Two types of *clamps* are used by the woodworker in a large variety of ways; perhaps the most common use is clamping pieces together for gluing. The wooden *handscrew* is relatively limited with regard to both scope and pressure. The *steel bar clamp* applies a very strong pressure and can be set (by moving the *adjustable head* outward) to a very wide scope.

A *handscrew* is shown in Fig. 9; a *steel bar clamp* in Fig. 10. The size of a handscrew is designated by the length of the jaw in inches; sizes range from 6″ to 18″. The size of a steel bar clamp is designated by the length of the bar in feet; sizes range from 2′ to 8′.

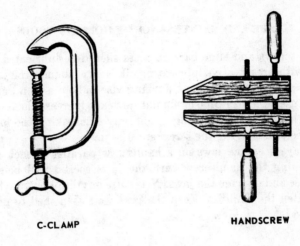

**C-CLAMP**                **HANDSCREW**

**Fig. 9.** C-clamp and handscrew.

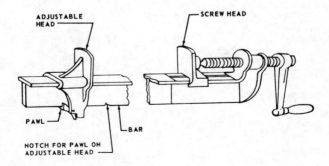

**Fig. 10.** Steel bar clamp.

A *metal C-clamp* is also shown in Fig. 9. When one of these is used for wood, the wood must be protected against damage from the metal jaw and the screw swivel on the clamp. C-clamps are designed chiefly for clamping metal. Size is designated by the maximum scope between the screw swivel and the jaw.

(*See* Chap. 1, Woodworking Tools and How To Use Them; *see also* Chap. 6, Power Tools.)

### CARE AND MAINTENANCE OF HOLDING TOOLS

The screws and slide bars on vises should be lubricated regularly with preservative lubricating oil. Never hammer the jaws of a vise, and never use a woodworking vise to hold a metal article. Never use a piece of pipe or similar device to increase the leverage of the handle. There is danger, not only of breaking the handle, but also of damaging the screw and the jaws.

Always keep the jaws on a handscrew parallel to each other. Tightening the handscrew with the jaws cocked will bend the spindles and damage the jaws. *Never* use anything but the hands to tighten the spindles. Keep the jaws well varnished to protect the wood.

## CHAPTER 3

# Power Tools

## PORTABLE ELECTRIC SAWS

Portable electric saws are available in various sizes, ranging from 6½″ for the amateur builder, up to 9¼″ for the more advanced or professional worker.

**Motor.** These saws are equipped with a "Universal" type motor and will operate either on D.C. or A.C. current at 25, 40, 50, or 60 cycles, of the specified voltage. Standard voltages are 115 or 220, with 125 or 240 volts available.

Inspect carbon brushes in the motor at regular intervals, and if worn away replace immediately to prevent damage to the motor armature. The manufacturer's service department will be glad to instruct you in brush inspection and furnish the correct brushes.

**Current.** Be sure to specify the voltage when purchasing a portable electric saw. *Always* check the voltage specifications on the nameplate of your equipment with the voltage of your supply line.

**Cable.** Three-conductor cable is used on all saws. The third wire is for "grounding." Do not permit the cable to lie in grease or oil which ruins the rubber. Wipe it off occasionally and avoid rough handling. When not in use coil it loosely without sharp bends or kinks and keep it off the floor. Extension cables are described in this chapter.

**Grounding.** Every electric tool *should be* grounded while in use to protect the operator against shock. Proper grounding is a good habit to develop under all circumstances, but is especially important where dampness is present. The unit is equipped with approved 3-conductor cord and 3-blade grounding type attachment plug cap to be used with the proper grounding type receptacle, in accordance with the National Electrical Code. The green colored conductor in the cord is the grounding wire which is connected to the metal frame of the unit inside the housing and to the longest blade of the attachment plug cap. *Never* connect the green wire to a "live" terminal.

If your unit has a *plug* that looks like the one shown in Fig. 1, A, it will fit directly into the latest type of 3-wire grounding receptacles. The unit is then grounded automatically each time it is plugged in. A special grounding adaptor (Fig. 1, B) is supplied to permit using 2-wire receptacles until the correct receptacle is properly installed. The green grounding wire extending from the side of the adaptor must be connected to a permanent ground, such as a properly grounded outlet box, conduit or water pipe before plugging in the tool.

If the unit has a *plug* like the one shown in Fig. 1, C, no adaptor is furnished and it should be used in the proper standard matching 3-wire grounding receptacle. The unit is then grounded automatically each time it is plugged in.

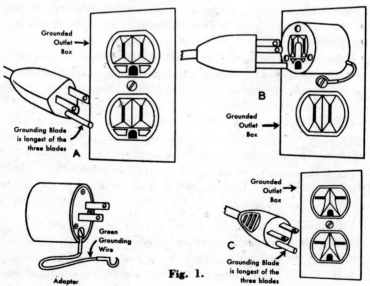

Grounded Outlet Box

Grounding Blade is longest of the three blades A

B

Grounded Outlet Box

Green Grounding Wire

Adapter

C

Grounding Blade is longest of the three blades

Grounded Outlet Box

**Fig. 1.**

## OPERATION

Connect the grounding-wire first, as described previously in this chapter, and then plug into power supply. Before pressing trigger switch to start motor, rest front of saw "shoe or base on the work and line up blade with cutting line. Be sure that blade teeth are not yet in contact with work and that lower blade guard is free. Pull trigger and guide saw through its cut with firm pressure, but without forcing. Undue force actually slows down the cutting and produces a rougher cut.

**Keep blades sharp.** Dull or incorrectly set teeth may cause the saw to swerve or stall under pressure. If the saw stalls *do not* release trigger switch, but *back* the saw until the blade momentum is regained. Then either shut off motor or start to cut again. This procedure will greatly increase the life of your saw switch.

To make a *pocket cut*, first set the saw shoe at the desired cutting depth. Then rest the toe or heel of shoe against the work (heel, when using 6½" saw). Carefully draw back the lower blade guard by lifting the provided lever *before starting the motor*. Next, lower the saw until the blade teeth lightly contact the cutting line. This will allow you to release the lower blade guard as contact with the work will keep it in position to open freely as the cut is started. *Now*, start the motor and gradually lower the saw until its shoe rests flat on the work. Advance along the cutting line as in normal sawing. For starting each new cut, proceed as above for your own protection. *Do not* tie back the lower blade guard.

**Caution!** To insure against accidents *always* disconnect the cable plug before making adjustments or inspection. *Always* disconnect the saw cable when not in active use.

## ADJUSTMENTS

**Cutting depth adjustments.** In cutting any material with steel blades the most efficient depth adjustment is one that permits the tooth depth only of the blade to project below the material (except when using carbide tipped blades, when just ½ of the tooth tip should project below the material). This keeps blade friction at a minimum, removes sawdust from the cut and results in cooler, faster sawing (Fig. 2).

**For 6½″, 7¼″, 8″ saws.** Correct cutting depth is obtained by adjusting the quick clamping lever on the side at the rear of the saw. Adjustment of the clamping lever on the 6½″, 7¼″ and 8″ saws is made by loosening the set screw, removing and indexing the lever to its proper clamping location, replacing it and tightening the set screw.

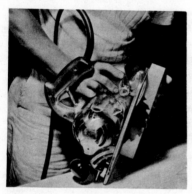
Fig. 2.

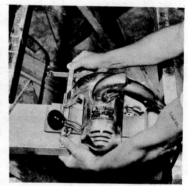
Fig. 3.

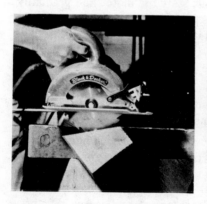
Fig. 4.

Fig. 5.

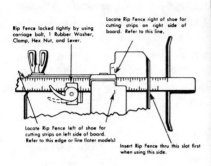

Rip Fence locked tightly by using carriage bolt, 1 Rubber Washer, Clamp, Hex Nut, and Lever.

Locate Rip Fence right of shoe for cutting strips on right side of board. Refer to this line.

Locate Rip Fence left of shoe for cutting strips on left side of board. Refer to this edge or line (later models)

Insert Rip Fence thru this slot first when using this side.

**Fig. 6.**

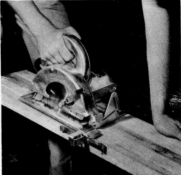

**Fig. 7.**

**For 8¼", 9¼" saws.** Correct cutting depth for these saws is obtained by adjusting either or both of the built-in front and rear cutting depth adjustments. By using both adjustments, the handle remains in the most comfortable cutting position. *Always* be sure to retighten wing nuts securely after making adjustments.

**Bevel Angle Adjustments.** The 6½", 7¼", 8", 8¼" and 9¼" saws have an adjustable shoe which permits bevel cutting at any angle between 45° and 90°. The quadrant on the front of these saws is calibrated for accurate adjustment. Loosen the wing nut and tilt the shoe to angle desired. Retighten wing nut securely. See Figs. 3 and 4.

### ACCESSORIES

**Protractor.** This is a surprisingly simple and practical device that is calibrated in degrees and can be set to cut any angle by moving the holding arm to correct degree. Use the bevel adjustment on the saw in conjunction with the protractor for compound mitres. To operate, the saw shoe (either side) is lined up with the protractor's straightedge and is advanced along this edge (Fig. 5).

A protractor is also useful for laying out any carpentry work involving angles.

**Rip fence.** The rip fence saves time in rip sawing (Fig. 6), eliminating the need to scribe guide lines. It greatly improves ripping accuracy. Fence is calibrated to $\frac{1}{8}$ of an inch. It may be used on either right or left hand side of the saw. To attach, slide fence through proper openings provided in the shoe as shown in Fig. 7. Clamp firmly at desired position with quick acting lever.

BLADES

**Changing blades.** To change a saw blade, first disconnect the cable plug to prevent injury or damage resulting from accidental pressure on the trigger switch. Then insert nail through hole in blade so that it rests against bottom of saw shoe and prevents blade from turning. With a wrench, turn holding screw counterclockwise to loosen and remove screw and washer. Retract lower guard and lift off blade. Remove inner clamp washer and clean both faces of each clamp washer, blade, and blade screw threads —this prevents uneven seating of the blade. Replace inner clamp washer, new blade—trade-mark side out (with teeth pointing toward front of saw), outer clamp washer, and blade holding screw and tighten holding screw clockwise with wrench until secure.

**Combination blades.** This is the latest type, precision engineered, fast-cutting blade for general service ripping and crosscutting (Fig. 8, A). Each blade carries the correct number of teeth to cut chips rather than scrape sawdust. Blade teeth receive less wear and stay sharp longer, and give definitely smoother cuts. Cutting efficiency has been increased by using redesigned sturdier teeth, reduces any tendency of the blade to "flutter" or vibrate.

Extensive tests have shown that a greater number of teeth reduces cutting efficiency, because of an increased scraping action. On the other hand, a lesser number increases the toothload to a point where the cutting edges rapidly become dull and burnt.

**Crosscut blades.** Crosscut blades were designed specifically for fast, smooth crosscutting (Fig. 8, B). They make a smoother cut than the combination blades.

**Planer blades.** This blade makes very smooth cuts, both rip and crosscut (Fig. 8, C). It is ideal for interior wood working, and is hollow-ground to produce the finest possible saw-cut finish.

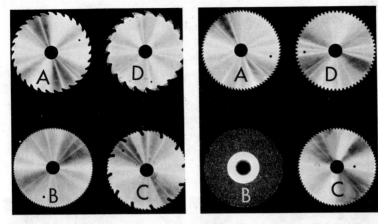

Fig. 8. Fig. 9.

**Carbide-tipped blades.** The carbide-tipped blade is the keenest and most durable blade yet developed for cutting building materials (Fig. 8, D). This blade stays sharp thirty times longer than normal steel blade when cutting lumber. The carbide tips are brazed into a special alloy steel blade. It has been established that the diamond-like hardness of these tips will retain their edges up to 50 times longer than steel.

**Flooring blades.** Flooring blades should be used on jobs where occasional nails may be encountered (Fig. 9, A). They are especially useful in cutting through flooring, sawing reclaimed lumber and in opening boxes and crates.

**Abrasive discs.** These blades are all of the top-quality resinoid-bonded, abrasive cut-off type (Fig. 9, B). They are used for cutting and slotting in ceramics, slate, marble, tile, transite, etc. Also for cutting thin gauge, non-ferrous metals.

**Non-ferrous metal-cutting blades.** These blades have teeth shaped and set for cutting soft, non-ferrous metals, including lead (Fig. 9, C).

**Friction blades.** Friction blades are ideal for cutting corrugated galvanized sheets. They cut faster, with less dirt, than abrasive discs. Blade is taper-ground for clearance (Fig. 9, D).

### COMBINATION ELECTRIC SCREW-DRILL

A completely new combination tool, the electric screw-drill, is an efficient tool for craftsmen, builders, and hobbyists. It is equipped with a positive-clutch electric screw-driving mechanism. The screw-drill has a locking collar that permits operator to quickly convert to direct drive for general-purpose drilling. The unit is amply powered by a "Universal" motor for 115 volts, A.C. or D.C., and includes a 3-jaw geared chuck and key, and screw-driving bit and finder assembly.

Fig. 10.                              Fig. 11.

Used as a drill, the unit is capable of drilling holes up to ⅜″ diameter in steel. It can also be used to drive hole saws, masonry bits and wood augers (Fig. 10).

In its screw-driving position, the screw-drill drives wood screws up to #10 x 1½″ size, or self-tapping metal screws up to size #12 (Fig. 11).

### OPERATION

**Chuck.** When operating, first, always bottom the bit in the chuck. This permits the chuck jaws to grip the shank fully and prevents cocking the jaws. Second, use *all three holes* in the chuck body to tighten as much as possible. Only one hole is needed to release the bit. Third, use *only* a chuck key to tighten or loosen the chuck jaws. If you lose the chuck key, obtain a new one at once.

To obtain maximum life from the jaw assembly, lock your chuck firmly with the key to prevent drill slippage, and when the chuck is not in use, leave it with the jaws open.

**Removing the chuck.** To remove the chuck, place the chuck key in the chuck and strike key a sharp blow using a hammer or other object in the same direction that tool normally runs. This will loosen the chuck so that it can be easily unscrewed by hand. *Disconnect* tool before making any changes or adjustments.

**Switch.** Grasp the tool firmly before pressing trigger switch "ON". The tool will remain "ON" as long as pressure is maintained on the trigger. Releasing trigger automatically turns the motor "OFF".

*To lock the switch* "ON" pull trigger and hold it "ON"; press in locking button and hold it in; then release trigger. Motor will now stay "ON" until trigger is again squeezed and released— the trigger will snap out and the motor will turn "OFF". Practice this a few times.

**Drilling.** To adjust the unit for drilling, viewing the unit from the chuck end, rotate the adjustment collar counterclockwise until the word "drill" is at the top of the unit. If the collar stops before reaching this point, turn the chuck slightly; the adjustment collar can then be rotated to the proper position (Fig. 12).

For screw-driving rotate the adjustment collar in a clockwise direction until the word "screw" is at the top of the unit. This will disengage the clutch teeth which will automatically be engaged when pressure is applied in driving screws.

The two Allen set screws located in the front part of the gear case are properly adjusted by the factory and should not be readjusted unless the adjusting collar is loose.

Mark exact center of hole with a center punch or nail to guide the drill bit. Clamp or anchor the work securely to insure accuracy and prevent damage or injury. Thin metal should be backed up with a wooden block to prevent bending or distortion

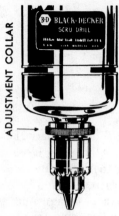

ADJUSTMENT COLLAR

Fig. 12.

Fig. 13.

of the work. Keep bits sharp and use a lubricant when drilling ferrous metals other than cast iron. Relieve pressure on the tool when bit is about to break through to avoid "stalling" the motor. Be sure that the chuck jaws are tightened securely and do not constantly overload the tool. In general, high speed and light feed are recommended.

When drilling wood, particularly deep holes, partially remove the bit from the hole several times while in motion. This will clear the chips, speed up drilling and prevent overheating (Fig. 13).

In drilling brick, cement, cinder block or similar materials, use carbide tipped masonry drill bits. Ordinary steel bits would be dulled rapidly in this type of work.

**Driving screws.** Adjust the collar to the screw driving position, then insert the correct screw driving bit into the chuck. (See Fig. 11). Make sure that the chuck jaw rests squarely on the "flats" of the bit. Tighten chuck jaws securely so that there is no chance of slippage. Turn on the unit and the chuck and bit will idle until the bit is engaged in the screw head and pressure is applied. The unit should be grasped firmly with both hands and a steady forward pressure applied—the screw will be driven down tight. At this point the clutch comes into operation and will ratchet or slip until the unit is removed from the screw.

It is suggested that you practice by driving a few screws into a scrap piece of lumber until you get the "feel" of this procedure (Fig. 11).

## MAINTENANCE

**Brushes.** Inspect carbon brushes frequently and replace them when badly worn. Cartridge-type brush holders are used to make this operation easy for you. Merely remove the end cover on the switch handle by taking out screws which hold cover in place. Then remove brush caps with a screwdriver and take out the brush and spring assemblies. Springs should have enough tension to hold the brush firmly against the commutator. Be sure to replace badly worn brush assemblies.

Always keep brushes clean and sliding freely in their guides. After several brush replacements, the commutator should be inspected for excess wear. If a groove has been cut by the brushes, the tool should be sent to the manufacturer for repair.

**Cable.** The cable is the "life line" of your tool, therefore keep it clean by wiping it off occasionally. Be sure to keep it out of oils and greases which ruin the rubber. Coil it neatly when not in use and avoid dragging it across sharp surfaces or using it as a handle to lift the tool.

When using the tool at a considerable distance from power source, an extension cable of adequate size must be used to prevent loss of power. Use the table below for 115 volt current.

| *Extension Cable Length in Feet* | *Gauge of Cable Wire Required* |
|---|---|
| 25, 50, 75, 100, 200 | 18, 18, 18, 18, 16 |

**Lubrication.** The gears should be re-lubricated regularly in from sixty days to six months, depending on use. Remove gear housing, flush out all old grease with kerosene and, with gears in place, refill the housing only half full. The commutator and armature bearing may be lubricated by one or two drops of oil on the armature shaft through the hole provided in the handle cover.

## ELECTRIC HAND FINISHING SANDER

This new dustless finishing sander for use in the home and shop has been designed for simple, quick attachment to any vacuum cleaner, and the unit gives the cleanest sanding jobs possible. Dust is instantly removed from the work surface to provide more healthful working conditions and keeps the abrasive paper sharp for more efficient sanding.

It operates on an orbital-action principle, powered by a special sander motor to deliver 4300 orbits per minute, producing a satin-smooth finish upon any surface. Speed and power of the unit permit sanding *with, against,* or *across* the grain of wood surfaces without danger of swirl marks or scratches. Light, compact, and easy to handle, this sander permits even a novice to get professional results effortlessly, on all sanding or refinishing jobs (Fig. 14).

**Fig. 14.**

**Abrasive Paper.** "Electro coated," aluminum oxide abrasive paper is the best to use with your finishing sander; 150 or 4/0 fine grit, open grain paper will give you the smoothest finish; and 60 or 1/2/0 coarse grit, open grain will give you the greatest material removal consistent with the proper wood finishing practice.

*Do not* use ordinary sand paper as its coating qualities are inferior. However, in certain metal sanding applications, emory cloth of various grits will prove to be more durable.

**Attaching abrasive paper.** The dustless finishing sander is supplied with a dust collecting skirt, snap-in hose connector, hose and coupling. To attach the abrasive paper to this unit the dust collecting skirt should be removed. Two studs on either side of the skirt clamp around the bottom of the sander housing. With thumb pressure on both sides of skirt and two index fingers on inner edge of skirt, pull out and up. This will release studs and allow skirt to be removed (Fig. 15, A). The sandpaper tightening sprockets are now completely exposed.

After selecting the correct grade of grit apply the abrasive paper between the sprocket and the platen and tighten the sprocket by using the T-shaped key provided, or a screwdriver. (Key may be attached to cable, using the slot provided in the key.) This sprocket should be tightened until the abrasive paper is about ¼″ underneath the sprocket (Fig. 15, B).

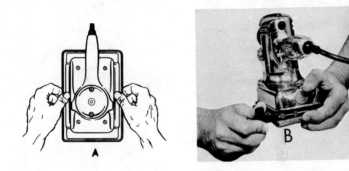

**Fig. 15.**

Fasten the other edge of the abrasive paper in the same manner. You will find this new type clamping mechanism holds the abrasive paper taut. If it should become loose during operation, tighten the sprockets immediately. This will preserve the life of your abrasive paper.

### ASSEMBLY

The finishing sander, after the abrasive paper has been mounted in place, can be converted to a dustless unit by assembling the dustless equipment as follows:

Remove round plug (Fig 16, A) in the rear of the finishing sander by prying under the edge with a screwdriver or knife. Snap on the dust collecting skirts so that the two studs (Fig. 16, I) fit firmly over the lower edge of the sander housing. Insert the metal coupling (Fig. 16, B) with the detent pin inserted in the rear end of the sander. It may be necessary to manually depress the detent pin. Now attach the hose to the coupling using the smaller hose end (Fig 16, C). To the other end of the hose attach a vacuum cleaner (any type). In connecting the hose to the vacuum cleaner use either the adapter supplied, or hose end itself (which may be attached over or into the inlet). See Fig. 16, depending upon the type of vacuum cleaner connection.

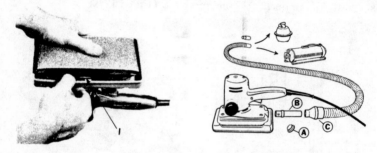

**Fig. 16.**

## OPERATION

Before using the finishing sander, examine the trigger switch. Squeezing this trigger turns the tool "ON"; releasing it turns the tool "OFF". However, on most sanding applications it is more convenient to lock the switch "ON", with the locking pin, which projects from the side of the switch handle, just above the trigger. To do this, first squeeze the trigger and hold it "ON", and press in the locking pin. Then release the trigger. The switch will remain "ON". To turn the motor "OFF", merely pull the trigger and release it. The black molded knob may be screwed into any of three positions to suit the operator. The knob can be threaded into either side or in front of the motor housing.

After turning on the vacuum cleaner, which is attached to your finishing sander, grasp both control handles of the sander firmly, and use the tool freely without forced effort or unnecessary downward pressure. Excessive pressure will slow cutting action and reduce abrasive life. The weight of the tool itself, in most cases, will prove to be sufficient (Fig. 17).

It is not necessary to sand only with the grain of the wood. Move the sander in any direction over the work area to effect rapid and convenient coverage. Sand only long enough to obtain a smooth surface, as the cutting action of the tool is rapid and too much material may be removed with prolonged sanding (Fig. 18).

**Fig. 17.**

**Fig. 18.**

For best results sand progressively with coarse paper first; then, medium; then, fine paper. To obtain what might be called a "superfinish", wet the surface with a sponge or rag and let it dry. The grain of the wood will rise slightly and the surface feel rough. Now, re-sand with 150 or 4/0 grit paper for extra-smooth results.

Of course, the more effective your vacuum cleaner, the more dust removal; therefore, the bag of the vacuum cleaner should be emptied periodically to assure maximum suction.

**Note:** To remove metal coupling (Fig. 16), rotate coupling so that arrow is on top and then remove.

## MAINTENANCE

**Motors.** This finishing sander is equipped with a "Universal" motor which can be used, at the voltage specified on the nameplate, with either alternating current at 25, 40, 50 or 60 cycles, or with direct current. Voltage should not vary more than 5 per cent, over or under the voltage shown on the nameplate, or serious overheating and loss of power can result. All motors are tested by the manufacturer, and if the tool fails to operate, proceed as follows: (1) Check supply line for blown fuses; (2) see that plug and receptacle are making good contact; and (3) inspect carbon brushes and replace them if they are worn away.

**Brushes.** Inspect carbon brushes frequently and replace when badly worn. Cartridge-type brush holders are used to make this operation easy. After disconnecting tool, merely remove both brush caps with a screwdriver and take out the brush and spring assemblies. Springs should have enough tension to hold the brush firmly against the commutator. Be sure to replace badly worn brush assemblies.

Be sure to keep brushes clean and sliding freely in their guides. After several brush replacements, the commutator should be inspected for excess wear. If a groove has been cut by the brushes, the tool should be sent to the manufacturer for repair.

**Cable.** Be sure to keep the cable clean by wiping it off occasionally as it is the "life line" of your tool. Keep it out of oils and greases which ruin the rubber. Coil it neatly when not in use and avoid dragging it across sharp surfaces or using it as a handle to lift the tool.

When using the tool at a considerable distance from power source, an extension cable of adequate size must be used to prevent loss of power. Use the table below for 115 volt current.

| *Extension Cable Length in Feet* | *Gauge of Cable Wire Required* |
|---|---|
| 25, 50, 75, 100, 200 | 18, 18, 17, 14, 12 |

**Lubrication.** The gears should be re-lubricated regularly from sixty days to six months, depending on use. Remove gear housing, flush out all old grease with kerosene and, with gears in place, refill the housing only half full. The commutator and armature bearing may be lubricated by one or two drops of oil on the armature shaft through the hole provided in the top of the tool.

## ELECTRIC HAND POWER PLANE

This hand power plane is designed for a comfortable operating balance. Handles and thumb-rest are so placed as to provide an accurate planing "feel" and afford the correct "inward and downward" pressure for each planing operation.

**Motors.** The power plane shown in Fig. 19 is equipped with a "Universal" motor which can be used, at the voltage specified on the nameplate, with either alternating current at 25, 40, 50 or 60 cycles, or with direct current. Voltage should not vary more than 10 per cent, over or under, the voltage shown on the nameplate or serious overheating and loss of power can result. All motors are tested by the manufacturer, and if the tool fails to operate take the following action: (1) Check your supply line for blown fuses; (2) see that the plug and receptacle are making good contact; and (3) inspect carbon brushes and replace them if they are worn away.

**Fig. 19.**

**Brushes.** Inspect carbon brushes frequently and replace them when badly worn. Cartridge-type brush holders are used to make this operation easy for you. Merely remove both brush caps with a screwdriver and take out the brush and spring assemblies. Springs should have enough tension to hold the brush firmly against the commutator. Be sure to replace badly worn brush assemblies.

Keep brushes clean and sliding freely in their guides. After several brush replacements, the commutator should be inspected for excess wear. If a groove has been cut by the brushes, the tool should be sent to the manufacturer for repair.

**Cable.** When using a power plane at a considerable distance from power source, an extension cable of adequate size must be used to prevent loss of power. Use the table below for 115 volt current.

| *Extension Cable Length in Feet* | *Gauge of Cable Wire Required* |
|---|---|
| 25, 50, 75, 100, 200 | 18, 16, 16, 12, 10 |

**Grounding.** As previously described.

**Adjustments.** Place a straightedge or scale along the rear shoe of the plane and with a screwdriver, turn adjusting screw (Fig. 20), until the highest cutting edge of the cutter touches the scale of straightedge. This adjustment must be accurate, or poor results would be obtained and, when once adjusted properly, the adjustment should not be changed unless the cutter is replaced or resharpened.

To adjust the depth of cut, place a straightedge or a piece of wood along the rear shoe of the plane and turn the knurled knob (Fig. 21) for the depth of cut desired. This is determined by the space between the front shoe and the straightedge or piece of wood (Fig. 21). The depth of cut is adjustable from zero to $\frac{3}{32}''$. A depth of cut of $\frac{1}{32}''$ is recommended.

The adjustments referred to above are necessary each time a cutter is replaced or sharpened.

To adjust the vertical guide at right angles to the shoe of the plane, slightly loosen wing nuts (Fig. 22, A) and using a square, move the vertical guide so that it is at 90° to the shoe.

The vertical guide is adjustable outward to a 120° obtuse angle and inward to a 45° angle for bevel planing. To adjust the vertical guide for bevel planing, loosen wing nuts (Fig. 22, A) and adjust it to the degree of bevel required. The quadrants at the wing nuts are graduated, however, for very accurate work, a protractor or similar device should be used when adjusting the vertical guide,

Fig. 20.

Fig. 21.

Fig. 22.

after which wing nuts (Fig. 22, A) should be tightened securely.

Lock screws (Fig. 22, B) are used to apply tension on both the front and rear shoes of the plane. These screws are properly tensioned at the factory, but after a long period of use it may be necessary to slightly tighten them with a screwdriver.

## OPERATION

When using the power plane, grasp both handles firmly and place the thumb of the left hand on the recess of the top of the shoe (Fig. 19). Place the plane on the board using downward pressure with the left hand until the cutter engages, after which downward pressure is applied by both hands, and the vertical guide should be engaged against the side of the board using side pressure. At the completion of the cut, pressure is relieved from the left hand and exerted to the right hand at the rear of the tool, and the forward feed should be reduced so as to minimize chipping at the end of the cut.

The forward movement of the plane in operation depends upon the type of wood being planed. Softwood such as pine planes very rapidly; however, when planing hardwood and particularly plywood, the forward feed of the plane should be slowed down so that the cutter will cut freely.

If the plane is moved forward too slowly the cutter will have a tendency to burn certain kinds of lumber, and if moved too fast, the speed of the motor would be reduced, causing it to be overloaded and result in premature wear on the cutter. The fact that wood has different densities and occasional knots will be encountered, it is impossible to predetermine the forward movement of the plane. The user will soon learn by the sound of the motor when the forward movement of the plane is correct.

It is suggested that a piece of scrap lumber be used to familiarize the user with the tool. There are instances where the wood being planed would have high spots, and these spots should be removed before making a complete cut the length of the board. This is best done by drawing an accurate line on the side of the board, so that the high spots can be easily located.

To get the most out of your plane keep it clean, blow dust and chips from it when necessary, and always keep both the vertical guide and shoes free of resin or any other foreign matter so that smooth surfaces will always be applied to the board being planed. For the best results keep the cutter sharp at all times. When not in use, store the plane in a dry place. A thin coat of oil or paste wax will retard rust.

**Safety procedures.** Always disconnect the plane from the power supply when making any adjustments. Be sure to disconnect the plane from the power supply when not in use. Handle sharp cutters carefully to avoid injury.

**Lubrication.** The power plane is completely lubricated at the factory. All ball bearings are of the closed-type and lubricant lasts the life of the bearings.

## ELECTRIC HEAVY DUTY HAND ROUTER

The hand operated router shown in Fig. 23 is the latest development in electric woodworking tools. It is efficiently designed for speed and accuracy in performing the finest joinery, and most beautiful cabinet work such as beading, grooving, routing, fluting, cove-cutting, dovetailing, dadoing, rabbeting, making joints, and similar operations. Its use enables the home woodworker to rapidly accomplish inlay work, decorative edges, and many types of bas-relief carving and wood-finishing. (See Parts shown in Fig. 23)

This router is powered by a special router motor, and operates on a direct-drive principle, no gears are necessary, and the motor speeds up to 21,000 r.p.m. Feeding properly into the work it leaves an extremely smooth finish that requires little or no sanding.

## GENERAL OPERATING PROCEDURES

The router consists of two major parts—the *motor* and the *base* (Fig. 24). The motor housing is designed in such a way that it forms a firm support for the router in an inverted position. This extra convenience feature leaves both of the operator's hands free to insert or remove bits and cutters. The base is equipped with a smooth surface sub-base, held in place by three countersunk screws. This sub-base protects the working surface from mars or scratches while doing fine cabinet work. It may be

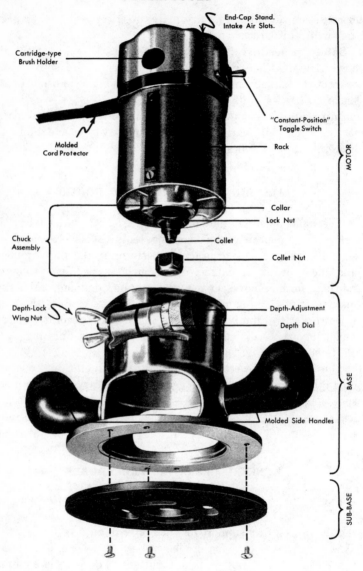

End-Cap Stand.
Intake Air Slots.

Cartridge-type
Brush Holder

"Constant-Position"
Toggle Switch

Molded
Cord Protector

Rack

MOTOR

Collar
Lock Nut

Chuck
Assembly

Collet

Collet Nut

Depth-Lock
Wing Nut

Depth-Adjustment

Depth Dial

BASE

Molded Side Handles

SUB-BASE

**Fig. 23.**

easily removed to facilitate use of large bits and cutters, or to add depth-of-cut when a longer bit or arbor is not available.

### ASSEMBLY

Figure 25 shows the assembled motor and base. To *assemble,* loosen the wing nut (A) on the base, and insert the motor into the base until the rack and pinion (B) which regulates the depth-of-cut, engages. Tighten wing nut and set router up in inverted position. The unit is now ready for inserting a bit or an arbor to hold cutters.

Fig. 24.

Fig. 25.

### MAINTENANCE AND CARE

**Motor and current.** The router is powered by a "Universal" router motor. It operates at nameplate voltage on alternating current (25 to 60 cycles), or on direct current. Voltage variation of more than ten per cent will cause loss of power and overheating. Be sure to check the voltage specifications on the nameplate of your equipment with the voltage of your supply line. Inspect the carbon brushes in the motor at regular intervals, and if worn away replace them immediately to prevent damage to the motor armature as instructed by the manufacturer.

**Cable.** Every router is equipped with a *three-conductor cable*. The third wire is for "grounding." (See Grounding in section on Portable Electric Saws, Chap. 3.) *Do not* permit cable to lie in grease or oil which ruins the rubber. Wipe it off occasionally and avoid rough handling. When not in use coil the cable loosely without sharp bends or kinks, and keep it off the floor.

If an extension cable is necessary to reach a power outlet, be sure that the cable is made of a wire size large enough to carry current to the router without too great a drop in voltage. A long extension cable of inadequate size will cause a voltage drop, loss of power and damage to the motor through overheating. When using an extension make sure that it is a 3-conductor cable. Connect the third wire of the cable on the tool to the third wire of the extension. Then ground the other end of the extension with the third wire, as described under Grounding. If more than one extension cable is used, connect the various third wires, grounding the one nearest the electrical receptacle.

Use the following table for 115 volt current.

| *Extension Cable Length In Feet* | *Gauge of Cable Wire Required* |
| --- | --- |
| 25, 50, 75, 100, 200 | 18, 16, 14, 12, 10 |

### OPERATION SAFETY

*Make sure* that the tool is *properly grounded* before operating. To operate, grasp the tool firmly, not gingerly in your hand. *Do not* turn the power "ON" until you are in working position. Then place the tool in working position and press the toggle switch.

Always pull the plug before you change bits or cutters.

Every tool is thoroughly tested before leaving the factory and should be in perfect operating condition when it reaches the user. If, at any time, your unit fails to operate, it will save you time and expense to check the following possible causes of failure:

1. Is your supply line dead? Check for blown fuses.
2. Are the receptacle and plug making good contact? Check for bent prongs and loose wires.
3. Are both brushes touching commutator? Check for good

brush contact. Carbon brushes should be inspected at regular intervals and if worn away should be replaced immediately to avoid motor damage.

4. Check voltage specifications on the nameplate with the voltage of your supply line. See Motor and Current previously described in this chapter.

**Lubrication.** All *routers* are completely lubricated at the factory and are ready for use. All *ball bearings* are of the closed type and are grease sealed with sufficient lubricant packed in them to last the life of the bearing.

### ATTACHING BITS AND CUTTERS

Figure 26 illustrates how a straight bit is inserted into the collet-type chuck. The shank of the bit or cutter arbor should be inserted to a depth of at least ½″. *Make sure electric current is disconnected when performing this operation.*

**Fig. 26.**          **Fig. 27.**

After the bit is inserted, the two open-end wrenches are employed to tighten the chuck, as shown in Fig. 27. One of the two wrenches is fitted to the upper, or collet nut, and the other is attached to the collar at the bottom. Hold the lower wrench stationary and turn the upper wrench from right to left to tighten bit or arbor in chuck securely. Reverse the procedure to loosen and to remove the bit when necessary.

Located between the collet nut and the collar is a *lock nut*, which neither wrench will fit, and which is tightened before the unit leaves the factory. This lock nut needs no further attention from the operator.

## REGULATING CUTTING DEPTH

Place the router on flat surface, on its base, loosen wing nut (A), and turn knurled knob (C) until the bit very lightly touches the surface on which it is resting (Fig. 28). Tighten the wing nut and set router up on end.

With router inverted, the built-in micrometer-type depth adjustment (D) is set on the zero calibration. Each graduation on the depth dial represents $\frac{1}{64}$ of an inch. To set bit to desired cutting depth, loosen wing nut, turn outer knob (C), reading depth on dial (D); then tighten the wing nut. The graduated scale provides direct depth-reading in 64ths of an inch, without measuring, up to 1 inch.

## OPERATING THE ROUTER

There are a number of fixtures and attachments used to control and guide the router—the straight and circular guide, slot and circle cutting attachment, template guides, dovetail joint fixture, and the hinge mortising template. These, as well as other fixtures such as a home-made T-square are illustrated and described in this chapter.

In using the router, the base should be held firmly and flat on the surface, and the tool should be moved from left to right in straight cutting at a rate sufficient to maintain a high motor speed. In irregular or circular cutting move the router counter-clockwise. Feeding the router too slowly may cause the bit or cutter to burn the wood, whereas excessive speed in feeding will cause undue wear on the bits and cutters and at the same time result in an inferior cut.

Various wood densities make it impossible to set down just how fast this feeding should be done. After short practice in using the router, you will soon acquire the *feel* of the tool for the correct feeding speed.

In some instances, such as extremely hard wood, it is necessary to make several passes at varying depths until the desired depth-of-cut is obtained.

Bits and cutters should be kept sharp at all times.

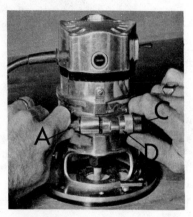

**Fig. 28.**

**Free-hand routing.** Although the router is more widely used with some form of guiding device for greater cutting accuracy, there are many applications to which it is put *free-hand*, that is, routing that is guided only by the operator's skill. Raised letter work. A variation of this is routing the letters themselves out of a flat surface. Surface stock removal may be accomplished free-hand, carefully following a pencilled layout. Skilled wood carvers often use a router to gouge out background and prepare work for final carving. The results and beauty of work that can be done in this fashion are limited only by the artistic ability and skill of the operator.

**T-square guide.** A simple device for guiding the router when making straight cuts on flat surfaces is the home-made T-square (Fig. 29). This T-square can be easily made out of scrap lumber, but make sure its edges are perfectly smooth and straight. It is

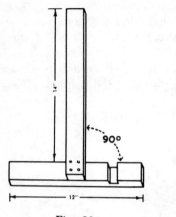

Fig. 29.

Fig. 30.

placed on the surface being routed and held in position by means of a clamp, as shown in Fig. 30. The base of the router is guided firmly along the edge of the T-square to make a straight cut. Measurements shown in the illustration are ideal for most applications with the router. They may, however, be altered to suit your specific needs. Other home-made guiding devices are discussed later in this chapter.

### STRAIGHT AND CIRCULAR GUIDE

The straight and circular guide (Fig. 31) is the most popular device used with the router. It enables the operator to make straight, curved, or angular cuts with ease and accuracy.

**Attaching and adjusting.** Figure 32 shows how the straight and circular guide is attached with four screws through the metal brackets, and firmly tightened to the router base. The two wing nuts (A) are loosened and the guide is adjusted along the length of the round metal rods and positioned in relation to the bit or cutter where the cut is to be made, after which wing nuts (A) are tightened.

The guide has a built-in vernier-type adjustment device that is used to adjust the guide accurately. In making fine adjustments, tighten the wing nut (B), loosen two wing nuts (A), and turn the knurled knob (C) to either right or left until the guide is accurately positioned, then tighten wing nuts (A) securely. Figure 33 shows operating position.

There are times when the length of the guide is insufficient to give the router ample support. When such is the case, a piece of wood may be attached to the front end of the guide using two wood screws and a piece of smooth lumber about 8″ or 10″ long and 2″ to 3″ wide (Fig. 34). Two holes are provided in the straight edge for this purpose.

**Fig. 31.**

**Fig. 32.**

**Fig. 33.**

**Fig. 34.**

**Straight cuts.** When routing along the edge of straight pieces, the straight edge (Fig. 31) is attached to the guide and held against the straight edge of the work as the router is fed along cutting line as shown in Fig. 33.

**Curved and angular cuts.** Routing is accurately accomplished along curved or angular edges by removing the straight edge, (AA), from the straight and circular guide. This leaves two points of contact to guide the router along irregularly shaped edges. Figure 35 illustrates this operating position, using the router to put a decorative edge around circular table top.

Fig. 35.

Fig. 36.

Fig. 37.

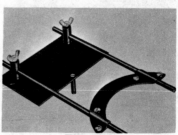

Fig. 38.

**Inside cuts.** When cutting inside edges such as rabbeting for screens, the straight and circular guide is attached in the reverse position as illustrated in Fig. 36.

**Measuring feature.** For added accuracy, the straight and circular guide features a slotted recess along the bottom which permits the insertion of a rule or scale for use in adjusting the edge of the guide in relation to the cutting edge of the bit. Figure 37 shows how this measurement is made, assuring precision results on any routing project.

### SLOT AND CIRCLE CUTTING ATTACHMENT

The slot and circle cutting attachment is used with the router for cutting evenly spaced slots and grooves, discs, circular holes and concentric designs. In circle cutting, or slot cutting, the attachment can be adjusted for diameters or lengths from 1″ to 22″ (Fig. 38).

Figure 39 shows the router in operating position when cutting a medium sized circle. Move the router always in a counterclockwise direction. Figure 40 illustrates the completed operation. *Note* that a ¼″ hole was first drilled in the center of the circle to hold the attachment guide pin. A straight bit of sufficient depth to pass through the wood was used—with a scrap piece of lumber being placed underneath the work to prevent cutting into the workbench.

Fig. 39.                    Fig. 40.

Interesting circular designs can be made using this attachment such as the one shown in Fig. 41. *Note* that two different bits were used to obtain an artistic result. *Note* how a circular opening can be improved by routing an attractive molding as shown in Fig. 42.

Fig. 41.

Fig. 42.

With the circle cutting pin removed and a guide bar assembled in its place, this attachment serves as a guide for cutting slots and grooves. In the example shown in Fig. 43, the first slot was made by using the end of the lumber as a guide, and the second slot was cut in the same manner as illustrated. This operation can be repeated, or the distance between slots varied by adjusting the two wing nuts on the attachment.

## PORTABLE ELECTRIC DRILLS

The *portable electric drill* shown in Fig. 44 is probably the most frequently used power tool. Although it is especially designed for drilling holes, by adding various accessories you can adapt it for different jobs. Sanding, sawing, buffing, polishing, screwdriving, wire brushing, and paint mixing are examples of possible uses. The sizes of portable electric drills are classified by the maximum-size straight-shank drill it will hold. That is,

**Fig. 43**.

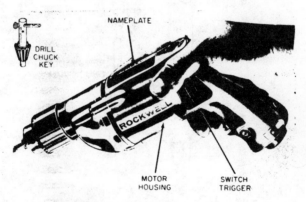

**Fig. 44.** ¼″ portable drill.

a ¼″ electric drill will hold a straight-shank drill up to and including ¼″.

The revolutions per minute (rpm) and power the drill will deliver are most important when choosing a drill for a job. You will find that the speed of the drill motor decreases with an increase in size, primarily because the larger units are designed to turn larger cutting tools or to drill in heavy materials, and both these factors require slower speed.

If you are going to do heavy work, such as drilling in masonry or steel, then you would probably need to use a drill with a ⅜" or ½" capacity. If most of your drilling will be forming holes in wood or small holes in sheet metal, then a ¼" drill will probably be adequate.

The *chuck* is the clamping device into which the drill is inserted. Nearly all electric drills are equipped with a three-jaw chuck. Some of the drill motors have a hand-type chuck that you tighten or loosen by hand, but most of the drills used have gear-type, three-jaw chucks which are tightened and loosened by means of a chuck key (Fig. 45). *Do not* apply further pressure with pliers or wrenches after you hand-tighten the chuck with the **chuck key**.

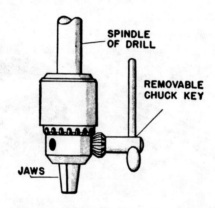

**Fig. 45.** Three-jaw chuck and chuck key.

*Always* remove the key *immediately* after you use it. Otherwise the key will fly loose when the drill motor is started and may cause serious injury to you or others. The chuck key is generally taped on the cord of the drill; but if it is not, be sure you put it in a safe place where it will not get lost.

Most portable electric drills have controls similar to the ones shown on the ¼" drill in Fig. **44**. This drill has a momentary contact trigger switch located in the handle. The switch is squeezed to start the electric drill and released to stop it.

The trigger latch is a button in the bottom of the drill handle. It is pushed in, while the switch trigger is held down, to lock the trigger switch in the "ON" position. The trigger latch is released by squeezing and then releasing the switch trigger.

### SANDERS

*Portable sanders* are tools designed to hold and operate abrasives for sanding wood, plastics, and metals. The most common types are the disc, belt, and reciprocating orbital sanders.

### DISC SANDER

*Electric disc sanders* (Fig. **46**) are especially useful on work where a large amount of material is to be removed quickly such as scaling surfaces in preparation for painting. This machine *should not* be used where a mirror smooth finish is required.

The disc should be moved smoothly and lightly over the surface. *Never* allow the disc to stay in one place too long because it will cut into the material and leave a large depression.

**Fig. 46.** Portable electric sander.

### BELT SANDER

The *portable belt sander* (Fig. **47**) is commonly used for surfacing lumber used for interior trim, furniture, or cabinets. Wood floors are almost always made ready for final finishing by using a belt sander. Whereas these types of sanding operations were once laborious and time-consuming, it is now possible to perform the operations quickly and accurately with less effort.

The belt sanders use endless sanding belts that can be obtained in many different grades (grits). The belts are usually 2″, 3″, or 4″ wide and can be easily changed when they become worn or when you want to use a different grade of sanding paper.

**Fig. 47.** Portable belt sander.

When preparing to use the sander, *be sure* that the object to be sanded is firmly secured. Then, after the motor has been started verify that the belt is tracking on center. Any adjustment to make it track centrally is usually made by aligning screws. The moving belt is then placed on the surface of the object to be sanded with the rear part of the belt touching first. The machine is then leveled as it is moved forward. When you use the sander, *do not* press down or *ride* it, because the weight of the machine exerts enough pressure for proper cutting. (Excessive pressure also causes the abrasive belt to clog and the motor to overheat.) Adjust the machine over the surface with overlapping strokes, always in a direction parallel to the grain.

By working over a fairly wide area and avoiding any machine tilting or pausing in any one spot, an even surface will result. Upon completion of the sanding process, lift the machine off the work and then stop the motor.

Some types of sanders are provided with a bag that takes up the dust that is produced. Be sure to use it if it is available.

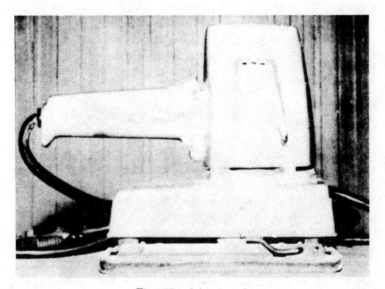

**Fig. 48.** Orbital sander.

## ORBITAL SANDER

The *orbital sander* (Fig. 48) is so named because of the action of the sanding pad. The pad moves in a tiny orbit, with a motion that is hardly discernible, so that it actually sands in all directions. This motion is so small and so fast that, with fine paper mounted on the pad, it is nearly impossible to see any scratches on the finished surface.

The pad, around which the abrasive sheet is wrapped, usually extends beyond the frame of the machine so it is possible to work in tight corners and against vertical surfaces.

Some models of the orbital sanders have a bag attached to catch all dust that is made from the sanding operation. Orbital sanders (pad sanders) do not remove as much material as fast as the belt sander or disc sander but do a better job on smoothing a surface for finishing. If both a belt or disc sander and an orbital sander are available, you should use the belt or disc sander for rough, preliminary work and the orbital sander for finishing. The sandpaper used on the sander may be cut to size from a bulk sheet of paper or may be available in the correct size for the sander you are using. The paper is wrapped around a pad on the sander and is fastened to the pad by means of levers on the front and rear of the sander. The lever action fasteners make changing the paper easy and quick.

## PORTABLE CIRCULAR SAW

The *portable circular saw* is becoming more and more popular as a woodworking tool because of the time and labor it saves, the precision with which it works, and its ease of handling and maneuverability.

Because of the many changes being made in the design of these saws, only general information will be given in this section. Information concerning a particular saw can be found by checking with the manufacturer.

The sizes of portable electric saws range from one-sixth horsepower with a 4″ blade to one-and-one-half horsepower with a 14″ blade. They are so constructed that they may be used as a carpenter's handsaw, both at the job site or on a bench in the woodworking shop.

The portable electric saw (Fig. 49) is started by pressing a trigger inserted in the handle and stopped by releasing it. The saw will run only when the trigger is held.

Most saws may be adjusted for crosscutting or for ripping. The ripsaw guide shown in Fig. 49 is adjusted by the two small knurled nuts at the base of the saw. When the guide is inserted in the rip guide slot to the desired dimensions, the nuts are then tightened to hold it firmly in place.

In crosscutting a guideline is generally marked across the board to be cut. Place the front of the saw base on the work so that the guide mark on the front plate and the guide line on the work are aligned. *Be sure* the blade is clear of the work. Start the saw and allow the cutting blade to attain full speed. Then advance the saw, keeping the guide mark and guide line aligned. If the saw stalls, back the saw out. *Do not release* the starting trigger. When the saw resumes cutting speed, start cutting again.

Additional adjustments include a depth knob and a bevel thumbscrew. The depth of the cut is regulated by adjusting the depth knob. The bevel-adjusting thumbscrew is used for adjusting the angle of the cut. This permits the base to be tilted in relation to the saw. The graduated scale marked in degrees on the quadrant (Fig. **49)** enables the operator to measure his adjustments and angles of cut.

The bottom plate of the saw is wide enough to provide the saw with a firm support on the lumber being cut. The blade of the saw is protected by a spring guard which opens when lumber is being cut but snaps back into place when the cut is finished. Many different sawblades may be placed on the machine for special kinds of sawing. By changing blades, almost any building material from slate and corrugated metal sheets to fiberglass can be cut.

To change saw blades, first disconnect the power. Remove the blade by taking off the saw clamp screw and flange, using the wrench provided for this purpose. Attach the new saw blade making certain the teeth are in the proper cutting direction (pointing upward toward the front of the saw) and tighten the flange and clamp screw with the wrench.

*Caution: Do not* put the saw blade on backwards. Most blades have instructions stamped on them with the words *this side out.*

The *portable electric saw* is one of the *most dangerous power tools* in existence when it is not properly used. *Be sure* the board you are sawing is properly secured so it will not slip or turn. After making a cut *be sure* the saw blade has come to a stand-

**Fig. 49.** Portable electric circular saw.

still before laying the saw down.

When using an electric saw remember that all the blade you can normally see is covered and that the portion of the blade that projects under the board being cut is not covered. The exposed teeth under the work are dangerous and can cause serious injury if any part of your body should come into contact with them.

The blade of a portable circular saw should be kept sharp at all times. The saw blade will function most efficiently when the rate of feed matches the blade's capacity to cut. You will not have to figure this out: you will be able to feel it. With a little practice you will know when the cut is smooth and you will know when you are forcing it. Let the blade do its own cutting. The tool will last longer and you will work easier because it is less fatiguing.

### SABER SAW

The *saber saw* (Fig. 50) is a power-driven jigsaw that will let you cut smooth and decorative curves in wood and light metal. Most saber saws are light-duty machines and are not designed for extremely fast cutting.

There are several different blades designed to operate in the saber saw and they are easily interchangeable. For fast cutting of wood, a blade with coarse teeth may be used. A blade with fine teeth is designed for cutting metal.

The best way to learn how to handle this type of tool is to use it. Before trying to do a finished job with the saber saw, clamp down a piece of scrap plywood and draw some curved as well as straight lines to follow. You will develop your own way of

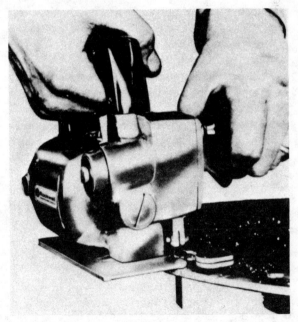

**Fig. 50.** Saber or bayonet saw operations.

gripping the tool, and this will be affected somewhat by the particular tool you are using. On some tools, *for example*, you will find guiding easier if you apply some downward pressure on the tool as you move it forward. If you are not firm with your grip, the tool will tend to vibrate excessively and this will roughen the cut. Do not force the cutting faster than the design of the blade allows or you will break the blade.

### ELECTRIC IMPACT WRENCH

The *electric impact wrench* (Fig. **51**) is a portable hand-type reversible wrench. The one shown has a ½″ square impact-driving anvil over which ½″ square drive sockets can be fitted. Wrenches also can be obtained that have impact-driving anvils ranging from ⅜″ to 1″. The driving anvils are not interchangeable, however, from one wrench to another.

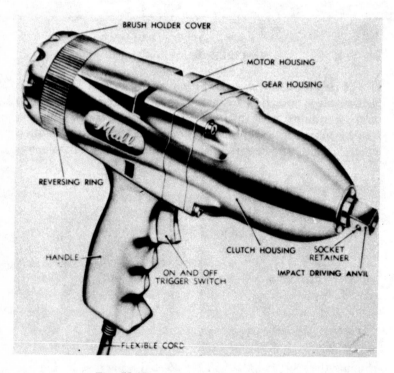

**Fig. 51.** Reversible electric impact wrench.

The electric wrench with its accompanying equipment is primarily intended for applying and removing nuts, bolts, and screws. It may also be used to drill and tap wood, plastics, metal, and other material, and drive and remove socket-head, Phillips-head, or slotted-head wood, machine, or self-tapping screws.

Before you use an electric impact wrench depress the on-and-off trigger switch and allow the electric wrench to operate a few seconds, noting carefully the direction of rotation. Release the trigger switch to stop the wrench. Turn the reversing ring located at the rear of the tool. The ring should move easily in one direction (which is determined by the current direction of rotation). Depress the on-and-off trigger again to start the electric wrench. The direction of rotation should now be reversed. Continue to operate for a few seconds in each direction to be sure that the wrench and its reversible features are functioning correctly. When you are sure the wrench operates properly, place the suitable equipment on the impact-driving anvil and go ahead with the job at hand.

## WOODWORKING SAWS

Mechanical woodworking saws range in size and power from small shop jigsaws to huge handsaws used in west coast sawmills to saw redwood trees into lumber. Mechanical saws for sawmill work are beyond the scope of this chapter. Of the types of mechanical saws, the various members of the *circular saw* family are the most widely used.

## TILT-ARBOR BENCH SAW

A *tilt-arbor bench saw* is shown in Fig. 52. This saw is called a tilt-arbor saw because the saw blade can be tilted for cutting bevels and the like by tilting the arbor. In the earlier types of bench saws the saw blade remained stationary and the table was tilted. A canted (tilted) saw table is hazardous in many ways, however, and most modern bench saws are of the tilt-arbor type.

For ripping stock, the *cutoff gages* are removed and the *ripping fence* is set a distance away from the saw which is equal to the desired width of the piece to be ripped off. The piece is placed with one edge against the fence and fed through with the fence as a guide.

For cutting stock off square, the cutoff gage is set at 90° to the line of the saw and the ripping fence is set to the outside edge of the table, away from the stock to be cut. The piece is then placed with one edge against the cutoff gage, held firmly, and fed through by pushing the gage along its slot.

The procedure for cutting stock off at an angle other than 90° (called *miter cutting*) is similar, except that the cutoff gage is set to bring the piece to the desired angle with the line of the saw.

For ordinary ripping or cutting off, the distance the saw blade should extend above the table top is ⅛″ plus the thickness of the piece to be sawed. The vertical position of the saw is controlled by the *depth of cut handwheel* shown in Fig. 52. The angle of the saw blade is controlled by the *tilt handwheel*. The guard *must be kept in place* except when its removal is absolutely unavoidable. Blade guards are shown in Figs. 52 and 53.

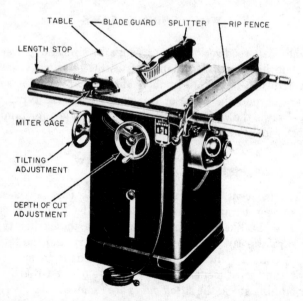

**Fig. 52.** Tilt-arbor bench saw.

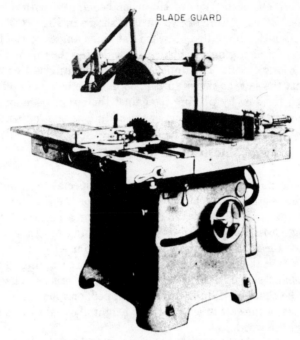

BLADE GUARD

**Fig. 53.** Tilt-arbor bench saw with sliding table section.

The slot in the table through which the saw blade extends is called the *throat*. The throat is contained in a small, removable section of the table called the *throat plate*. The throat plate is removed when it is necessary to insert a wrench to remove the saw blade. The blade is held on the arbor by a nut called the *arbor nut*. A saw is usually equipped with several throat plates, containing throats of various widths. A wider throat is required when a *dado head* is used on the saw. A dado head consists of two outside *grooving saws* (which are much like combination saws) and as many intermediate chisel-type *cutters* (called chippers) as are required to make up the designated width of the groove or dado. Grooving saws are usually ⅛″ thick; consequently, one grooving saw will cut a ⅛″ groove , and the two, used together, will cut a ¼″ groove. Intermediate cutters come in various thicknesses.

A more elaborate type of tilt-arbor bench saw with a *sliding table section* consisting of two parts is shown in Fig. 53. The sliding section can be pulled outward (at right angles to the line of the saw) for changing saw blades, for widening the throat, and for making long cutoffs. The upper part of the sliding section can be slid past the saw, as shown in Fig. 53. A piece being cut off is fed through the saw by placing it against the cutoff gage and then pushing the whole upper part of the sliding section past the saw.

## CIRCULAR SAW SAFETY

All equipment should be operated with special care, but here are some operating precautions especially for the circular saw.

Do not use a ripsaw for crosscutting or a crosscut saw for ripping. Crosscut saws can be used for ripping but they are not intended for such work and should not be so used.

See that the saw is in good condition before starting to use it. This means sharp, unbroken, and free from cracks. The blade should be changed if dull, cracked, chipped, or warped.

Be sure the saw is set at proper height above the table to cut through the wood.

Avoid "kickbacks" by standing to one side of the saw—not in line with it.

Always use a push stick to push short, narrow pieces between the saw and the gage.

Keep material of any kind from accumulating on the saw table and in the immediate working area.

*Never* reach over the saw to obtain material from the other side.

When cutting, do not feed wood into the saw faster than the saw will cut freely and cleanly.

*Never* leave the sawing machine unattended with the power turned on.

## RADIAL-ARM SAW

A *radial-arm saw* is shown in Fig. 54. The motor and arbor are pivoted in a *yoke* which can be swung in any direction. The yoke

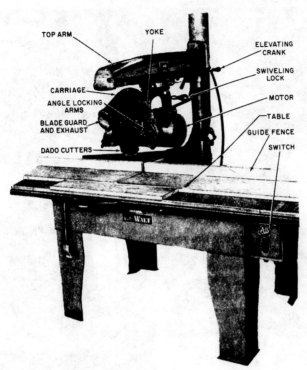

**Fig. 54.** A radial arm saw.

slides back and forth on an *arm* (or *overarm*) which can also be swung in any direction. These arrangements make the radial saw adaptable to almost any conceivable type of cutting, as indicated in Fig. 55. Equipped with a grooving head, the saw can be used for *grooving* and *rabbeting*. Equipped with a *shaper head*, it can be used as a *shaper*. Equipped with a *router bit*, it can be used for *routing*. In short, the radial saw is just about the most versatile power tool in a workshop.

## RADIAL-ARM SAW SAFETY

Make sure the saw blade is mounted on the arbor so that the

CROSSCUTTING WITH OVERARM SAW

MITER CUTTING

RIPPING

ANGLE CUT-OFF

COMPOUND MITER CUTTING

BEVEL RIPPING

**Fig. 55.** Saw cutting with the radial arm saw.

teeth of the saw point toward the operator.

When crosscutting stock, make sure the stock is flat on the

table and that the back edge of the stock is held firmly against the fence.

Always make sure that the saw is back as far as it will go before starting to use it for crosscutting work.

When crosscutting long stock, make sure the ends are supported at the same level as the table.

Always keep the saw guards in place.

Adjust the saw for the correct depth before starting the saw.

Never use a dull saw. Pinching or binding indicates a dull saw.

Make sure the anti-kickback guard is properly adjusted whenever ripping stock.

Never rip stock without the stock having a straight edge.

Always feed the stock to be ripped against the rotation of the saw blade.

Never make any adjustments while the motor is turning.

Always remember that the radial-arm saw cuts on the "pull" stroke.

## BAND SAW

While the band saw is designed primarily for making curved cuts, it can also be used for straight cutting. Unlike the circular saw, the band saw is frequently used for freehand cutting.

The band saw has two large wheels on which a continuous narrow saw blade or *band* turns, just as a belt is turned on pulleys. The *lower wheel*, located below the *working table*, is connected to the motor directly or by means of pulleys or gears and serves as the driver pulley. The *upper wheel* is the driven pulley.

The saw blade is guided and kept in line by two sets of *blade guides*, one fixed set below the table and one set above with a vertical sliding adjustment. The alignment of the blade is adjusted by a mechanism on the back side of the upper wheel. *Tensioning* of the blade—tightening and loosening—is provided by another adjustment located just back of the upper wheel.

Cutoff gages and ripping fences are sometimes provided for use with band saws, but you will do most of your work freehand with the table clear. With this type of saw it is difficult to make accurate cuts when gages or fences are used.

The size of a band saw is designated by the diameter of the wheels. Common sizes are 14″ (Fig. 56), 16″, 18″, 20″, 30″, 36″, 42″, and 48″ machines. The 14″ size is the smallest practical band saw. With the exception of capacity, all band saws are much alike as regards maintenance, operation, and adjustment.

Blades or bands for band saws are designated by *points* (tooth points per inch), *thickness* (gage), and *width*. The required length of a blade is found by adding the circumference of one wheel to twice the distance between the wheel centers. Length can vary within a limit of twice the tension adjustment range. Blades are set and filed much the same as with a hand ripsaw.

## BAND SAW SAFETY

Here are some safety pointers to keep in mind when you are

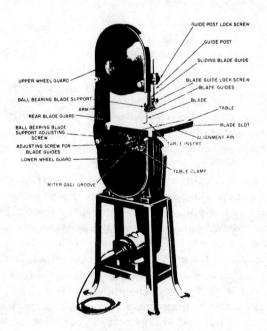

**Fig. 56.** Bandsaw.

operating a band saw.

Keep your fingers away from the moving blade.

Keep the table clear of stock and scraps so your work will not catch as you push it along.

Keep the upper guide just above the work, not excessively high.

Do not stand to the right of the machine while it is running and do not lean on the table at any time.

Bandsaw wheels should be tested by experienced men or women at least once a week with a small machinist's hammer to detect cracks or loose spokes. The sound of a cracked or broken wheel is dull and flat.

Cracked blades should not be used. If a blade develops a "click" as it passes through the work, the operator should shut off the power, as the click is a signal that the blade is cracked and may be ready to break. After the saw blade has stopped moving, it should be replaced with one in proper condition.

If the saw blade breaks, the operator should shut off the power and not attempt to remove any part of the saw blade until the machine is completely stopped.

If the work binds or pinches on the blade, the operator should never attempt to back the work away from the blade while the saw is in motion, since this may break the blade. He should always see that the blade is working relatively freely through the cut.

A band saw should not be operated in a location where the temperature is below 45°F., as it may break when the machine is started.

Using a small saw for large work or forcing a wide saw on a small radius is bad practice. The saw blade should in all cases be as wide as the nature of the work will permit.

Band saws should not be stopped by thrusting a piece of wood against the cutting edge or side of the band saw blade immediately after the power has been shut off because the blade may break. Band saws 36" and larger should have a hand or foot brake.

Particular care should be taken when sharpening or brazing a band saw blade to see that the blade is not overheated and that the brazed joints are thoroughly united and are finished to the same thickness as the rest of the blade. *It is recommended that all*

*bandsaw blades be butt welded where possible, as this method is*
*much superior to the old style of brazing.*

## JIGSAW

A *jigsaw* performs basically the same function as a band saw,
but is usually capable of cutting more intricate curves. Instead
of a flexible band-type blade, the jigsaw has a short, straight,
rigid blade that is rapidly oscillated vertically by the power
mechanism.

## PORTABLE FIELD SAW UNIT

There are several types of portable units used. The *portable
field saw unit* shown in Fig. 57 is portable and self-contained for
field construction.

**Fig. 57.** Woodworking trailer mounted shop.

## CARE AND MAINTENANCE OF POWER SAWS

The most important factors in the care and maintenance of a mechanical saw are the proper lubrication of all moving parts and the proper conditioning of the saw blade. A saw blade that is dull, or one in which the teeth are incorrectly shaped or improperly set, will "labor" in the wood. This in turn will place an excessive strain on the driving mechanism. The correct shapes of ripsaw and cutoff saw teeth are shown in Fig. 58. In a combination saw, the *rip* or *raker* teeth are shaped like ripsaw teeth and the *crosscut* teeth like cutoff saw teeth, as shown in Fig. 59. As is the case with handsaws, the front and backslope of a circular cutoff saw are beveled, as shown in Fig. 58.

Complete reconditioning of a circular saw consists of (1) jointing, (2) gumming, (3) setting, and (4) sharpening, as follows.

**Jointing.** *Jointing* is done when wear and repeated sharpenings have caused the points on the saw to become unrounded. The procedure for jointing is as follows:

*Put on goggles.* Remove all sawdust from working area. Install blade in reverse order. Crank blade below table surface. Place and secure stone over blade. Start the saw and crank blade into stone slowly. When each tooth shows a bright spot the jointing process has been completed.

**Gumming.** *Gumming* is done when wear and repeated sharpenings have caused the gullets to become too shallow. It is very similar to the handsaw procedure called *shaping*. The first step in gumming is to lay out the shapes of several teeth on the saw as shown in Figs. 60 and 61. For a ripsaw (Fig. 60), draw a circle on the saw with a diameter equal to half that of the saw, and draw a line from each point tangent to the circle. This line indicates the correct angle for the front of the tooth. Lay off the correct angle for the top of the backslope (15° as shown in Fig. 58) and free-hand in the gullet until it looks about right. Draw a circle (the *gum line* shown in Fig. 60) through the bottom of the gullet and all the way around the saw to indicate the correct gullet depths of all the teeth. A cutoff saw is marked for gumming as shown in Fig. 61. Draw two circles on the saw, one with a diameter equal to one-quarter that of the saw, the other with a diameter equal to three-

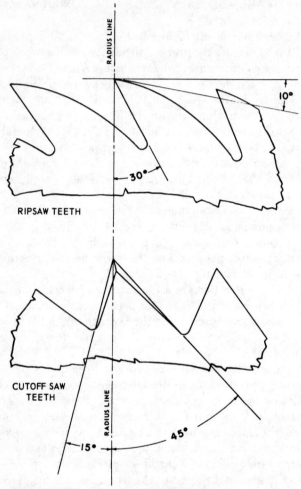

**Fig. 58.** Correct shapes of circular ripsaw and cutoff saw teeth.

quarters that of the saw. A tangent drawn from the smaller circle to the point of each tooth gives the line of the front of the tooth; a tangent drawn from the larger circle to the point of a tooth gives the line of the backslope of the tooth. Make the gum-line circle

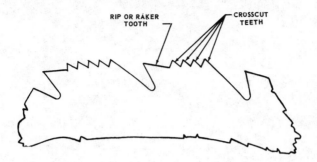

**Fig. 59.** Teeth on a combination saw.

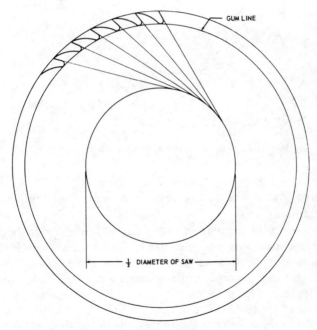

**Fig. 60.** Laying out a circular ripsaw for gumming.

large enough to run a little above the points of intersection of fronts and backslopes to allow for a slight rounding of the gullet.

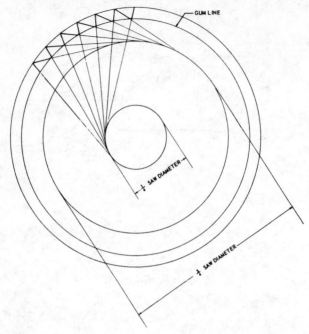

**Fig. 61.** Laying out a circular cutoff saw for gumming.

A gullet that is filed to a corner has a tendency to crack at the corner.

A ripsaw may be gummed with a hand file of suitable shape or with a *saw sharpener* and *gummer* like the one shown in Fig. 62. The procedure with the saw sharpener and gummer is as follows:

1. Place the saw blade in the gumming machine and adjust so that the face of the grinding wheel is exactly in line with the correct line of the front of a tooth.

2. Bring the wheel into light contact with the front of the tooth and then grind the bullet down to the gum line.

3. File down the backslope to the correct angle and shape by hand.

4. A cutoff saw may be gummed with a hand file of suitable shape or with the *saw-filing machine* shown in Fig. 63. This ma-

**Fig. 62.** Circular saw sharpener and gummer.

chine is a mechanical filer that works a file with a cross section of the same shape as that of the gullet. The machine is used in just about the same manner as the saw sharpener and gummer, with the exception that it files the front of one tooth and the backslope of the tooth directly ahead in a single operation.

**Setting.** A circular saw is *set* in a *saw setting machine.* The *arbor* is set to the radius of the saw and the *anvil* is set to produce the desired amount of set on a tooth. Procedure for setting is as follows:

1. Move a tooth that is already bent downward onto the anvil.

2. Strike the anvil a single blow with a medium-weight *ball-peen hammer,* held so as to bring the face of the hammer flush on the anvil.

3. Repeat on every other tooth all the way around.

4. Turn the saw over and perform the same operation on the teeth bent the other way.

**Sharpening.** *Sharpening* may be done with a hand file of suitable shape, or with the *saw sharpener* and *gummer* (ripsaw) or

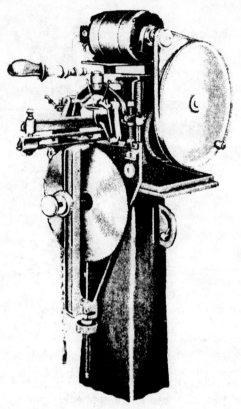

**Fig. 63.** Saw filing machine.

the *saw filing machine* (cutoff saw) already mentioned. For the ripsaw the machine must be set, or the file must be held, so as to grind or file the fronts of the teeth at 90° to the line of the saw. For the cutoff saw the machine must be set, or the file must be held, so as to file the front of one tooth and the backslope of the tooth directly ahead at the correct bevel angle, which is about 45° to the line of the saw. Procedure for sharpening is as follows:

1. Set the machine to the correct front angle and correct crosswise angle (90° for a ripsaw, and 45° for a cutoff saw).

2. Grind or file the front of each tooth that is *set toward the machine*.

3. Reverse the saw blade and grind or file the fronts of the remaining teeth.

For the combination or miter saw, the reconditioning procedures are those of the ripsaw for the rip or raker teeth and those of the cutoff saw for the crosscut teeth. The points of the rip teeth should be slightly lower than the points of the cutoff teeth to get a smooth-cutting saw. To test the saw for this factor, make a shallow cut in a piece of waste wood. If the bottom of the cut is perfectly flat, the points of the rip teeth are higher than the points of the crosscut teeth. If two sharp lines are scored on either side of the bottom of the cut, the points of the crosscut teeth are higher than the points of the rip teeth, as they should be.

*Band saw* teeth are shaped like the teeth in a hand ripsaw, which means that their fronts are filed at 90° to the line of the saw. Reconditioning procedures are the same as they are for a hand ripsaw, except that very narrow bandsaws with very small teeth must usually be set and sharpened by special machines.

## SHAVING TOOLS

To get the smooth surface or edge desired on certain materials, various operations must be performed with shaving tools. The following sections are provided to aid you in conducting these operations safely.

## JOINTER

The *jointer* is a machine for power-planing stock on faces, edges, and ends. The planing is done by a revolving *cutterhead* equipped with two or more *knives* as shown in Fig. 65. Setting up on the *set screws* forces the *throat piece* against the knife to hold the knife in position. Loosening the set screws releases the knife for removal. The size of a jointer is designated by the width in inches of the cutterhead—sizes range from 4″ to 36″. A 6″ jointer is shown in Fig. 65.

The principle on which the jointer functions is illustrated in Fig. 66. The *table* consists of two parts on either side of the cutterhead. The stock is started on the *infeed table* and fed past the

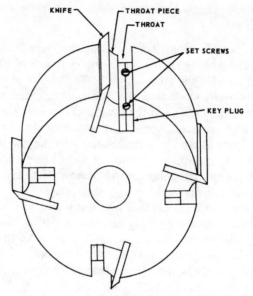

**Fig. 64.** Four-knife cutterhead for a jointer.

cutterhead onto the *outfeed table*. The surface of the outfeed table must be exactly level with the highest point reached by the knife edges. The surface of the infeed table is depressed below the surface of the outfeed table, an amount equal to the desired depth of cut. The usual depth of cut is about 1/16″ to ⅛″.

The level of the outfeed table must be frequently checked to ensure that the surface is exactly even with the highest point reached by the knife edges. If the outfeed table is too high, the cut will become progressively more shallow as the piece is fed through. If the outfeed table is too low, the piece will drop downward as its end leaves the infeed table, and the cut for the last inch or so will be too deep.

The outfeed table can be set to correct height as follows.

Feed a piece of waste stock past the cutterhead until a few inches of it lie on the outfeed table. Then stop the machine and look under the outfeed end of the piece. If the outfeed table is too low, there will be a space between the surface of the table and the

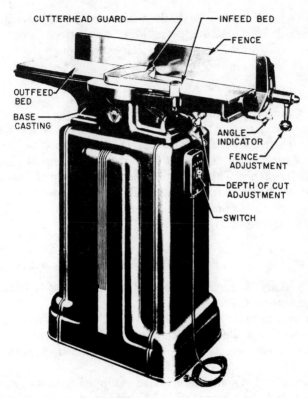

**Fig. 65.** Six-inch jointer.

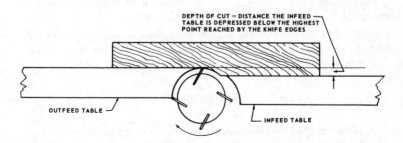

**Fig. 66.** Principle of operation of the jointer.

lower face of the piece. Raise the outfeed table until this space is eliminated. If no space appears, lower the outfeed table until a space does appear. Now run the stock back through the machine. If there is still a space, then raise the table just enough to eliminate it.

Note that the cutterhead cuts toward the infeed table. Therefore, in order to cut the grain, you must place the piece with the grain running toward the infeed table. A piece is *edged* by feeding it through on edge with one of the faces held against the *fence*. A piece is *surfaced* by feeding it through flat with one of the edges against the fence. This operation, however, should if possible be limited to straightening the face of the stock. The fence can be set at 90° to produce squared faces and edges, or at any desired angle to produce beveled edges or ends.

## JOINTER SAFETY

Only sharp and evenly balanced knives should be used in a jointer cutting head.

The knives must be securely fastened after the machine has been standing in a cold building over a period of time.

When pieces shorter than 18″ are machined, a push block should be used.

Each hand-fed jointer should be equipped with a cylindrical cutting head, the throat of which should not exceed 7/16″ in depth nor ⅝″ in width. It is strongly recommended that no cylinder be used in which the throat exceeds ⅜″ in depth or ½″ in width.

Each hand-fed jointer should have an automatic guard that will cover all the sections of the head on the working side of the fence or gage. The guard should automatically adjust horizontally for edge jointing and vertically for surface work, and should remain in contact with the material at all times.

## SURFACER

A *single surfacer* (also called a *single planer*) is shown in Fig. 67. This machine surfaces stock on one face (the upper face) only. Double surfacers that surface both faces at the same time are used

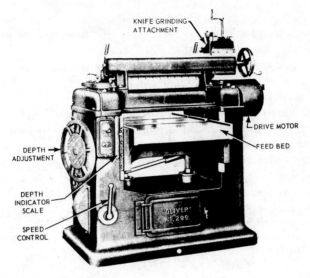

**Fig. 67.** Single surfacer.

only in large planing mills.

The surfacer cuts with a cutterhead like the one on the jointer, but on the single surfacer the cutterhead is located above instead of below driven rollers, and the part adjacent to the cutterhead is pressed down against the *feed bed* by two members, the *chip breaker* (just ahead of the cutterhead) and the *pressure bar* (just behind the cutterhead). The pressure bar temporarily straightens out any warp a piece may have. In effect, a piece that goes into the surfacer warped will come out still warped. This is not a defect in the machine. The surfacer is designed for surfacing only, not for truing warped stock. If true, planed surfaces are desired, one face of the stock (the face that goes down in the surfacer) must be trued on the jointer before the piece is fed through the surfacer. If the face that goes down in the surfacer is true, the surfacer will plane the other face true.

## SURFACER SAFETY

Each surfacing machine should have all cutting heads covered by a metal guard. If the guard is constructed of sheet metal, the material used should not be less than 1/16″ thick; if cast iron is used, it should not be less than 3/16″ thick.

Where an exhaust system is used, the guards should form part or all of the exhaust hood and should be constructed of metal of a thickness not less than the above.

Feed rolls should be guarded by a hood or a semicylindrical guard to prevent the hands of the operator from coming in contact with the in-running rolls at any point. The guard should be fastened to the frame carrying the rolls so as to remain adjusted for any thickness of the stock.

Sectional feed rolls should be provided for surfacers. Where solid feed rolls are used, the sectional finger devices should be used to prevent kickbacks.

## WOOD SHAPER

The *wood shaper* is designed primarily for edging curved stock and for cutting ornamental edges, as on moldings. But the shaper can also be used for *rabbeting, grooving, fluting,* and *beading.* A *flute* is a straight groove with a curved rather than a rectangular cross-section. A *bead* might be called the reverse of a flute. A shaper is shown in Fig. 68.

The flat cutter or knives on a shaper are mounted on a vertical *spindle* and held in place by a hexagonal *spindle nut.* A grooved *collar* is placed below and above the cutter or knives to receive the edges of the knives. Ball bearing collars are available for use as guides on irregular work where the fence is not used. The part of the edge that is to remain uncut runs against the ball bearing collar, as shown in the bottom view of Fig. 69.

A *three-wing cutter* fits over the spindle as shown in the upper view of Fig. 69. *Flat-knife* cutters are assembled in pairs between collars. Both cutters and knives come with cutting edges in a great variety of shapes. *Blank* flat knives are available which may be ground to any desired shape of cutting edge. This is done only by experienced operators.

For shaping the side edges on a rectangular piece, a light-duty shaper has an *adjustable fence* like the one shown on the shaper in

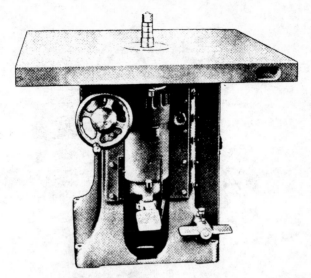

**Fig. 68.** Wood shaper.

Fig. 70. For shaping the end edges on a rectangular piece, a machine of this type has a *sliding fence* similar to the cutoff gage on a circular saw. The sliding fence slides in the groove shown in the table top.

On larger machines the fence consists of a board straightedge, clamped to the table with a handscrew as shown in Fig. 71. A semi-circular opening is sawed in the edge of the straightedge to accommodate the spindle and the cutters or knives. Whenever possible, a guard of the type shown in Fig. 71 should be placed over the spindle.

For shaping curved edges there are usually a couple of holes in the table, one on either side of the spindle, in which vertical *starter pins* can be inserted. When a curved edge is being shaped, the piece is guided by and steadied against the starter pin and the ball bearing collar on the spindle.

Like the jointer and surfacer, the shaper cuts toward the infeed side of the spindle, which is against the rotation of the spindle. Stock should therefore be placed with the grain running toward the infeed side.

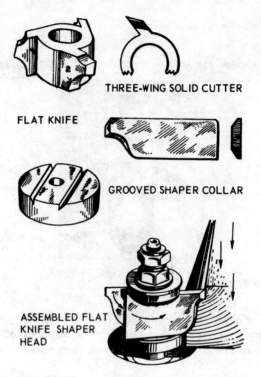

THREE-WING SOLID CUTTER

FLAT KNIFE

GROOVED SHAPER COLLAR

ASSEMBLED FLAT
KNIFE SHAPER
HEAD

**Fig. 69.** Three-wing cutter and flat knives
for a shaper.

## SHAPER SAFETY

Make sure the knives are sharp and are well secured.

If curved or irregularly shaped edges are to be shaped, place the stock in position and check to see that the collar will rub against part of the edge which will not be moved.

Whenever the straight fence cannot be used, always use a starting pin in the table top.

Never make extremely deep cuts.

Make sure the shaper knives rotate toward the work.

Whenever possible, always use a guard, pressure bar, hold-down, or holding jig.

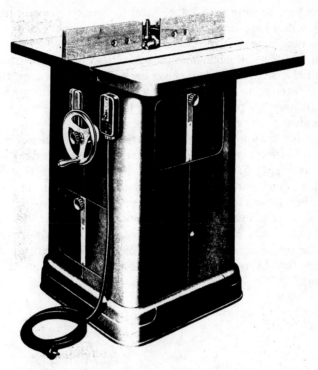

**Fig. 70.** Light-duty shaper with adjustable fence.

If possible, place the cutter on the shaper spindle so that the cutting will be done on the lower side of the stock.

Do not attempt to shape small pieces of wood.

Check all adjustments before turning on the power.

The *spindle shaper* is probably one of the most *dangerous* machines used in the workshop. Use extreme caution at all times.

## CARE AND MAINTENANCE OF POWER SHAVING TOOLS

The two most important factors in the care and maintenance of a jointer, surfacer, or shaper are the proper lubrication of all moving parts and the proper sharpening and adjustment of the knives and/or cutters. Dull knives and cutters deteriorate the machinery by causing it to "labor" and to "chatter" or vibrate. Besides, a dull knife or cutter on a power shaving machine is a very dangerous hazard. A dull knife or cutter tends to "catch" in the wood and, since the machine is cutting toward the operator, the result of a catch is a violent throw-back of the stock toward the operator; even more serious than this is the fact that the operator's hands, when the piece is torn out of them, may be driven against the knives or the cutters.

The best way to sharpen the knives on a jointer or surfacer is with a *knife-grinding attachment* like the one shown on the surfacer in Fig. 71. With one of these devices, the knives can be sharpened without removing them from the cutterhead. The knife-grinding attachment consists of a small motor-driven grinding wheel mounted in a *saddle* that can be cranked back and forth on a steel bar called a *bridge*. The bridge can be mounted over the cutterhead by means of a couple of *bridge brackets*. The general procedure for sharpening with a knife-grinding attachment is as follows.

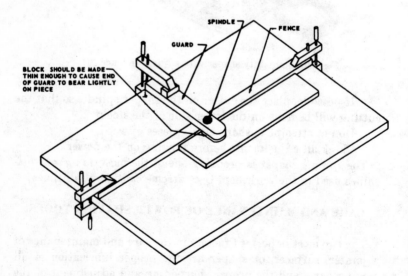

**Fig. 71.** Shaper table, showing straightedge fence and guard.

Open the starting switch on the machine and lock it open. If the power line has a main switch that can be opened, open that switch as well.

Revolve the cutterhead by hand until a knife is in a position where the cutterhead *locking pin* can be put on. The locking pin holds the uppermost knife in correct grinding position.

Loosen the set screws until they are holding the knife only lightly, and move the knife up about 1/12 of an inch. The best way to do this and still keep the knife level is to use a *three-pronged knife gage*. This device has two prongs that fit against the cutterhead on either side of the knife, and a third prong in the center that can be set to any desired amount of protrusion of the knife edge. When the knife has been set at the desired height, tighten the set screws.

Adjust the knife edges of the other knives to the same height.

Set the grinding attachment in place, bring the grinder down to contact the bevel on the first knife, and crank the grinder back and forth over the knife several times. Take a light cut, and crank fast enough to keep the knife from overheating. Repeat on the other two knives.

When the first knife is again under the grinder, lower the grinder slightly and repeat the above procedure on all three knives. Repeat this whole process, lowering the grinder a little every time you get back to the first knife, until all nicks have been ground away and there is a perfect bevel on every knife in the cutterhead.

The next step is *jointing* the knives, which means, as in the case of a circular saw, ensuring that the knife edges form a perfect circle as the cutterhead revolves.

Remove the motor from the saddle and install a *jointing attachment*. A jointing attachment is a device with a fine whetstone attached to its lower end. The whetstone can be set so that it barely touches the knife edges. Set it in this fashion, revolving the cutterhead by hand to ensure that there is the barest contact and no more.

Start the machine and crank the jointing attachment back and forth several times over the revolving knives. Stop the machine and examine the knife edges. If they have not all been slightly touched, lower the stone just a little and repeat the process until every knife edge has been touched.

In the absence of a knife-grinding attachment, the knives must be removed from the cutterhead and ground on an oilstone grinder or in some other manner.

To readjust the knives in the cutterhead of a jointer, place a builder's level or a wooden straightedge on the outfeed table and line the highest point reached by each knife edge with the lower edge of the straightedge as follows. Place the knife in the cutterhead and set the screws up lightly. Place the straightedge over one end of the knife and raise or lower the knife until the edge barely contacts the straightedge when the cutterhead is rotated by hand. Move the straightedge to the other end of the knife and repeat the same procedure. Tighten the setscrews and make a final check for correct height at both ends of the knife. Repeat the same procedure with the remaining knives.

A flat shaper knife with a straight cutting edge is ground and whetted like a plane iron or a chisel. As is the case with a jointer or surfacer, the knives in a shaper must be exactly equal in size and weight. Three-way cutters and knives with curved edges must be sharpened "free-hand" with a small portable grinding wheel, called a "grinding pencil." The greatest care must be taken to keep pairs of knives and the cutting extensions in a three-way cutter exactly alike in size, weight, and shape.

## DRILL PRESS

*Portable electric drills* are not used much in woodworking. Many woodworkers and carpenters have a stationary drill which is usually called a *drill press* (Fig. 72). Besides boring, the drill press (equipped with a *router bit* like the one shown on the radial saw in Fig. 40) is used for *routing,* and also (when equipped with a *shaper head* and shaper knives or cutters) for shaping.

When it is used for boring, a portable or stationary power-driven drill always uses a twist drill, never an auger bit. The most important care and maintenance factors are proper lubrication of moving parts and the use of properly conditioned twist drills.

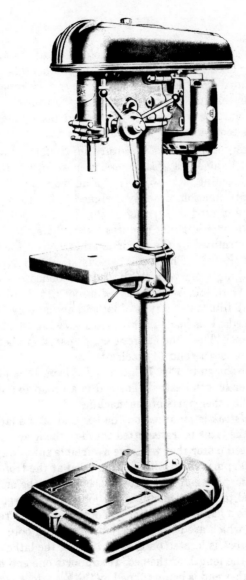

**Fig. 72.** Drill press.

## THE LATHE

The *lathe* is without question the oldest of all woodworking machines. In its early form, it consisted of two holding centers with the suspended stock being rotated by an endless rope belt. It was operated by having one person pull on the rope hand-over-hand while the cutting was done by a second person holding crude hand-lathe tools on an improvised beam rest.

The actual operations of woodturning performed on a modern lathe are still done to a great degree with woodturner's handtools. However, machine lathe work is coming more and more into use with the introduction of newly designed lathes for that purpose.

The lathe is used in turning or shaping round billets, drums, disks, and any object that requires a true diameter. The size of a lathe is determined by the maximum diameter of the work it can swing over its bed. There are various sizes and types of wood lathes, ranging from very small sizes for delicate work to large surface or "bull lathes" that can swing jobs 15' in diameter.

Figure 73 illustrates a type of lathe that you may find suitable for your needs. It is made in three sizes to swing 16", 20", and 24" diameter stock. The lathe has four major parts: (1) bed, (2) headstock, (3) tailstock, and (4) toolrest.

The lathe shown in Fig. 73 has a *bed* of iron. It can be obtained in any other length desired. The bed is a broad flat surface that supports the other parts of the machine.

The *headstock* is mounted on the left end of the lathe bed. All power for the lathe is transmitted through the headstock. It has a fully enclosed motor that will give a variable spindle speed (from 600 to 3600 rpm). The *spindle* is threaded at the front end to receive the *faceplates*. A faceplate attachment to the motor spindle is furnished to hold or mount small jobs having large diameters. There is also a flange on the rear end of the spindle to receive large faceplates, which are held securely by four stud bolts.

The *tailstock* is located on the right end of the lathe and is movable along the length of the bed. It supports one end of the work while the other end is being turned by the *headstock spur*. The tail center may be removed from the stock simply by backing the screw. The shank is tapered to automatically center the point.

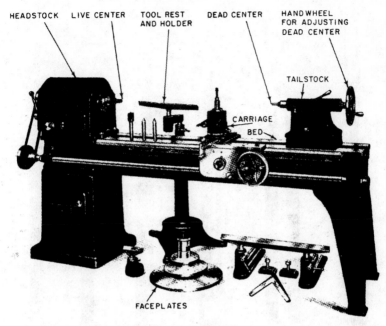

HEADSTOCK   LIVE CENTER   TOOL REST AND HOLDER   DEAD CENTER   HANDWHEEL FOR ADJUSTING DEAD CENTER

TAILSTOCK

CARRIAGE

BED

FACEPLATES

**Fig. 73.** A woodturning lathe with accessories.

Most large sizes of lathes are provided with a *power-feeding carriage.* A cone-pulley bolt arrangement provides power from the motor, and ways are cast to the side of the bed for sliding the carriage back and forth. All machines have a metal bar that may be attached to the bed of the lathe between the operator and the work. This serves as a *handtool rest* and provides support for the operator in guiding tools along the work. It may be of any size and is adjustable to any desired position.

In lathe work, wood is rotated against the special cutting tools illustrated in Fig. 74. The special lathe tools include turning gouges; skew chisels; parting tools; round-nose, square-nose, and spear-point chisels; toothing irons; and auxiliary aids such as calipers, dividers, and templates.

*Turning gouges* are used chiefly to rough out nearly all shapes in spindle turning. The gouge sizes vary from ⅛ of an inch to 2 or more inches, with ¼", ¾", and 1" sizes being most common.

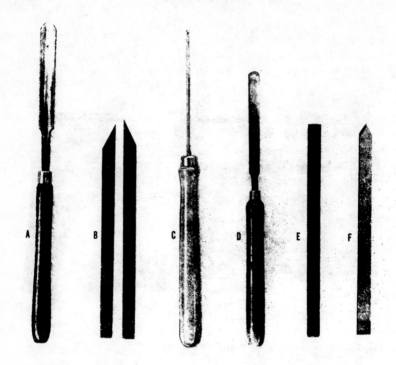

A. Turning gouge
B. Skew chisels
C. Parting tool
D. Round-nose chisel
E. Square-nose chisel
F. Spear-point chisel

**Fig. 74.** Lathe cutting tools.

*Skew chisels* are used for smoothing cuts to finish a surface, turning beads, trimming ends or shoulders, and for making V-cuts. They are made in sizes from ⅛″ to 2½″ in width and in pairs, right-handed and left-handed.

*Parting tools* are used to cut recesses or grooves with straight sides and a flat bottom and also to cut off finished work from the faceplate. These tools are available in sizes ranging from ⅛″ to ¾″.

*Scraping tools* of various shapes are used for the most accurate turning work, especially for most faceplate turning. A few of the more commonly used shapes are shown in *D*, *E*, and *F* of Fig. 74.

The chisels shown in *B, E,* and *F* are actually old jointer blades which have been ground to the required shape. The wood handles for these homemade chisels are not shown in the illustration.

A *toothing iron* is basically a *square-nose turning chisel* with a series of parallel grooves cut into the top surface of the iron. (*See* Fig. 75.) These turning tools are used for rough turning of segment work mounted on a faceplate. The points of the toothing iron created by the parallel grooves serve as a series of *spear-point chisels.* Therefore, the tool is not likely to catch and dig into the work like a square-nose turning chisel. The toothing iron is made with coarse, medium, and fine parallel grooves and varies from ½″ to 2″ in width.

DETAIL "A"

**Fig. 75.** Toothing iron lathe tool.

Lathe turning may be divided into two categories—center-to-center turning (also called between turning and spindle turning) and faceplate turning.

Being aware of the many dangers when using a lathe, you should follow and insist upon strict adherence to the following safety rules.

Use the tool rest as much as possible.

Adjust and set the compound or the tool rest for the start of the cut before turning the switch on.

Take very light cuts, especially when using handtools.

Never attempt to use calipers on interrupted surfaces while the work is in motion.

(*See* Chap. 1, Woodworking Hand Tools and How To Use Them.)

## CHAPTER 4

# Methods of Fastening

The most commonly used fastening devices are usually made of metal—nails, screws, bolts, driftpins, and corrugated fasteners.

## NAILS

The standard nail used by the woodworker is the *wire nail*, so named because it is made from steel wire. There are many types of nails, all of which are classified according to use and form. The wire nail is round-shafted, straight, pointed, and may vary in size, weight, size and shape of head, type of point, and finish. All normal requirements of construction and framing are filled by one of the nail types below. There are a few general rules to be followed in the use of nails in building. A nail, whatever the type, should be at least three times as long as the thickness of the wood it is intended to hold. Two-thirds of the length of the nail is driven into the second piece for proper anchorage while one-third provides the necessary anchorage of the piece being fastened. Nails should be driven at an angle slightly toward each other and should be carefully placed to provide the greatest holding power. Nails driven with the grain do not hold as well as nails driven across the grain. A few nails of proper type and size, properly placed and properly driven, will hold better than a great many driven close together. Nails can generally be considered the cheapest and easiest fasteners to be applied. In terms of holding power alone, nails provide the least; screws of comparable size provide more, and bolts provide the greatest amount.

*Common wire nails* and *box nails* are the same except that the wire sizes are one or two numbers smaller for a given length of the box nail than they are for the common nail. The common wire nail (*A*, Fig. 1) is used for housing-construction framing. The common wire nail and the box nail are generally used for structural construction.

The *finishing nail* (*B*, Fig. 1) is made from finer wire and has a smaller head than the common nail. It may be set below the surface of the wood into which it is driven and will leave only a small hole that is easily puttied up. It is generally used for interior or exterior finishing work, particularly in finished carpentry and cabinetmaking.

The *duplex nail* (*C*, Fig. 1) is made with what may appear to be two heads. The lower head, or shoulder, is provided so that the nail may be driven securely home to give maximum holding power while the upper head projects above the surface of the wood to make its withdrawal simple. The reason for this design is that the duplex nail is not meant to be permanent. It is used in the construction of temporary structures such as scaffolding and staging and is classified for temporary construction.

*Roofing nails* (*D*, Fig. 1) are round-shafted, diamond-pointed, galvanized nails of relatively short length and comparatively large heads. They are designed for fastening flexible roofing materials and for resisting continuous exposure to weather. Several general rules apply to the use of roofing nails, especially their use with asphalt shingles. If shingles or roll roofing are being applied over old roofing, the roofing nails selected must be of sufficient length to go through the old material and secure the new. Asphalt roofing material is fastened with corrosion resistant nails, never with plain nails. Nailing is begun in the center of the shingle, just above the cutouts or slots, to avoid buckling.

## NAIL SIZES

*Nail sizes* are designated by the use of the term penny. This term designates the length of the nail (1–penny, 2–penny, and so on), which is the same for all types. The approximate number of nails per pound varies according to the type and size. The wire gage number varies according to type. Figure 1 provides the information implicit in the term penny for each of the type of nails

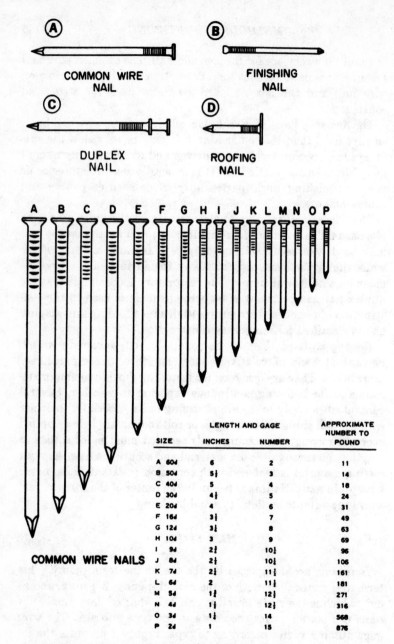

Fig. 1. Types of common nails and nail sizes.

referred to in this chapter. The "d" adjacent to the numbers in the *size column* is the accepted abbreviation of the word penny as used in nail sizing and should be read 2–penny, 3–penny, and so on. Table 1 gives the general size and type of nail preferable for specific applications.

## SCREWS

The use of *screws,* rather than nails, as fasteners may be dictated by a number of factors. These would include the type of material to be fastened, the requirement for greater holding power than could be obtained by the use of nails, the finished appearance desired, and the fact that the number of fasteners that can be used is limited. The use of screws, rather than nails, is more expensive in terms of time and money but is often necessary to meet requirements for superior results. The main advantages of screws are that they provide more holding power; can be easily tightened to draw the items being fastened securely together; are neater in appearance if properly driven; and may be withdrawn without damaging the material. The common wood screw is usually made of unhardened steel, stainless steel, aluminum, or brass. The steel may be bright-finished or blued, or zinc-, cadmium-, or chrome-plated. Wood screws are threaded from a gimlet point for approximately two-thirds of the length of the screw and are provided with a slotted head designed to be driven by an inserted driver.

*Wood screws* as shown in Fig. 2 are designated according to head style. The most common types are flathead, ovalhead, and roundhead, both in slotted and Phillips heads. To prepare wood for receiving the screws, bore a pilot hole the diameter of the screw to be used in the piece of wood that is to be fastened (Fig. 3). Then bore a smaller, starter hole in the piece of wood that is to act as anchor to hold the threads of the screw. The starter hole is drilled with a diameter less than that of the screw threads and to a depth one-half or two-thirds the length of the threads to be anchored. The purpose of this careful preparation is to assure accuracy in the placement of the screws, to reduce the possibility of splitting the wood, and to reduce the time and effort required to drive the screw. Properly set slotted and Phillips flathead and ovalhead

TABLE 1

*Size, type, and use of nails*

| Size | Lgth (in.)[1] | Diam (in.) | Remarks | Where used |
|---|---|---|---|---|
| 2d | 1 | .072 | Small head | Finish work, shop work. |
| 2d | 1 | .072 | Large flathead | Small timber, wood shingles, lathes. |
| 3d | 1¼ | .08 | Small head | Finish work, shop work. |
| 3d | 1¼ | .08 | Large flathead | Small timber, wood shingles, lathes. |
| 4d | 1½ | .098 | Small head | Finish work, shop work. |
| 4d | 1½ | .098 | Large flathead | Small timber, lathes, shop work. |
| 5d | 1¾ | .098 | Small head | Finish work, shop work. |
| 5d | 1¾ | .098 | Large flathead | Small timber, lathes, shop work. |
| 6d | 2 | .113 | Small head | Finish work, casing, stops, etc., shop work. |
| 6d | 2 | .113 | Large flathead | Small timber, siding, sheathing, etc., shop work. |
| 7d | 2¼ | .113 | Small head | Casing, base, ceiling, stops, etc. |
| 7d | 2¼ | .113 | Large flathead | Sheathing, siding, subflooring, light framing. |
| 8d | 2½ | .131 | Small head | Casing, base, ceiling, wainscot, etc., shop work. |
| 8d | 2½ | .131 | Large flathead | Sheathing, siding, subflooring, light framing, shop work. |
| 8d | 1¼ | .131 | Extra-large flathead | Roll roofing, composition shingles. |
| 9d | 2¾ | .131 | Small head | Casing, base, ceiling, etc. |
| 9d | 2¾ | .131 | Large flathead | Sheathing, siding, subflooring, framing, shop work. |
| 10d | 3 | .148 | Small head | Casing, base, ceiling, etc., shop work. |
| 10d | 3 | .148 | Large flathead | Sheathing, siding, subflooring, framing, shop work. |
| 12d | 3¼ | .148 | Large flathead | Sheathing, subflooring, framing. |
| 16d | 3½ | .162 | Large flathead | Framing, bridges, etc. |
| 20d | 4 | .192 | Large flathead | Framing, bridges, etc. |
| 30d | 4½ | .207 | Large flathead | Heavy framing, bridges, etc. |
| 40d | 5 | .225 | Large flathead | Heavy framing, bridges, etc. |
| 50d | 5½ | .244 | Large flathead | Extra-heavy framing, bridges, etc. |
| 60d | 6 | .262 | Large flathead | Extra-heavy framing, bridges, etc. |

[1] This chart applies to wire nails, although it may be used to determine the length of cut nails.

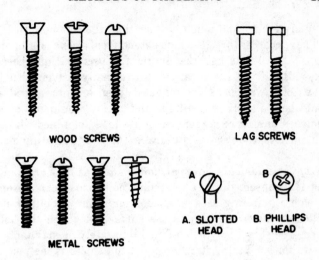

**Fig. 2.** Types of screws.

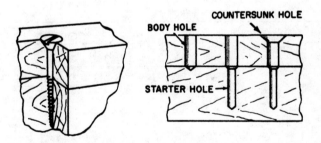

**Fig. 3.** Sinking screw properly.

screws are countersunk sufficiently to permit a covering material to be used to cover the head. Slotted roundhead and Phillips roundhead screws are not countersunk, but are driven so that the head is firmly flush with the surface of the wood. The slot of the roundhead screw is left parallel with the grain of the wood.

The proper name for a *lag screw* (Fig. 2) is lag bolt, wood screw type. These screws are often required in construction building.

They are longer and much heavier than the common wood screw and have coarser threads which extend from a cone or gimlet point slightly more than half the length of the screw. Squarehead and hexagonhead lag screws are also externally driven, usually by means of a wrench. They are used when ordinary wood screws would be too short or too light and spokes would not be strong enough. For sizes of lag screws see Table 2. Combined with expansion anchors, they are used to frame timbers to existing masonry.

*Expansion shields,* or *expansion anchors* as they are sometimes called, are inserted into a predrilled hole, usually in masonry, to provide a gripping base or anchor for a screw, bolt, or nail intended to fasten an item to the surface in which the hole was bored. The shield may be obtained separately or may include the screw, bolt, or nail. After the expansion shield is inserted in the predrilled hole, the fastener is driven into the hole in the shield, expanding the shield and wedging it firmly against the surface of the hole.

TABLE 2
*Lag screws*

| Lengths (inches) | ¼ | Diameters (inches) | | |
|---|---|---|---|---|
| | | ⅜, ⁷⁄₁₆, ½ | ⅝, ¾ | ⅞, 1 |
| 1 _____ | x | x | | |
| 1½ _____ | x | x | x | |
| 2, 2½, 3, 3½, etc., 7½, 8 to 10_ | x | x | x | x |
| 11 to 12_____ | | x | x | x |
| 13 to 16_____ | | | x | x |

For the assembly of metal parts, *sheet metal screws* are used. These screws are made regularly in steel and brass with four types of heads—flat, round, oval, and fillister, as shown in that order in Fig. 2.

*Wood screws* come in sizes that vary from ¼″ to 6″. Screws up to 1″ in length increase by eighths, screws from 1″ to 3″ increase by quarters, and screws from 3″ to 6″ increase by half-inches. Screws vary in length and size of shaft. Each length is made in a number of shaft sizes specified by an arbitrary number that represents no particular measurement but indicates relative differences in the diameter of the screws. Proper nomenclature of a screw, as illustrated in Fig. 4, includes the type, material, finish, length, and screw size number that indicates the wire gage of the body, drill or bit size for the body hole, and drill or bit size for the starter hole. Tables 3 and 4 provide size, length, gage, and applicable drill and auger bit sizes for screws. Table 4 gives length and diameters of lag screws.

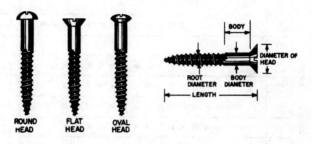

**Fig. 4.** Types of wood screws and nomenclature.

## BOLTS

*Bolts* are used in construction when great strength is required or when the work under construction must be frequently disassembled. Their use usually implies the use of nuts for fastening and sometimes the use of washers to protect the surface of the material they are used to fasten. Bolts are selected for application to specific tasks in terms of length, diameter, thread, style of head, and type. Proper selection of head style and type of bolt will result in good appearance as well as good construction. The use of washers between the nut and a wood surface or between both the nut and the head and their opposing surfaces will avoid marring the surfaces and permit additional torque in tightening.

## TYPES OF BOLTS

*Carriage bolts* fall into three categories—*square neck bolt, finned neck bolt,* and *ribbed neck bolt* (Fig. 5). These bolts have

TABLE 3
*Screw sizes and dimensions*

| Length (in.) | 0 | 1 | 2 | 3 | 4 | 5 | 6 | 7 | 8 | 9 | 10 | 11 | 12 | 13 | 14 | 15 | 16 | 17 | 18 | 20 | 22 | 24 |
|---|---|---|---|---|---|---|---|---|---|---|---|---|---|---|---|---|---|---|---|---|---|---|
| 1/4 | × | × | × | × | × | × | × | × | × | × | × | × | × |  |  |  |  |  |  |  |  |  |
| 3/8 | × | × | × | × | × | × | × | × | × | × | × | × | × |  | × |  |  |  |  |  |  |  |
| 1/2 |  | × | × | × | × | × | × | × | × | × | × | × | × |  | × |  | × |  |  |  |  |  |
| 5/8 |  | × | × | × | × | × | × | × | × | × | × | × | × |  | × |  | × |  |  |  |  |  |
| 3/4 |  |  | × | × | × | × | × | × | × | × | × | × | × |  | × |  | × |  | × | × |  |  |
| 7/8 |  |  | × | × | × | × | × | × | × | × | × | × | × |  | × |  | × |  | × | × |  |  |
| 1 |  |  |  | × | × | × | × | × | × | × | × | × | × |  | × |  | × |  | × | × |  | × |
| 1 1/4 |  |  |  | × | × | × | × | × | × | × | × | × | × |  | × |  | × |  | × | × |  | × |
| 1 1/2 |  |  |  |  | × | × | × | × | × | × | × | × | × |  | × |  | × |  | × | × |  | × |
| 1 3/4 |  |  |  |  | × | × | × | × | × | × | × | × | × |  | × |  | × |  | × | × |  | × |
| 2 |  |  |  |  |  | × | × | × | × | × | × | × | × |  | × |  | × |  | × | × |  | × |
| 2 1/4 |  |  |  |  |  | × | × | × | × | × | × | × | × |  | × |  | × |  | × | × |  | × |
| 2 1/2 |  |  |  |  |  |  | × | × | × | × | × | × | × |  | × |  | × |  | × | × |  | × |
| 2 3/4 |  |  |  |  |  |  |  | × | × | × | × | × | × |  | × |  | × |  | × | × |  | × |
| 3 |  |  |  |  |  |  |  |  | × | × | × | × | × |  | × |  | × |  | × | × |  | × |
| 3 1/2 |  |  |  |  |  |  |  |  | × | × |  |  | × |  | × |  | × |  | × | × |  | × |
| 4 |  |  |  |  |  |  |  |  |  |  |  |  | × |  | × |  | × |  | × | × |  | × |
| 4 1/2 |  |  |  |  |  |  |  |  |  |  |  |  |  |  | × |  | × |  | × | × |  | × |
| 5 |  |  |  |  |  |  |  |  |  |  |  |  |  |  | × |  | × |  | × | × |  | × |
| 6 |  |  |  |  |  |  |  |  |  |  |  |  |  |  |  |  | × |  | × | × |  | × |
| Threads per inch | 32 | 28 | 26 | 24 | 22 | 20 | 18 | 16 | 15 | 14 | 13 | 12 | 11 |  | 10 |  | 9 |  | 8 | 8 |  | 7 |
| Diameter of screw (in.) | .060 | .073 | .086 | .099 | .112 | .125 | .138 | .151 | .164 | .177 | .190 | .203 | .216 |  | .242 |  | .268 |  | .294 | .320 |  | .372 |

Size numbers

TABLE 4
*Drill and auger bit sizes for wood screws*

| Screw size No. | 1 | 2 | 3 | 4 | 5 | 6 | 7 | 8 | 9 | 10 | 12 | 14 | 16 | 18 |
|---|---|---|---|---|---|---|---|---|---|---|---|---|---|---|
| Nominal screw Body diameter | .073 | .086 | .099 | .112 | .125 | .138 | .151 | .164 | .177 | .190 | .216 | .242 | .268 | .294 |
| Pilot hole — Drill size | 5/64 | 3/32 | 7/64 | 7/64 | 1/8 | 9/64 | 5/32 | 11/64 | 3/16 | 3/16 | 7/32 | 1/4 | 17/64 | 19/64 |
| Pilot hole — Bit size | — | — | — | — | — | — | — | — | — | — | 4 | 4 | 5 | 5 |
| Starter hole — Drill size | — | 1/16 | 1/16 | 5/64 | 5/64 | 3/32 | 7/64 | 7/64 | 1/8 | 1/8 | 9/64 | 5/32 | 3/16 | 13/64 |
| Starter hole — Bit size | — | — | — | — | — | — | — | — | — | — | — | — | — | 4 |

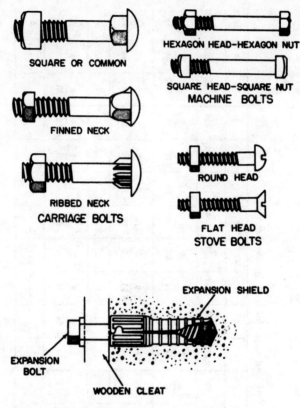

**Fig. 5.** Types of bolts.

roundheads that are not designed to be driven. They are threaded only part of the way up the shaft; usually the threads are two to four times the diameter of the bolt in length. In each type of carriage bolt the upper part of the shank, immediately below the head, is designed to grip the material in which the bolt is inserted and keep the bolt from turning when a nut is tightened down on it or removed. The finned type is designed with two or more fins extending from the head to the shank. The ribbed type is designed with longitudinal ribs, splines, or serrations on all or part of a shoulder located immediately beneath the head. Holes bored to receive carriage bolts are bored to be a tight fit for the body of the bolt and counterbored to permit the head of the bolt to fit flush with, or below the surface of, the material being fastened. The bolt is then driven through the hole with a hammer. Carriage bolts are chiefly for wood-to-wood application but may also be used for wood-to-metal applications. If used for wood-to-metal application, the head should be fitted to the wooden object. Metal surfaces are sometimes predrilled and countersunk to permit the use of carriage bolts metal-to-metal. Carriage bolts can be obtained from ¼″ to 1″ in diameter, and from ¾″ to 20″ long. (*See* Table 5.)

TABLE 5
*Carriage bolts*

| Lengths (inches) | Diameters (inches) | | | |
|---|---|---|---|---|
| | ³⁄₁₆, ¼, ⁵⁄₁₆, ⅜ | ⁷⁄₁₆, ½ | ⁹⁄₁₆, ⅝ | ¾ |
| ¾ | x | | | |
| 1 | x | x | | |
| 1¼ | x | x | x | |
| 1½, 2, 2½, etc., 9½, 10 to 20 | x | x | x | x |

A common flat washer should be used with carriage bolts between the nut and the wood surface.

*Machine bolts* (Fig. 5) are made with cut National Fine or National Coarse threads extending in length from twice the diameter of the bolt plus ¼″ (for bolts less than 6″ in length), to twice the diameter of the bolt plus ½″ (for bolts over 6″ in length). They are precision-made and generally applied metal-to-metal where close tolerance is desirable. The head may be square, hexagonal, rounded, or flat countersunk. The nut usually corresponds in shape to the head of the bolt with which it is used. Machine bolts are externally driven only. Selection of the proper machine bolt is made on the basis of head style, length, diameter, number of threads per inch, and coarseness of thread. The hole through which the bolt is to pass is bored to the same diameter as the bolt. Machine bolts are made in diameters from ¼″ to 3″ and may be obtained in any length desired. (*See* Table 6.)

TABLE 6
*Screw, cap (machine bolts)*

| Lengths (inches) | Diameters (inches) | | | | |
|---|---|---|---|---|---|
| | ¼, ⅜ | ⁷⁄₁₆ | ½, ⁹⁄₁₆, ⅝ | ¾, ⅞, 1 | 1⅛, 1¼ |
| ¾ | x | | | | |
| 1, 1¼ | x | x | x | | |
| 1½, 2, 2½ | x | x | x | x | |
| 3, 3½, 4, 4½, etc., 9½, 10 to 20. | x | x | x | x | x |
| 21 to 25 | | | x | x | x |
| 26 to 39 | | | | x | x |

*Stove bolts* (Fig. 5) are less precisely made than machine bolts. They are made with either flat or round slotted heads and may have threads extending over the full length of the body, over part of the body, or over most of the body. They are generally used with square nuts and applied metal-to-metal, wood-to-wood, or wood-to-metal. If flatheaded, they are countersunk; if roundheaded, they are drawn flush to the surface.

An *expansion bolt* (Fig. 5) is a bolt used in conjunction with an expansion shield to provide anchorage in substances in which a threaded fastener alone is useless. The shield, or expansion anchor, inserted in a predrilled hole expands when the bolt is driven into it and becomes wedged firmly in the hole, providing a secure base for the grip of the fastener.

*Driftpins* are long, heavy, threadless bolts used to hold heavy pieces of timber together (Fig. 6). The term "driftpin" is almost universally used in practice. However, for supply purposes the correct designation is "driftbolt."

Driftpins have heads that vary in diameter from ½" to 1", and in length from 18" to 26".

To use the driftpin, a hole slightly smaller than the diameter of the pin is made in the timber. The pin is driven into the hole and is held in place by the compression action of the wood fibers.

The *corrugated fastener* is one of the many means by which joints and splices are fastened in small timber and boards. It is used particularly in the miter joint. Corrugated fasteners are

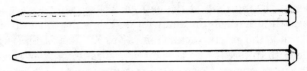

**Fig. 6.** Driftpins (driftbolts).

made of sheet metal of 18 to 22 gage with alternate ridges and grooves. The ridges vary from 3/16″ to 5/16″, center to center. One end is cut square, the other end is sharpened with beveled edges. There are two types of corrugated fasteners—one with the ridges running parallel (Fig. 7), the other with ridges running at a slight angle to one another (Fig. 7). The latter type has a tendency to compress the material since the ridges and grooves are

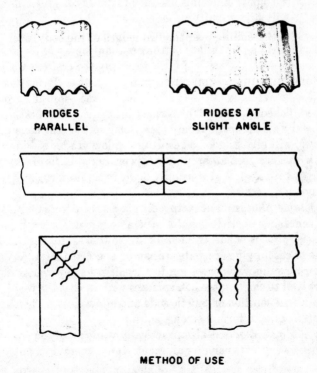

RIDGES
PARALLEL

RIDGES AT
SLIGHT ANGLE

METHOD OF USE

**Fig. 7.** Corrugated fasteners and their uses.

closer at the top than at the bottom. These fasteners are made in several different lengths and widths. The width varies from ⅝″ to 1⅛″, while the length varies from ¼″ to ¾″. The fasteners also are made with different numbers of ridges, ranging from three to six ridges per fastener. Corrugated fasteners are used in a number of ways: to fasten parallel boards together, as in fastening tabletops; to make any type of joint; and as a substitute for nails where nails may split the timber. The fasteners have a greater holding power than nails in small timber. The proper method of using the fasteners is also shown in Fig. 7.

## GLUE

One of the oldest materials used for fastening is glue. In museums you will find furniture, assembled with glue hundreds of years ago, that is still in good condition. Good glue properly applied will form a joint that is stronger than the wood itself.

There are several classes of glue. Probably the best one for joint work and furniture construction is *animal glue*. It may be obtained commercially in a variety of forms—liquid, ground, chipped, flaked, powdered, or formed into sticks. The best grades of animal glue are made from hides. Some of the best bone glues, however, will give as good a result as the low grades of hide glue.

*Fish glue* is a good all-around woodworking glue, but it is not as strong as animal glue. It is usually made in liquid form, and it has a disagreeable odor.

*Vegetable glue* is manufactured by a secret process for use in some veneering work. It is *not* a satisfactory glue for wood joints.

*Casein glue* is made from milk in powdered form. The best grades of casein glue are water-resistant and are, therefore, excellent for forming waterproof joints. Casein glue, however, does not adhere well to oak. To join oak surfaces with it, coat the wood with a 10 per cent solution of caustic soda and allow to dry. Then apply the casein glue to form a strong joint.

*Blood albumin glue* is also practically waterproof, but to use it you need very expensive equipment. It is, therefore, not often used.

*Plastic resin glue* may be procured in either liquid or powder form. It is durable and water resistant but, like casein glue, it does not adhere too well to oak. Plastic resin glue is used in the manufacture of balsa wood and plywood life floats.

Each type of glue must be prepared and used in a special manner if you are to get the strongest possible joint. Instructions are always found on the label of the container. Study these carefully before you attempt to use the glue. There are also certain general principles that you should follow when you apply any glue.

A lot depends on the wood itself. Dry wood makes stronger joints than wood which is not well seasoned. This is easy to understand if you will remember that water in the wood will decrease the amount of glue that can be absorbed.

(*See* Chap. 1, Woodworking Hand Tools and How To Use Them, and Chap. 2, Equipment for Holding Work.)

# Lumber, Joints, and Frame Construction

Know something about the grade of lumber you purchase. The most basic skill in the art of woodworking—making joints and splices.

An overview of frame construction—layout, cutting, and erection of formwork members; plates, joists, studs, girders, bridging, bracing, rafters, sheathing, and subflooring.

Methods of reducing your building costs.

# CHAPTER 5
# Lumber

Any piece of wood is made up of a number of small cells as shown in Fig. 1. The size and arrangement of the cells determine the grain of the wood and many of its properties. (*See* Fig. 2.)

There are two methods of sawing up logs: *slash cutting* and *rift cutting* (Fig. 3).

Lumber that is specially cut to provide edge grain on both faces is said to be rift cut. If hardwood is being cut, the lumber is said to

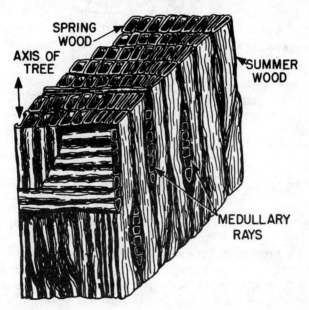

**Fig. 1.** Structure of wood.

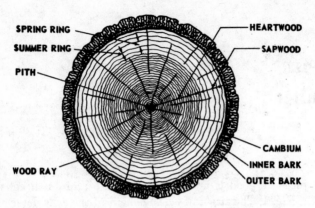

**Fig. 2.** Cross section of a tree.

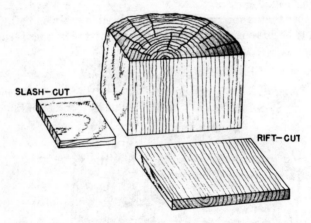

**Fig. 3.** Slash and rift cutting.

be *quartersawed* (Fig. 4). If softwood is being sawed, it is called *edge-grain lumber*. If an entire log is slash cut, several boards from near the center of the log will actually be rift cut.

Slash-cut lumber is usually cheaper than rift-cut lumber because it takes less time to slash cut a log, and there is less waste. Circular or oval knots appearing in slash-cut boards affect the strength and surface appearance much less than do spike knots

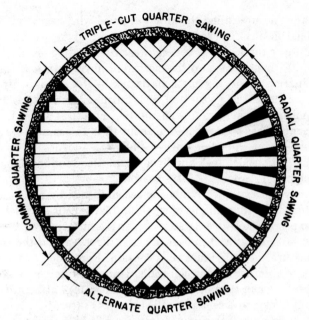

**Fig. 4.** Rift cutting—four methods of quartersawing.

which may appear in rift-cut boards. If, however, a log is sawed to produce all slash-cut lumber, more boards will contain knots than would be the case if the log were sawed to produce the maximum amount of rift-cut material. Another advantage of slash cutting is that shakes and pitch pockets, when present, will extend through fewer boards.

Rift-cut lumber is preferred because it offers more resistance to wear than does slash-cut lumber. Rift-cut lumber also shrinks and swells less in width. Another advantage of rift-cut lumber as compared with slash-cut lumber is that it twists and cups less and splits less when used. Rift-cut lumber usually holds paint better.

After being sawed, lumber must be thoroughly dried before it is suitable for most uses. The old method—and one still preferred for some uses—was merely to air-dry the lumber in a shed or stack it in the open. This method requires considerable time—up to seven years for some of the hardwoods.

A faster method is known as kiln-drying. The wood is placed in a tight enclosure called the kiln and dried with heat supplied by artificial means. The length of time required for drying varies from two or three days to several weeks, depending on the kind of wood, its dimensions, and the method of drying. In most cases, a combination of drying methods is used—the wood is air-dried from six months to a year and then finished off in a kiln.

Lumber is considered dry enough for most uses when the moisture content has been reduced to about 12 or 15 per cent. As a user of lumber you will soon learn to judge the dryness of wood by color, weight, smell, feel, and by a visual examination of shavings and chips.

Briefly, seasoning of lumber is accomplished by removing the moisture from the millions of small and large cells of which wood is composed. Moisture (water or sap) occurs in two separate forms—*free water* and *embedded water*. Free water is the amount of moisture the individual cells contain. Embedded water is the moisture absorbed by the cell walls. During drying or seasoning, the free water in the individual cells evaporates until a minimum amount of moisture remains, called the *fiber saturation point*. The moisture content of this point varies from 25 to 30 per cent. Below the fiber saturation point, the embedded water is extracted from the porous cell walls; this process causes a reduction of the thickness of the walls. Wood shrinks across the grain when the moisture content is lowered below the fiber saturation point. *Shrinking* and *swelling* of the wood cells, caused by varying amounts of moisture, change the size of the cells. Therefore, the *lowering* or *raising* of the moisture content causes lumber to shrink or swell.

The loss of moisture during seasoning causes wood to be harder, stronger, stiffer, and lighter in weight.

## CLASSIFICATION OF LUMBER

Lumber is classified into three major use categories as follows:

*Yard-lumber grades* for general building purposes where the piece is to be used as a whole.

*Factory* and *shop-lumber grades* where the lumber is to be cut up in further manufacture.

*Structural material* of relatively large dimension where the piece is to be used as a whole and where strength factors are definitely appraised independent of appearance factors.

An *important exception* to this generally applicable classification according to use is that boxes and containers are produced largely from the yard lumber grades rather than factory grades.

## SIZE OF LUMBER

The *nominal* cross section dimensions of a piece of lumber (2 × 4, 1 × 2, 8 × 10, and so on) are always larger than the actual *dressed* dimensions. Dressed lumber is lumber that has been *surfaced* (planed smooth) on two or four sides. Lumber that has been surfaced on two sides is designated as S2S (surfaced two sides); lumber that has been surfaced on all four sides is designated as S4S (surfaced 4 sides). Most lumber used in general construction is S4S. The nominal sizes and the actual dressed (S4S) dimensions of some common sizes of boards follow:

| Nominal Size | Dressed Dimensions |
|---|---|
| 1 × 6 | 25/32 × 5⅝ |
| 1 × 8 | 25/32 × 7½ |
| 1 × 10 | 25/32 × 9½ |

The nominal sizes and the actual dressed (S4S) dimensions of some common sizes of dimension lumber are as follows:

| Nominal Size | Dressed Dimensions |
|---|---|
| 2 × 2 | 1⅝ × 1⅝ |
| 2 × 4 | 1⅝ × 7½ |
| 2 × 6 | 1⅝ × 9⅝ |
| 2 × 8 | 1⅝ × 7½ |
| 2 × 10 | 1⅝ × 9½ |
| 2 × 12 | 1⅝ × 11½ |
| 4 × 4 | 3⅝ × 3⅝ |

All softwood framing lumber, and most other softwood lumber, is cut to even-numbered feet lengths, such as 10′, 12′, 14′, and so on. Hardwood is sometimes cut to odd-numbered as well as even-numbered feet lengths.

## BOARD MEASURE

*Board measure* is a method of measuring lumber in which the basic unit is an abstract volume 1' long by 1' wide by 1" thick. This abstract volume or unit is called a *board foot.*

There are several formulas for calculating the number of board feet in a piece of given dimensions. Since lumber dimensions are most frequently indicated by width and thickness in inches and length in feet, the following formula is probably the most practical.

$$\frac{\text{Thickness in in.} \times \text{width in in.} \times \text{length in ft.}}{12} = \text{board ft.}$$

Suppose you are calculating the number of board feet in a 14' long 2 × 4. Applying the formula, you get:

$$\frac{\overset{1}{\cancel{2}} \times \overset{2}{\cancel{4}} \times 14}{\underset{\underset{3}{\cancel{6}}}{\cancel{12}}} = \frac{28}{3} = 9\tfrac{1}{3} \text{ board feet}$$

The chief practical use of board measure is in cost calculations, since lumber is bought and sold by the board foot. Any lumber less than 1" thick is presumed to be 1" thick for board measure purposes. Board measure is calculated on the basis of the *nominal,* not the *actual,* dimensions of lumber. As described previously, the actual size of a piece of dimension lumber (such as a 2 × 4, for example) is usually less than the nominal size.

## DEFECTS AND BLEMISHES

A *defect* in lumber is any flaw that tends to affect the strength, durability, or utility value of the lumber. A *blemish* is a flaw that mars the appearance of the lumber only. A blemish that affects the utility value of the lumber (such as a blemish in wood intended for fine cabinet work) is also a defect.

Common defects and blemishes are as follows.

A *bark pocket* is a patch of bark over which the tree has grown and which it has entirely or almost entirely enclosed.

A *check* is a separation along the lengthwise grain, caused by too rapid or nonuniform drying.

*Cross-grained lumber* is lumber in which the grain does not parallel the lengthwise axis of the piece, or in which the grain spirals around the lengthwise axis.

*Decay* is deterioration caused by various kinds of fungi.

A *knot* is the root section of a branch. It may appear on a surface in cross section or in lengthwise section. A knot that appears in lengthwise section is a *spike knot;* a spike knot is always a defect. A *loose knot* of the cross-section type is also a defect. A *tight knot* of this type may be a defect if it mars the appearance of wood intended for fine cabinet work or the like; otherwise it is usually considered to be only a blemish.

A *pitch pocket* is a deposit of solid or liquid pitch enclosed in the wood.

A *shake* is a separation along the lengthwise grain. It is not the same as a *check* because it already exists when the tree is cut, while a check develops as the cut lumber dries. *Heart shake* moves outward from the center of the tree; *wind shake* follows the circular lines of the annual rings. Heart shake is caused by decay at the center of the trunk. The cause of wind shake is not definitely known.

*Blue stain* is a blemish caused by a mold fungus. It does not weaken the wood.

*Wane* is a term applied to any edge or corner defect that causes that particular part of a board or timber to be less than its full-size dimensions.

*Warp* is a general term applied to the various types of shrinkage distortions that were previously described.

## GRADING LUMBER

Lumber is graded for quality in accordance with American

Lumber Standards set by the National Bureau of Standards for the United States Department of Commerce. The two major quality grades, in descending order of quality, are *select lumber* and *common lumber*. Each of these grades has subdivisions in descending order of quality as follows.

*Grade A* lumber is select lumber that is practically free of defects and blemishes.

*Grade B* lumber is select lumber that contains a few minor blemishes.

*Grade C* lumber is finish item lumber that contains more numerous and more significant blemishes than grade B. All of these must be capable of being easily and thoroughly concealed with paint.

*Grade D* lumber is finish item lumber that contains more numerous and more significant blemishes than grade C, but that is still capable of presenting a satisfactory appearance when painted.

*No. 1 common* lumber is sound, tight-knotted stock, containing only a few minor defects. It must be suitable for use as watertight lumber.

*No. 2 common* lumber contains a limited number of significant defects, but no knotholes or other serious defects. It must be suitable for use as graintight lumber.

*No. 3 common* lumber contains a few defects that are larger and coarser than those in No. 2 common—occasional knot holes, for example.

*No. 4 common* lumber is low-quality material, containing serious defects like knotholes, checks, shakes, and decay.

*No. 5 common* lumber is capable only of holding together under ordinary handling.

The grades *construction, standard, utility,* and *economy* are used in some associations.

All species are covered by the grading rules and size standards of some association or grading bureau. In the case of softwood lumber, standards are set by a regional manufacturer's association. In the case of hardwood lumber, there is but one national association. In a few cases, a softwood species growing in more than one region is graded under rules of two different associations.

There is great advantage to the purchaser, whether large or small, to buy according to these association grades rather than to attempt to buy according to individual specifications unless the requirements are actually very unusual. Occasionally a departure from the standard grade provision is necessary to cover unusual requirements. This is best handled as an exception to a standard grade rather than as an entirely special grade.

## HANDLING AND STORAGE OF LUMBER

The advances made in the mechanized handling of lumber have to a great extent changed storage and handling methods. The development of handling equipment, such as forklifts and straddle trucks or carriers, that can be used to pile, unpile, and transport lumber, has brought about revolutionary changes in storage and handling practices, the most notable being the handling of lumber in packages (drafts). Regardless of whether lumber is handled by mechanized equipment or by manual labor, the objectives of storage and handling are unchanged.

The objective of lumber storage is to maintain the lumber at or bring it to a moisture content suitable for its end use with a minimum of deterioration. The objective of lumber handling is to load, transport, unload, pile, and unpile lumber economically and without damage. Both of these objectives are obtained easily if good handling and storage practices are followed. Adequate protection of lumber in storage will help prevent attack by fungi, insects, and changes in moisture content that will result in checking, warping, and staining in lumber which render it unsuitable for the intended use.

Available space limits the location of the storage yard, but it is preferably near the spot where the lumber is received or used. The best location is on high ground that is level, well drained, and remote from water bodies or wind-obstructing objects such as tall trees or buildings. A low site is likely to be sheltered from the full sweep of the winds and to be damp—conditions that may retard drying and expose the lumber to stain and decay.

## LAMINATED LUMBER AND PLYWOOD

*Laminated lumber* is made up of layers of wood that are glued face-to-face with the grain of adjacent layers parallel (Fig. 5). The component parts that are glued together to make laminated lumber may be thin sliced sheets of veneer or they may be sawed boards. Plywood frequently alternates grain to give the member the qualities of nonsplitting and stability. (*Note:* Plywood alternates grain each ply and laminated wood never alternates grain.)

One advantage of laminated wood is that it can be made up in unlimited thicknesses. Also, by staggering the ends of individual layers it is possible to secure members that are much longer than solid timbers.

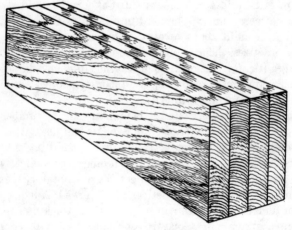

**Fig. 5.** Laminated lumber.

*Plywood* (Fig. 6) is made up of thin layers of wood that are glued face-to-face at right angles to one another. It always has an odd number of plies. Veneered stock for use in the manufacture of furniture usually has five layers. A thick layer, called the core, is in the center. The layers glued on with their grain running across that of the faces are called *crossbands*. The surface layers or faces are placed so that their grain runs parallel to the long direction of the panel.

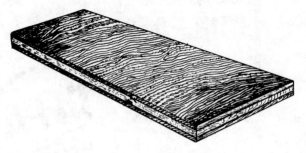

**Fig. 6.** Plywood.

Ordinarily ¼″ and ⅛″ plywood (fir) has only three plies. Thicker plywood may have as many as 15 plies, but always an odd number. The standard size of plywood sheets is 4′ wide by 6′ to 12′ long, though smaller and larger sizes are available. Because of the cross-grain effect, it is almost impossible to split plywood, and shrinking and swelling are negligible.

The development of special glues and other bonding materials has made possible a type of plywood highly resistant to water.

## GRADES OF PLYWOOD

There are two types of plywood—*interior* and *exterior*. Most plywood produced is of the interior type. Although it can stand an occasional wetting and subsequent normal drying without losing its original form and strength, interior plywood is unreliable in wet places. Exterior type plywood will retain its original form and strength when repeatedly wet and dried and otherwise subjected to the elements. It is suitable for permanent exterior use. Most plywood is branded or stamped on the edge with the symbol "EXT." or "INT." (interior). In addition, other markings carrying more complete information are stamped on the back of the plywood sheet. A typical Douglas fir back stamp, with all symbols explained, is shown in Fig. 7.

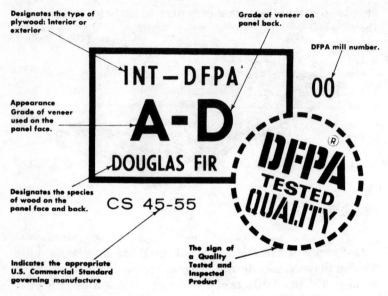

**Fig. 7.** Typical Douglas fir back stamp.

Plywood is graded by the quality of the face veneers, with "A" being the best and "D" the poorest (Fig. 7). The grading is based upon the number of defects, such as knotholes, pitch pockets, and splits, and the presence of streaks, discolorations, sapwood, shims, and patches in each face of the panel. Plywood also comes with resin-impregnated fiber faces that provide better painting surfaces and better wearing qualities.

## PLYWOOD STORAGE

Because of the conditions of its manufacture, plywood can generally be assumed to be dry when received. It should therefore be stored in a closed shed. For long storage in winter or the rainy season, a heated storage building is recommended.

Plywood is commonly solid piled. Under humid conditions there is some tendency for edges to swell because of exposed end-grain, and this swelling causes *dishing*, especially in the upper panels of high piles. Dishing can be minimized by placing strips in the pile at intervals. Enough strips should be used so that plywood will not bend between them. Dry 1″ strips are suitable for supporting plywood.

*Plywood reusable concrete forms* should be stacked flat on dry, level platforms after use. Wet faces should be separated with strips to permit drying. If unused for long periods, forms should be stored indoors after being cleaned and dried. Before reuse, the faces should be oiled with standard wood form oil or pale oil. Newly cut edges should be sealed with white lead and oil or some other sealer.

## WALLBOARD

According to Webster's, *wallboard* is considered as any boarding designed to be used against a wall, or an artificial board of wood fiber (or the like) made in large sheets and used for the interior sheathing of the walls of rooms.

## FIBERBOARD

*Fiberboard* conforming to Federal Specification LLL-F-321 is made of wood or vegetable fiber, and is compressed to form sheets or boards. It is available in sizes from ½″ to 1″ in thickness, 2′ to 4′ in width, and 8′ to 12′ in length. The boards are comparatively soft and provide good insulation and sound-absorbing qualities. Fiberboard usually has a rough surface, but is also available with finished surfaces.

## GYPSUM WALLBOARD

*Gypsum wallboard* conforming to Federal Specification SS-W-0051 is composed of gypsum between two layers of heavy paper. The most common sizes are ¼″, ⅜″, ½″, and ⅝″. Heavier gypsum wallboard is also available. The width is 4′ and the lengths vary from 8′ to 12′.

Some types have unfinished surfaces, while others have finishes that represent wood grain or tile. The joints of the unfinished type may be covered with strips to form panels. Another commonly used type of board has depressed or tapered edges. The joints are filled with a special cement and tape, so that the wall can be painted and the joints will not show.

## HARDBOARD

*Hardboard* is known by several trade names. They are all made by separating and treating wood fibers which are then subjected to heat and heavy pressure. Hardboard is available in thickness from 1/16" to 5/16". The most common size of sheet is 4' by 8' but other sizes are available. The finish may be obtained in a plain smooth surface or in any of a number of glossy finishes, some of which imitate tile or stone. Where moisture resistance or extra strength is required, Class B treated hardboard should be used; otherwise Class A is satisfactory.

## PLYWOOD

*Plywood* for interior walls is made in the same manner and comes in the same sizes as plywood for other purposes. Plywood may be purchased with both sides good (G2S) or good on one side (G1S). It may be obtained with faces of walnut, mahogany, gum or other decorative woods. Single veneers or thin two-ply panels may be obtained to bend around curved surfaces.

(*See* Chap. 6, Woodworking Joints and Splices.)

## CHAPTER 6

# Woodworking Joints and Splices

This chapter will explain some of the methods used in woodworking by explaining the procedures involved in developing various woodworking *joints* and *splices*.

## PLANING AND SQUARING TO DIMENSION

*Planing* and *squaring* a small board to dimension is what you might call the first lesson in woodworking; like a good many other things, it looks easy until you try it. The six major steps in the process are illustrated and described in Fig. 1. You should practice them until you can get a smooth, square board with a minimum of planing.

## JOINTS AND JOINING

Simple joints like the *butt joint* (Figs. 2 and 3), the *lap joint* (Fig. 4), and the *miter joint* (Fig. 5) are used mostly in rough or finish carpentry, though they may also be used occasionally in millwork and furniture making. More complex joints like the *rabbet joint* (Fig. 6), the *dado* and *gain joint* (Fig. 7), the *mortise-and-tenon* and *slip tenon joint* (Fig. 8), the *box corner joint* (Fig. 9), and the *dovetail joint* (Fig. 10) are used mostly in furniture, cabinet, and mill work. Of the edge joints shown in Fig. 11, the *dowel* and *spline* are used mainly in furniture and cabinet work, while the *plain butt* and the *tongue-and-groove* are used in practically all types of woodworking.

The joints used in rough and finish carpentry are for the most part simply nailed together. Nails in a 90° plain butt joint may be

## 1. WORK FACE

PLANE ONE BROAD SURFACE SMOOTH AND STRAIGHT. TEST IT CROSSWISE, LENGTHWISE, AND FROM CORNER TO CORNER. MARK THE WORK FACE X.

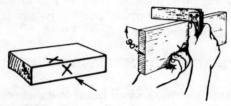

## 2. WORK EDGE

PLANE ONE EDGE SMOOTH, STRAIGHT AND SQUARE TO THE WORK FACE. TEST IT FROM THE WORK FACE. MARK THE WORK EDGE X.

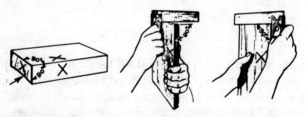

## 3. WORK END

PLANE ONE END SMOOTH AND SQUARE. TEST IT FROM THE WORK FACE AND WORK EDGE. MARK THE WORK END X.

**Fig. 1.** Planing and squaring to dimensions.

driven through the member abutted against and into the end of the abutting member, or they may be *toenailed* at an angle through the faces of the abutting member into the face of the member abutted against, as shown in Fig. 12. Studs and joists are

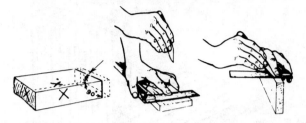

### 4. SECOND END

MEASURE LENGTH AND SCRIBE AROUND THE STOCK A LINE SQUARE TO THE WORK EDGE AND WORK FACE. SAW OFF EXCESS STOCK NEAR THE LINE AND PLANE SMOOTH TO THE SCRIBED LINE. TEST THE SECOND END FROM BOTH THE WORK FACE AND THE WORK EDGE.

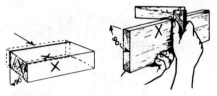

### 5. SECOND EDGE

FROM THE WORK EDGE GAUGE A LINE FOR WIDTH ON BOTH FACES. PLANE SMOOTH, STRAIGHT, SQUARE AND TO THE GAUGE LINE. TEST THE SECOND EDGE FROM THE WORK FACE.

### 6. SECOND FACE

FROM THE WORK FACE GAUGE A LINE FOR THICKNESS AROUND THE STOCK. PLANE THE STOCK TO THE GAUGE LINE. TEST THE SECOND FACE AS THE WORK FACE IS TESTED.

**Fig. 1.** (continued).

usually toenailed to sole plates and sills. (*See* Chap. 4, Methods of Fastening.)

The more complex furniture and cabinet-making joints are usually fastened with glue, with additional strength provided as

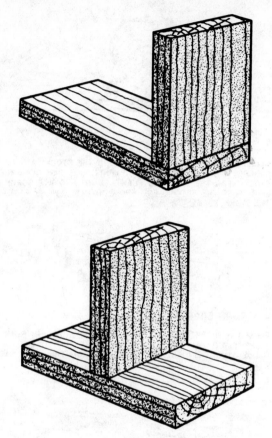

**Fig. 2.** 90-degree plain butt joints.

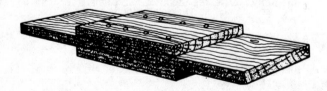

**Fig. 3.** End butt joint with fish plates.

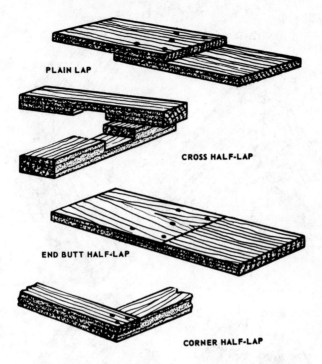

PLAIN LAP

CROSS HALF-LAP

END BUTT HALF-LAP

CORNER HALF-LAP

**Fig. 4.** Lap joints.

necessary by dowels, splines, corrugated fasteners, slip feathers, keys, and other types of joint fasteners. In the dado joint, the gain joint, the mortise-and-tenon joint, the box corner joint, and the dovetail joint, the interlocking character of the joint is an additional factor in fastening.

The two pieces that are to be joined together are called *members* and the two major steps in joining are the layout of the joint on the ends, edges, or faces of the members and the cutting of the members to the required shapes for joining.

The chief instruments for laying out joints are: the try, miter, combination square, sliding T-bevel; the marking or mortising gage; and a scratch awl, sharp pencil, or knife for scoring lines. For cutting the more complex joints by hand the hacksaw, dovetail saw, and various chisels are essential, and the rabbet-and-fil-

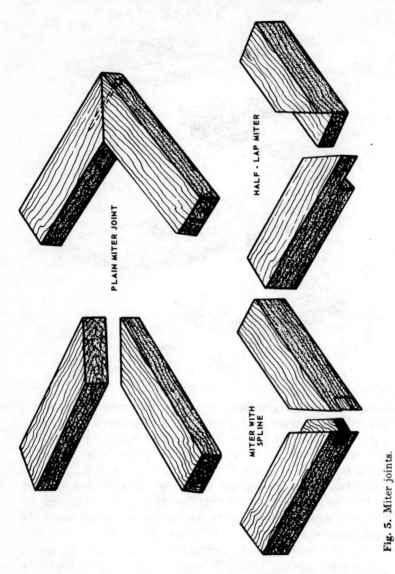

PLAIN MITER JOINT

HALF - LAP MITER

MITER WITH SPLINE

**Fig. 5.** Miter joints.

lister plane (for rabbet joints) and the router plane (for smoothing the bottoms of dados and gains) are very helpful. (*See*

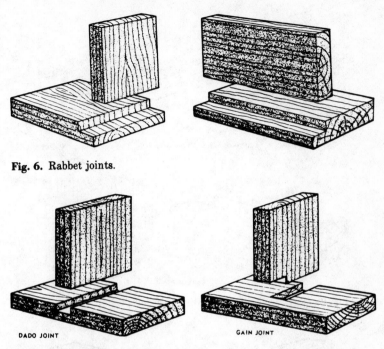

**Fig. 6.** Rabbet joints.

DADO JOINT      GAIN JOINT

**Fig. 7.** Dado and gain joints.

Chap. 1, Woodworking Hand Tools and How To Use Them.)

With the possible exception of the dovetail joint, all the joints that have been mentioned can be cut either by hand or by machine. (*See* Chap. 3, Power Tools.) Whatever the method used, and whatever the type of joint, always remember the following important rule. To ensure a tight joint, always cut on the *waste side* of the line, never on the line itself. Preliminary grooving *on the waste side* of the line with a knife or chisel will help a backsaw to get a smooth start.

## HALF LAP JOINTS

For *half lap joints* the members to be joined are usually of the same thickness, and the following discussion is based on the as-

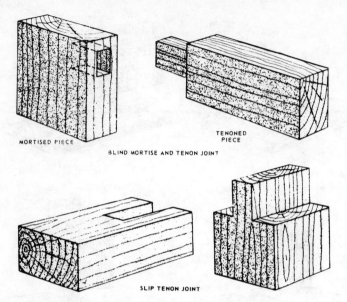

MORTISED PIECE

TENONED PIECE

BLIND MORTISE AND TENON JOINT

SLIP TENON JOINT

**Fig. 8.** Mortise-and-tenon and slip-tenon joints.

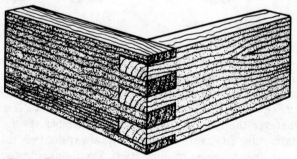

**Fig. 9.** Box corner joint.

sumption that this is the case. The method of laying out and cutting an end butt half lap or a corner half lap is as follows.

For the *end butt half lap*, measure off the desired amount of lap from the end of each member and square a line all the way around at this point. For the *corner half lap*, measure off the width of a member from the end of each member and square a line all the

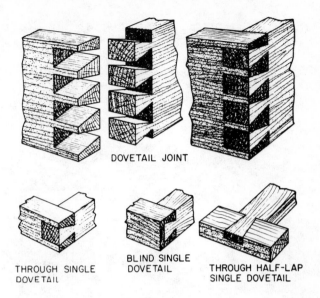

**Fig. 10.** Dovetail joints.

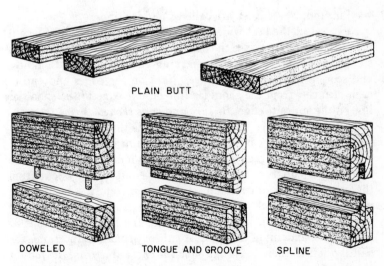

**Fig. 11.** Edge joints.

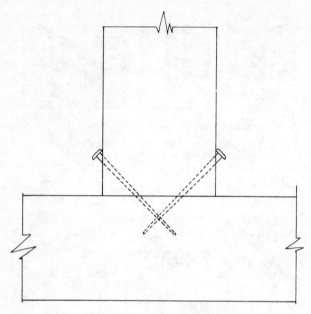

**Fig. 12.** Toenailing.

way around. These lines are called *shoulder* lines.

Next, select the best wide surface of each member and place it upward. Call this surface the *face* of the member, call the opposite surface the *back*. Next set the marking gage to half the thickness and score a line (called the *cheek line*) on the edges and end of each member, from the shoulder line on one edge to the shoulder line on the opposite edge. *Be sure and gage the cheek line from the face of each member.* The reason for this is that if you gage from both faces they will come flush after the joint is cut, regardless of whether or not the gage was set to exactly half the thickness. Too much waste cut from one member will be offset by less cut from the other. On the other hand, if you gage from the face of one member and the back of the other and the gage happens to be set to more or less than half the thickness, the faces will be out of flush by the amount of the error. A rule of primary importance for half lap joints, then, is *always gage the cheek line from the face of the member.*

Next, make the *shoulder cuts* by sawing along the shoulder line down to the waste side of the cheek line, sawing from the *back* of the lapping member and from the *face* of the lapped member. Use a bench hook if possible; if not, clamp a piece of wood along the starting groove to steady the saw.

The *cheek cuts* (sometimes called the *side cuts*) are made next, along the *waste side* of the cheek line. Clamp the member in the vise so that it leans diagonally *away* from you. With the member in this position you can see the end and the upper edge, and when the saw reaches the shoulder line on the upper edge it will still be some distance away from the shoulder line on the edge you cannot see. Reverse the member in the vise and saw exactly to the shoulder line on that edge.

Completing the shoulder cut will detach the waste. When both shoulder cuts have been made, the members should fit together with faces, ends, and edges flush or near enough to it to be brought flush by a little paring with the chisel.

A *cross half lap joint* between members of equal cross section dimensions is laid out and cut as follows.

If the members are of the same length and they are to lap each other at the midpoint, place them face-to-face with ends flush and square a center line all the way around. To test the accuracy of the center calculation, reverse one of the members end-for-end. If the center lines still meet, the center location is correct.

Lay off half the width of a member on either side of the center lines and square shoulder lines all the way around. Again check for accuracy by reversing a member end-for-end. If the shoulder lines meet, the layout is accurate. Next, gage half the thickness of a member *from the face of each member* and score cheek lines on the edges, between the shoulder lines. Next make the shoulder cuts, sawing from the *back* of the lapping member and from the *face* of the lapped member.

In this type of joint the waste must be chiseled out rather than sawed out. To make the work of chiseling easier, remove as much stock as possible with the saw first, by sawing a series of kerfs between the shoulder cuts. In chiseling make a roughing cut first, down to just above the cheek line, with a firmer chisel and mallet, holding the chisel bevel-down. Then finish off the bottom with a paring chisel, holding the chisel bevel-up. For fine work, smooth the bottom with a router plane if you have one.

End butt half lap and corner half lap joints are known generally as *end half lap joints,* as distinguished from *cross half lap joints.* A third type of half lap joint, much used in frame construction for tying partition plates to wall plates, is the so-called *middle half lap joint,* in which the end of one member is half-lapped to the other member at a point other than the end. In this joint the end of the lapping member is recessed as it would be for an end half lap joint, while the lapped member is recessed as it would be for a cross half lap joint.

End half lap joints may be cut with the circular saw by the method described for cutting tenons. Equipped with the dado head, the circular saw can be used to cut both *end half lap recesses* and *cross half lap recesses.*

For an end half lap recess proceed as follows.

Set the dado head to protrude above the table a distance equal to half the thickness of a member, and adjust the fence so that when the end of the member bears against it the dado head will cut on the waste side of the shoulder line. Place the member against the universal gage, set at 90° to the fence, and make the shoulder cut. Then take out the remaining waste by making as many recuts as necessary, each made with the member moved a little less than the thickness of the dado head to the left.

For a cross half lap recess set the dado head so that its height above the table is equal to half the thickness of a member, and adjust the ripping fence so that when the end of the member is placed against it the dado head will cut on the waste side of the left-hand shoulder line. Make the shoulder cut. Then reverse the piece end-for-end and repeat the same procedure to make the opposite shoulder cut. Take out the remaining waste between the shoulder cuts by making as many recuts as necessary, each made with the member moved a little less than the thickness of the dado head to the left.

## MITER JOINTS

A *miter joint* is made by *mitering* (cutting at an angle) the ends or edges of the members that are to be joined together. The angle of the miter cut is half the angle that will be formed by the joined members. In rectangular mirror frames, door casings, boxes, and the like, adjacent members form a 90° angle; the correct angle for mitering is consequently half of 90°, or 45°. For members that will form an equal-sides figure with other than four sides (such as an octagon or a pentagon), the correct mitering angle can be found by dividing the number of sides the figure will have into 180 and subtracting the result from 90. For an octagon (8-sided figure), the mitering angle is 90 minus 180/8, or 67½°. For a pentagon (5-sided figure), the angle is 90 minus 180/5, or 54°.

Members can be end-mitered to 45° in the wooden miter box and to any angle in the steel miter box (by setting the saw to the desired angle) or on the circular saw (by setting the universal gage to the desired angle). Members can be edge-mitered to any angle on the circular saw by tilting the saw to the required angle. Sawed edges are unsuitable for gluing, however, and if the joint is to be glued, the edges should be mitered on a jointer.

Since abutting surfaces of end-mitered members do not hold well when they are merely glued, they must usually be reinforced. One type of reinforcement is the *corrugated fastener,* a corrugated strip of metal with one edge sharpened for driving into the joint. The fastener is placed at a right angle to the line between the members, half on one member and half on the other, and driven down flush with the members. (*See* Chap. 4, Methods of Fastening, section on Corrugated Fasteners.)

The corrugated fastener mars the appearance of the surface into which it is driven and is therefore used only on the backs of picture frames and the like. A more satisfactory type of fastener for a joint between end-mitered members is the *slip feather,* a thin piece of wood or veneer that is glued into a kerf cut in the thickness dimension of the joint. Saw about halfway through from the outer to the inner corner, apply glue to both sides of the slip feather, and push the slip feather into the kerf. Clamp tight and allow the glue to dry. After it has dried, remove the clamp and chisel off the protruding portion of the slip feather. (*See* Chap. 4, Methods of Fastening, section on Glue.)

A joint between edge-mitered members may be reinforced with a *spline,* a thin piece of wood that extends across the joint into grooves cut in the abutting surfaces. A spline for a plain butt edge joint is shown in Fig. 5. The groove for a spline can be cut by hand by laying out the outline of the groove, removing the major part of the waste by boring a series of holes with a bit of suitable size, and smoothing with a mortising chisel. The best way to cut a groove, however, is on the circular saw.

## GROOVED JOINTS

A *groove* is a three-sided recess running with the grain. A similar recess running across the grain is called a *dado.* A groove or dado that does not extend all the way across the piece is called a *stopped groove* or a *stopped dado.* A stopped dado is also known as a *gain* (Fig. 7).

A two-sided recess running along an edge is called a *rabbet* (Fig. 6). Dados, gains, and rabbets are not, strictly speaking, grooves, but joints which include them are generally called *grooved joints.*

Grooves on edges and grooves on faces of comparatively narrow stock can be cut by hand with the plow plane. The matching plane will cut a groove on the edge of one piece and a tongue to match it on the edge of another. A dado can be cut by hand with the backsaw and chisel by the same method used to cut a cross half lap joint by hand. Rabbets on short ends or edges can be sawed out by hand with the backsaw.

A *long rabbet* can be cut by hand with the rabbet-and-fillister plane as follows.

First be sure that the side of the plane iron is exactly in line with the machined side of the plane; then set the width and depth gages to the desired width and depth of the rabbet. *Be sure to measure the depth from the edge of the plane iron, not from the sole of the plane.* If you measure from the sole of the plane, the rabbet will be too deep by the amount that the edge of the iron extends below the sole of the plane. Clamp the pieces in the vise, hold the plane exactly perpendicular, press the width gage against the face of the board, and plane down with even, careful strokes until the depth gage prevents any further planing.

A groove or dado can be cut on the circular saw as follows. (*See* Chap. 3, Power Tools.)

Lay out the groove or dado on the end wood (for a groove) or edge wood (for a dado) that will first contact the saw. Set the saw to the desired depth of the groove above the table, and set the fence at a distance from the saw, which will cause the first cut to run on the waste side of the line that indicates the left side of the groove. Start the saw and bring the piece into light contact with it; then stop the saw and examine the layout to ensure that the cut will be on the waste side of the line. Readjust the fence if necessary. When the position of the fence is right, make the cut. Then reverse the piece and proceed to set and test as before for the cut on the opposite side of the groove. Then make as many recuts as are necessary to remove the waste stock between the side kerfs.

The procedure for grooving or dadoing with the dado head is about the same, except that in many cases the dado head can be built up so as to take out all the waste in a single cut. The two outside cutters alone will cut a groove ¼″ wide. Inside cutters vary in thickness from 1/16″ to ¼″.

A stopped groove or stopped dado can be cut on the circular saw, using either a saw blade or a dado head as follows.

If the groove or dado is stopped at only one end, clamp a *stop block* to the rear of the table in a position that will stop the piece from being fed any further when the saw has reached the place where the groove or dado is supposed to stop. If the groove or dado is stopped at both ends, clamp a stop block to the rear of the table and a *starting block* to the front. The starting block should be placed so that the saw will contact the place where the groove is supposed to start when the infeed end of the piece is against the block. Start the cut by holding the piece above the saw, with the infeed end against the starting block and the edge against the fence. Then lower the piece gradually onto the saw and feed it through the stop block.

A *rabbet* can be cut on the circular saw as follows.

The cut in the face of the piece is called the *shoulder cut* and the cut in the edge or end is called the *cheek cut*. To make the shoulder cut (which should be made first) set the saw to extend above the table a distance equal to the desired depth of the shoulder, and set the fence a distance away from the saw equal to the desired depth of the cheek. Be sure to measure this distance from a saw tooth *set to the left,* or *away from* the ripping fence. If you measure it from a tooth set to the right, or toward the fence, the cheek will be too deep by an amount equal to the width of the saw kerf.

Make the shoulder cut first. Then place the face of the piece that was down for the shoulder cut against the fence and make the cheek cut. If the depth of the shoulder and the depth of the cheek are the same, the cheek cut will be made with the saw at the same height as for the shoulder cut. If the depth of the cheek is different, the height of the saw will have to be changed to conform before the cheek cut is made.

By using the dado head you can cut most ordinary rabbets in a single cut. First build up a dado head equal in thickness to the desired width of the cheek. Next set the head to protrude above the table at a distance equal to the desired depth of the shoulder. Clamp a 1″ board to the fence to serve as a guide for the piece, and set the fence so that the edge of the board barely contacts the right side of the dado head. Set the piece against the universal gage (set at 90°), hold the edge or end to be rabbeted against the 1″ board, and make the cut.

On some jointers, a *rabbeting strip* on the outboard edge of the outfeed table can be depressed for rabbeting. The strip is outboard of the end of the cutterhead. To rabbet on a jointer of this type, you depress the infeed table and the rabbeting strip the depth of the rabbet below the outfeed table, and set the fence the width of the rabbet away from the outboard end of the cutterhead. When the piece is fed through, the unrabbeted part feeds onto the rabbeting strip.

Some jointers are equipped with a *rabbeting arm.* The rabbeting arm is bolted to the infeed table and moves up and down with it. To rabbet on a jointer of this type, you depress the infeed table the depth of the rabbet below the outfeed table and get the fence the width of the rabbet away from the outboard end of the cutterhead. The rabbeted part of the piece feeds onto the outfeed table, and the unrabbeted part feeds onto the section of the rabbeting arm that extends beyond the cutterhead.

Various combinations of the grooved joints are used in woodworking. The well-known *tongue-and-groove joint* is actually a combination of the groove and the rabbet, the tongued member simply being a member that is rabbeted on both faces. In some types of panel work the tongue is made by rabbeting only one face; a tongue of this kind is called a *barefaced tongue*. A joint often used in making boxes, drawers, cabinets and the like is the *dado* and *rabbet joint* shown in Fig. 13. As you can see, one of the members here is rabbeted on one face to form a barefaced tongue.

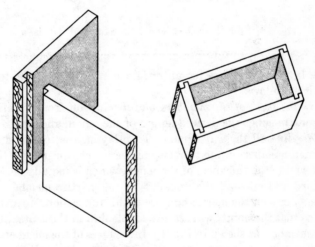

**Fig. 13.** Dado and rabbet joint.

## MORTISE-AND-TENON JOINTS

The *mortise-and-tenon* joint is the most important and most frequently used of the joints in furniture and cabinet work. In the *blind* mortise-and-tenon joint (Fig. 8) the tenon does not penetrate all the way through the mortised member. A joint in which the tenon does penetrate all the way through is a *through* mortise-and-tenon joint. Besides the ordinary *stub* joint (Fig. 8 and the first view of Fig. 14), there are *haunched* joints (second view of Fig. 14) and *table-haunched* joints (third view of Fig. 14). Haunching and table-haunching increase the strength and rigidity of the joint.

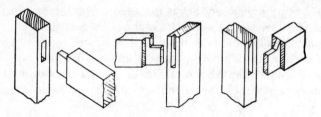

**Fig. 14.** Stub, haunched, and table-haunched mortise-and-tenon joints.

The layout procedure for an *ordinary stub* mortise-and-tenon joint is as follows.

*Mark the faces of the members plainly.* Lay off from the end of the tenon member the desired length of the tenon, and square the *shoulder line* all the way around. Then lay off the total width of the tenon member on the mortise member as shown in Fig. 15.

Determine the thickness of the tenon, which is usually between one-third and one-half the thickness of the mortise member, and set the points on the mortising gage to this dimension. Adjust the block so that the points will score a double line on the center of the tenon member, as shown in Fig. 15. If the faces of the members are to be flush, use the same gage setting to score a double line on the mortise member, remembering to gage from the *face* of the member. If the face of the tenon member is to be set back from the face of the mortise member (as is often the case with table rails and the like), the mortising gage setting must be increased by the amount of the setback. Remember, however, that the setting of the *points* remains the same. Last, lay off from the end of the mortise member and from the appropriate edge of the tenon member the amount of end stock that is to be left above the mortise, as indicated also in Fig. 15, and square lines as shown. For a *slip tenon joint* like the one shown in Fig. 8, you would not need this last

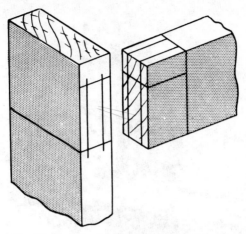

**Fig. 15.** Layout of stub mortise-and-tenon joint.

phase of the layout.

Tenons can be cut by hand with the backsaw using the same method previously described for cutting corner and end half lap joints. Mortises can be cut by hand with the mortising chisel. As in the case of a spline groove cut by hand, you can remove the major part of the waste by boring a series of holes with a twist drill of a diameter slightly smaller than the width of the mortise. For a blind mortise-and-tenon joint use a depth gage or a wooden block to prevent the drill from boring below the correct depth of the mortise.

Tenons can be cut with the circular saw as follows.

To make the shoulder cuts, set the saw the depth of the shoulder above the table and set the ripping fence the length of the tenon away from the saw. Remember to measure from a saw-tooth *set to the left*.

Set the saw the depth of the cheek above the table, set the fence the width of the shoulder away from the saw, and make the cheek cuts. To maintain the stock upright, use a *push board*.

Tenons can be cut with the dado head using the same method previously described for cutting end half lap joints. Mortises are cut mechanically on a *hollow-chisel mortising machine* like the one shown in Fig. 16. The cutting mechanism on this machine

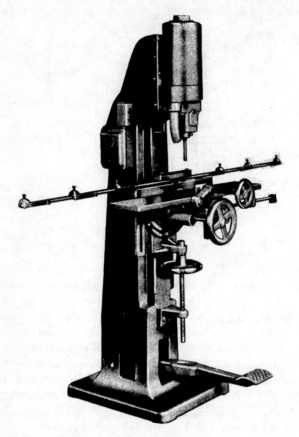

**Fig. 16.**  Hollow-chisel mortising machine.

consists of a boring bit encased in a square, hollow steel chisel. As the mechanism is pressed into the wood, the bit takes out most of the waste while the chisel pares the sides of the mortise square. Chisels come in various sizes, with corresponding sized bits to match.

The procedure for cutting a mortise on the machine is as follows.

Install a chisel and bit of the proper size, making sure that the rear edge of the chisel is exactly parallel to the fence on the machine. Place the piece to be mortised against the fence, clamp it to the table, and adjust the position of the table to bring one end of the mortise layout exactly under the chisel. Start the machine and press the foot pedal down to make a cut to about half the depth of the mortise. If you go too deep on the first cut, the cutter may bind in the wood causing overheating and making extraction difficult. Extract the cutter by releasing the foot pedal, move the table the required distance to the left by operating the large-table lateral-motion handwheel, and again cut to half the depth of the mortise. Continue this process to the end of the mortise; then work the other way, cutting this time to the full depth of the mortise.

In some mortise-and-tenon joints, such as those between rails and legs in tables, the tenon member is much thinner than the mortise member. Sometimes a member of this kind is too thin to shape in the customary manner, with shoulder cuts on both faces. When this is the case a *barefaced* mortise-and-tenon joint may be used. In a barefaced joint the tenon member is shoulder-cut on one side only. The cheek on the opposite side is simply a continuation of the face of the member.

Mortise-and-tenon joints are fastened with glue and with additional fasteners as required. One or more wood or metal dowels may be driven through the joint. A through- mortise-and-tenon joint may be fastened by sawing kerfs in the tenon and driving wedges into the kerfs after the joint is assembled, so as to jam the tenon tightly in the mortise. In a *keyed* mortise-and-tenon joint the tenon extends some distance beyond the mortised member. The extending part contains a *keyway*, into which a tapered *key* is driven. The key jams against the mortised member so as to hold the joint tightly together.

## DOVETAIL JOINTS

The *dovetail joint* (Fig. 10) is the strongest of all the woodworking joints. It requires a good bit of labor and is therefore used only for the finer grades of furniture and cabinet work, where it is used principally for joining sides and ends of drawers.

In the dovetail joint, one or more *pins* on the *pin member* fit tightly into the openings between two or more *tails*—or in the case of a single dovetail joint between two *half-tails*—on the *tail member*. A joint containing only a single pin is called a *single dovetail joint*. A joint containing two or more pins is called a *multiple dovetail joint*. A joint in which the pins pass all the way through the tail member is a *through dovetail joint*. A joint in which they pass only part-way through is a *blind dovetail joint*.

About the simplest of the dovetail joints is the *dovetail half lap joint* shown in Fig. 17. This joint is first laid out and cut like an ordinary end half lap, after which the end of the lapping member is laid out for shaping into a dovetail as follows.

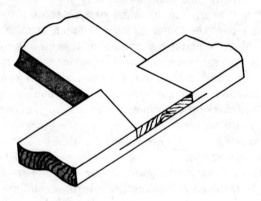

**Fig. 17.**  Dovetail half-lap joint.

Set the sliding T-bevel to 10°, which is the correct angle between the vertical axis and the sides of a dovetail pin or tail. You can set the sliding T-bevel with a protractor or with the protractor head on the combination square. If you do not have either of these, use the method shown in Fig. 18. Select a board with a straight edge, square a line across it, and lay off an interval of appropriate length six times on the line as shown. From the sixth mark lay off the same interval perpendicularly to the right. A line drawn from this point to the starting point of the first line drawn will form a 10° angle with that line.

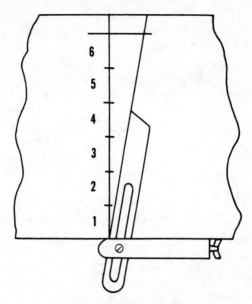

**Fig. 18.** Laying off 10-degree angle for dovetail joint.

Lay off this angle from the end corners of the lapping member to the shoulder line, as shown in Fig. 19, and saw out the waste as indicated. The lapping member now has a dovetail on it. Place this dovetail over the other member, in the position it is supposed to occupy, and score the outline of the recess. Then saw and chisel out the recess, remembering to saw on the *waste* side of the lines.

For a through multiple dovetail joint, the end of the tail member is laid out for cutting as shown in Fig. 20. A joint in which the pins and tails are the same size is the strongest type of dovetail, but for ease in cutting the pins are usually made somewhat smaller than the tails, as shown in the illustration. Determine the appropriate number of pins and the size you want to make each pin. Lay off a half pin from each edge of the member and then locate the center lines of the other pins at equal intervals across the end of the piece. Lay off the outlines of the pins at 10° to the center lines, as indicated. Then measure back from the end of the member a distance equal to the thickness of the tail member and

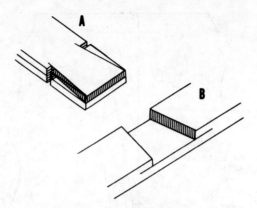

**Fig. 19.** Making a dovetail half-lap joint.

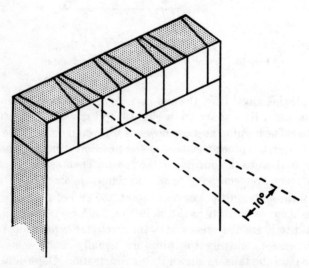

**Fig. 20.** Laying out pin member for through-multiple-dovetail joint.

square a line all the way around. This line indicates the bottoms of the openings between the pins.

Cut out the pins by sawing on the waste sides of the lines and then chiseling out the waste. Chisel halfway through from one side, as shown in Fig. 21; then turn the member over and chisel through from the other side.

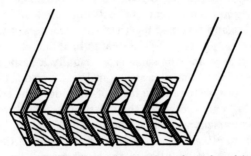

**Fig. 21.** Chiseling out waste in a through-multi-ple-dovetail joint.

When you have finished cutting out the pins, lay the tail member flat and set the ends of the pins in exactly the position they are to occupy. Score the outlines of the pins, which will also be the outlines of the tails. Square lines across the end of the tail member and saw and chisel out the waste between the tails just as you did the waste between the pins.

### BOX CORNER JOINTS

With the exception of the obvious difference in the layout, the *box corner joint* (Fig. 9) is made in just about the same manner as the through multiple dovetail joint.

### SIMPLE DETAILS FOR FABRICATING FURNITURE

The construction details for various kinds of furniture and cabinets are similar. Dressers, chests, kneehole desks, and built-in-cabinets all have drawers for storage purposes and are constructed in a similar manner.

A number of pieces of stock glued edge-to-edge should provide sufficient width for the *cabinet side.* The sides usually range in width from 16″ to 20″ and finished ¾″ thick. Some constructions require the use of a square post in each corner of the case. If the square posts are used, they are usually connected with the rails. (*See* Chap. 4, Methods of Fastening, section on Glue.)

Division rails and bearing rails are used to make up the *drawer division frames*. These frames are usually made of stock ¾" thick and 2" wide and fastened together at the corners with blind mortise-and-tenon joints. The frames are glued and checked to ensure they are square and the same size. Usually a gain is cut on the front edge of the frames, as shown in Fig. 22, and fitted and glued into the dados on the inside faces of the sides. The frames should be made ¼" narrower than the sides when ¼" plywood is used. This measurement will allow the plywood back to be glued and fastened into place. To keep dust and insects out of the case, a plywood panel can be installed in the lower frame.

The *cabinet bases* should be similar to the other furniture located in the room. The bases usually vary from a straight mitered frame, legs, or a slanted base with hopper-type joints.

The *drawers* should have special attention so they will fit accurately. Drawers have been known to expand or shrink in the front, sides, and back; therefore, some allowance must be made accordingly. It will be helpful to you if you would remember *wood shrinks or expands mostly across the grain and very little lengthwise or with the grain*. The height of the drawer opening should be ⅛ to 3/16 of an inch wider than the drawer sides and back. The edges and ends should be slightly beveled toward the back face and the drawer front fitted to the opening. (The lip-type drawer may be fitted more loosely because the lip extension will cover the opening at the ends and top.)

There are several types of joints that can be used to join the drawer sides to the front: the plain rabbet joint, half blind dovetail, and the dado tongue and rabbet.

The bottom of the drawer is usually grooved into all four sides of the drawer and a plain grooved- or dovetail center-guide fastened to the bottom. After the drawer has been fitted into place and the front lined up with the front face of the case, the center guide is fastened permanently to the drawer rails with screws. You may find it to be more convenient if you leave the back off the case until the drawer guides have been fastened to the drawer

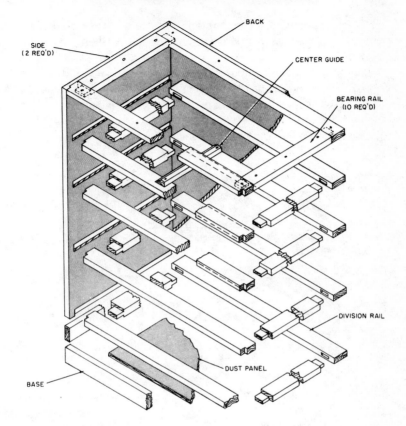

**Fig. 22.** Cabinet details.

rails.

To minimize expansion and shrinkage of the wood, a sealer coat of finish should be applied to the inside surfaces of all cases as well as drawers.

## CONTOUR CUTTING

The term *contour cutting* refers to the cutting of ornamental face curves on stock that is to be used for molding or other trim. Most contour cutting is done on the shaper, equipped with a cutter or blades or with a combination of cutters and/or blades, arranged to produce the desired contour. (*See* Chap. 3, Power Tools.)

The simple molding shapes are the *quarter round*, the *half round*, the *scotia* or *cove*, the *cyma recta* and the *cyma reversa* (Fig. 23). The quarter round and half round form convex curves, the cove molding forms a concave curve, and the cyma moldings are combinations of convex and concave curves.

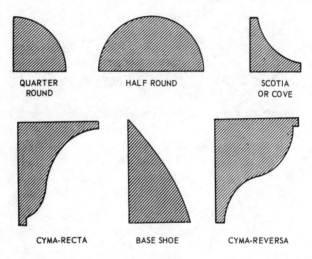

QUARTER ROUND    HALF ROUND    SCOTIA OR COVE

CYMA-RECTA    BASE SHOE    CYMA-REVERSA

**Fig. 23.** Simple modeling shapes.

## COPING JOINTS

Inside corner joints between molding trim members are usually made by butting the end of one member against the face of the other. Figure 24 shows the method of shaping the end of the abutting member to fit the face of the other member. First saw off the end of the abutting member square, as you would for an ordinary butt joint between ordinary flat-faced members. Then miter the end to 45° as shown in the first and second views of Fig. 24. Then set the coping saw at the top of the line of the miter cut, hold the

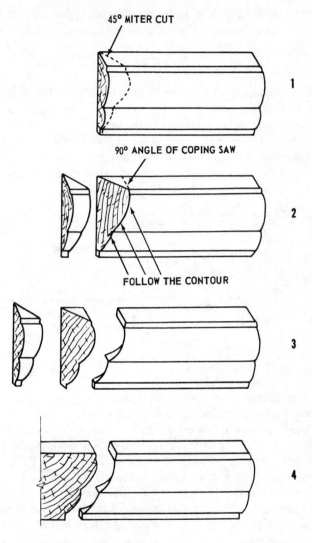

**Fig. 24.** Making a coping joint.

saw at 90° to the lengthwise axis of the piece, and saw off the segment shown in the third view, following closely the face line left by the 45° miter cut. The end of the abutting member will then match the face of the other member as shown in the third view. A joint made in this manner is called a *coping joint*.

## SPLICES

*Splices* connect two or more pieces of lumber so they will be as strong as a single piece of lumber the same length and the joint will be as strong as the unjoined portions. The type of splice used is determined by the way in which the spliced lumber is to be subjected to the stress and strain it must support. Lumber subjected to direct longitudinal stress such as vertical supports (*1*, Fig. 25),

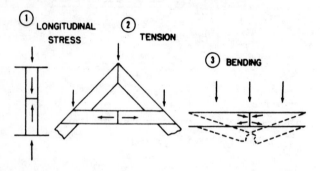

**Fig. 25.** Splice stresses.

or used in exerting pressure require splices designed to resist compression. Lumber subjected to transverse and angular stresses when used as trusses, braces, or joists require splices designed to resist tension (*2*, Fig. 25). Lumber used as horizontal supports require splices designed to resist bending (*3*, Fig. 25). Splices for resisting compression are usually worthless for tension or bending. Therefore, splices should be made to meet the conditions for which they are used. The carpenter should know each type of splice and should be able to make and apply each properly. (*See* Chap. 5, Lumber.)

## COMPRESSION RESISTANT SPLICES

*Compression resistant splices* support weight or exert pressure and will resist compression stress only. The butt splice and the halved splice are the most common types of compression resistant splices.

## BUTT SPLICE

The *butt splice* is constructed by butting the squared ends of two pieces of lumber together and securing them in this position by means of two wood or metal pieces fastened on opposite sides of the lumber (*1* and *2*, Fig. 26). The two short supporting pieces keep the splice straight and prevent buckling. Metal plates used as supports in constructing a butt splice are called *fishplates* (*1*, Fig. 26). Wood plates are called *scabs* (*2*, Fig. 26). Fishplates are fastened in place with bolts or screws. Bolts, nails, or corrugated fasteners may be used to secure scabs. If nails are used with scabs, they are staggered and driven at an angle away from the splice. Too many nails or nails that are too large will weaken a splice. (*See* Chap. 4, Methods of Fastening.)

## HALVED SPLICE

The *halved splice* is made by cutting away half the thickness of equal lengths from the ends of two pieces of lumber and fitting the complementary tongues or laps together. The laps should be long enough to have enough bearing surfaces. Nails or bolts may be used to fasten the halved splice (*3*, Fig. 26). In order to give this type of splice resistance to some tension as well as compression, fishplates or scabs may be used as with the butt splice.

## TENSION RESISTANT SPLICES

In tension members such as trusses, braces, and joists, the joint undergoes stress that is exerted in more than one direction and creates a tension tending to buckle the member in a predictable direction. *Tension splices* are designed to provide the greatest practicable number of bearing surfaces and shoulders within the splice to resist the buckling tension.

The *square splice* is a modification of the compression halved

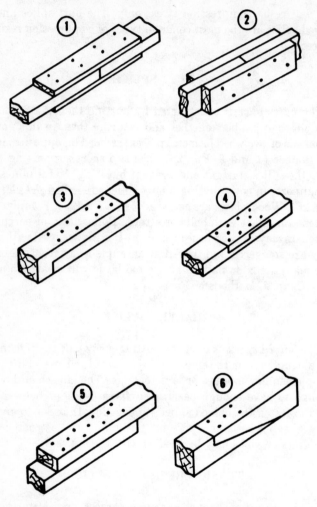

**Fig. 26.** Compression, tension, and bending splices.

splice. Notches are cut in the tongues or laps to provide an additional locking shoulder (*4*, Fig. 26). The square splice may be fastened with nails or bolts or may be greatly strengthened by the use of fishplates or scabs. (*See* Chap. 4, Methods of Fastening.)

A hasty substitute for the square splice is the long *plain splice* (5, Fig. 26). A long overlap of the two pieces is desirable to provide adequate bearing surface and enough room for fasteners to make up for the lack of shoulder lock.

## BEND RESISTANT SPLICES

Horizontal lumber supporting weight undergoes stress at a splice resulting in a compression of the upper part that has a tendency to crush the fibers and in a tension of the lower part that tends to pull the fibers apart. *Bend resistant splices* resist both compression and tension. They combine the features of the compression and tension splices.

The bend resistant splice is constructed by cutting oblique complementary laps in the ends of two pieces of lumber. The upper tongue (bearing surface) is squared to butt against the square of the complementary lap (6, Fig. 26) to offer maximum resistance to crushing, and the lower tongue is beveled. A scab or fishplate may be fastened along the bottom of the splice to resist the tendency of the pieces to separate. In any case where it is not desirable to lap or halve the lumber ends for a splice subjected to tension, a butt joint secured by fishplates may be used.

## CHAPTER 7

# Methods of Frame Construction

The methods of frame construction may be divided into two types, the built-in-place method or the panel method.

**Built-in-place.** In this method each piece is separately erected in its proper place.

**Panel method.** In this method a complete section is built up as a unit and then set in the building in the proper place. It is used extensively because it makes for greater speed, better control over workers, and better use of manpower. It also allows the use of a standard list of sizes for each similar section. Standard plans further simplify construction.

## BUILT-IN-PLACE METHOD

The steps in the built-in-place method are as follows:
1. Lay out the foundation.
2. Grade and excavate.
3. Lay out and cut the various sizes of material.
4. Carry material to the cutting and erecting workers.

Parts are built in the following order: footings, piers, sills, joists, floor, soles, studs, plates, girts, rafters, bracing, siding, sheathing, roofing, doors, windows, steps, and inside finish (if used). (*See* Chap. 9, Building Layout—Tools and Materials.)

## PANEL METHOD

The panel method (preassembly method) requires careful planning before the actual construction. Most buildings are now built by this method as follows:

1. Before measuring and cutting the lumber, the number and size of sections that are alike should be determined from the blueprint. This insures the correct numbers of each piece. The carpenter cuts and assembles one section. In most cases, a template is built as a guide for assembling the section. It should be built square, correct in size, and level. (*See* Chap. 5, Lumber.)

2. The number and size of each piece in a section is given to the worker. The lumber is cut to the correct length with a handsaw or power saw. The length is measured by the use of a square and tape. After one piece has been cut, it may be used as a pattern for marking the remaining pieces. The pattern is set up by nailing two blocks to the piece of correct size, one near each end as shown in Fig. 1. These blocks act as stops to hold the pattern in place on the lumber to be marked. Several cutting and assembling parties may be used at one time on different types of sections. (*See* Chap. 1, Woodworking Hand Tools, and Chap. 3, Power Tools.)

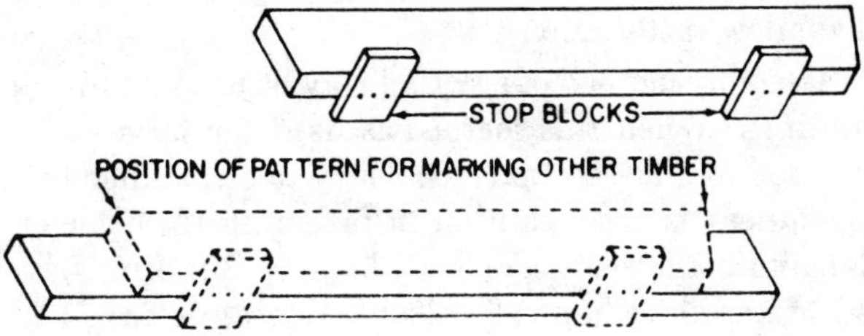

**Fig. 1.** Marking a pattern.

3. The plate and sole are placed in the template with the studs and girts between; then the door and window posts, if any, are placed (Fig. 2). The girts, sole, and plate are nailed to the studs with 16- or 20-penny nails. If insulation board is used, it and the wall sheathing are put on the section before it is taken out of the template by applying the wall finish before raising the section. No scaffold or ladders need be used.

4. The erecting worker(s) sets the sections into place, braces them temporarily, and nails them together. The end section should be first, and it may be erected on graded earth. The side-wall sections are next and should be erected so as to keep the two

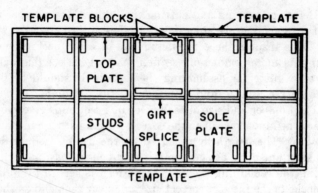

**Fig. 2.** Template for framing walls.

walls even. The rafter worker(s) can then place the rafters on the walls. Procedures are as follows: layout, cutting, assembling, carrying, erecting sidewalls, erecting rafters, sheathing, roofing, and door-and-window installation.

The preassembly method of erection may be used for all types of small buildings. When this method is used for large buildings, cranes are used to place sections too heavy to be handled by hand. Where machinery is used, caution in fastening the cable or rope avoids damaging the section. (*See* Chap. 9, Building Layout—Tools and Materials; Chap. 11, Floor Framing; Chap. 12, Wall Framing; Chap. 13, Framing Layout and Erection; Chap. 14, Wall Sheathing; Chap. 16, Roofing; Chap. 17, Reroofing; Chap. 20, Exterior Frames, Windows, and Doors; and Chap. 26, Interior Doors.)

CHAPTER 8

# Methods of Reducing
# Building Costs

The average homebuilder is interested in reducing the overall
cost of his or her house, but not at the expense of its livability or
resale value. This is often somewhat difficult to do for a single
custom-built house.

Operators of large housing developments often build hundreds
of houses each year. Because of their need for huge volumes of materials, they buy direct from the manufacturer. They also develop
the building sites from large sections of land. Much of the work,
such as installation of the roofing, application of gypsum-board
interiors, and painting, is done by subcontractors. Their own
crews are specialists, each crew becoming proficient in its own
phase of the work. Central shops are established where all material is cut to length and often preassembled before being trucked
to the site. These methods reduce the cost of the individual house
in a large building project, but few of them can be applied to an
individual house built by the owner.

If a home builder pays attention to various construction details
and to the choice of materials, this information will usually aid in
reducing costs. The following suggestions are intended as possible
ways for the owner to lower the cost of the house.

## DESIGN

The first area where costs of the house may be reduced somewhat is during the design stages. However, such details should not
affect the architectural lines or appearance of the house, but

rather the room arrangement and other factors. The following design elements might be considered before final plans are chosen.

**Size.** The size of the house, width and length, should be such that standard-length joists and rafters and standard spacings can be used without wasting material. The architect or contractor will have this information available. Also reflected in the house size is the use of standard-width sheets of sheathing materials on the exterior as well as in the interior. Any required waste or ripping adds to both the labor and material costs.

The rooms should be arranged so that the plumbing, water, and heating lines are short and risers can serve more than one room. An "expandable" house may mean the use of a steeper pitched roof to provide space for future rooms in the attic area. It might also be desirable to include second-floor dormers in the original design. Additional rooms can thus be provided at a much lower cost than by adding to the side or rear of the house at a future date. Roughing in plumbing and heating lines to the second floor will also reduce future costs when the second floor is completed, yet not add appreciably to the original construction costs.

While a rectangular plan is the most economical from many standpoints, it should not always govern final design. A rectangular plan of the house proper with a full basement can be enhanced by a garage or porch wing of a different size or alignment. Such attachments require only shallow footings, without the excavation necessary for basement areas.

**Foundation.** The type of foundation to be used, such as slab, crawl space, or basement, is an important consideration. Base this selection on climatic conditions and needs of the family for storage, hobby, or recreation space. While basement space in areas below grade is not as desirable as in areas above grade, its cubic-foot cost is a great deal lower. The design of a slab-type house usually includes some additional space for heating, laundry, and storage. This extra area may often cost as much as a full basement. Many multilevel houses include habitable rooms over concrete slabs as well as a full basement. Consult local architects or contractors for their opinions on the most desirable type of home in your area from the cost standpoint. (*See* Chap. 10, Foundation Construction, and Chap. 22, Basement Rooms.)

**Roof.** Many contemporary house designs include a flat or low-pitched roof that allows one type of member to serve as both ceiling joist and rafter. This generally reduces the cost compared to that of a pitched roof, both in materials and labor. However, all styles of houses are not adaptable to such a roof. Many contractors incur savings by using preassembled roof trusses for pitched roofs. Dealers who handle large quantities of lumber are usually equipped to furnish trusses of this type. (*See* Chap. 16, Roofing, and Chap. 17, Reroofing.)

Pitched roofs are of *gable* or *hip* design, with the *gambrel* roof a variation of each. While the hip roof is somewhat more difficult to frame than the gable roof, it usually requires less trim and siding. Furthermore, painting is much simpler in the hip roof: there is less wall area by elimination of the gable and it affords greater accessibility. In the gambrel roof, which is adapted to two-story houses, roof shingles serve also as siding over the steep-pitched portions. Furthermore, a roof of this type provides a greater amount of headroom (perhaps the original purpose of this design) than the common gable type.

## CHOICE OF MATERIALS

The type and grade of materials used in a house can vary greatly and savings can be effected in their choice. It is poor practice to use a low grade or inferior material that could later result in excessive maintenance costs. On the other hand, it is not economical to use a material of too high a grade when not needed for strength or appearance.

Several points might be considered as a means of reducing costs. (Your contractor or lumber dealer, who is familiar with these costs, will aid you in your final selection.)

1. Consider the use of concrete blocks for foundation walls as opposed to the use of poured concrete. It is less costly to provide a good water-resistant surface on a poured wall than on a block wall. On the other hand, a common hollow concrete block has better insulating properties than a poured concrete wall of equal thickness. Costs often vary by areas. (*See* Chap. 10, Foundation Construction.)

2. If *precast* blocks are available, consider them for chimneys. These blocks are made to take flue linings of varied sizes and are laid up more rapidly than brick. Concrete block units are also used in laying up the base for a first-floor fireplace, rather than bricks. Prefabricated, lightweight chimneys that require no masonry may also save money.

3. Dimension material varies somewhat in cost by species and grade. Use the better grades for joists and rafters and the lower cost grades for studs. Do not use better grades of lumber than are actually needed. Conversely, grades that involve excessive cutting and selection would dissipate the saving by increased labor costs. Proper moisture content is an important factor. (*See* Chap. 5, Lumber.)

4. Conventional items such as cabinets, moldings, windows, and other millwork, which are carried as stock or can be easily ordered, also reduce costs. Any special, nonstandard materials that require extra machine setups will be much more expensive. This need not restrict the home builder in his or her design, as there are numerous choices of millwork components from many manufacturers. (*See* Chap. 20, Exterior Frames, Windows, and Doors, and Chap. 26, Interior Doors and Trim.)

5. The use of a single material for wall and floor covering will provide a substantial saving. A combination subfloor underlayment of ⅝″ or ¾″ tongued- and-grooved plywood will serve both as a subfloor and as a base for resilient tile or similar material, as well as for carpeting. Panel siding consisting of 4′ wide full-height sheets of plywood or similar material serves both as a sheathing and a finish siding. For example, exterior particle-board with a painted finish and corner bracing on the stud wall may also qualify as a panel siding. Plywood may be obtained with a paper overlay, as well as rough-sawn, striated, reverse board and batten, brushed, and other finishes. (*See* Chap. 25, Floor Coverings.)

6. In planning a truly low-cost house where each dollar is important, a crawl space design with the use of a treated wood post foundation is worth investigating. This construction utilizes treated wood foundation posts bearing on concrete footings. The posts support floor beams upon which the floor joists rest. A variation of this design includes spacing of the beams on 48″ cen-

ters and the use of 1⅛″ thick tongue-and-groove plywood, eliminating the need for joists as such.

7. Costs of exterior siding or other finish materials often vary a great deal. Many factory-primed sidings are available that require only finish costs after they are applied. A rough-sawn, low-grade cedar or similar species in board and batten pattern with a stained finish will often reduce the overall cost of exterior coverings. Many species and textures of plywood are available for the exterior. When these sheet materials are of the proper thickness and application, they might also serve as sheathing. Paintability of species is also important. Edge-grained boards or paper-overlaid plywood provide good bases for paint. (*See* Chap. 18, Exterior Wood Coverings.)

In applying all exterior siding and trim, galvanized or other rust resistant nails reduce the need for frequent treatment or refinishing. Stainless steel or aluminum nails on siding having a natural finish are a must. Corrosion resistant nails will add slightly to the cost but will save many dollars in reduced maintenance costs. (*See* Chap. 4, Methods of Fastening.)

8. Interior coverage also deserves consideration. While gypsum board dry-wall construction may be lower in cost per square foot, it requires decorating before it can be considered complete; plaster walls do not require immediate decorating. (*See* Chap. 7, Methods of Frame Construction.) These costs vary by location, depending largely on the availability of the various trades. However, prefinished or plastic-faced gypsum board (available in a number of patterns) with a simple "V" joint or with a joint flap of the same covering and the use of adhesive for application will result in an economical wall and ceiling finish. (*See* Chap. 5, Lumber, and Chap. 23, Interior Wall and Ceiling Finish.)

9. There are many cost-related considerations in the choice of flooring, trim, and other interior finish. Areas that will be fully carpeted do not require a finished floor. However, there is a trend to provide a finish floor under the carpeting. The replacement cost of the carpeting may be substantially greater than the cost of the original finish floor. (*See* Chap. 11, Floor Framing, and Chap. 25, Floor Coverings.)

Species of trim, jambs, and other interior moldings vary from a relatively low-cost softwood to the higher cost hardwoods such as oak or birch. Softwoods are ordinarily painted, while the hardwoods have a natural finish or are lightly stained. The softwoods, though lower in cost, are less resistant to blows and impacts.

Another consideration is the selection of panel and flush doors. Flush doors can be obtained in a number of species and grades. Unselected gum, for example, might have a paint finish while the more costly woods are best finished with a varnish or sealer. Hollow-core flush doors are lower in cost and are satisfactory for interior use, but exterior flush doors should be solid core to better resist warping. The standard exterior panel door can be selected for many styles of architecture. (*See* Chap. 20, Exterior Frames, Windows, and Doors, and Chap. 26, Interior Doors and Trim.)

## CONSTRUCTION

Methods of reducing construction costs are primarily based on reducing on-site labor time. The progressive contractor often accomplishes this in several ways, but the size of the operation generally governs the method of construction. A contractor might use two carpenter crews—one for framing and one for interior finishing. Close cooperation with the subcontractors—such as plumbers, plasterers, and electricians—avoids wasting time. Delivery of items when needed so that storage is not a problem also reduces on-site costs. Larger operators may preassemble components at a central shop to permit rapid on-site erection. While the small contractor building individual houses cannot always use the same cost-saving methods, he follows certain practices.

1. Power equipment, such as a radial-arm saw, skill saw, or an automatic nailer, aids in reducing the time required for framing and is used by most progressive contractors. Such equipment not only reduces assembly time for floor, wall, and roof framing and sheathing, but is helpful in applying siding and exterior and interior trim. For example, with a radial-arm saw on the job, studs can be cut to length, headers and framing members prepared, and entire wall sections assembled on the floor and raised in place. Square cuts, equal lengths, and accurate layouts result in better nailing and more rigid joints. (*See* Chap. 3, Power Tools.)

2. Where a gypsum-board dry-wall finish is used, many contractors employ the horizontal method of application. This brings the taped joint below eye level, and large room-size sheets may be used. Vertical joints may be made at window or door openings. This reduces the number of joints to be treated and results in a better looking wall.

3. Staining and painting of the exterior and interior surfaces and trim are important. For example, one cost study of interior painting indicated that prestaining of jambs, stops, casing, and other trim before application would result in a substantial saving. These are normally stained or sealed after they have been fitted and nailed. (*See* Section 6, Chaps. 27, 28, 29, and 30; *see also* Chap. 4, Methods of Fastening.)

4. During construction, the advantages of a simple plan and the selection of an uncomplicated roof will be obvious. There will be less waste by cutting joists and rafters, and erection will be more rapid than on a house where intricate construction is involved. (*See* Chap. 16, Roofing, and Chap. 17, Reroofing.)

# Building Construction

Layout of materials and work area prior to construction.
The foundation of your building.
The erection of wall framing, floor framing, and roofing.
The sheathing for your walls and your roof.
Forms for concrete.

## CHAPTER 9

# Building Layout— Tools and Materials

Tools and materials used in layout must be carefully selected. The most commonly used are as follows. Some are shown in Fig. 1. (*See also* Chap. 1, Woodworking Hand Tools and How to Use Them, and Chap. 3, Power Tools.)

## TOOLS AND MATERIALS

**Sledge hammer or maul.** The sledge hammer or maul is used to sink corner stakes or batter-board posts.

**Post-hole auger.** The post-hole auger is used to dig the holes required to set posts properly in some soils.

**Handsaw.** The handsaw is used to cut batter boards and posts.

**Chalkline.** A chalkline is a white, twisted mason's line consisting of a reel, line, and chalk. It is coated with chalk and stretched taut between points to be connected by a straight line, just off the surface. When snapped, the line makes a straight guideline.

**Tracing tape.** Tracing tape is a cotton tape approximately 1″ wide. It is generally a 200′ length for laying out excavation or foundation lines.

**Ax or hatchet.** The ax or hatchet is used to sharpen batter boards and stakes.

**Hammer.** The hammer is used for building batter boards.

**Posts and stakes.** Batter-board posts are made from 2 × 4 or 4 × 4 material; corner stakes, from 4 × 4's. Batter boards are made from 1 × 4 or 1 × 6 pieces.

**Carpenter's level.** The carpenter's level (*3*, Fig. 1) determines levelness of surface and sights level lines. It may be used directly

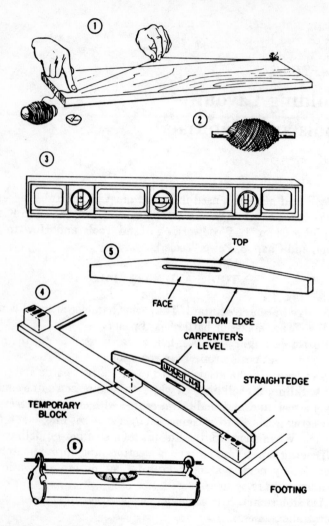

**Fig. 1.** Layout tools.

on the surface or used with a straightedge (4, Fig. 1). Levelness is determined by the bubbles suspended within glass tubes parallel to one or more surfaces of the level.

**Straightedge.** The straightedge usually has a handhole, a bottom edge at least 30″ long used as a leveling surface, and a top edge 8″ to 10″ long used as a working surface. It may be used with the level to increase the area checked (*5*, Fig. 1). It is most often used to lay out straight lines between points close enough together to use the edge as a ruler.

**Line level.** The line level has a spirit bubble to show levelness; it can be hung from a line (*6*, Fig. 1). Placement halfway between the points to be leveled gives the greatest accuracy.

**Engineer's transit or leveling instrument.** The engineer's transit establishes reference points or grade lines that permit building up or down with accuracy as to vertical level. It locates corners and lays out lines for buildings or excavation.

**Engineer's transit.** The engineer's transit has an adjustable tripod and head. It measures horizontal or vertical angles (Fig. 2).

**Locator's hand level.** The locator's hand level measures approximate differences in elevation and can establish grades over limited distances (Fig. 3). The landscape, level bubble, and index line are seen in the tube.

## USE OF THE ENGINEER'S TRANSIT

The carpenter ordinarily does not use the engineer's transit but many learn how to do so on the job. The following guide will help those who wish to review the procedure.

1. Set up the transit directly over station mark (*A*, Fig. 4), the point from which layout is sighted. A bench mark (*B*) may be provided by surveying engineers as a point of reference. The bench mark may be on the foundation of an adjacent building or a buried stone marker. If bench marks have been established in the area and the architect's drawings have been created specifically for that particular area, the bench mark will appear on the drawings and the plans will be oriented to that point. If no bench mark exists, a post may be driven into the ground to provide this reference point. This post can establish floor levels, foundation levels, or any definite point of elevation. When setting up the engineer's transit or leveling instrument, a plumb bob may be used to center

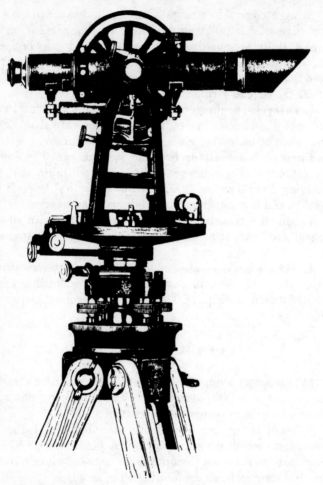

**Fig. 2.** Engineer's transit.

the instrument directly over the selected station mark.

2. Adjust the tripod so that it rests firmly on the ground with the sighting tube at eye level. Level up the head of the instrument by turning the leveling screws, so that the sight tube and head are level when turned in any direction. Once set up, all contact with

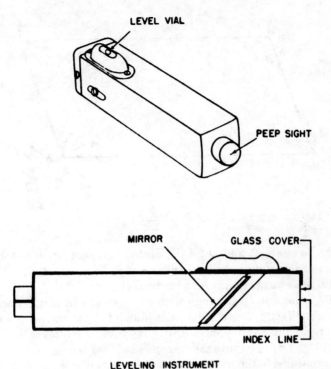

**Fig. 3.** Leveling instrument.

the legs of the tripod should be avoided.

3. Place a leveling rod (*C*) upright on any point to be checked, and sight through the sight tube of the instrument at the leveling rod. In accurate work, a spirit level may be attached to the leveling rod. An assistant should hold the leveling rod, and should move the target on the rod up or down until the crossline on the target comes in line with the cross-hair sights in the sighting tube.

4. To obtain the difference in elevation between two points, such as the surveyor's bench mark (*B*) and the target point(*D*), hold the rod on the point (*B*) and take a rod reading. This will be the length of the bottom of the rod below the line of sight. Take a rod reading at point (*D*). The difference between the two rod readings is the difference.

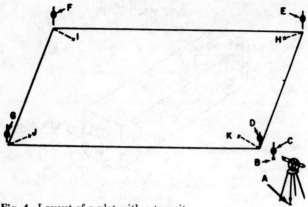

**Fig. 4.** Layout of a plot with a transit.

5. To establish a level for the depth of an excavation or for the level of foundation walls, measure equal distances at all corners from these target points to the desired elevations (*H*, *I*, *J*, and *K*).

6. To lay out a right angle with an engineer's transit, set up the transit directly over the line (use plumb bob) at the point where the right angle is to occur (*A*, Fig. 5). Sight a reference point on that line (*B*) to be sure the transverse axis of the engineer's transit is parallel to the line. Turn the eyepiece end of the sight tube to the left until the scale indicates that an arc of 90° has been completed. Establish a leveling rod in position along this line of sight at the desired distance. A line extended from the leveling rod (*D*)

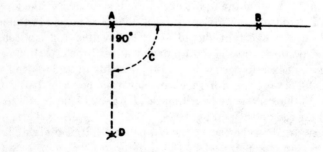

**Fig. 5.** Laying out a right angle with an engineer's transit.

to the point from which the sight was taken will be perpendicular to the base line and will form a right angle at the point at which they bisect (*DAB*).

## STAKING OUT

When the location and alignment of a building have been determined, a rectangle comprising the exterior dimensions of the structure is *staked out*. If the building is other than rectangular, a rectangle large enough to comprise the major outline of the irregular structure is staked out and the irregularities plotted and proved by smaller rectangles within or without the basic form.

## LAYING OUT A RECTANGLE WITHOUT A TRANSIT

If the construction is parallel to an identifiable line that can be used as a guide, staking out may be accomplished without a builder's transit. If a clearly defined line that construction is to parallel is present (*AB*, Fig. 6) and the maximum outer perimeter of the building area (*AC, CD, DB*) is known, proceed in the following manner.

1. Measure away from the front line (*AB*) along the side lines (*AC* and *BD*) the distances (*AO* and *BO*) desired to the dimension of the project that is to run parallel to the front line.

2. Stretch a line tightly from point *O* to *O*. This line will mark out what will be the frontage of the project.

3. Measure in from lines *AC* and *BD* along line *OO* half the difference between the length of *OO* and the desired length of the project. The points (*X* and *X*) will constitute the front corners of the project.

4. The two distances, *OX* and *XO*, establish the distance *E* and *F*. Extending lines from the two front corners, *X* and *X*, parallel to *AC* and *BD* at the distances established as *E* and *F* for the required depth of the project, provide the side lines of the project *XG* and *XH*.

5. Joining the extreme ends of side lines *XG* and *XH* will provide the rear line of the project.

6. After the four corners (*X, X, G,* and *H*) have been located,

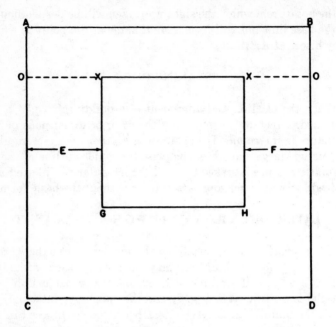

**Fig. 6.** Laying out a rectangular without use of a transit.

drive stakes at each corner. Batter boards may be erected at these points either after all the stakes have been set or while they are being set. Dimensions are determined accurately during each step.

7. If the building is not rectangular, several lines such as *OO* may be run and appropriate adjacent rectangles constructed from these lines in the same fashion as indicated above.

## LAYING OUT A SIMPLE RECTANGLE WITH AN ENGINEER'S TRANSIT OR LEVELING INSTRUMENT

1. Working from an established line *AB* (Fig. 7) such as a road, street line, property line, or other established reference line, select a point to represent the lateral limit for a front corner of the project.

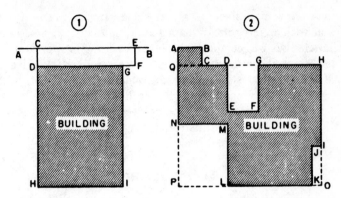

**Fig. 7.** Laying out regular and irregular projects.

2. Set up the engineer's transit at point $C$ and establish point $D$, a front corner of the project.

3. Set up the engineer's transit at a point $E$ a greater distance along line $AB$ from point $C$ than the intended length of the project. Set a stake at $F$, the same distance from $AB$ as $D$. $CD$ and $EF$ are equal.

4. Establish the front line of the project by marking off the length of the project $DG$ along the established line $DF$. The two front corners of the project will be located at $D$ and $G$.

5. With engineer's transit at point $C$, shoot $E$ and then swing the transit 90° and sight along the position to establish $H$, the rear corner of the project.

6. With the engineer's transit set up at $G$, sight $D$ and swing the transit sight tube 90° and shoot $I$, the other rear corner of the project.

7. To prove the work, set up the transit at $I$ and take a sighting on $H$. If $IH$ is equal to $DG$ the work is correct. If it is not, the work must be repeated until correct.

### LAYING OUT AN IRREGULARLY SHAPED PROJECT

Where the outline of the building is not a rectangle, the procedure in establishing each point is the same as previously described, but more points have to be located and the final proving of the work is more likely to reveal a small error. It is usually advisable with an irregularly shaped building to lay out first a large rectangle that will comprise the entire building or a greater part of it. This is shown in *2*, Fig. 7, as the rectangle *HOPQ*. Having once established this accurately, the remaining portion of the layout will consist of small rectangles each of which can be laid out and proved separately. The other rectangles, *LMNP*, *ABCQ*, *DEFG*, and *LJKO*, are illustrated in *2*, Fig. 7.

## BATTER BOARDS

**Staking procedure.** At the points at which the various corners of the project are located, a corner stake is driven to mark the exact spot (Fig. 8). If the area must be excavated for a foundation, the excavating will disturb the pegs. *Batter boards* are therefore set up to preserve definite and accurate building lines to work toward or from. This is done by stretching heavy or fine cord from one batter board to the other to define the lines of excavation.

**Locating batter boards.** Right-angle batter boards are erected 3′ or 4′ outside each corner stake (Fig. 8). Straight batter boards are erected 3′ or 4′ outside of the line stakes set at points provided for the extension of foundation lines (Fig. 8) which intercept side lines.

**Construction of batter boards.** Batter-board stakes may be 2 × 4's, 2 × 6's, or 4 × 4's. Right-angle batter boards usually are two 1 × 6 boards and three stakes. They can be nailed or bolted to the stakes either before or after they are sunk. Batter boards are firmly anchored. Since the boards should be at the exact height of the top of the foundation, it may be desirable to adjust the height by nailing the boards to the stakes after the stakes have been sunk. Right-angle batter boards may be nailed at close to perpendicular by the use of a framing square and should be leveled by means of a carpenter's level before they are secured. When the final adjustments have been made for accuracy and squareness, saw cuts may be made or nails driven into the tops of the boards to hold the lines and keep them in place. Separate cuts or nails may be used for the building line, the foundation line, footing line and excavation

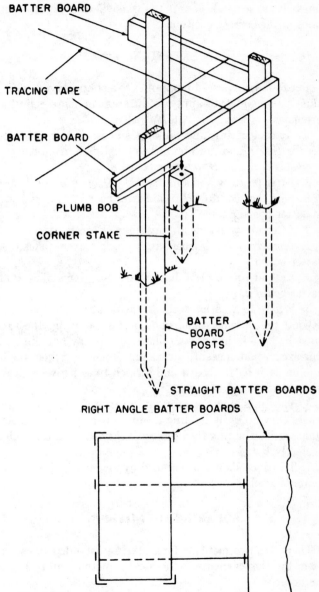

**Fig. 8.** Batter boards.

lines. These grooves permit the removal and replacement of the lines in the correct position.

## EXTENDING LINES

The following procedure applies to a simple layout (Fig. 9) and must be amended to apply to different or more complex layout problems.

1. After locating and sinking stakes *A* and *B*, erect batter boards *1*, *2*, *3*, and *4*. Extend the chalkline *X* from batter board *1* over stakes *A* and *B* to batter board *3*.

2. After locating and sinking stake *C*, erect batter boards *5* and *6*. Extend the chalkline *Y* from batter board *2* over stakes *A* and *C* to batter board *6*.

3. After locating and sinking stake *D*, erect batter boards *7* and *8*. Extend chalkline *Z* from batter board *5* over stakes *C* and *D* to batter board *7*.

4. Extend line *O* from batter board *8* over stakes *D* and *B* to batter board *4*.

5. Where foundation walls are wide at the bottom and extend beyond the outside dimensions of the building, the excavation must be larger than the size laid out. To lay out dimensions for this excavation, measure out as far as required from the building line on each batter board and stretch lines between these points and outside the first layout.

6. The lines may be brought to an approximate right angle where they cross by holding a plumb bob over the corner layout stakes and adjusting the lines until they touch the plumb-bob line perfectly.

7. The lines should be checked by means of a line level, or carpenter's level.

## SQUARING FOUNDATION LINES

There are two methods for squaring extended lines commonly used by the carpenter—the 6-8-10 method and the diagonal method.

**6-8-10 method** (Fig. 9). After lines have been extended and

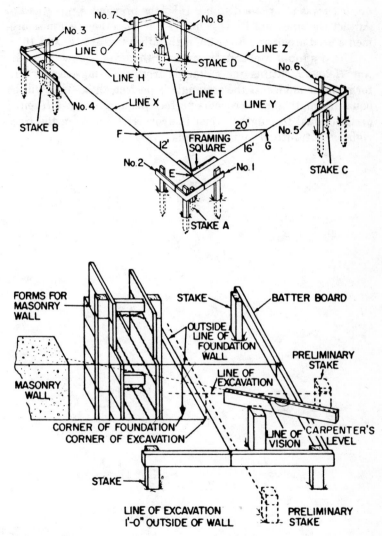

**Fig. 9.** Laying out building lines from batter boards.

are in place, measure the distance $EF$ 6′ or a multiple thereof, such as 12′. Measure off $EG$ to a distance of 8′ if the previous figure used was 6', or to a distance 16' if the previous figure was 12'. Adjust the lines until *FG* equals 10' if the other two measurements used are 6' and 8', or 20' if the other two are 12' and 16'.

**The diagonal method** (Fig. 9). If the layout is rectangular, line *H* and *I* cutting the rectangle from opposing corners will form two triangles. If the rectangle is perfect, these lines will be equal in length and the corners perfectly square. If lines *H* and *I* are not equal in length, adjust the corners by moving the lines right or left until *H* and *I* are equal.

## CHAPTER 10

# Foundation Construction

The two major parts of a building are (1) the foundation, and (2) the part above the foundation, which is called the *superstructure*. A *frame* building is one in which the skeleton of the superstructure consists of a framework of wooden structural members. This framework is called the *framing* of the building, and the framing is subdivided into *floor framing, wall framing,* and *roof framing.* Floor framing consists for the most part of horizontal members called *joists,* wall framing for the most part of vertical members called *studs,* and roof framing for the most part of inclined members called *rafters.* (*See* Chap. 11, Floor Framing; Chap. 12, Wall Framing; Chap. 16, Roofing; and Chap. 17, Reroofing.)

The most common framing method is *platform framing* (also called western and story-by-story framing). In platform framing there are separate studs for each floor, anchored on *sole plates* laid on the subflooring as shown in Fig. 1.

## FOUNDATIONS

*Foundations* vary according to their use, the bearing capacity of the soil, and the type of material available. The material may be cut stone, rock, brick, concrete, tile, or wood, depending upon the weight which the foundation is to support. Foundations may be classified either as wall or column (pier) foundations.

## WALL FOUNDATIONS

*Wall foundations* are built solid, the walls of the building being

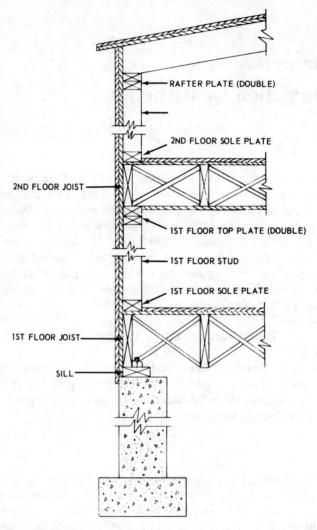

**Fig. 1.** Platform-frame wall section.

of continuous heavy construction for their entire length. Solid walls are used when there are heavy loads to be carried or where the earth has low supporting strength. These walls may be made of concrete, rock, brick, or cut stone, with a footing at the bottom (Fig. 2). The rule of thumb for determining the width or depth of a footing for a foundation is: width = two times thickness of wall; thickness of footing = same as thickness of the wall. This rule of thumb is illustrated in Fig. 3. (*See* Chap. 15, Forms for Concrete.) This type of wall should be used only when other types cannot be used because of the time, labor, and material required. Steel rod reinforcements should be used in all concrete walls.

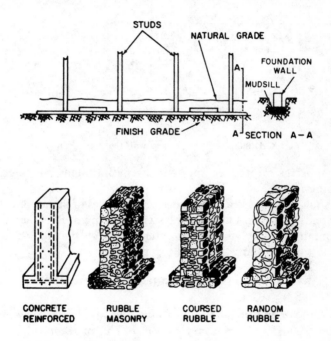

**Fig. 2.** Foundation walls.

*Rubble stone masonry* is used for walls both above and below ground and for bridge abutments. It is used when form lumber or masonry units are not available. Rubble masonry may be laid up with or without mortar. If strength and stability are desired, mortar must be used.

*Coursed rubble* is assembled of roughly squared stones in such a

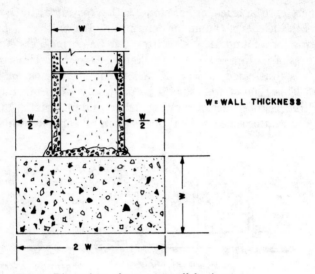

**Fig. 3.** Dimensions of masonry wall footings.

manner as to produce approximately continuous horizontal bed joints.

*Random rubble* is the crudest of all types of stonework. Little attention is paid to laying the stone in courses. Each layer must contain bonding stones that extend through the wall. This produces a wall that is well tied together.

## COLUMN OR PIER FOUNDATIONS

*Column* or *pier* foundations save time and labor. They may be constructed from masonry or wood. The piers or columns are spaced according to the weight to be carried. In most cases, the spacing is from 6' to 10'. Figure 4 shows the different types of piers with different types of footing. Wood piers are generally used since they are installed with the least time and labor. Where wood piers are used, braces are necessary (Fig. 5).

## SILL FRAMING

The work involved in sill construction is very important. The

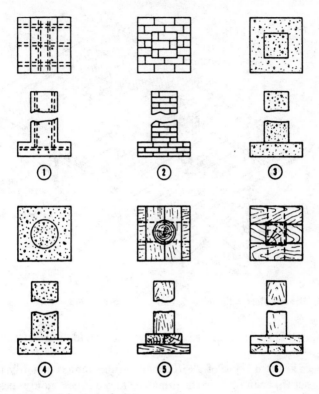

**Fig. 4.** Column and piers.

foundation wall is the support upon which all structures rest. The sill is the foundation on which all framing structures rest and it is the real stepping-off point for actual building and joinery activities. The sills are the first part of the frame to be set in place. They rest either directly on the foundation piers or on the ground, and may extend all around the building; they are joined at the corners and spliced when necessary. Figure 6 shows some common types of sills. The type used depends upon the general type of construction used in the frame.

*Box sills* are often used with the very common style platform framing, either with or without the sill plate. In this type of sill, the part that lies on the foundation wall or ground is called the

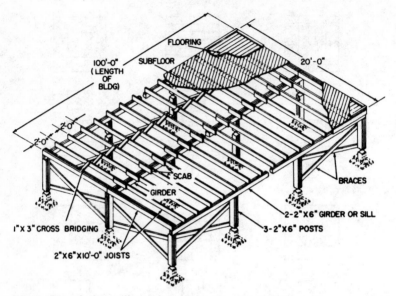

**Fig. 5.** Braced piers, sills, girders, and joist construction.

sill plate. The sill is laid edgewise on the outside edge of the sill plate.

There are two types of *T-sill* construction—one commonly used in the south, or in dry, warm climates,, and one commonly used in the east, or colder climates. Their construction is similar except that in the case of the eastern T-sill the joists are nailed directly to the studs, as well as to the sills, and headers are used between the floor joists.

The sill shown in the lower portion of Fig. 6 is generally used in braced-framing construction. The floor joists are notched out and nailed directly to the sill and studs.

Where built-up sills are used the joints are staggered (Fig. 7). The corner joints are made as shown in Fig. 7.

If *piers* are used in the foundation, heavier sills are used. These sills are of single heavy timbers or are built up of two or more pieces of timber. Where heavy timber or built-up type sills are used, the joints should occur over piers. The size of the sill depends upon the load to be carried and upon the spacing of the

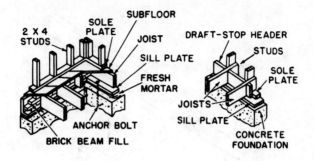

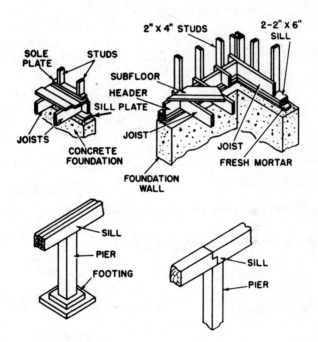

**Fig. 6.** Types of sills.

piers. The sill plates are laid directly on graded earth or on piers. Where earth floors are used, the studs are nailed directly to the sill plate.

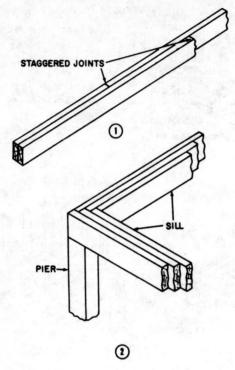

**Fig. 7.** Sill fabrication.

## CHAPTER 11

# Floor Framing

The *floor framing* in a wood frame house consists specifically of the posts, beams, sill plates, joists, and subfloor. (*See* Chap. 25, Floor Coverings.) When these are assembled on a foundation, they form a level, anchored platform for the rest of the house. The posts and center beams of wood or steel, which support the inside ends of the joists, are sometimes replaced with a wood frame or masonry wall when the basement area is divided into rooms. Wood frame houses may also be constructed upon a concrete floor slab or over a crawl-space area with floor framing similar to that used for a full basement.

## DESIGN

One of the important factors in the design of wood floor systems is to equalize shrinkage and expansion of the wood framing at the outside walls and at the center beam. This is usually accomplished by using approximately the same total depth of wood at the center beam as the outside framing. Therefore, as beams and joists approach moisture equilibrium or the moisture content they reach in service, there are only small differences in the amount of shrinkage. This will minimize plaster cracks and prevent sticking doors and other inconveniences caused by uneven shrinkage. If there is a total of 12″ of wood at the foundation wall (including joists and sill plate), this should be balanced with about 12″ of wood at the center beam.

Moisture content of beams and joists used in floor framing should not exceed 19 per cent. However, a moisture content of about 15 per cent is much more desirable. Dimension material can be obtained at these moisture contents when so specified. When moisture contents are in the higher ranges, it is good practice to allow joists and beams to approach their moisture equilibrium before applying inside finish and trim, such as baseboard, base shoe, door jambs, and casings.

Grades of dimension lumber vary considerably by species. For specific uses in this book, a sequence of first-, second-, third-, fourth-, and sometimes fifth-grade material is used. In general, the first grade is for a high or special use, the second for better than average, the third for average, and the fourth and fifth for more economical construction. Joists and girders are usually second-grade material of a species, while sills and posts are usually of third or fourth grade. (*See* Chap. 5, section on Lumber Grades.)

## NAILING PRACTICES

Of primary consideration in the construction of a house is the method used to fasten the various wood members together. These connections are most commonly made with nails, but on occasion metal straps, lag screws, bolts, and adhesives may be used. (*See* **Chap. 4, Methods of Fastening.**)

Proper fastening of frame members and covering materials provides the rigidity and strength to resist severe windstorms and other hazards. Good nailing is also important from the standpoint of normal performance of wood parts. *For example,* proper fastening of intersection walls usually reduces plaster cracking at the inside corners.

Nailing practices for the framing and sheathing of a well-constructed wood frame house is shown in Table 7.

## POSTS AND GIRDERS

*Wood* or *steel posts* are generally used in the basement to support wood girders or steel beams. Masonry piers may also be used for this purpose and are commonly employed in crawl-space houses.

The round steel post can be used to support both wood girders and steel beams and is normally supplied with a steel bearing

## Table 7.

*Recommended schedule for nailing the framing and sheathing of a well-constructed wood-frame house*

| Joining | Nailing method | Number | Size | Placement |
|---|---|---|---|---|
| | | | **Nails** | |
| Header to joist | End-nail | 3 | 16d | |
| Joist to sill or girder | Toenail | 2 | 10d or | |
| | | 3 | 8d | |
| Header and stringer joist to sill | Toenail | 3 | 10d | 16 in. on center |
| Bridging to joist | Toenail each end | 2 | 8d | |
| Ledger strip to beam, 2 in. thick | | 3 | 16d | At each joist |
| Subfloor, boards: | | | | |
| 1 by 6 in. and smaller | | 2 | 8d | To each joist |
| 1 by 8 in. | | 3 | 8d | To each joist |
| Subfloor, plywood: | | | | |
| At edges | | | 8d | 6 in. on center |
| At intermediate joists | | | 8d | 8 in. on center |
| Subfloor (2 by 6 in., T&G) to joist or girder | Blind-nail (casing) and face-nail | 2 | 16d | |
| Soleplate to stud, horizontal assembly | End-nail | 2 | 16d | At each stud |
| Top plate to stud | End-nail | 2 | 16d | |
| Stud to soleplate | Toenail | 4 | 8d | |
| Soleplate to joist or blocking | Face-nail | 2 | 16d | 16 in. on center |
| Doubled studs | Face-nail, stagger | 2 | 10d | 16 in. on center |
| End stud of intersecting wall to exterior wall stud | Face-nail | 2 | 16d | 16 in. on center |
| Upper top plate to lower top plate | Face-nail | 2 | 16d | 16 in. on center |
| Upper top plate, laps and intersections | Face-nail | 2 | 16d | 16 in. on center |

| Joining | Nailing method | Number of nails | Nail size | Placement |
|---|---|---|---|---|
| Continuous header, two pieces, each edge | | | 12d | 12 in. on center |
| Ceiling joist to top wall plates | Toenail | 3 | 8d | |
| Ceiling joist laps at partition | Face-nail | 4 | 16d | |
| Rafter to top plate | Toenail | 2 | 8d | |
| Rafter to ceiling joist | Face-nail | 5 | 10d | |
| Rafter to valley or hip rafter | Toenail | 3 | 10d | |
| Ridge board to rafter | End-nail | 3 | 10d | |
| Rafter to rafter through ridge board | Toenail | 4 | 8d | |
| | Edge-nail | 1 | 10d | |
| Collar beam to rafter: | | | | |
|   2 in. member | Face-nail | 2 | 12d | |
|   1 in. member | Face-nail | 3 | 8d | |
| 1-in. diagonal let-in brace to each stud and plate (4 nails at top) | Face-nail | 2 | 8d | |
| Built-up corner studs: | | | | |
|   Studs to blocking | Face-nail | 2 | 10d | Each side |
|   Intersecting stud to corner studs | Face-nail | | 16d | 12 in. on center |
| Built-up girders and beams, three or more members | Face-nail | 2 | 20d | 32 in. on center, each side |
| Wall sheathing: | | | | |
|   1 by 8 in. or less, horizontal | Face-nail | 2 | 8d | At each stud |
|   1 by 6 in. or greater, diagonal | Face-nail | 3 | 8d | At each stud |
| Wall sheathing, vertically applied plywood: | | | | |
|   3/8 in. and less thick | Face-nail | | 6d | 6 in. edge |
|   1/2 in. and over thick | Face-nail | | 8d | 12 in. intermediate |
| Wall sheathing, vertically applied fiberboard: | | | | |
|   1/2 in. thick | Face-nail | | 1½ in. roofing nail | 3 in. edge and |
|   25/32 in. thick | Face-nail | | 1¾ in. roofing nail | 6 in. intermediate |
| Roof sheathing, boards, 4-, 6-, 8-in. width | Face-nail | 2 | 8d | At each rafter |
| Roof sheathing, plywood: | | | | |
|   3/8 in. and less thick | Face-nail | | 6d | 6 in. edge and 12 in. intermediate |
|   1/2 in. and over thick | Face-nail | | 8d | |

plate at each end. Be sure to secure anchoring to the girder or beam (Fig. 1).

*Wood posts* should be solid and not less than 6″ by 6″ in size for freestanding use in a basement. When combined with a framed wall, they may be 4″ by 6″ to conform to the depth of the studs. Wood posts should be squared at both ends and securely fastened to the girder (Fig. 2). The bottom of the post should rest on and be pinned to a masonry pedestal 2″ to 3″ above the finish floor. In moist or wet conditions it is good practice to treat the bottom end of the post or use a moisture-proof covering over the pedestal. (*See* Chap. 3, section on Posts.)

Both wood girders and steel beams are used in present-day house construction. The standard *I-beam* and wide *flange beam* are the most commonly used steel beam shapes. Wood girders are of two types—*solid* and *built up*. The built-up beam is preferred because it can be made up from drier dimension material and is more stable. Commercially available glue-laminated beams may be desirable where exposed in finished basement rooms.

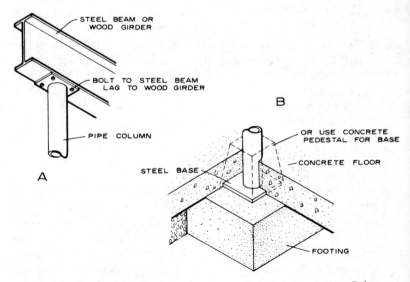

**Fig. 1.** Steel post for wood or steel girder. *A,* connection to beam. *B,* base plate also may be mounted on and anchored to a concrete pedestal.

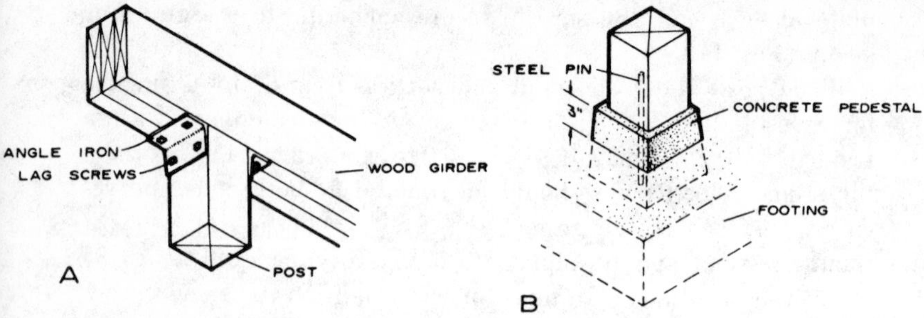

**Fig. 2.** Wood post for wood girder. *A,* connection to girder. *B,* base.

The built-up girder (Fig. 3) is usually made up of two or more pieces of 2″ dimension lumber spiked together, the ends of the pieces joining over a supporting post. A two-piece girder may be nailed from one side with tenpenny nails, two at the end of each piece and others driven stagger-fashion 16″ apart. A three-piece girder is nailed from each side with twentypenny nails, two near each end of each piece and others driven stagger-fashion 32″ apart.

Ends of wood girders should bear at least 4″ on the masonry walls or pilasters. When wood is untreated, a ½″ air space should be provided at each end and at each side of wood girders framing into masonry (Fig. 3). In termite-infested areas, these pockets should be lined with metal. The top of the girder should be level with the top of the sill plates on the foundation walls, unless *ledger strips* are used. If steel plates are used under ends of girders, they should be of full bearing size.

### GIRDER-JOIST INSTALLATION

The simplest method of floor joist framing is one where the joists bear directly on the wood girder or steel beam, in which case the top of the beam coincides with the top of the anchored sill (Fig. 3). This method is used when basement heights provide adequate headroom below the girder. When wood girders are used in this manner, the main disadvantage is that shrinkage is usually greater at the girder than at the foundation.

For more uniform shrinkage at the inner beam and the outer

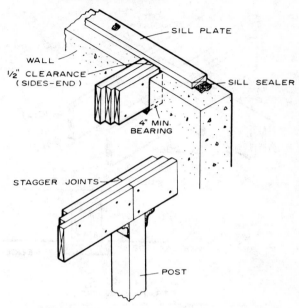

WALL

1/2" CLEARANCE
(SIDES-END)

SILL PLATE

SILL SEALER

4" MIN.
BEARING

STAGGER JOINTS

POST

**Fig. 3.** Built-up wood girder.

wall and to provide greater headroom, joist hangers or a supporting ledger strip are commonly used. Depending on sizes of
joists and wood girders, joists may be supported on the ledger
strip in several ways (Fig. 4). Each provides about the same
depth of wood subject to shrinkage at the outer wall and at the
center wood girder. A continuous horizontal tie between exterior
walls is obtained by nailing notched joists together (*A*, Fig. 4).
Joists must always bear on the ledgers. In *B*, Fig. 4, the connecting scab at each pair of joists provides this tie and also a
nailing area for the subfloor. A steel strap is used to tie the
joists together when the tops of the beam and the joists are level
(*C*, Fig. 4). It is important that a small space be allowed above
the beam to provide for shrinkage of the joists.

When a space is required for heat ducts in a partition supported on the girder, a *spaced wood girder* is sometimes necessary (Fig. 5). Solid blocking is used at intervals between the
two members. A single post support for a spaced girder usually
requires a bolster, preferably metal, with sufficient span to support the two members.

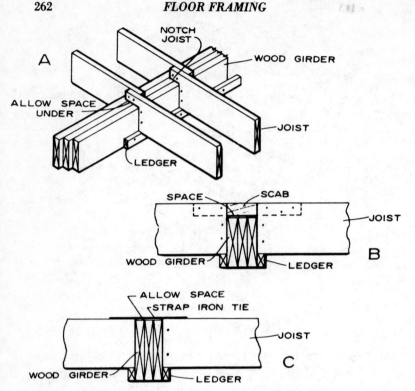

**Fig. 4.** Ledger on center wood girder. *A*, notched joist. *B*, scab tie between joist. *C*, flush joist.

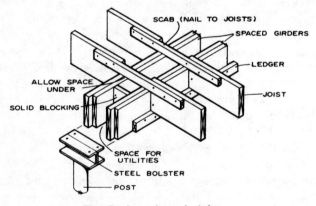

**Fig. 5.** Spaced wood girder.

Joists may be arranged with a steel beam generally the same way as illustrated for a wood beam. Perhaps the most common methods used, depending on joist sizes, are as follows:

1. The joists rest directly on the top of the beam.

2. Joists rest on a wood ledger or steel angle iron, which is bolted to the web (*A*, Fig. 6).

3. Joists bear directly on the flange of the beam (*B*, Fig. 6). In the third method, wood blocking is required between the joists near the beam flange to prevent overturning.

## WOOD SILL CONSTRUCTION

The two general types of wood sill construction used over the foundation wall conform either to platform or balloon framing. The *box sill* is commonly used in platform construction. It consists of a 2″ or thicker plate anchored to the foundation wall over a sill sealer which provides support and fastening for the joists and header at the ends of the joists (Fig. 7). Some houses are constructed without benefit of an anchored sill plate although

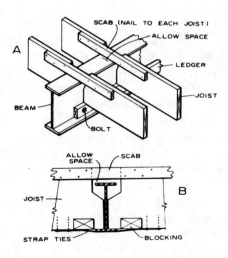

**Fig. 6.**  Steel beam and joists. *A,* bearing on ledger. *B,* bearing on flange.

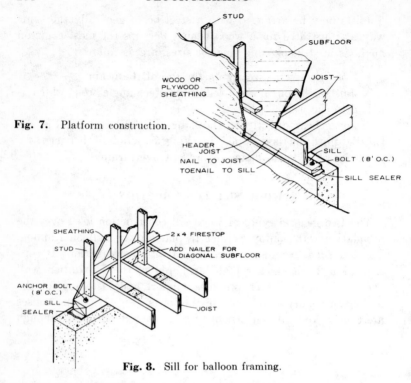

**Fig. 7.**   Platform construction.

**Fig. 8.**   Sill for balloon framing.

this is not entirely desirable.   (*See* Chap. 5, Lumber, Chap. 10, Foundation Constructions, and Chap. 12, Wall Framing.)   The floor framing should then be anchored with metal strapping installed during pouring operations.

*Balloon frame* construction uses a nominal 2″ or thicker wood sill upon which the joists rest. The studs also bear on this member and are nailed both to the floor joists and the sill. The subfloor is laid diagonally or at right angles to the joists and a firestop added between the studs at the floorline (Fig. 8). When diagonal subfloor is used, a nailing member is normally required between joists and studs at the wall lines.

Because there is less potential shrinkage in exterior walls with balloon framing than in the platform type, balloon framing is usually preferred over the platform type in full two-story brick or stone-veneer houses.

## FLOOR JOISTS

Floor joists are selected primarily to meet strength and stiffness requirements. Strength requirements depend upon the loads to be carried. Stiffness requirements place an arbitrary control on deflection under load. Stiffness is also important in limiting vibrations from moving loads that are often a cause of annoyance to occupants. Other desirable qualities for floor joists are **good nail-holding ability and freedom from warp.** (*See* **Chaps. 11, 12, and 13 on Framing.**)

Wood-floor joists are generally of 2″ (nominal) thickness and of 8″, 10″, or 12″ (nominal) depth. The size depends upon the loading, length of span, spacing between joists, and the species and grade of lumber used. As previously mentioned, grades in species vary a great deal. *For example,* the grades generally used for joists are *Standard* for Douglas fir, *No. 2* or *No. 2KD* for southern pine, and comparable grades for other species.

## JOIST INSTALLATION

After the sill plates have been anchored to the foundation walls or piers, the joists are located according to the house design. (Sixteen-inch center-to-center spacing is commonly used.)

Any joists having a slight bow edgewise should be so placed that the crown is on top. A crowned joist will tend to straighten out when subfloor and normal floor loads are applied. Since knots on the upper side of a joist are on the compression side of the member and will have less effect on strength, the largest edge knots should be placed on top.

The header joist is fastened by nailing into the end of each joist with three sixteenpenny nails. In addition, the header joist and the stringer joists parallel to the exterior walls in platform construction (Fig. 9) are toenailed to the sill with tenpenny nails spaced 16″ on center. Each joist should be toenailed to the sill and center beam with two tenpenny or three eightpenny nails. Then the joists should be nailed to each other with three or four sixteenpenny nails when they lap over the center beam. If a nominal 2″ scab is used across the butt ended joists, it should be nailed to each joist with at least three sixteenpenny nails at each side of the joint. These and other nailing patterns and

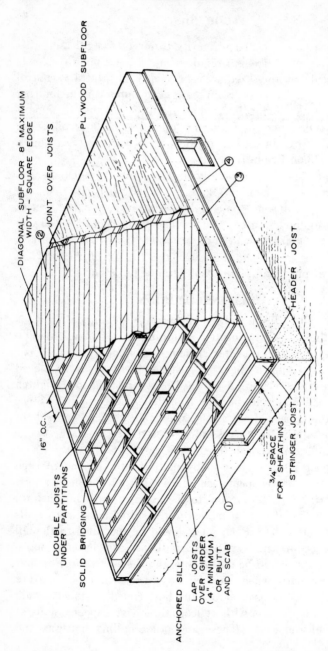

PLYWOOD SUBFLOOR

DIAGONAL SUBFLOOR 8" MAXIMUM
WIDTH - SQUARE EDGE

② JOINT OVER JOISTS

16" O.C.

DOUBLE JOISTS
UNDER PARTITIONS

SOLID BRIDGING

ANCHORED SILL

LAP JOISTS
OVER GIRDER
( 4" MINIMUM )
OR BUTT
AND SCAB

①

STRINGER JOIST

3/4" SPACE
FOR SHEATHING

HEADER JOIST

③

④

**Fig. 9.** Floor framing. (1) Nailing bridging to joists. (2) Nailing board subfloor to joists. (3) Nailing header to joists. (4) Toenailing header to sill.

practices are shown in Table 7.

The *in-line* joist splice is sometimes used in framing the floor and ceiling joists. This system normally allows the use of one smaller joist size when center supports are present. It consists of uneven length joists; the long overhanging joist is cantilevered over the center support, then spliced to the supported joist (Fig. 10). Overhang joists are alternated. Depending on the span, species, and joist size, the overhang varies between 1' 10" and 2' 10". Plywood splice plates are used on each side of the end joints.

It is good practice to double joists under all parallel-bearing partition walls. If spacing is required for heat ducts, solid blocking is used between the joists (Fig. 9).

## FRAMING FOR FLOOR OPENINGS

When framing for large openings such as stairwells, fireplaces, and chimneys, the opening should be doubled. A method of framing and nailing for floor openings is shown in Fig. 11.

Joist hangers and short sections of angle iron are often used to support headers and tail beams for large openings. (*See* Chap. 21, Construction of Stairs.)

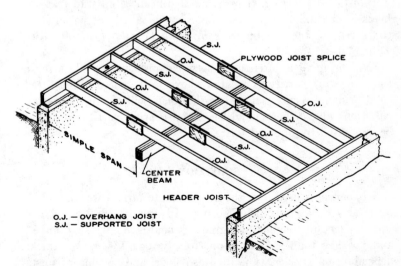

**Fig. 10.** "In-line" joist system. Alternate extension of joists over the center support with plywood gusset joint allows the use of a smaller joist size.

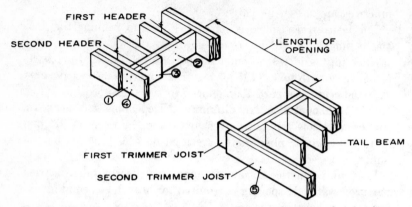

**Fig. 11.** Framing for floor openings. (1) Nailing trimmer to first header. (2) Nailing header to tail beams. (3) Nailing header together. (4) Nailing trimmer to second header. (5) Nailing trimmers together.

## BRIDGING

*Cross bridging* between wood joists has often been used in house construction, but research by several laboratories has questioned the benefits of bridging in relation to its cost, especially in normal house construction. Even with tight-fitting, well-installed bridging, there is no significant ability to transfer loads after subfloor and finish floor are installed. Some building codes require the use of *cross bridging* or *solid bridging*. (*See* Table 7.)

*Solid bridging* is often used between joists to provide a more rigid base for partitions located above joist spaces. Well-fitted solid bridging securely nailed to the joists will aid in supporting partitions above them (Fig. 9). Load-bearing partitions should be supported by doubled joists.

## SUBFLOOR

*Subflooring* is used over the floor joists to form a working platform and base for finish flooring. It usually consists of (a) square-edge or tongued-and-grooved boards no wider than 8″ and not less than 3/4″ thick or (b) plywood 1/2″ to 3/4″ thick, depending on species, type of finish floor, and spacing of joists (Fig. 9). (*See* Chap. 25, Floor Coverings.)

## BOARDS

Subflooring may be applied either *diagonally* (common) or at *right angles* to the joists. When subflooring is placed at right angles to the joists, the finish floor should be laid at right angles to the subflooring. Diagonal subflooring permits finish flooring to be laid either parallel or at right angles (common) to the joists. End joints of the boards should always be made directly over the joists. Subfloor is nailed to each joist with two eight-penny nails for 8″ widths.

The joist spacing should not exceed 16″ on center when finish flooring is laid parallel to the joists or where parquet finish flooring is used. The spacing should not exceed 24″ on center when finish flooring at least $25/32$″ thick is at right angles to the joists.

Where balloon framing is used, blocking should be installed between ends of joists at the wall of nailing the ends of diagonal subfloor boards (Fig. 8).

## PLYWOOD

Plywood can be obtained in a number of grades designed to meet a broad range of end-use requirements. All interior-type grades are also available with waterproof adhesive identical with those used in exterior plywood. This type is useful where a hazard of prolonged moisture exists, such as in underlayments or subfloors adjacent to plumbing fixtures and for roof sheathing which may be exposed for long periods during construction. Under normal conditions and for sheathing used on walls, standard sheathing grades are satisfactory.

Plywood suitable for subfloor, such as standard sheathing, Structural I and II, and C-C Exterior grades, has a panel identification index marking on each sheet. These markings indicate the allowable spacing of rafters and floor joists for the various thicknesses when the plywood is used as roof sheathing or subfloor. *For example,* an index mark of $32/16$ indicates that the plywood panel is suitable for a maximum spacing of 32″ for rafters and 16″ for floor joists. Therefore, no problem of strength differences between species is involved since the correct identification is shown for each panel.

Normally, when some type of underlayment is used over the

plywood subfloor, the minimum thickness of the subfloor for species such as Douglas fir and southern pine is ½″ when joists are spaced 16″ on center and ⅝″ for such plywood as western hemlock, western white pine, ponderosa pine, and similar species. These thicknesses of plywood might be used for 24″ spacing of joists when a finish $^{25}/_{32}$″ strip flooring is installed at right angles to the joists. It is very important to have a solid and safe platform for the workmen during construction of the remainder of the house. For this reason, it is necessary to have a slightly thicker plywood subfloor, especially when joist spacing is greater than 16″ on center.

Plywood can also serve as combined plywood subfloor and underlayment, eliminating separate underlayment because the plywood functions as both a structural subfloor and as a good substrate. This is applied to thin resilient floorings, carpeting, and other nonstructural finish flooring. The plywood used in this manner must be tongued-and-grooved or blocked with 2″ lumber along the unsupported edges. Following are recommendations for its use:

*Grade:* Underlayment, underlayment with exterior glue, C-C plugged.

*Spacing* and *thickness:*

(a) For species such as Douglas fir (coast type) and southern pine: ½″ minimum thickness for 16″ joist spacing, ⅝″ for 20″ joist spacing, and ¾″ for 24″ joist spacing.

(b) For species such as western hemlock, western white pine, and ponderosa pine: ⅝″ minimum thickness for 16″ joist spacing, ¾″ for 20″ joist spacing, and ⅞″ for 24″ joist spacing.

Plywood should be installed with the grain direction of the outer plies at right angles to the joists and be staggered so that end joints in adjacent panels break over different joists. Plywood should be nailed to the joist at each bearing with eight-penny common or sevenpenny threaded nails for plywood ½″ to ¾″ thick. Space nails 6″ apart along all edges and 10″ along intermediate members. When plywood serves as both subfloor and underlayment, nails may be spaced 6″ to 7″ apart at all joists and blocking. Use eightpenny or ninepenny common nails or sevenpenny or eightpenny threaded nails.

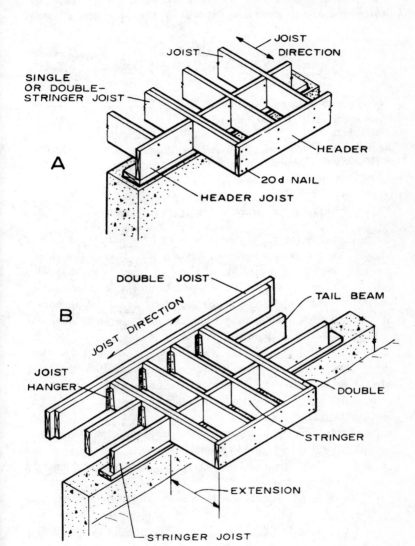

**Fig. 12.** Floor framing at wall projections. *A*, projection of joists for bay window extensions. *B*, projection at right angles to joists.

For the best performance, plywood should *not* be laid up with tight joints, whether used on the interior or exterior. The following spaces are recommendations by the American Plywood Association:

| Plywood Location and Use | Spacing | |
|---|---|---|
| | Edges (Inches) | Ends (Inches) |
| Underlayment or interior wall lining | $\frac{1}{32}$ | $\frac{1}{32}$ |
| Panel siding and combination subfloor underlayment | $\frac{1}{16}$ | $\frac{1}{16}$ |
| Roof sheathing, subflooring, and wall sheathing. (Under wet or humid conditions, spacing should be doubled.) | $\frac{1}{8}$ | $\frac{1}{16}$ |

## FLOOR FRAMING AT WALL PROJECTIONS

The framing for wall projections—such as a *bay window* or first- or second-floor extensions beyond the lower wall—should generally consist of projection of the floor joists (Fig. 12). This extension normally should not exceed 24″ unless designed specifically for great projections, which may require special anchorage at the opposite ends of the joists. The joists forming each side of the bay should be doubled. Nailing, in general, should conform to that for stair openings. The subflooring is carried to and sawed flush with the outer framing member. Rafters are often carried by a header constructed in the main wall over the bay area, which supports the roofload. Therefore, the wall of the bay has less load to support.

Projections at right angles to the length of the floor joists should generally be limited to small areas and extensions of not more than 24″. In this construction, the stringer should be carried by doubled joists (*B*, Fig. 12). Joist hangers or a ledger will provide good connections for the ends of members.

CHAPTER 12

# Wall Framing

*Wall framing* (Fig. 1) is composed of regular studs, diagonal bracing, cripples, trimmers, headers, and fire blocks and is supported by the floor sole plate. The vertical members of the wall framing are the studs, which support the top plates and all of the weight of the upper part of the building or everything above the top plate line. They provide the framework to which the wall sheathing is nailed on the outside and which supports the lath, plaster, and insulation on the inside. (*See* Chap. 13, Framing Layout and Erection.)

*Walls* and *partitions* which are classed as framed constructions are composed of structural elements (Fig. 2) which are usually closely spaced, slender, vertical members called *studs*. These are arranged in a row with their ends bearing on a long horizontal member called a bottom plate or sole plate, and their tops capped with another plate, called a top plate. Double top plates are used in bearing walls and partitions. The bearing strength of stud walls is determined by the strength of the studs.

## CORNER POSTS

The studs used at the corners of the frame construction are usually built up from three or more ordinary studs to provide greater strength. These built-up assemblies are corner-partition posts. After the sill and first-floor joists are in place, the subfloor is placed to give a surface upon which to work. The *corner posts* are set up, plumbed, and temporarily braced. The corner posts may be made in several different ways (Fig. 3).

A corner post may consist of a 4 by 6 with a 2 by 4 nailed on

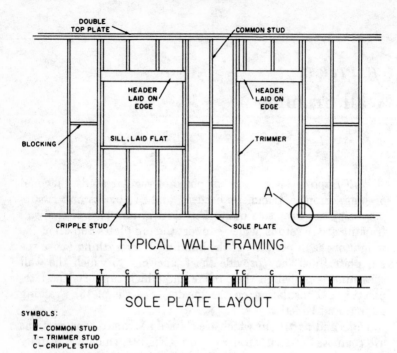

**Fig. 1.** Typical wall frame details.

the board side, flush with one edge. This type corner is for 4″ wall. Where walls are thicker, heavier timber is used. A 4 by 4 may be used with a 2 by 4 nailed to two of the adjoining sides.

Two 2 by 4's may be nailed together with blocks between and a 2 by 4 flush with one edge.

A 2 by 4 may be nailed to the edge of another 2 by 4, the edge of one flush with the side of the other. This type is used extensively where no inside finish is required.

Whenever a *partition* meets an outside wall, a stud wide enough to extend beyond the partition on both sides is used—this affords a solid nailing base for the inside wall finish. This type of stud is called a *T-post* and is made in several different ways (Fig. 4).

A 2 by 4 may be nailed and centered on the face side of a 4 by 6.

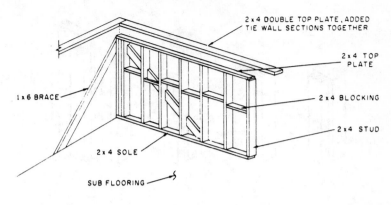

2 x 4 DOUBLE TOP PLATE, ADDED
TIE WALL SECTIONS TOGETHER

2 x 4 TOP
PLATE

1 x 6 BRACE

2 x 4 BLOCKING

2 x 4 STUD

2 x 4 SOLE

SUB FLOORING

WALL SECTION INPLACE
WITH TEMPORARY BRACING

**Fig. 2.** Typical wall construction.

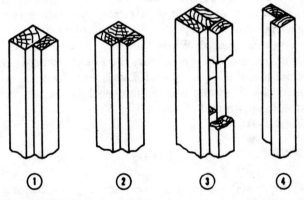

① ② ③ ④

**Fig. 3.** Corner post construction.

A 2 by 4 may be nailed and centered on two 4 by 4's nailed together.

Two 2 by 4's may be nailed together with a block between them and a 2 by 4 centered on the wide side.

A 2 by 4 may be nailed and centered on the face side of a 2 by 6, with a horizontal bridging nailed behind them to give support and stiffness.

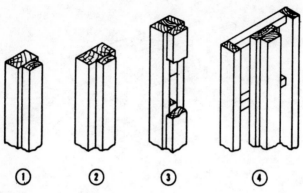

**Fig. 4.** T-post construction.

Where a partition is finished on one side only, the *partition post* used consists of a simple stud set in the outside wall, in line with the side of the partition wall, and finished as stud *A* in *1*, Fig. 5. These posts are nailed in place along with the corner post. The exact position of the partition walls must be determined before the posts are placed. Where the walls are more than 4″ thick, wider timber is used. In special cases, for example where partition walls cross, a double T-post is used. This is made by using methods previously described and nailing another 2 by 4 to the opposite wide side, as shown in *2*, *3*, and *4*, Fig. 5.

## STUDS

After the posts, plates, and braces are in place, the studs are placed and nailed with two 16- or 20-penny nails through the top plate. Before the studs are set in place, the window and door openings are laid out. Then the remaining or intermediate studs are laid out on the sole plates by measuring from one corner the distances the studs are to be set apart. Studs are normally spaced 12″, 16″, and 24″ on centers, depending upon the type of building and the type of outside and inside finish. Where vertical siding is used, studs are set wider apart since the horizontal girts between them afford nailing surface.

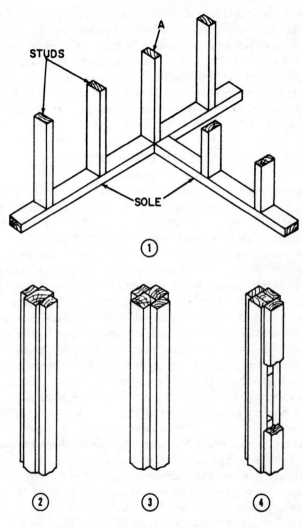

**Fig. 5.** Partition posts.

When it is desirable to double the post of the door opening, first place the outside studs into position and nail them securely. Then cut short studs, or *filler studs,* the size of the opening and nail these to the inside face of the outside studs as shown in Fig. 1. In making a window opening, a bottom header must be framed; this header is either single or double. When it is doubled, the bottom piece is nailed to the opening studs at the proper height and the top piece of the bottom header is nailed into place flush with the bottom section. The door header is framed as shown in Fig. 1. The filler stud rests on the sole at the bottom.

## TOP PLATE AND SOLE PLATE

The *top plate* serves two purposes—to tie the studding together at the top and form a finish for the walls, and to furnish a support for the lower ends of the rafters (Fig. 1). The top plate serves as a connecting link between the wall and the roof, just as the sills and girders are connecting links between the floors and the walls. The plate is made up of one or two pieces of timber of the same size as the studs. (In cases where the studs at the end of the building extend to the rafters, no plate is used at the end of the building.) When it is used on top of partition walls, it is sometimes called the *cap.* Where the plate is doubled, the first plate or bottom section is nailed with 16- or 20- penny nails to the top of the corner posts and to the studs; the connection at the corner is made as shown in *1,* Fig. 6. After the single plate is nailed securely and the corner braces are nailed into place, the top part of the plate is then nailed to the bottom section by means of 16- or 20- penny nails, either over each stud or spaced with two nails every two feet. The edges of the top section should be flush with the bottom section and the corner joints lapped as shown in *1* and *2,* Fig. 6.

All partition walls and outside walls are finished either with a 2 by 4 or with a piece of lumber corresponding to the thickness of the wall. This lumber is laid horizontally on the floor or joists. It carries the bottom end of the studs (Fig. 1). The 2 by 4 or lumber is called the *sole* or *sole plate.* The sole should be nailed with two 16- or 20- penny nails at each joist that it crosses. If it is laid lengthwise on top of a girder or joist, it should be nailed with two nails every two feet. (*See* Chap. 5, Lumber; Chap. 4, Methods of Fastening; and Chap. 6, Woodworking Joints and Splices.)

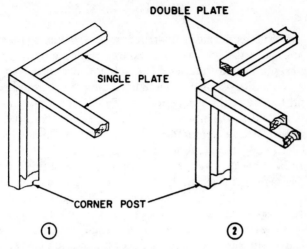

**Fig. 6.** Plate construction.

## PARTITION

*Partition walls* are walls that divide the inside space of a building. These walls in most cases are framed as part of the building. In cases where floors are to be installed after the outside of the building is completed, the partition walls are left unframed. There are two types of partition walls—the bearing and the non-bearing types. The bearing type supports ceiling joists. The non-bearing type supports only itself. This type may be put in at any time after the other framework is installed. Only one cap or plate is used. A sole plate should be used in every case, as it helps to distribute the load over a larger area. Partition walls are framed in the same manner as outside walls, and door openings are framed as outside openings. Where there are corners or where one partition wall joins another, corner posts or T-posts are used, as in the outside walls. These posts provide nailing surfaces for the inside wall finish. Partition walls in a one-story building may or may not extend to the roof. The top of the studs has a plate when the wall does not extend to the roof; but when the wall extends to the roof, the studs are joined to the rafters.

## BRACES

Bracing stiffens framed construction and helps it to resist winds, storms, twists, or strains stemming from any cause. Good bracing keeps corners square and plumb and prevents warping, sagging, and shifts resulting from lateral forces that would otherwise tend to distort the frame and cause badly fitting doors and windows as well as the cracking of plaster. There are three commonly used methods of bracing frame structures. (*See* Chap. 7, Methods of Frame Construction.)

**Let-in bracing** (*1*, Fig. 7). Let-in bracing is set into the edges of studs so as to be flush with the surface. The studs are always cut to let in the braces; the braces are *never* cut. Usually 1 by 4's or 1 by 6's are used, set diagonally from top plates to sole plates.

**Cut-in bracing** (*2*, Fig. 7). Cut-in bracing is toenailed between studs. It usually consists of 2 by 4's cut at an angle to permit toenailing, inserted in diagonal progression between studs running up and down from corner posts to sill or plates.

**Diagonal sheathing** (*3*, Fig. 7). The type of bracing with the highest strength is diagonally applied sheathing. Each board acts as a brace of the wall. If plywood sheathing ⅝″ thick or more is used, other methods of bracing may be omitted. (*See* Chap. 14, Wall Sheathing.)

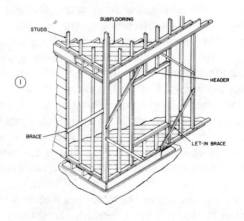

**Fig. 7.** Common types of bracing.

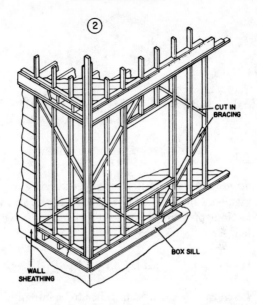

②

CUT IN BRACING

BOX SILL

WALL SHEATHING

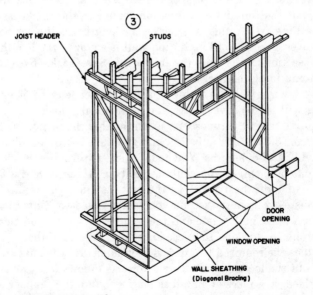

③

JOIST HEADER     STUDS

DOOR OPENING

WINDOW OPENING

WALL SHEATHING
(Diagonal Bracing)

**Fig. 7.** (continued).

## CHAPTER 13

# Framing Layout and Erection

*Framing layout* consists principally of laying out the various framing members for cutting to correct lengths and marking the correct locations of members on other members to which they are to be joined.

## SILL LAYOUT

The *sill* is normally the first member to be laid out. As shown in Chap. 10, Fig. 1, the edge of the sill is usually set back from the edge of the foundation a distance equal to the thickness of the sheathing. When this is the case, the length of sill stock required to cover a section of foundation wall is equal to the length of the wall section minus twice the amount of the setback. (*See* Chap. 10, Foundation Construction.)

To make up this length you should select lengths of sill stock that will most conveniently and economically make up the total required length. Suppose, for example, that the section of the wall calls for 33′ of 2 × 8 sill stock and you have 2 × 8 available in 18′, 16′, 14′, and 6′ lengths. You could select two 18′ pieces and cut 3′ off one of them, or you could select two 14′ pieces and a 6′ piece and cut 1′ off the 6′ piece. In the first instance, you would have 3′ of waste, while in the second you would have two joints in the sill. To minimize both waste and the number of joints, you should select one 18′ and one 16′ piece and cut 1′ off one of them.

Once the required length has been made up, the next step is to lay out the locations of the bolt holes as follows.

Place each piece of sill stock on the foundation, inboard of the bolts, but otherwise in exactly the position it is to occupy, and square a line across the stock from the center of each bolt. To lay out the bolt-hole center on each of these lines, measure the distance from the center *of each bolt* to the outer edge of the foundation; subtract the amount of the sill set back from this distance and lay off the remainder *on the corresponding bolt line*, measuring from what is to be the outer edge of the sill.

The reason you must lay out each bolt hole separately is that the bolts may be set at slightly varying distances from the edge of the foundation and from each other.

## SILL PLACEMENT

Bore the bolt holes with an auger bit ⅛″ larger in diameter than the bolt diameter, to allow for making slight adjustments in the location of the sill. When all the holes have been bored, try the stock for the whole section on the bolts for a fit. If the fit is satisfactory, remove the pieces of stock and place a thin layer of mortar on top of the foundation. Replace the pieces and check the whole sill for line and level. Place small wedges, if necessary, to hold pieces level until the mortar sets. Then place the washers on the bolts, screw on the nuts, and bolt the sill down.

## JOIST LAYOUT

A *common joist* is a full-length joist, as distinguished from a *cripple joist*. The best way to lay out common joists for cutting is to figure the correct length of a common joist, cut a piece of stock to this length, notch for identification, and use the piece as a *pattern* from which to cut the other common joists. The best way to lay out cripples for cutting is to postpone the cripple layout until after the headers have been placed; then measure the spaces that are to be spanned by the cripples.

In platform framing, the outer ends of the joists usually butt against a header joist that is set flush with the outer edge of the sill. In this case the length of a wall-to-wall common joist will be the distance between the outer edges of the sills, minus twice the thickness of a header joist.

The length of common joist required to cover a given span between an outside wall and a girder varies with the character of the wall framing and also with the manner in which the joists are framed to the girder. The length of common joist required to cover a given span between two girders varies with the manner in which the joists are framed to the girders. Joists that lap a girder with full bearing (meaning joists that extend all the way across the top of the girder) must obviously be longer than joists that butt each other on the top of a girder. Joists in hangers, which butt against the sides of a girder, are shorter than joists that butt each other on top of a girder.

The whole floor-framing situation, then, must be studied closely before a common joist pattern is cut. Whenever possible, the cutting of a pattern should be delayed until the sills, headers, and other supporting or abutting members are erected. The joist length can then be determined by measurements taken on the actual structure. Whenever possible, the common joist pattern should be tried on the actual structure for a fit before any joists are cut from it.

## JOIST LOCATION LAYOUT

The location of a joist end is marked on a sill or a header joist by squaring a line across and drawing an X alongside it. The X indicates the side of the line on which the joist end-section is to be placed.

The location of one of the outside joists is marked first, and the locations of the others are then measured off from this one in accordance with the specified spacing of joists on center (O.C.).

Figure 1 shows the method of laying out joist locations on the header joists in a platform-frame box sill, in which the headers and outside joists come flush with the outer edges of the sill.

Before you start laying out the joist locations you should study the floor framing plan to learn the locations of any double trimmers around floor openings. Locations of double trimmers are marked with two lines and two X's. The locations of cripples are marked the same as the locations of common joists, but with the word *crip* written in alongside.

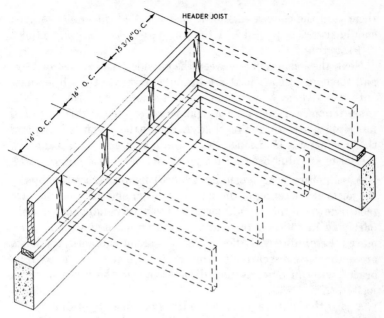

**Fig. 1.** Joist location layout-platform-frame box sill assembly with header joists.

## JOIST ERECTION

The usual procedure for erecting joists is as follows.

If there are any header joists, these joists are cut and erected first. As a general rule, the length of a platform-frame header is equal to the shortest distance between the outer edges of the sills. Header joists are toenailed to the sills with 16-penny nails spaced 16″ O.C.

As soon as a common joist pattern has been laid out and cut as previously described, the workers start cutting common joists. As each joist is cut, two men should carry it to its location and lay it flat across the span. Two men (one man at each end of the span) erect the outside joists first. Each of these joists is toenailed down to the sill or plate with 16-penny nails spaced 16″ O.C. and end-nailed through the headers with two 20-penny nails driven into each joist end. Incidentally, many joists have a slight curve to them, and the convex edge of a joist is called the *crown*. A joist should always be placed with the crown up. (*See* Chap. 4, Methods of Fastening.)

Next, the joists lying between the outside joists are set on edge and the ends of each joist are toenailed down to the sill or plate with two 16-penny nails, one on each side of the joist. Only the inner trimmer of each pair of trimmers is erected at this time, and no cripples are cut at this time. After all the common joists and the trimmers as mentioned have been set on edge and toenailed, the joists are plumbed and temporarily braced as follows.

A temporary brace (usually a 1 × 6) is laid across the tops of the joists at the center of the span. The outer ends of this brace are tacked down to the outside joists with 8-penny nails, driven only part way in to allow for extracting later when the brace is removed. Beginning with the joist next to an outside joist, the joists are plumbed consecutively, and as each joist is plumbed it is braced with an 8-penny nail driven through the brace into the joist.

A joist that butts against a header is plumbed by lining up the joist end with the perpendicular location line on the header. When the joist is in plumb position, it is nailed at the ends with 20-penny nails, two to each end, driven through the header into the joist.

After all the common joists plus the inside trimmers (if there are any) have been plumbed and braced, the framing around a floor opening (if there is one) is installed. First the locations of the headers are determined by measurement of the shortest distance between the inside trimmers. The four pieces of joist stock that will form the double headers are then cut to correct length, after which the outside header of each pair is set in place and fastened to the inside trimmers with 20-penny nails, three to each end, driven through the trimmers into the ends of the headers as shown in Fig. 2.

Once the outside headers are in place, the lengths of the cripple joists can be determined by simple measurement. The cripples are cut, set in place, plumbed, fastened at the outer ends like common joists, and fastened at the floor-opening ends with 20-penny nails, three to each cripple, driven through the outside headers into the

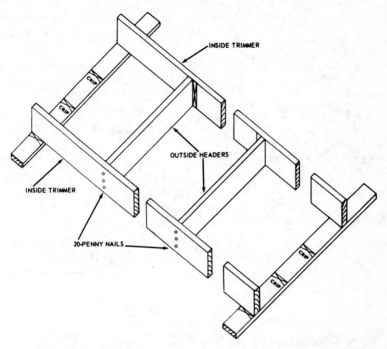

**Fig. 2.** First step in framing around floor opening.

ends of the cripples as shown in Fig. 3.

Next, the inside headers are set in place, fastened to the outside headers with 16-penny nails spaced 6″ O.C., and fastened to the inside trimmers with 20-penny nails, three to each end, driven through the trimmers into the ends of the headers (Fig. 4). Finally, the outside trimmers are set in place and nailed to the inside trimmers with 16-penny nails spaced 12″ O.C., as shown in Fig. 5.

As soon as enough common joists have been erected, the installation of bridging begins. Cross-bridging struts are nailed (usually with 8-penny nails) at the top ends only at this time. Bottom ends will be nailed from below, after the joists have adjusted themselves to the weight of the subflooring. Remember the joist should be placed with the crown up, so that any settlement

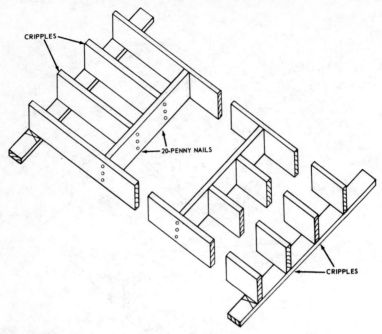

**Fig. 3.** Second step in framing around floor opening.

under the weight of the flooring will tend toward a level instead of toward a sag.

After the bridging is installed, the subflooring is laid as previously described. In the meantime, the layout and cutting of studs begins.

## LAYING OUT STUDS FOR CUTTING

Before you can lay out any studs for cutting, you must calculate how long the studs must be. The best way to do this is to lay out to full scale on a piece of stud stock certain data obtained from the wall sections and elevations, and then use the piece of stock as a pattern for cutting studs.

The next step is to lay out the segments of the gable-end studs that extend above the level of the top of the rafter plate. In order

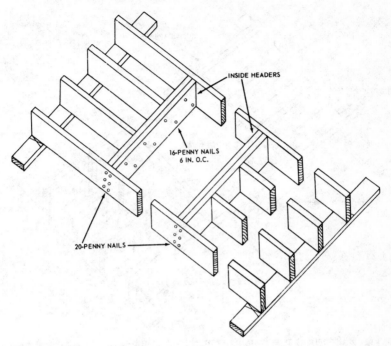

**Fig. 4.** Third step in framing around floor opening.

to do this you must calculate the *common difference* of gable-end studs as follows.

In Fig. 6, the line *AC* indicates the level of the side-wall rafter plate, and line *AB* indicates the roof line of the building. Somewhere on the elevations you will find a small triangle like the one shown in the upper left illustration. This is called the *roof triangle,* and it gives the proportion of run to rise in the roof. In this case this is also the proportion of run to rise between line *AC* and line *AB;* this proportion is 8″ of rise to every 12″ of run. (*See* Chap. 16, Roofing, and Chap. 17, Reroofing.)

The lines *DE* and *FG* represent the portions of two gable-end studs that extend above the level of the top of the side-wall rafter plate. You can calculate the length of *DE* as follows.

Since the studs are spaced 16″ O.C., the run of the right triangle *AED* is 16″. The rise of this triangle is the length of the line

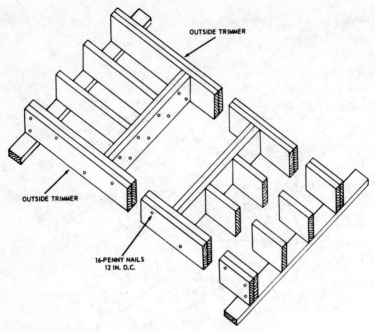

**Fig. 5.** Fourth step in framing around floor opening.

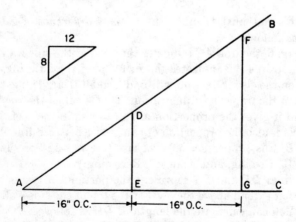

**Fig. 6.** Calculating common difference of gable-end studs.

*DE*. From the roof triangle you know that the rise of a similar triangle with a run of 12″ is 8″. If the rise of a right triangle with a run of 12″ is 8″, the rise of a similar right triangle with a run of 16″ must be the value of x in the proportional equation 12:8 :: 16:x, or 10⅔″. The length of *DE*, therefore, is 10⅔″. Rounded off to the nearest 1/16″, this is 10 11/16″. The common difference may also be found as follows. Multiply the cut of the roof, expressed as a fraction, by the spacing of the studs. Assume a roof cut of 8″ and 12″ and a stud spacing of 16″. The common difference in the length of the gable stud is 16″ × 8/12″ = 10⅔″. Expressed as a formula, stud spacing × cut of the roof = common difference.

If the rise of a right triangle of 16″ of run is 10 11/16″, the rise for twice as much run, or 32″, must be twice as much, or 2 × 10 11/16″; the rise for three times as much run must be 3 × 10 11/16″, and so on. This means that, moving inboard from the rafter plates, each gable-end stud is 10 11/16″ longer than the preceding gable-end stud.

Knowing this, you can lay off the lengths of the gable-end studs by laying off 10 11/16″ (which is called the *common difference* of gable-end studs) progressively for each stud, from the shortest to the longest, in either side of the end wall. The top end cut of the gable stud is laid out by using the cut of the roof and marking on the rise side.

A pattern layout for platform-frame studs is shown in Fig. 7. Since the bottom of a platform-frame stud rests on the sole plate, which in turn rests on the subflooring, you should first lay off the vertical distance between the finish floors, *minus* the thickness of the sole plate, *plus* the thickness of the finish floor. This is distance *1* in Fig. 7; laying it off will give you the level of the upper finish floor. Lay off back from this level the combined thickness of the upper-floor flooring, the depth of an upper-floor joist, and the thickness of the top plate. You now have the length of a stud, as shown in the illustration.

## STUD LOCATION LAYOUT

Stud locations are marked on sole plates in the same manner as joist locations. The sole plate is marked first, as shown in Fig. 8.

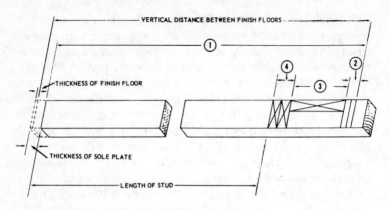

**Fig. 7.** Pattern layout for platform-frame studs.

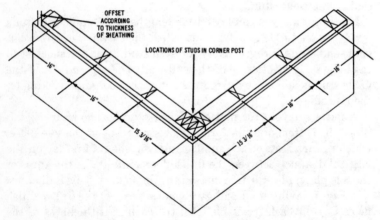

**Fig. 8.** Stud location layout.

These marks are then transferred to the corresponding top plate or rafter plate, by "matching" the top plate or rafter plate against the marked sole plate and squaring the marks across.

The studs around wall openings require special treatment. First locate the center line of the opening by examining the floor plan. Let us say that the opening is a door, and that the plan shows that the center line of this door lies 7′ 5″ from one of the building corners. Measure this off and square a line across the sill or plate at this point. Next look on the door schedule and find the width of this door. Let us say that it is door A, and you find that door A is 3′ wide. Lay off half of this, or 1½′, on either side of the center line and square the lines across.

## FRAMING ALLOWANCE

These lines mark the boundaries of the *finished* door opening. The trimmer studs on either side of the opening must be located at the boundaries of the *rough* opening. To get the width of the rough opening you add a *framing allowance* to the width of the finished opening. First, the width of the rough opening must exceed the width of the finished opening by the combined thicknesses of the *side jambs* on the door less the combined width of the rabbets, if the door fits into rabbets cut in the side jambs.

Besides the allowance for the thickness of the jambs, you must make an additional *framing allowance*. As you will see later, the side jambs are wedged in place with wooden wedges driven between the jambs and the trimmers. The usual wedging allowance is ½″ on either side.

The width of the finished opening (which is the same as the width of the door) is the horizontal distance between the side jambs. The width of the rough opening is the same horizontal distance, plus the combined width of the jambs, plus the combined width of the wedging allowance.

To locate the trimmers, then, lay off, on either side of the center line, half the width of the door, plus the thickness of a side jamb (which should be measured on the actual stock), plus the wedging allowance (usually ½″). Mark the trimmer locations with the word *trim* and postpone the cutting of the trimmers until after the header has been cut and set in place.

The header will be nailed between the first two full-length studs lying outside the boundaries of the finished opening. To locate the header at the right height, you must add to the height of the door a framing allowance as follows.

Make allowance for the thickness of the head jamb, and also for the depth of the *side-jamb lugs*. The side-jamb lugs are the portions of the side jambs that extend above the head-jamb dados. Since you will be measuring from the top of the subflooring and since the bottom of the door will have to clear the finish flooring, you must allow for the thickness of the finish flooring. If there will be no threshold, you must add a *clearance allowance* that will permit the door to swing clear of any rugs or carpets. The usual clearance allowance is ⅝″, which is also the usual thickness of a threshold. If the carpeting is to be extra thick, the clearance allowance may have to be more than ⅝″.

The framing allowance for a window opening is calculated as follows.

Locate and mark the window center line and lay off on either side of the center line half the width of the window, as obtained from the window schedule. This will locate the limits of the finished window opening. The top header and subsill header will be set between the first two full-length studs lying outside these limits.

Further window-opening layout should be postponed until the subsill header has been set in place. The height of the subsill header is obtained as follows.

Determine by examining the appropriate elevation the height of the top of the window sill above the finish flooring. Since you will be measuring from the subflooring, add the thickness of the finish flooring. From this, subtract the thickness of the window sill, plus the sill *bevel allowance,* or amount that the sill will be raised by tilting. This is usually about ¾″. To sum up, the height of the top of the subsill header above the finish flooring will be the vertical distance between the top of the window sill and the top of the finish floor, *minus* the thickness of the window sill, the sill bevel allowance (usually ¾″), and the thickness of the finish flooring.

The next step is to locate the top header at the proper height. On the elevation you will find the vertical distance between the finished first floor line and the bottom of the window head jamb. Since you will measure this distance from the top of the subfloor, add to it the thickness of the finish floor. Next add the thickness of the head lugs, which are similar to those on a door. The total will be the vertical distance between the top of the subfloor and the bottom of the top header.

When you have located the level of the bottom of the top header, check the whole layout as follows. You know that the height of the rough opening should be the height of the window (as given on the schedule) plus the total framing allowance. Calculate the total framing allowance you have applied and add it to the window height. The result should be the same as the measured vertical distance between the top of the subsill header and the bottom of the top header. If it is not, you have made a mistake somewhere.

To locate the trimmers proceed as follows.

Transfer the window center line to the subsill header and lay off on either side of it half the width of the window, as obtained from the window schedule. For a window without sash pockets, add on either side a framing allowance consisting of the thickness of the side jamb plus a wedging allowance of ½″. If the window is a double-hung window with sash weights, add the thickness of the side jamb plus 2″ for the width of the sash pocket. (*See* Chap. 20, Exterior Frames, Windows, and Doors, and Chap. 24, Window and Door Screens, and Hood or Canopy.)

## WALL FRAMING ERECTION

The steps in erecting a frame wall are to erect and plumb each of the corner posts as follows.

Set the post in exact position on the plate and toenail it down with 8-penny nails, two to each stud in the corner post. Attach temporary braces at the top, and nail a couple of short blocks to the subflooring at the approximate points where the ends of the braces will be fastened. Set nails in the floor ends of the braces, ready to be driven into the blocks when the exact position of each end is found.

While one man applies and reads the level, another worker should be ready to nail the brace to the block as soon as correct position is found. This worker works the end of the brace back and forth, on signal from the man at the level, until he gets the word that the bubble is centered. He then nails the end of the brace to the block. When this procedure has been followed with both braces, the corner post will be plumb all around.

Erection of the section of wall laying between the corner posts may be either by the *piece-by-piece* method or by the *section* method. In the piece-by-piece method, the wall is erected a piece at a time, meaning that each of the studs is raised and toenailed in place separately, after which the top plate or rafter plate is nailed on. In the section method the entire wall section, with the exception usually of the framing around openings and the upper member of the top plate or rafter plate, is assembled lying flat on the subflooring. The section is then heaved up into place and fastened at the top and bottom. Nowadays the section method is used for almost all platform-frame walls. (*See* Chap. 12, Wall Framing.)

The full-length studs are laid out adjacent to their location marks on the sole plate. As previously mentioned, the lower member of the top plate or rafter has already been matched against the sole plate, and marked with the corresponding stud locations. After the full-length studs have all been laid out flat, the lower member of the top plate or rafter plate is nailed to the tops of the studs with 16-penny nails, two to each stud, driven through the plate into the studs.

The wall section is then heaved up into place and temporarily braced. The bottoms of the braces are only tacked to the floor blocks at this time, so that their positions can be adjusted later when the wall is straightened. Each of the studs is toenailed down to its mark on the sole plate with 8-penny nails, two to each side of a stud. An adjoining wall section is then erected in the same manner, after which the upper members of the top plates or rafter plates are nailed to the lower members with 10-penny nails spaced 16″ O.C. End laps between adjoining plates are nailed down with 16-penny nails, two to each lap.

When all four walls have been erected, each wall is straightened as follows.

A guide line is stretched between the tops of the corner posts, and the bottoms of the temporary braces are released from the floor blocks. Beginning at one end of the wall, each brace is adjusted so as to bring the outer edge of the top plate in exact contact with the line. The bottom of the brace is then again nailed to the floor block.

The next step is to frame the rough openings. The procedure for this is much the same as it is for framing a floor opening. Trimmers are nailed to full-length studs, or to each other, with 10-penny nails spaced 16″ O.C. Headers are nailed to full-length studs with 8-penny nails, two to each end of a header member, driven through the full-length studs into the ends of the headers. Double headers are nailed to each other with 10-penny nails spaced 16″ O.C. (*See* Chap. 11, Floor Framing.)

Next step is to cut gains for diagonal bracing (if any) in studs and plates. Lay out these gains by placing the 1 × 6 bracing material in position against the framing members and scoring the outline on each stud or plate. Nail bracing on with two 8-penny nails to each stud or plate crossing.

## CHAPTER 14

# Wall Sheathing

*Wall sheathing*, because it strengthens and braces the wall framing, is considered a structural element and therefore a part of the framing.

## TYPES OF SHEATHING

The four most common types of sheathing used on modern structures are *wood, plywood, fiberboard,* and *gypsum.*

*Wood sheathing* consists usually of 1 x 6 or 1 x 8 boards, but thicker and/or wider stock is sometimes used. Boards may be square-edged for ordinary edge-butt joining, or they may be *shiplap* or *tongue-and-groove* (Fig. 1). "Dressed-and-matched" is simply a term that is used instead of tongue-and-groove with reference to sheathing, siding, or flooring.

*Plywood sheathing* is normally used in 4' by 8' sheets that are usually applied *vertically* or with the 8' dimension vertical. The type of plywood used is called *sheathing grade*. For studs spaced 16" O.C., the minimum thickness is 5/16".

*Fiberboard* (sometimes called *insulation board*) is a synthetic material that may be coated or impregnated with asphalt to increase water resistance. Edges are usually shiplap or tongue-and-groove for joining. Thickness is normally 25/32".

*Gypsum sheathing* consists of a treated gypsum filler faced on both sides with a light-weight paper. Sheets are usually dressed-and-matched, with V-shaped grooves and tongues. (*See* Chap. 5, Lumber.)

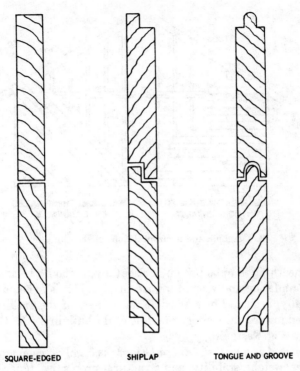

SQUARE-EDGED　　　　SHIPLAP　　　　TONGUE AND GROOVE

**Fig. 1.** Types of wood sheathing.

## APPLICATION OF SHEATHING

As soon as all the wall openings have been framed, the application of the sheathing begins.

*Wood wall sheathing* can be obtained in almost all widths, lengths, and grades. Generally, widths are from 6″ to 12″, with lengths selected for economical use. Almost all solid wood wall sheathing used is 13/16″ thick and either square or matched edge. This material may be nailed on horizontally or diagonally (Fig. 2). Diagonal application contributes much greater strength to the structure. Sheathing should be nailed on with three 8-penny common nails to each bearing if the pieces are over 6″ wide. Wooden sheathing is laid on tight, with all joints made over the studs. If

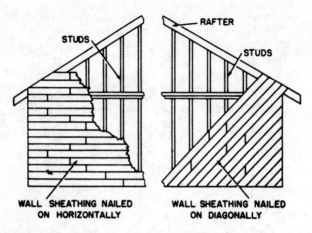

**Fig. 2.** Diagonal and horizontal wooden sheathing.

the sheathing is to be put on horizontally, it should be started at the foundation and worked toward the top. If it is to be put on diagonally, it should be started at the corners of the building and worked toward the center or middle of the building. (*See* Chap. 4, Methods of Fastening.)

*Plywood* as a *wall sheathing* (Fig. 3) is highly recommended by its size, weight, stability, and structural properties, plus the ease and rapidity of application. It adds considerably more strength to the frame than does diagonally applied wood boards. When plywood sheathing is used, corner bracing can be omitted. Large size panels effect a major saving in the time required for application and still provide a tight, draft-free installation that contributes a high insulation value to the wall. Minimum thicknesses of plywood wall sheathing are 5/16″ for 16″ stud spacing and ⅜″ for 24″ stud spacing. The panels should be installed with the face grain parallel to the studs. However, a little more stiffness can be gained by installing them across the studs, but this requires more cutting and fitting. Use 6-penny common nails for 5/16″, ⅜″, and ½″ panels and 8-penny common nails for ⅝″ and 13/16″ panels. Space the nails not more than 6″ on center at the edges of the panels and not more than 12″ on center elsewhere.

*Fiberboard sheets* are applied vertically or horizontally. The

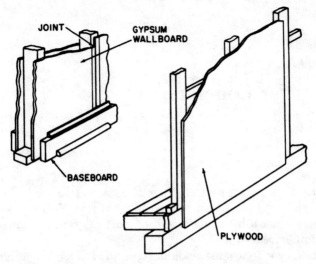

**Fig. 3.** Gypsum and plywood sheathing.

material is nailed on with 2″ galvanized roofing nails. A nail should be started at least ⅜″ away from the edge of a sheet.

*Gypsum-board sheathing* (Fig. 3) is made by casting a gypsum core within a heavy water-resistant fibrous envelope. The long edges of the 4′ by 8′ boards are tongued and grooved. Each board is a full ½″ thick. Its use is mostly with wood siding that can be nailed directly through the sheathing and into the studs. Gypsum sheathing is fireproof, water resistant, and windproof, does not warp or absorb water, and does not require the use of building papers.

*CHAPTER 15*

# Forms for Concrete

*Forms* are a major part of concrete construction work. They must support the plastic concrete until it hardens. Forms protect the concrete, assist in curing it, and support any reinforcing rods or conduit embedded in it.

Forms for concrete must be tight, rigid, and strong. If not tight, loss of mortar may cause a honeycomb effect or loss of water may cause sand streaking. The forms must be braced enough to stay in alignment. Special care is needed in bracing and tying down forms, such as for retainer walls, where the mass of concrete is large at the bottom and tapers toward the top. In this type of construction and in the first pour for walls and columns, the concrete tends to lift the form above its proper elevation.

## CONSTRUCTION MATERIALS

Forms are generally constructed from one of four different materials—earth, metal, wood, or fiber. The carpenter usually constructs wood and fiber forms. (*See* Chap. 5, Lumber.)

## WOOD

*Wood forms* are the most common in building construction; they are economical, easy to handle, easy to produce, and adaptable to many shapes. Form lumber can be reused for roofing, bracing, or similar purposes.

*Lumber* should be straight, strong, and only partially seasoned. Kiln-dried timber tends to swell when soaked with water. Swelling

302

may cause bulging and distortion. If green lumber is used, allowance should be made for shrinkage or it should be kept wet until the concrete is in place. Softwoods (pine, fir, and spruce) are the most economical, are light, easy to work, and are generally available.

*Wood* coming in contact with concrete should be surfaced (smooth) on the side towards the concrete and on both edges. The edges may be square, shiplap, or tongue-and-groove. Tongue-and-groove lumber makes a more watertight joint, which reduces warping.

*Plywood* can be used economically for wall and floor forms if made with waterproof glue and marked for use in concrete forms. Plywood is warp resistant and can be used more often than other lumber. It is made in thicknesses of ¼, ⅜, 9/16, ⅝, and ¾ of an inch and in widths up to 48″. The 8′ lengths are most commonly used. The ⅝″ and ¾″ thicknesses are most economical. Thinner plywood requires solid backing to prevent deflection. The ¼″ thickness is useful for curved surfaces.

## WATERPROOF CARDBOARD

*Waterproof cardboard* and other fiber materials are used for round concrete columns and other preformed shapes. Forms are made by gluing layers of fiber together and molding them to the right shape. The advantage is that fabrication at the job site is not necessary.

## OILING OR WETTING

**Oiling.** Before concrete is placed, forms are treated with oil or other coating material to prevent the concrete from sticking. The oil should penetrate the wood and prevent water absorption. A light-bodied petroleum oil will do. On plywood, shellac is more effective than oil. If forms are to be reused, painting helps preserve the wood. Occasionally, lumber contains enough tannin to cause softening of the concrete surface; if so, the form surface should be treated with whitewash or limewater before the oil is used.

**Wetting.** If form oil is not available, wetting with water may be substituted to prevent sticking, but only in an emergency.

## FORM REMOVAL

Forms should be built so as to permit easy removal without danger to the concrete. When necessary to wedge against the concrete, only wood wedges should be used rather than a pinchbar or other metal tool. Forms should not be jerked off after wedging has been started at one end, to avoid breaking the edges of the concrete. Forms to be reused should be cleaned and oiled immediately. Nails should be removed as forms are stripped.

## COMPONENTS OF WALL FORMS

Figure 1 shows the various parts of a wall form. These parts are described as follows.

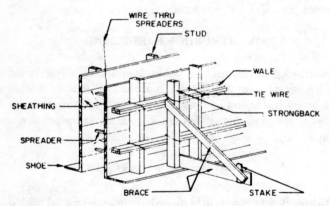

**Fig. 1.** Form for a concrete wall.

**Sheathing.** Sheathing forms the surface of the concrete. It should be smooth, especially if the finished surface is to be exposed. Since concrete is plastic when placed in the form, sheathing should be watertight. Tongue-and-groove lumber or plywood gives a watertight surface.

**Studs.** The weight of the concrete causes the sheathing to bulge if it is not reinforced. Vertical studs make the wall form rigid. They are generally made from 2‾4 or 3‾6 lumber.

**Wales (walers).** Studs also require reinforcing when they extend more than four or five feet. Double wales give this reinforcing; they also tie prefabricated panels together and keep them in a straight line. They run horizontally and are lapped at the corners.

**Braces.** Many types of braces give the forms stability. The most common brace is a horizontal member and a diagonal member nailed to a stake and to a stud or wale. The diagonal member should make a 30 angle with the horizontal member. Additional bracing may be in the form of strongbacks (vertical members) behind the wales or in the corner formed by intersecting wales. Braces are not part of the form design and do not provide additional strength.

**Shoe plates.** The shoe plate is nailed into the foundation or footing and must be carefully placed to maintain the wall dimensions and alignment. Studs are tied into the shoe.

**Spreaders.** Spreaders are cut to the same length as the thickness of the wall and placed between the forms. They are not nailed but held in place by friction because they must be removed before the concrete hardens. A wire is attached to the spreaders to pull them out of the form after the concrete has put enough pressure on the walls to permit easy removal.

**Tie wires.** Tie wires hold the forms secure against the lateral pressure of unhardened concrete. Double strands are always used.

## CONSTRUCTION OF WALL FORMS

*Wall panels* should be about 10′ long so they can be easily handled. Panels are made by nailing the sheathing to the studs. Sheathing is normally 1″ (13/16″ dressed) tongue-and-groove lumber or ¾″ plywood. Figure 2 shows how panels are connected. Figure 3 shows details for the corner of a wall.

Figure 4 shows how to use a *wood strip* as a wedge when *curtain walls* and *columns* are placed at the same time. In removing the forms, the wedge is removed first.

*Ties* keep wall forms together as the concrete is poured—Figs. 5 and 6 show two ways of doing this. Figure 5 shows how to use wire

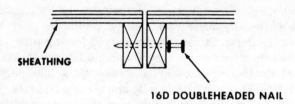

**SHEATHING**

**16D DOUBLEHEADED NAIL**

**Fig. 2.** Method of connecting wall form panels together.

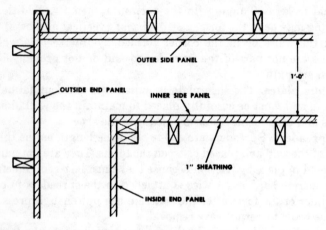

OUTER SIDE PANEL

1'-0'

OUTSIDE END PANEL

INNER SIDE PANEL

1" SHEATHING

INSIDE END PANEL

**Fig. 3.** Details of corner of wall form.

ties, which are for low walls only or when tie rods are not available. The wire should be No. 8 or No. 9 gage soft, black, annealed iron wire, but barbed wire can be used in an emergency. Tie spacing should be the same as the stud spacing, but never more than 3'. Each tie is formed by looping the wire around a wale, bringing it through the form, crossing it inside the form walls, and looping it around the wale on the opposite side. The tie wire is made taut by twisting it with a wedge.

*Spreaders* keep the wall forms together as the concrete is placed. Spreaders must be placed near each tie wire, and they are removed as the forms are filled so they will not become embedded in the concrete. Figure 7 shows how to remove spreaders. A wire fastened to the bottom spreader passes through a hole drilled in

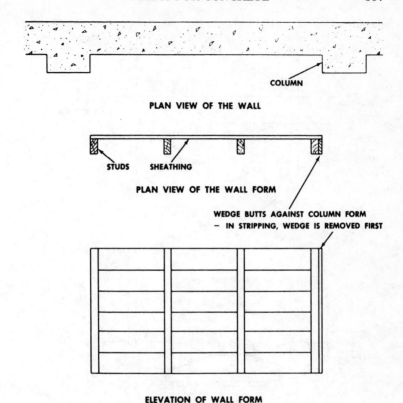

**PLAN VIEW OF THE WALL**

**STUDS**    **SHEATHING**

**PLAN VIEW OF THE WALL FORM**

**WEDGE BUTTS AGAINST COLUMN FORM — IN STRIPPING, WEDGE IS REMOVED FIRST**

**ELEVATION OF WALL FORM**

**Fig. 4.** Wall form for curtain walls.

each spreader above it. Pulling on the wire will remove the spreaders one after another as the concrete level rises in the forms. (*See* Chap. 10, Foundation Construction.)

Figure 6 shows a *tie rod* and *spreader combination*. After the form is removed, each rod is broken off at the notch. If appearance is important, the holes should be filled with a mortar mix.

## FOUNDATION AND FOOTING FORMS

When possible, earth is excavated to form a mold for concrete wall footings. If wood forms are needed, the four sides are built in

308 FORMS FOR CONCRETE

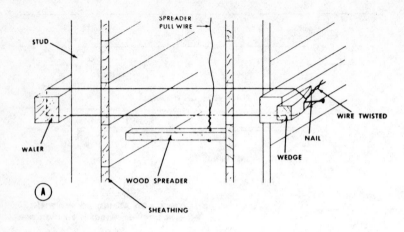

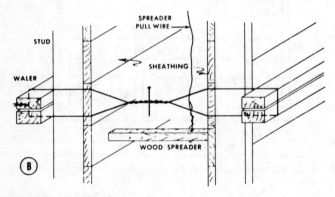

**Fig. 5.** Wire ties for form walls.

panels. Panels for two opposite sides are made at exact footing width (*a*, Fig. 8); the other pair (*b*, Fig. 8) have two end cleats on the inside spaced the length of the footing *plus* twice the sheathing thickness. The 1″ thick sheathing is nailed to vertical cleats spaced on 2′ centers. Two-inch dressed lumber should be used for the cleats.

*Panels* are held in place with form nails until the tie wire is installed; nails should be driven from the outside part way so they can be easily removed.

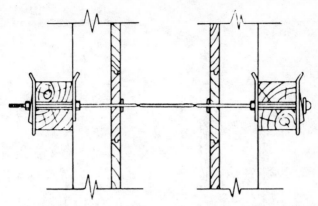

**Fig. 6.** Tie rod and spreader for wall form.

*Tie wires* are wrapped around the center cleats. Wire holes on each side of the cleat should be less than 1″ in diameter to prevent leakage of mortar. All reinforcing bars must be placed before the wire is installed.

For forms 4′ square or larger, *stakes* are driven as shown in Fig. 8. These stakes and 1 × 6 boards nailed across the top prevent spreading. Panels may be higher than the required depth of footing since they can be marked on the inside to show the top of the footing. If the footings are less than 1′ deep and 2′ square, forms can be constructed of 1″ sheathing without cleats as shown in Fig. 9.

## FOOTING AND PIER FORMS

When placing a *footing* and a small *pier* at the same time, the form is built as shown in Fig. 10. Support for the upper form must not interfere with the placement of concrete in the lower form. This is done by nailing 2 × 4 or 4 × 4 pieces to the lower form as shown. The top form is then nailed to these pieces.

## WALL FOOTINGS

Figures 11 and 12 show how to construct and brace forms for

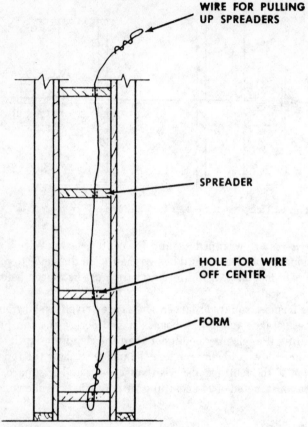

**Fig. 7.** Removing wood spreaders.

wall footings. The sides are 2″ lumber held in place by stakes and apart by spreaders. The short brace shown at each stake holds the form in line.

## COLUMN FORMS

Figure 13 shows elements of column forms.

**Components.** *Sheathing* runs vertically to save the number of sawcuts; *corner joints* are firmly nailed to insure watertightness.

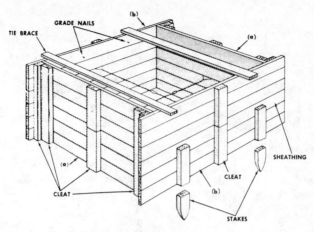

**Fig. 8.** Typical large footing form.

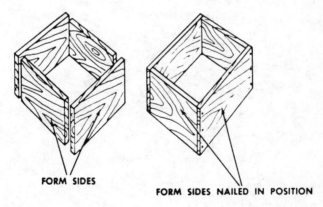

**Fig. 9.** Small footing forms.

*Batten* are narrow strips of boards (cleats) placed directly over the joints to fasten the several pieces of vertical sheathing together.

**Construction.** Figure 13 shows a column and footing form. The column form is erected after the steel reinforcing is assembled

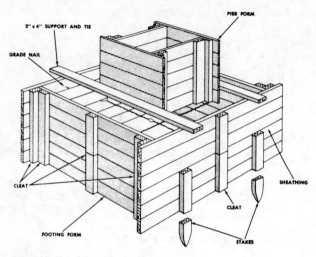

**Fig. 10.** Footing and pier form.

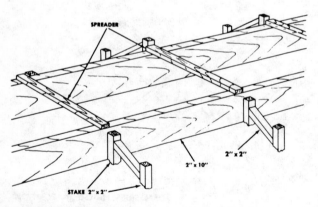

**Fig. 11.** Wall footing form.

and tied to dowels in the footing. The form should have a cleanout hole in the bottom to help remove debris.

## BEAM AND GIRDER FORMS

Figure 14 shows a *beam form*. The type of construction depends

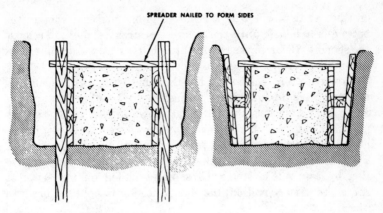

SPREADER NAILED TO FORM SIDES

**Fig. 12.** Bracing the wall footing form.

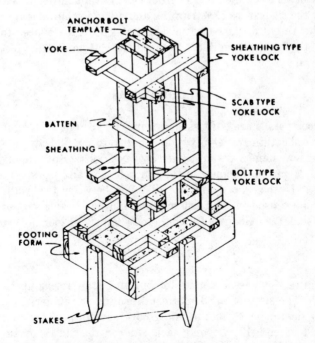

ANCHOR BOLT TEMPLATE

YOKE

SHEATHING TYPE YOKE LOCK

SCAB TYPE YOKE LOCK

BATTEN

SHEATHING

BOLT TYPE YOKE LOCK

FOOTING FORM

STAKES

**Fig. 13.** Form for a concrete column.

on whether the form is to be removed in one piece or whether the
bottom is to be left until the concrete is strong enough to remove
the shoring. Beam forms receive little bursting pressure but must
be shored at close intervals to prevent sagging.

**Construction.** The bottom has the same width as the beam and
is in one piece the full width. Form sides are 1″ tongue-and-groove
material and lap over the bottom as shown in Fig. 14. The sheath
is nailed to 2 × 4 struts placed on 3′ centers. A 1 × 4 piece is
nailed along the struts to support the joists for the floor panel.
The sides of the form are not nailed to the bottom but held in position by continuous strips. Crosspieces nailed on top serve as
spreaders. After erection, the slab-panel joints hold the beam in
place.

**Assembly.** Beam and girder assembly is shown in Fig. 14. The
beam bottom butts up tightly against the side of the girder and
rests on a 2 × 4 nailed to the girder side. Details in the illustration
show the clearances for stripping and allow for movement caused
by the weight of the concrete. The 4 × 4 posts are spaced to support the concrete and are wedged at bottom or top for easy
removal.

## FLOOR FORMS

Floor panels are built as shown in Fig. 16. The 1″ tongue-and-
groove sheathing or ¾″ plywood is nailed to 1 × 4 cleats on 3′ centers. These panels are supported by 2 × 6 joists. Spacing of joists
depends on the thickness of the concrete slab and the span of the
beams. If the slab spans the distance between two walls, the
panels are used in the same manner as when beams support the
floor slab. (*See* Chap. 5, Lumber, and Chap. 25, Floor Coverings.)

## STAIR FORMS

Figure 17 shows a method for building stair forms up to 3′ in
width. The sloping wood platform forming the underside of the
steps should be 1″ tongue-and-groove sheathing. This platform
should extend 12″ beyond each side of the stairs to support
stringer bracing blocks. The back of the panel is shored with 4 × 4

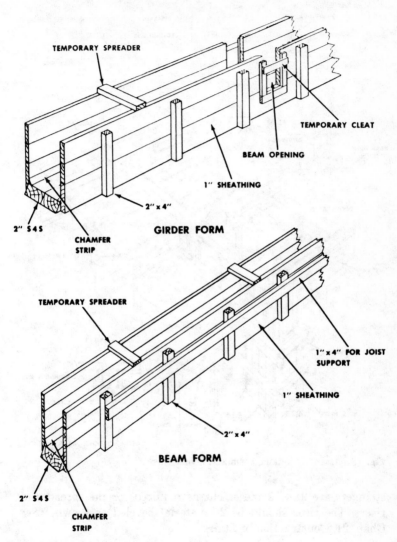

**Fig. 14.** Girder and beam forms.

pieces as shown. The 2 × 6 cleats nailed to the shoring should rest on wedges to make adjustment and post removal easy. The side

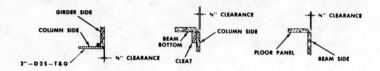

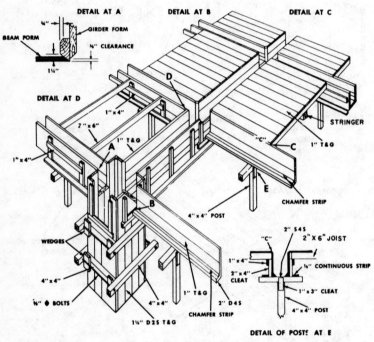

**Fig. 15.** Assembly details, beam and floor forms.

stringers are 2 × 12 pieces cut as required for the thread and risers. The riser should be 2″ material beveled as shown. (*See* Chap. 21, Construction of Stairs.)

## SAFETY PRECAUTIONS

The following rules apply to form construction and removal. During the construction phase:

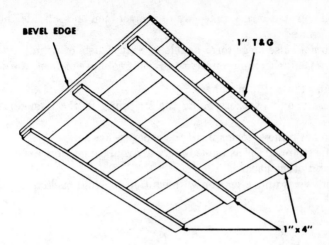

**Fig. 16.** Form for floor slab.

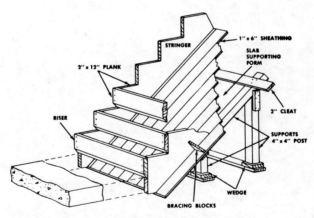

**Fig. 17.** Stairway form.

Consider protruding nails as the principal source of accidents on form work.

Inspect tools frequently.

Place mud sills under shoring that rests on the ground.

On elevated forms, take care to protect men on scaffolds and on the ground.

Do not raise large form panels in heavy gusts of wind.

Brace all shoring securely to prevent collapse of form work.

During the stripping phase:

Permit only workers doing the stripping in the immediate area.

Do not remove forms until the concrete has set.

Pile stripped forms immediately to avoid congestion, exposed nails, and other hazards.

Cut wires under tension with caution to avoid backlash.

## CHAPTER 16

# Roofing

*Ceiling joists* form the framework of the ceiling of the room. They are usually lighter than floor joists, but large enough and strong enough to resist bending and buckling, and to remain rigid. Ceiling joists are generally installed 16″ apart on centers, starting at one side of the building and continuing across. Extra joists, if needed, may be placed without affecting the spacing of the prime joists. The selection of the ceiling joists and their installation are much the same as those of floor joists. They are placed parallel with the rafters and extend in a continuous line across the structure. The ceiling joists are nailed to both the plates and the rafters, if possible, and lapped and spiked over bearing partitions. Joists that lie beside rafters on a plate are cut at the same slope as the pitch of the rafter, flush with the top of the rafter. They are installed crown or camber up. (*See* Fig. 1. *Also see* Chap. 13, Framing Layout and Erection, and Chap. 17, Reroofing.)

### ROOFS

The primary object of a *roof* in any climate is to keep out the rain and the cold. The roof must be sloped so as to shed water. Where heavy snows cover the roofs for long periods of time, roofs must be constructed more rigidly to bear the extra weight. They must also be strong enough to withstand high winds.

### TYPES OF ROOF CONSTRUCTION

The most commonly used types of roof construction include the gable, the lean-to or shed, the hip, and the gable and valley.

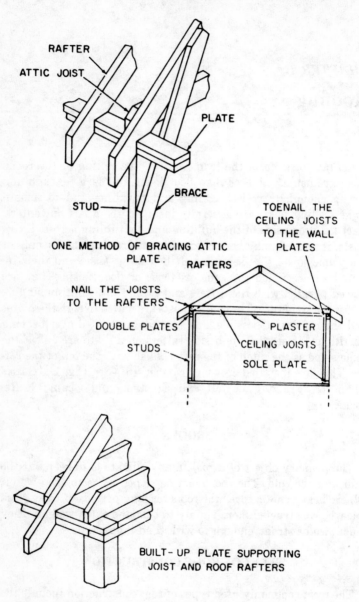

**Fig. 1.** Ceiling joists.

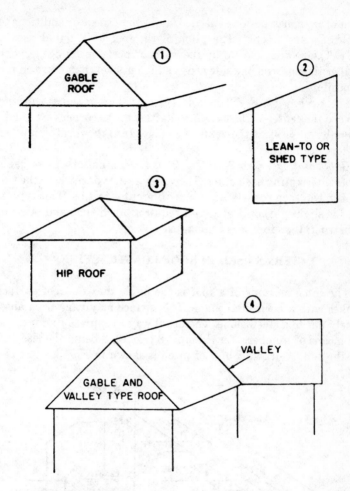

**Fig. 2.** Types of roofs.

The *gable roof* (*1*, Fig. 2) has two roof slopes meeting at the center, or ridge, to form a gable. This form of roof is the one most commonly used, since it is simple in design, economical to construct, and may be used on any type structure.

The *lean-to* or *shed roof* (*2*, Fig. 2) is a near flat roof and is used where large buildings are framed under one roof, where hasty or temporary construction is needed, and where sheds or additions to buildings are erected. The pitch of the roof is in one direction only. The roof is held up by the walls or posts on four sides; one wall or the posts on one side are at a higher level than those on the opposite side.

The *hip roof* (*3*, Fig. 2) consists of four sides or slopes running toward the center of the building. Rafters at the corners extend diagonally to meet at the center or ridge. Into these rafters, other rafters are framed.

*Gable and valley roof* (*4*, Fig. 2) is a combination of two gable roofs intersecting each other. The valley is that part where the two roofs meet, each roof slanting in a different direction. This type of roof is slightly complicated and requires much time and labor to construct; therefore it is seldom used.

## TERMS USED IN ROOF CONSTRUCTION

The *pitch* or *slope* of a roof is the angle that the roof surface makes with a horizontal plane. The surface may vary from absolutely flat to a steep slope. The usual way to express roof pitch is by means of numbers; for example 8 and 12, 8 being the rise and 12 the run. A drawing of roof pitch is shown in Fig. 3.

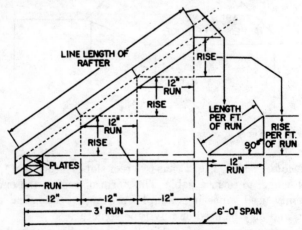

**Fig. 3.** Roof pitch.

The *span* (*1*, Fig. 4) of any roof is the shortest distance between the two opposite rafter seats. Stated another way, it is the measurement between the outside plates, measured at right angles to the direction of the ridge of the building.

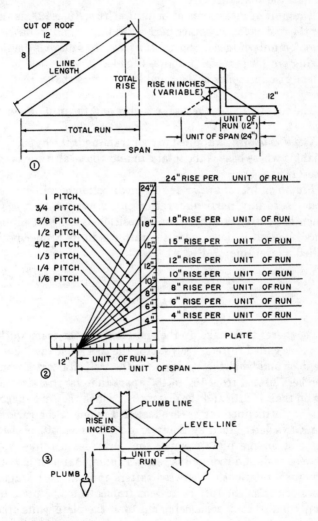

**Fig. 4.** Roof terms.

The *total rise* (*1*, Fig. 4) is the vertical distance from the plate to the top of the ridge.

The term *total run* (*1*, Fig. 4) always refers to the level distance over which any rafter passes. For the ordinary rafter, this would be half the span distance.

The unit of measurement or unit of run, 1' or 12", is the same for the roof as for any other part of the building. By the use of this common unit of measurement, the framing square is employed in laying out large roofs (*1* and *2*, Fig. 4).

The rise in inches is the number of inches that a roof rises for every foot of run.

The cut of a roof is the rise in inches and the unit of run (12", *2*, Fig. 4).

The *line length* as applied to roof framing is the hypotenuse of a triangle whose base is the total run and whose altitude is the total rise (*1*, Fig. 4).

*Plumb* and *level lines* refer to the direction of a line on a rafter and not to any particular rafter cut. Any line that is vertical when the rafter is in its proper position is called a plumb line. Any line that is level when the rafter is in its proper position is called a level line (*3*, Fig. 4).

## RAFTERS

The pieces that make up the main body of the framework of all roofs are called *rafters*. They do for the roof what the joists do for the floor and what the studs do for the wall. Rafters are inclined members spaced from 16" to 48" apart that vary in size, depending on their length and the distance at which they are spaced. The tops of the inclined rafters are fastened in one of the various common ways determined by the type of roof. The bottoms of the rafters rest on the plate member that provides a connecting link between wall and roof and is really a functional part of both. The structural relationship between rafters and wall is the same in all types of roofs. The rafters are not framed into the plate but are simply nailed to it, some being cut to fit the plate while others, in hasty construction, are merely laid on top of the plate and nailed in place. Rafters may extend a short distance beyond the wall to form the eaves and protect the sides of the building.

## TERMS USED IN CONNECTION WITH RAFTERS

Since rafters, with ridgeboards and plates, are the principal members of roof framing, it is important to understand the following terms that apply to them.

The *common rafters* (*1*, Fig. 5) extend from plate to ridgeboard, at right angles to both.

*Hip rafters* (*2*, Fig. 5) extend diagonally from the outside corners formed by perpendicular plates to the ridgeboard.

*Valley rafters* (*3*, Fig. 5) extend from the plates to the ridgeboard along the lines where two roofs intersect.

*Jack rafters* never extend the full distance from plate to ridgeboard. Jack rafters are subdivided into the hip jacks (*4*, Fig. 5), the lower ends of which rest on the plate and the upper ends against the hip rafter; valley jacks (*5*, Fig. 5), the lower ends of which rest against the valley rafters and the upper ends against the ridgeboard; and cripple jacks (*6*, Fig. 5), which are nailed between hip and valley rafters.

The *top* or *plumb cut* is the cut made at the end of the rafter to be placed against the ridgeboard or, if the ridgeboard is omitted, against the opposite rafters.

The *seat, bottom,* or *heel cut* is the cut made at the end of the rafter that is to rest on the plate.

The *side* or *cheek cut* is a bevel cut on the side of a rafter to fit it against another frame member.

*Rafter length* is the shortest distance between the outer edge of the plate and the center of the ridge line.

The *eave* or *tail* is the portion of the rafter extending beyond the outer edge of the plate.

The *measure line* is an imaginary reference line laid out down the middle of the face of a rafter. If a portion of a roof is represented by a right triangle (Fig. 6), the measure line will correspond to the hypotenuse, the rise to the leg, and the run to the base.

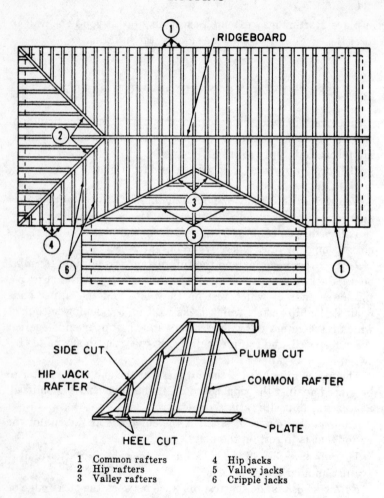

**Fig. 5.** Rafter terms.

| | | | |
|---|---|---|---|
| 1 | Common rafters | 4 | Hip jacks |
| 2 | Hip rafters | 5 | Valley jacks |
| 3 | Valley rafters | 6 | Cripple jacks |

## RAFTER LAYOUT

Rafters must be laid out and cut with slope, length, and overhang exactly right so that they will fit when placed in the position they are to occupy in the finished roof.

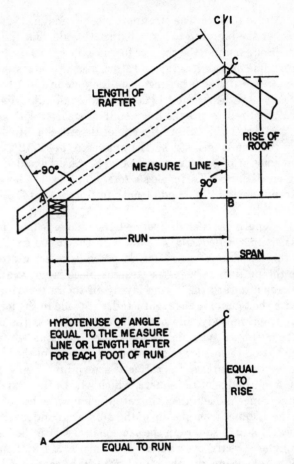

**Fig. 6.** Measure line.

The worker first determines the length of the rafter and the length of the piece of lumber from which the rafter may be cut. If he is working from a set of plans that include a roof plan, the rafter lengths and the width of the building may be obtained from this plan. If no plans are available, the width of the building must be measured with a tape.

To determine the rafter length, first find half of the distance between the outside plates. This distance is the horizontal distance that the rafter will cover. The amount of rise per foot has yet to be considered. If the building to be roofed is 20′ wide, half the span will be 10′. For example, the rise per foot is to be 8″. To determine the approximate overall length of a rafter, measure on a steel carpenter square the distance between 8 on the tongue and 12 on the blade, because 8 is the rise and 12 is the unit of run. This distance is 14 5/12″, and represents the line length of a rafter with a total run of 1′ and a rise of 8″. Since the run of the rafter is 10′, multiply 10 by the line length for 1′. The answer is 144 2/12″, or 12′ 1/6″. The amount of overhang, normally 1′, must be added if an overhang is to be used. This makes a total of 13′ for the length of the rafter, but since 13′ is an odd length for lumber, a 14′ piece of lumber is used.

After the length has been determined, the lumber is laid on sawhorses, sometimes called *saw benches,* with the crown or bow (if any) as the top side of the rafter. If possible, select a straight piece for the pattern rafter. If a straight piece is not available, have the crown toward the person laying off the rafter. Hold the square with the tongue in the right hand, the blade in the left, the heel away from the body, and place the square as near the upper end of the rafter as possible. In this case, the figure 8 on the tongue and 12 on the blade are placed along the edge of the lumber that is to be the top edge of the rafter as shown in *1,* Fig. 7. Mark along the tongue edge of the square, which will be the plumb cut at the ridge. Since the length of the rafter is known to be 12′ 1/6″, measure the distance from the top of the plumb cut and mark it on the lumber. Hold the square in the same manner with the 8 mark on the tongue directly over the 12′ 1/6″ mark. Mark along the tongue of the square to give the plumb cut for the seat (*2,* Fig. 7). Next measure off, perpendicular to this mark, the length of overhang along the lumber and make a plumb-cut mark in the same manner, keeping the square on the same edge of the timber (*3,* Fig. 6). This will be the tail cut of the rafter; often the tail cut is made square across the lumber.

The level cut or width of the seat is the width of the plate, measured perpendicular to the plumb cut, as shown in *4,* Fig. 7. Using the try square, square lines down on the sides from all level and plumb-cut lines. Now the rafter is ready to be cut.

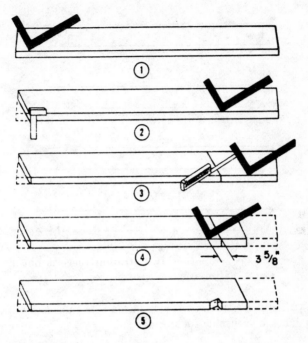

**Fig. 7.** Rafter layout—scale or measurement method.

If a building is 20′ 8″ wide, the run of the rafter would be 10′ 4″, or half the span. Instead of using the above method, the rafter length may be determined by *stepping it off* by successive steps with the square as shown in Fig. 8. Stake the same number of steps as there are feet in the run, which leaves four inches over a foot. These four inches are taken care of in the same manner as the full foot run; that is, with the square at the last step position, make a mark on the rafters at the 4″ mark on the blade, then move the square along the rafter until the tongue rests at the 4″ mark. With the square held for the same cut as before, make a mark along the tongue. This is the line length of the rafter. The seat cut and hangover are made as described above. When laying off rafters by any method, be sure to recheck the work carefully. When two rafters have been cut, it is best to put them in place to see if

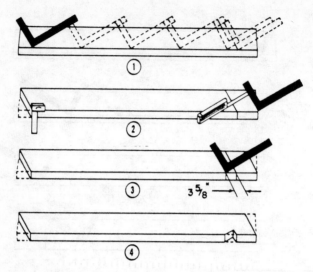

**Fig. 8.** Rafter layout—step-off method.

they fit. Minor adjustments may be made at this time without serious damage or waste of material.

## TABLE METHOD, USING RAFTER TABLE ON FRAMING SQUARE

The framing square may have one or two types of rafter tables on the blade. One type gives both the line length of any pitch or rafter per foot of run and the line length of any hip or valley rafter per foot of run. The difference in length of the jack rafter spaced 16″ or 24″ (on center) is also shown in the table. Where the jack rafter, hip, or valley rafter needs side cuts, the cut is given in the table. The other type of table gives the actual length of rafter for a given pitch and span.

The first type of table (Fig. 9) appears on the face of the blade. It is used to determine the length of the common, valley, hip, and jack rafters, and the angles at which they must be cut to fit at the ridge and plate. To use the table, the carpenter first must know

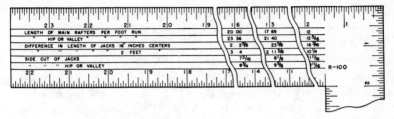

**Fig. 9.** Rafter table method (type 1).

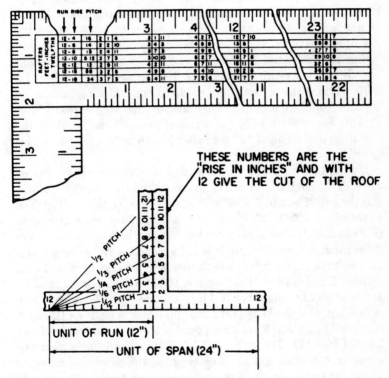

THESE NUMBERS ARE THE "RISE IN INCHES" AND WITH 12 GIVE THE CUT OF THE ROOF

UNIT OF RUN (12")

UNIT OF SPAN (24")

**Fig. 9a.** Rafter table method (type 2).

what each figure represents. The row of figures in the first line represents the length of common rafters per foot of run, as the title indicates at the left-hand end of the blade. Each set of figures under each inch division mark represents the length of rafter per foot of run with a rise corresponding to the number of inches over the number. For example, under the 16″ mark appears the number 20.00″. This number equals the length of a rafter with a run of 12″ and a rise of 16″. Under the 13″ mark appears the number 17.69″, which is the rafter length for a 12″ run and a 13″ rise. The other five lines of figures in the table will not be discussed as they are seldom used in the theater of operations.

These three columns of figures show that a rafter with a run of 12 and a rise of 4 has 1/6 pitch, 12 and 6 has ¼ pitch, and 12 and 12 has ½ pitch. To use this scale for a roof with 1/6 pitch (or the rise of one-sixth the width of the building) and a run of 12′, find 1/6 in the table, and follow the same line of figures to the right until directly beneath the figure 12. Here appear the numbers 12, 7, 10, which is the rafter length required and which represents 12′ 7″, and 10/12 of an inch. They are written as follows: 12′, 7-10/12″. For a pitch of ½ (or a rise of one-half the width of the building) and a run of 12′, the rafter length is 16, 11, 6, or 16′, 11-6/12″.

If the run is over 23′, the table is used as follows: For a run of 27′, find the length for a run of 23′, then, find the length for 4′ and add the two. The run for 23′ with a pitch of ¼ is 25′, 8 5/12″. For 4′, the run is 4′, 5 8/12′. When the run is in inches, the rafter table reads inches and twelfths instead of feet and inches. For example, if the pitch is ½ and the run is is 12′, 4″, add the rafter length of a 12′ run to that of a rafter length with a 4″ run, as follows: For a run of 12′ and ½ pitch, the length is 16′, 11 6/12″. For a run of 4″ and ½ pitch, the length is 5, 7, 11. In this case the 5 is inches, the 7 is twelfths, and the 11 is 11/12 of 1/12, which is nearly 1/12. Add it to the 7 to make it 8, making a total of 5 8/12″, then add the two lengths together. This sum is 17′, 5 2/12″. The lengths that are given in the table are the line lengths; the overhang must be added. After the length of the rafter has been found, the rafter is laid out as explained previously.

When the roof has an overhang, the rafter is usually cut square to save time. When the roof has no overhang, the rafter cut is plumb, but no notch is cut in the rafter for a seat. The level cut is made long enough to extend across the plate and the wall sheathing. This type of rafter saves material, although little protection is given to the side wall.

## BIRD'S MOUTH

A rafter with a projection has a notch in it called a *bird's mouth*, as shown in Fig. 10. The plumb cut of the bird's mouth, which bears against the side of the rafter plate, is called the *heel cut*. The level cut, which bears on the top of the rafter plate, is called the *seat cut*.

The size of the bird's mouth is usually stated in terms of the depth of the heel cut rather than in terms of the width of the seat cut. You lay out the bird's mouth in about the same way you lay out the seat on a rafter without a projection. Measure off the depth of the heel on the heel plumb line, set the square as shown in Fig. 11, and draw the seat line along the blade. For the roof surface, *all rafters* should be exact; therefore, the amount above the seat cut, rather than the bottom edge of the rafters, is the most important measurement. Suppose that on a hip roof, or an intersecting roof, the hips or valley rafters are 2 × 6 and the common rafters 2 × 4. The amount above the seat cut should be such as to adequately support the overhang of the roof, plus personnel working on the roof. The width of the seat cut is important as a bearing surface. The maximum width of the common rafter should not exceed the width of the plate.

## HIP RAFTER LAYOUT

Most hip roofs are *equal-pitch* hip roofs, in which the angle of slope on the roof end or ends is the same as the angle of slope on the sides. Unequal-pitch hip roofs do exist, but they are quite rare and they require special layout methods. The *unit length rafter table* on the framing square applies only to equal-pitch hip roofs.

In the following discussion of hip roof framing it will be assumed that in every case the roof is an equal-pitch hip roof.

The length of a hip rafter, like the length of a common rafter, is calculated on the basis of bridge measure times the unit of run.

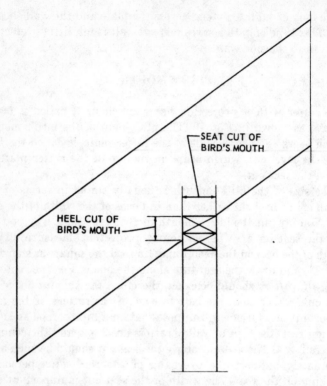

**Fig. 10.** Bird's mouth on a rafter with projection.

Any of the methods previously described for a common rafter may be used. Some of the basic data for a hip rafter are different.

Figure 12 shows part of a *roof framing diagram* for an *equal-pitch hip roof*. A roof framing diagram may be included among the working drawings. If it is not, you should lay one out for yourself. Lay the building lines out to scale first. You can find the span and the length of the building on the working drawings. Then draw a horizontal line along the center of the span.

In an equal-pitch hip roof framing diagram the lines that indicate the hip rafters (*FA, GA, IB,* and *KB* in Fig. 12) form 45° angles with the building lines. Draw these lines in at 45°, as shown in the illustration. The points where they meet the center

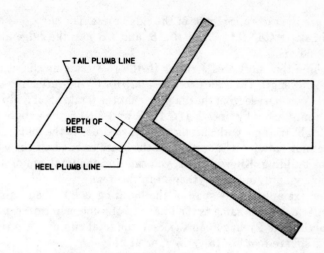

**Fig. 11.** Laying out a bird's mouth.

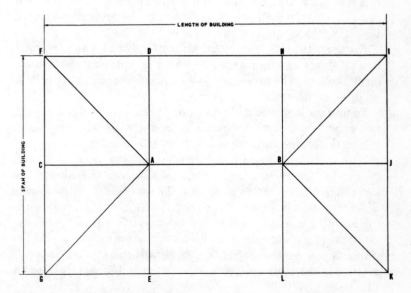

**Fig. 12.** Equal pitch hip roof framing diagram.

line are the *theoretical* ends of the ridge piece. The ridge-end common rafters *CA*, *DA*, *EA*, *HB*, *JB*, and *LB* join the ridge at the same points.

A line that indicates a rafter in the roof framing diagram is equal in length (to scale) to the *total run* of the rafter it represents. You can see from the diagram that the total run of a hip rafter (represented by lines *FA*, *GA*, *IB*, and *KB*) is the hypotenuse of a right triangle with shorter sides each equal to the total run of a common rafter—it is one-half of the span, or one-half the width of the building. Knowing this, you can find the total run of a hip rafter by applying the Pythagorean theorem.

For example, if the span of the building is 30', then half the span, which is the same as the total run of a common rafter, is 15'. Applying the Pythagorean theorem, the total run of a hip rafter is the square foot of $(15^2 + 15^2)$, or 21.21'.

What is the total rise? Since a hip rafter joins the ridge at the same height as a common rafter, the total rise for a hip rafter is the same as the total rise for a common rafter. Let us suppose that this roof has a unit run of 12 and a unit rise of 8. Since the total run of a common rafter is the value of x in the proportional equation 12:8 :: 15:x, the total run is 10'.

Knowing the total run of the hip rafter (21.21') and the total rise (10'), you can figure the line length by applying the Pythagorean theorem. The line length is the square root of $(21.21^2 + 10^2)$, or 23.44' or about 23' 5¼".

To find the length of a hip rafter on the basis of bridge measure, you must first determine the bridge measure. As with a common rafter, the bridge measure of a hip rafter is the length of the hypotenuse of a triangle with shorter sides equal to the unit run and unit rise of the rafter. The unit rise of a hip rafter is always the same as that of a common rafter, but the *unit run of a hip rafter is different.*

The unit run of a hip rafter in an equal-pitch hip roof is the hypotenuse of a right triangle with shorter sides each equal to the unit run of a common rafter. Since the unit run of a common rafter is 12, the unit run of a hip rafter is the sqaure root of $(12^2 + 12^2)$, or 16.97.

If the unit run of the hip rafter is 16.97 and the unit rise (in this particular case) is 8, the unit length of the hip rafter must be the square root of $(16.97^2 + 8^2)$, or 18.76. This means that for every 16.07 units of run the rafter has 18.76 units of length. Since the total run of the rafter is 21.21', the length of the rafter must be the value of x in the proportional equation 16.97:18.76 :: 21.21:x, or 23.44'.

Like the unit length of a common rafter, the bridge measure of a hip rafter may be obtained from the unit length rafter table on the framing square. If you turn back to Fig. 9, you will see that the second line in the table is headed "Length Hip Or Valley Per Foot Run." This means *per foot run of a common rafter in the same roof.* Actually, the unit length given in the tables is the unit length for every 16.97 units of run *of the hip rafter itself.* If you run across to the unit length given under 8, you will find the same figure, 18.76 units, that you calculated above.

An easy way to calculate the length of an equal-pitch hip roof rafter is to multiply the bridge measure by the number of feet in the total run of a common rafter, which is the same as the number of feet in half of the span of the building. Half of the span of the building in this case in 15'. The length of the hip rafter is therefore $18.76 \times 15$, or 281.40"; 281.40 divided by 12 equals 23.45'. Note that when you use this method you get a result in inches, which you must convert to feet. The slight difference of 0.01' between this result and the one previously obtained amounts to less than ⅛", and may be ignored.

You step off the length of an equal-pitch hip roof rafter just as you do the length of a common rafter, except for the fact that you set the square to a unit of run of 16.97" instead of to a unit of run of 12". Since 16.97" is the same as 16" and 15.52 sixteenths of an inch, setting the square to a unit of run of 17" is close enough for most practical purposes. Bear in mind that for any plumb-cut line on an equal-pitch hip roof rafter you set the square to the unit rise of a common rafter and to a unit run of 17.

You step off the same number of times as there are feet in the total run of a common rafter in the same roof; only the size of each step is different. For every 12" step in a common rafter a hip rafter has a 17" step. In the roof on which we are working, the total run of a common rafter is exactly 15'. This means that you would

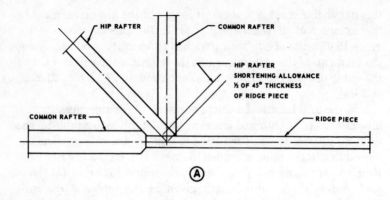

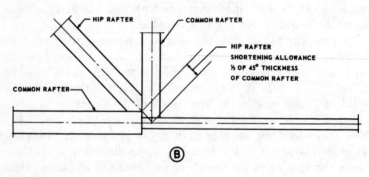

**Fig. 13.** Hip rafter shortening allowance.

step off the hip-rafter cut (17″ and 8″) exactly 15 times.

Suppose that there was an *odd unit* in the common rafter total run. Assume, for example, that the total run of a common rafter is 15′ 10½″. How would you make the odd fraction of a step on the hip rafter?

You remember that the unit run of a hip rafter is the hypotenuse of a right triangle with other sides each equal to the unit run of a common rafter. This being the case, the run of the odd unit on the hip rafter must be the hypotenuse of a right triangle with other sides each equal to the odd unit of run of the common rafter, which in this case is 10½″. You can figure this by the Pythagorean theorem (square root of $10.5^2 + 10.5^2$), or you can set the square on a true edge to 10½″ on the tongue and 10½″ on the blade and measure the distance between the marks. It comes to 14.84 inches, which rounded off to the nearest 1/16″ equals 14 13/16″.

To lay off the odd unit, set the tongue of the framing square to the plumb line for the last full step made and measure off 14-13/16″ along the blade. Place the tongue of the square at the mark, set the square to the hip rafter plumb cut of 8″ on the tongue and 17″ on the blade, and draw the line length cut line.

## HIP RAFTER SHORTENING ALLOWANCE

As is the case with a common rafter, the line length of a hip rafter does not take into account the thickness of the ridge piece. The size of the ridge-end shortening allowance for a hip rafter depends upon the manner in which the ridge end of the hip rafter is joined to the other structural members. As shown in Fig. 13, the ridge end of the hip rafter may be framed against the ridge piece ($A$, Fig. 13) or against the ridge-end common rafters ($B$, Fig. 13). If the hip rafter is framed against the ridge piece, the shortening allowance is half of the 45° thickness of a common rafter. To lay off the shortening allowance set the tongue of the framing square to the line length ridge-cut line, measure off the shortening allowance along the blade, set the square at the mark to the cut of the rafter (8″ and 17″), and draw the actual ridge plumb-cut line.

## HIP RAFTER PROJECTION

A *hip rafter projection*, like a common rafter, is figured as a separate problem. The run of a hip rafter projection, however, is not the same as the run of a common rafter projection in the same roof. Figure 14 shows you why. The run of the hip rafter projection, as you can see, is the hypotenuse of a right triangle with shorter sides each equal to the run of a common rafter overhang. If the common rafter projection is 18″, the run of the hip rafter would be the square root of ($18^2 + 18^2$), or 25.45″. Since the rafter rises 8 units for every 17 units of run, the total rise of the projection is the value of x in the proportional equation 17:8 ::

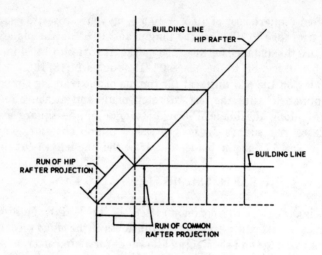

**Fig. 14.** Run of hip rafter projection.

25.45:x, or 11.9″. If the total run is 25.45″ and the total rise 11.9″, the length of the projection is the square root of $(25.45^2 + 11.9^2)$, or about 28″.

## HIP RAFTER SIDE CUTS

Since a common rafter runs at 90° to the ridge, the ridge end of a common rafter is cut square, or at 90° to the lengthwise line of the rafter. A hip rafter, however, joins the ridge, or the ridge ends of the common rafters, at an angle, and the ridge end of a hip rafter must therefore be cut to a corresponding angle, called a *side cut*. The angle of the side cut is more acute for a high unit rise than it is for a low one.

The angle of the side cut is laid out as shown in Fig. 15. Place the tongue of the framing square along the ridge-cut line as shown in the illustration, and measure off half the thickness of the hip rafter along the blade. Shift the tongue to the mark, set the square to the cut of the rafter (17″ and 8″), and draw the plumb line marked *A* in the illustration. Then turn the rafter edge-up, draw an edge-center line, and draw in the angle of the side cut as indicated in the lower view of Fig. 15. For a hip rafter that is to be

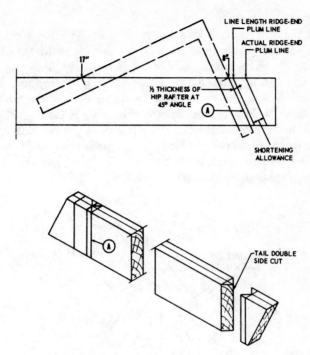

**Fig. 15.** Laying out hip rafter side cut.

framed against the ridge there will be only a single side cut, as indicated by the dotted line; for one that is to be framed against the ridge ends of the common rafters there will be a double side cut, as shown in Fig. 15. The tail of the rafter must have a double side cut at the same angle, but in the reverse direction.

The angle of the side cut on a hip rafter may also be laid out by referring to the unit length rafter table on the framing square. If you turn back to Fig. 9, you will see that the bottom line in the table is headed "Side Cut Hip Or Valley Use." If you follow this line over to the column headed by the figure 8 (for a unit rise of 8), you will find the figure 10⅞. If you place the framing square face-up on the rafter edge, with the tongue on the ridge-end cut line, and set the square to a cut of 10⅞" on the blade and 12" on the tongue, you can draw the correct side-cut angle along the tongue.

If the bird's mouth on a hip rafter had the same depth as the bird's mouth on a common rafter, the edges of the hip rafter would extend above the upper ends of the jack rafters as shown in Fig. 16. This can be corrected by either *backing* or *dropping* the hip rafter. Backing means to bevel the upper edge of the hip rafter. As shown in Fig. 16, the amount of backing is taken at the right angle to the roof surface, or the top edge of the hip rafter. Dropping means to deepen the bird's mouth so as to bring the top edge of the hip rafter down to the upper ends of the jacks. The amount of drop is taken on the heel plumb line.

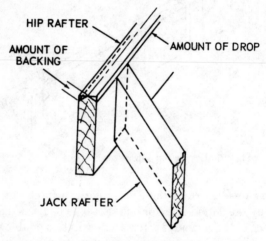

**Fig. 16.**  Backing or dropping a hip rafter.

The amount of backing or drop required is calculated as shown in Fig. 17. Set the framing square to the cut of the rafter (8″ and 17″) on the upper edge, and measure off half the thickness of the rafter from the edge along the blade. A line drawn through this mark parallel to the edge will indicate the bevel angle, as shown in the illustration, if the rafter is to be backed. The perpendicular distance between the line and the edge of the rafter will be the amount of drop—meaning the amount that the depth of the hip

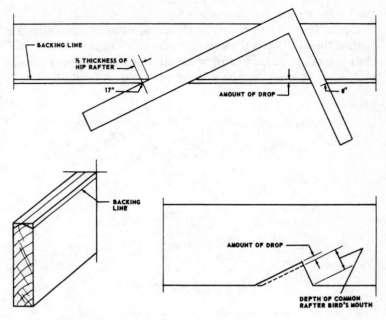

**Fig. 17.** Determining required amount of backing or drop.

rafter bird's mouth should exceed the depth of the common rafter bird's mouth.

## VALLEY RAFTER LAYOUT

A valley rafter follows the line of intersection between a main roof surface and a gable-roof addition or a gable-roof dormer surface. Most roofs that contain valley rafters are *equal-pitch* roofs, in which the pitch of the addition or dormer roof is the same as the pitch of the main roof. There are *unequal-pitch* valley-rafter roofs, but they are quite rare, and they require special framing methods. In the discussion of valley rafter layout it will be assumed that the roof is in every case an equal pitch roof, in which the unit of run and unit of rise of an addition or dormer common rafter is the same as the unit of run and unit of rise of a main-roof common rafter. In an equal-pitch roof the valley rafters always run at 45° to the building lines and the ridge pieces.

Figure 18 shows an *equal-span* framing situation, in which the span of the addition is the same as the span of the main roof. Since the pitch of the addition roof is the same as the pitch of the main roof, equal spans bring the ridge pieces to equal heights.

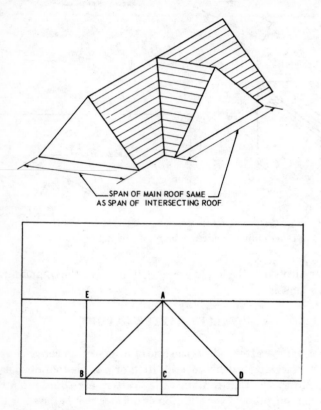

SPAN OF MAIN ROOF SAME
AS SPAN OF INTERSECTING ROOF

**Fig. 18.** Equal span main roof and intersection roof.

If you look at the roof-framing diagram in the figure, you will see that the total run of a valley rafter (indicated by $AB$ and $AD$ in the diagram) is the hypotenuse of a right triangle with shorter sides equal to the total run of a common rafter in the main roof.

The unit run of a valley rafter is therefore 16.97, the same as the unit run for a hip rafter. It follows that figuring the length of an equal-span valley rafter is the same as figuring the length of an equal-pitch hip roof hip rafter.

A valley rafter, however, does not require backing or dropping. The projection, if any, is figured just as it is for a hip rafter. Side cuts are laid out as they are for a hip rafter. The valley-rafter tail has a double side cut, like the hip-rafter tail, but in the reverse direction, since the tail cut on a valley rafter must form an inside rather than an outside corner. As indicated in Fig. 19, the ridge-end shortening allowance in this framing situation amounts to half of the 45° thickness of the ridge.

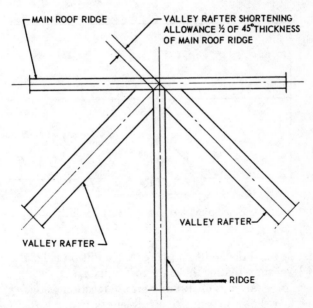

**Fig. 19.** Ridge-end shortening allowance for equal span intersection valley rafter.

Figure 20 shows a framing situation in which the span of the addition is shorter than the span of the main roof. Since the pitch of the addition roof is the same as the pitch of the main roof, the

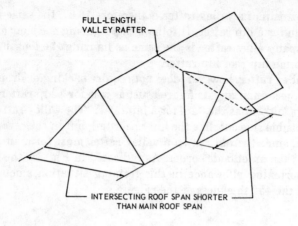

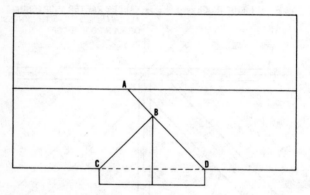

**Fig. 20.** Equal-pitch but unequal span framing situation.

shorter span of the addition brings the addition ridge down to a lower level than that of the main roof ridge.

There are two ways of framing an intersection of this type. By the method shown in Fig. 20, a full-length valley rafter (*AD* in the figure) is framed between the rafter plate and the ridge piece, and a shorter valley rafter (*CB* in the figure) is then framed to the longer one. If you study the framing diagram you will see that the total run of the longer valley rafter is the hypotenuse of a right triangle with shorter sides each equal to the total run of a common rafter *in the main roof*. The total run of the shorter valley rafter, on the other hand, is the hypotenuse of a right triangle with shorter sides each equal to the total run of a common rafter *in the addition*. The total run of a common rafter in the main roof is equal to half the span of the main roof; the total run of a common rafter in the addition is equal to half the span *of the addition*.

Knowing the total run of a valley rafter (or of any rafter, for that matter), you can always find the line length by applying the bridge measure times the total run. Suppose, for example, that the span of the addition in Fig. 20 is 30', and that the unit rise of a common rafter in the addition is 9. The total run of the shorter valley rafter is the square root of $(15^2 + 15^2)$, or 21.2'. If you refer back to the unit-length rafter table in Fig. 9, you will see that the bridge measure for a valley rafter in a roof with a common-rafter unit rise of 9 is 19.21. Since the unit run of a valley rafter is 16.97 and the total run of this rafter is 21.21', the line length must be the value of x in the proportional equation 16.97:19.21 :: 21.21:x, or 24.01'.

An easier way to find the length of a valley rafter is to simply multiply the bridge measure by the number of feet in half the span *of the roof to which the valley rafter belongs*. The length of the longer valley rafter in Fig. 20, for example, would be 19.21 times half the span *of the main roof*. The length of the shorter valley rafter is 19.21 times half the span *of the addition*. Since half the span of the addition is 15', the length of the shorter valley rafter is 15 × 19.21, or 288.15"; 288.15 divided by 12 equals 24.01'. Note again that when you use this method you get a result in inches, which you must change to feet.

Figure 21 shows the long and short valley-rafter shortening allowances. Note that the long valley rafter has a single side cut for framing to the main-roof ridge piece, while the short valley rafter is cut square for framing to the addition ridge.

Figure 22 shows another method of framing an equal-pitch unequal-span addition. In this method the inboard end of the addition ridge is nailed to a piece that hangs from the main roof ridge. As shown in the framing diagram, this method calls for two short valley rafters, each of which extends from the rafter plate to the addition ridge. The framing diagram shows that the total run of

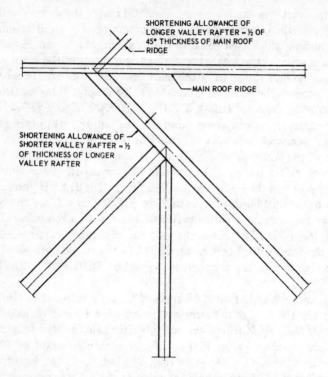

SHORTENING ALLOWANCE OF
LONGER VALLEY RAFTER = ½ OF
45° THICKNESS OF MAIN ROOF
RIDGE

MAIN ROOF RIDGE

SHORTENING ALLOWANCE OF
SHORTER VALLEY RAFTER = ½
OF THICKNESS OF LONGER
VALLEY RAFTER

**Fig. 21.** Long and short valley rafter shortening allowances.

each of these valley rafters is the hypotenuse of a right triangle with shorter sides each equal to the total run of a common rafter *in the addition.*

As indicated in Fig. 23, the shortening allowance of each of the short valley rafters is half of the 45° thickness of the addition ridge. Each rafter is framed to the addition ridge with a single side cut.

Figure 24 shows a method of framing a gable dormer without side walls. The dormer ridge is framed to a header set between a couple of doubled main-roof common rafters. The valley rafters are framed between this header and a lower header. As indicated in the framing diagram, the total run of a valley rafter is the hy-

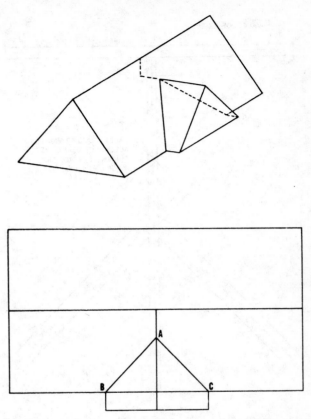

**Fig. 22.** Another method of framing equal-pitch unequal
span intersection.

potenuse of a right triangle with shorter sides each equal to the
total run of a common rafter *in the dormer*.

Figure 25 shows the arrangement and names of framing members in this type of dormer framing.

Figure 25 also shows that the upper edges of the headers must
be beveled to the cut of the main roof. Figure 26 shows that in this
method of framing the shortening allowance for the upper end of
a valley rafter is half of the 45° thickness of the inside member in
the upper doubled header. There is also a shortening allowance for
the lower end, consisting of half of the 45° thickness of the inside

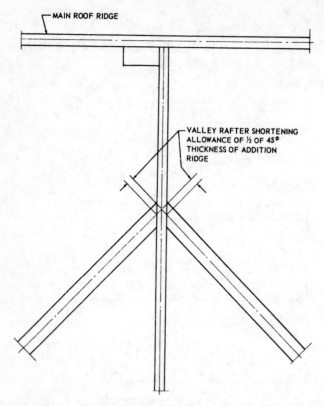

**Fig. 23.** Shortening allowance of valley rafters in suspended
ridge method of intersection roof framing.

member of the doubled common rafter. The figure also shows that
each valley rafter has a double side cut at the upper end and a
double side cut at the lower end.

Figure 27 shows a method of framing a gable dormer with side
walls. As indicated in the framing diagram, the total run of a valley rafter is again the hypotenuse of a right triangle with shorter
sides each equal to the run of a common rafter *in the dormer*. You
figure the lengths of the dormer corner posts and side studs just as
you do the lengths of gable-end studs, and you lay off the lower-
end cut-off angle by setting the square to the cut of the main roof.

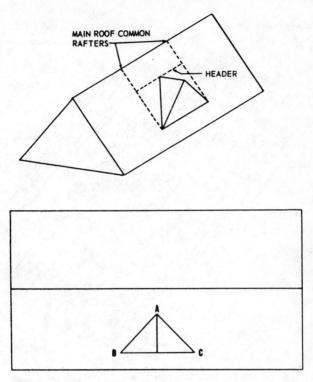

**Fig. 24.** Method of framing dormer without sidewalls.

Figure 28 shows the valley rafter shortening allowances for this method of framing a dormer with side walls.

## JACK RAFTER LAYOUT

A *jack rafter* is a part of a common rafter, shortened for framing to a hip rafter, a valley rafter, or both. This means that in an equal-pitch framing situation the unit rise of a jack rafter is always the same as the unit rise of a common rafter.

A *hip jack* rafter is one that extends from a hip rafter to a rafter plate. A *valley jack* rafter is one that extends from a valley rafter to a ridge. A *cripple jack* rafter is one which does not con-

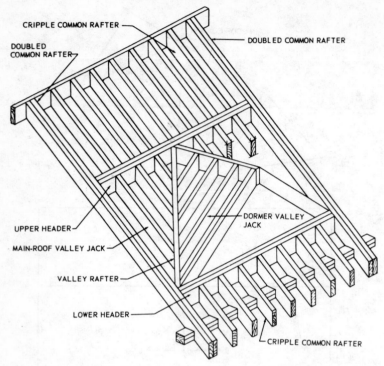

CRIPPLE COMMON RAFTER

DOUBLED COMMON RAFTER

DOUBLED COMMON RAFTER

UPPER HEADER

MAIN-ROOF VALLEY JACK

VALLEY RAFTER

LOWER HEADER

DORMER VALLEY JACK

CRIPPLE COMMON RAFTER

**Fig. 25.** Arrangement and names of framing members for dormer without sidewall.

tact either a rafter plate or a ridge. A *valley cripple jack* is one that extends between two valley rafters in the long-and-short valley rafter method of addition framing. A *hip-valley cripple jack* is one that extends from a hip rafter to a valley rafter. All types of jacks except cripple jacks are shown in Fig. 29. A valley cripple jack and a couple of hip-valley cripple jacks are shown in Fig. 30.

## LENGTHS OF HIP JACK RAFTERS

Figure 31 shows a roof framing diagram for a series of hip jack rafters. The jacks are always on the same spacing on center (O.C.) as the common rafters. Suppose that the spacing in this instance is 16″ O.C. You can see that the total run of the shortest jack is the

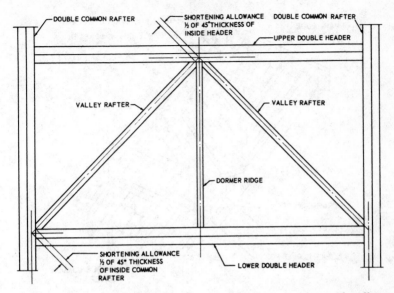

**Fig. 26.** Valley rafter shortening allowances for dormer without sidewall.

hypotenuse of a right triangle with shorter sides each 16″ long. The total run of the shortest jack is therefore the square root of $(16^2 + 16^2)$, or 22.62″.

Suppose that a common rafter in this roof has a unit rise of 8. The jacks, as you know, have the same unit rise as a common rafter. The unit length of a jack in this roof, then, is the square root of $(12^2 + 8^2)$, or 14.42. This means that a jack is 14.42 units long for every 12 units of run. The length of the shortest hip jack in this roof is therefore the value of x in the proportional equation 12:14.42 :: 16:x, or 19.23″.

This is always the length of the shortest hip jack when the jacks are spaced 16″ O.C. and the common rafter in the roof has a unit rise of 8. It is also the *common difference of jacks,* meaning that the next hip jack will be 2 × 19.23″ long, the next 3 × 19.23″ long, and so on.

The common difference for hip jacks spaced 16″ O.C., and also for hip jacks spaced 24″ O.C., is given in the unit length rafter table on the framing square for unit rises ranging from 2 to 18 in-

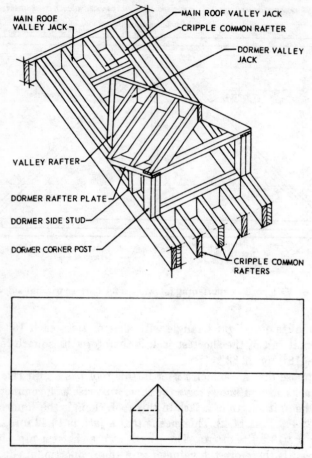

**Fig. 27.** Method of framing gable dormer with sidewalls.

clusive. See Fig. 9, which shows a segment of the unit length rafter table. Note the third line in the table, which reads "Diff. In Length Of Jacks 16 Inches Centers." If you follow this line over to the figure under 8 (for a unit rise of 8), you will find the same unit length (19.23 inches) that you worked out previously.

The best way to figure the length of a valley jack or a cripple

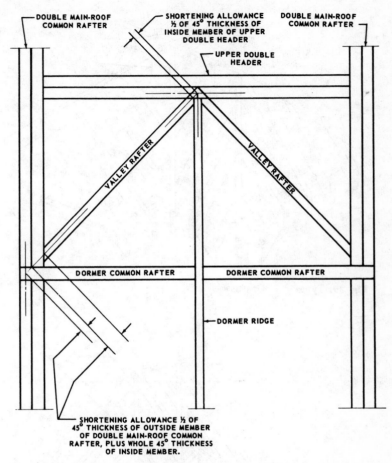

**Fig. 28.** Valley rafter shortening allowances for dormer with sidewall.

jack is to apply the bridge measure to the total run. The bridge measure of any jack is the same as the bridge measure of a common rafter having the same unit of rise as the jack. Suppose, for example, that the jack has a unit rise of 8. In Fig. 9 look along the line on the unit length rafter tables headed "Length Common Rafters Per Foot Run" for the figure in the column under 8, and you will find a unit length of 14.42. You should know by this time how

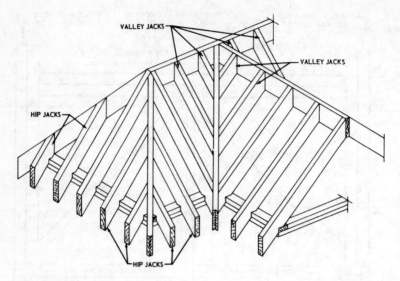

**Fig. 29.** Types of jack rafters.

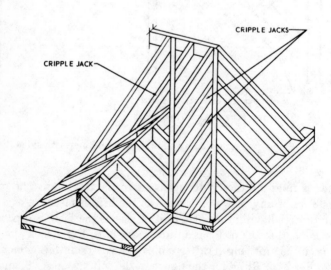

**Fig. 30.** Valley cripple jack and hip-valley cripple jacks.

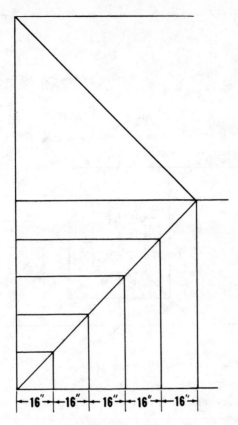

**Fig. 31.** Hip jack framing diagram.

to apply this to the total run of a jack to get the line length.

The best way to figure the total runs of valley jacks and cripple jacks is to lay out a framing diagram and study it to determine what these runs must be. Figure 32 shows part of a framing diagram for a main hip roof with a long-and-short valley rafter gable addition. By studying the diagram you can figure the total runs of the valley jacks and cripple jacks as follows.

1. The run of valley jack *No. 1* is obviously the same as the run of hip jack *No. 8*, which is the run of the shortest hip jack. The

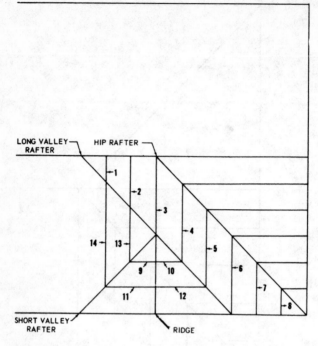

**Fig. 32.** Jack rafter framing diagram.

length of valley jack *No. 1* is therefore equal to the common difference of jacks.

2. The run of valley jack *No. 2* is the same as the run of hip jack *No. 7,* and the length is therefore twice the common difference of jacks.

3. The run of valley jack *No. 3* is the same as the run of hip jack *No. 6,* and the length is therefore three times the common difference of jacks.

4. The run of hip-valley cripple *No. 4,* and also of hip-valley cripple *No. 5,* is the same as the run of valley jack *No. 3.*

5. The run of valley jack *No. 9,* and also of valley jack *No. 10,* is equal to the spacing of jacks O.C. Therefore, the length of one of these jacks is equal to the common difference of jacks.

6. The run of valley jacks *Nos. 11* and *12* is twice the run of

valley jacks *Nos. 9* and *10,* and the length of one of these jacks is therefore twice the common difference of jacks.

7. The run of valley cripple *No. 13* is twice the spacing of jacks O.C., and the length is therefore twice the common difference of jacks.

8. The run of valley cripple *No. 14* is twice the run of valley cripple *No. 13,* and the length is therefore four times the common difference of jacks.

## JACK RAFTER SHORTENING ALLOWANCES

A hip jack rafter has a shortening allowance at the upper end consisting of half of the 45° thickness of the hip rafter. A valley jack rafter has a shortening allowance at the upper end, consisting of half of the thickness of the ridge, and another at the lower end, consisting of half of the 45° thickness of the valley rafter. A hip-valley cripple has a shortening allowance at the upper end, consisting of half of the 45° thickness of the long valley rafter, and another at the lower end, consisting of half of the 45° thickness of the short valley rafter.

## JACK RAFTER SIDE CUTS

The side cut on a jack rafter can be laid out by the method illustrated in Fig. 15 for laying out the side cut on a hip rafter. Another method is to use the fifth line of the unit length rafter table, which is headed "Side Cut Of Jacks Use" (Fig. 9). If you follow that line over to the figure under 8 (for a unit rise of 8), you will see that the figure given is 10. To lay out the side cut on a jack, set the square face up on the edge of the rafter to 12″ on the tongue and 10″ on the blade, and draw the side-cut line along the tongue.

## JACK RAFTER BIRD'S MOUTH AND PROJECTION

A jack rafter is a shortened common rafter; consequently, the bird's mouth and projection on a jack rafter are laid out just as they are on a common rafter.

## RIDGE LAYOUT

Laying out the ridge for a gable roof presents no particular problem, since the line length of the ridge is equal to the length of the building. The actual length would include any overhang. For a hip main roof, however, the ridge layout requires a certain amount of calculation.

As previously mentioned, in an equal-pitch hip roof the line length of the ridge amounts to the length of the building minus twice the total run of a main roof common rafter. The *actual* length depends upon the way in which the hip rafters are framed to the ridge.

As indicated in Fig. 33, the line length ends of the ridge are at the points where the ridge center line and the hip rafter center line cross. In Fig. 33 the hip rafter is framed against the ridge. In this method of framing, the actual length of the ridge exceeds the line length, at each end, by half of the thickness of the ridge, plus half of the 45° thickness of the hip rafter. In Fig. 33 the hip rafter

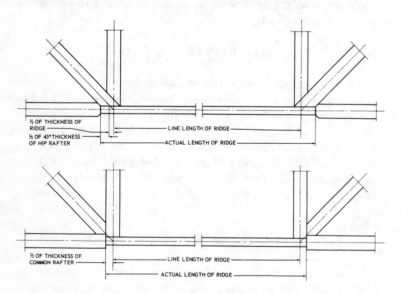

**Fig. 33.** Line and actual lengths of hip roof ridge.

is framed between the common rafters. In this method of framing, the actual length of the ridge exceeds the line length, at each end, by half of the thickness of a common rafter.

Figure 34 shows that the length of the ridge for an equal-span addition is equal to the length of the addition rafter plate, plus half the span of the building, minus the shortening allowance at the main roof ridge; the shortening allowance amounts to half the

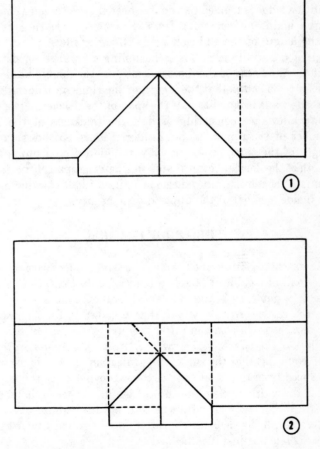

**Fig. 34.** Lengths of addition ridge.

thickness of the main roof ridge. Figure 34 also shows that the length of the ridge for an unequal-span addition varies with the method of framing the ridge. If the addition ridge is suspended from the main roof ridge, the length is equal to the length of the addition rafter plate plus half the span of the building. If the addition ridge is framed by the long-and-short valley rafter method, the length is equal to the length of the addition rafter plate, plus half the span of the addition, minus a shortening allowance consisting of half the 45° thickness of the long valley rafter. If the addition ridge is framed to a double header set between a couple of double main roof common rafters, the length of the ridge is equal to the length of the addition side-wall rafter plate, plus half the span of the addition, minus a shortening allowance consisting of half the thickness of the inside member of the double header.

Figure 35 shows that the length of the ridge on a dormer without side walls is equal to half the span of the dormer, less a shortening allowance consisting of half the thickness of the inside member of the upper double header. Figure 35 shows that the length of the ridge on a dormer with side walls amounts to the length of the dormer rafter plate, plus half the span of the dormer, minus a shortening allowance consisting of half the thickness of the inside member of the upper double header.

## SHED ROOF FRAMING

As previously described, a *shed* or *single-pitch* roof is essentially half of a gable or double-pitch roof. Like the full-length rafters in a gable roof, the full-length rafters in a shed roof are *common* rafters. *Note,* however, that as shown in Fig. 36, the total run of a shed-roof common rafter is equal to the span of the building *minus the width of the rafter plate on the higher rafter-end wall.* Note also that the run of the projection on the higher wall is measured from the *inner edge* of the rafter plate. To this must be added the width of the plate and the length of the overhang at the top. Shed-roof common rafters are laid out like gable-roof common rafters. A shed-roof common rafter has two bird's mouths, but they are laid out just like the bird's mouth on a gable-roof common rafter.

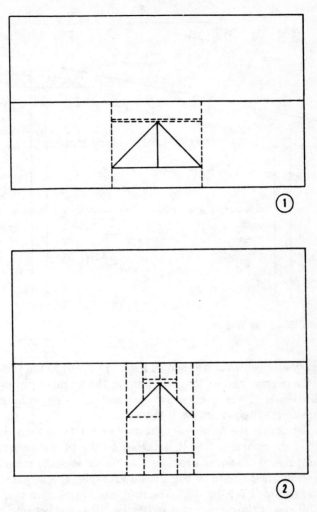

**Fig. 35.** Lengths of dormer ridge.

Figure 36 also shows that the height of the higher rafter-end wall must exceed the height of the lower by an amount equal to the total rise of a common rafter.

Figure 37 shows a method of framing a shed dormer. There are

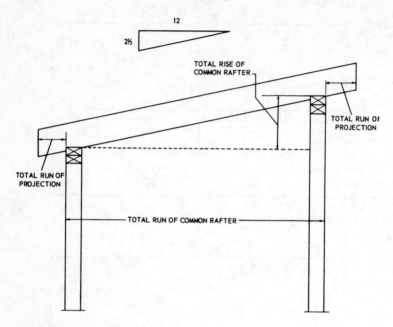

**Fig. 36.** Shed roof framing.

three layout problems to be solved here: (1) determining the total run of a dormer rafter, (2) determining the angle of cut on the inboard ends of the dormer rafters, and (3) determining the lengths of the dormer side-wall studs.

To determine the *total run* of a dormer rafter you divide the height of the dormer end wall, in inches, by the difference between the unit rise of the dormer roof and the unit rise of the main roof. Take the dormer shown in Fig. 38, for example. The height of the dormer end-wall is 9′ or 108″. The unit rise of the main roof is 8; the unit rise of the dormer roof is 2½; the difference between them is 5½. The total run of a dormer rafter is therefore 108 divided by 5½, or 19.63′. Knowing the total run and the unit rise, you can figure the length of a dormer rafter by any of the methods already described.

As indicated in Fig. 38 the *inboard ends* of the dormer rafters must be *cut* to fit the slope of the main roof. To get the angle of

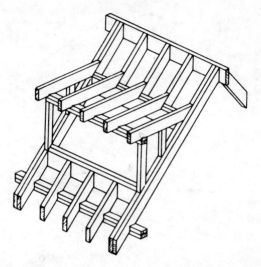

**Fig. 37.** Method of framing a shed dormer.

this cut, set the square on the rafter to the cut of the main roof, as shown in the third view of Fig. 38; measure off the unit size of the dormer roof from the heel of the square along the tongue as indicated; make a mark at this point, and draw the cut-off line through this mark from the 12″ mark.

You figure the lengths of the side-wall studs on a shed dormer as follows.

In the roof shown in Fig. 38, a dormer rafter rises 2½ units for every 12 units of run, and a main-roof common rafter rises eight units for every 12 units of run. If the studs were spaced 12″ O.C., the length of the shortest stud (which is also the *common difference* of studs) would be the difference between 8″ and 2½″, or 5½″. This being the case, if the stud spacing is 16″, the length of the shortest stud is the value of x in the proportional equation of 12:5½ :: 16:x, or 7 5/16″. The shortest stud, then, will be 7 5/16″ long; the next stud will be 2 × 7 5/16″ long, and so on. To get the lower end cut-off angle for studs you set the square on the stud to the cut of the main roof; to get the upper end cut-off angle you set it to the cut of the dormer roof.

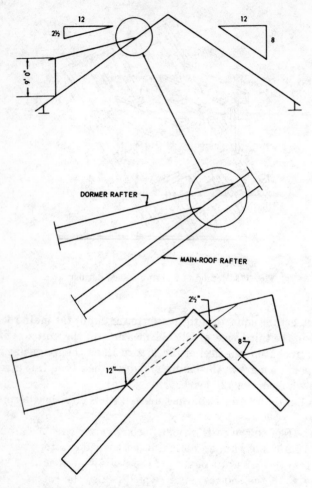

**Fig. 38.** Shed dormer framing calculations.

## RAFTER LOCATION LAYOUT

Rafter locations are laid out on plates, ridges, and other rafters with the same lines and X's used to lay out stud and joist locations. For a gable roof the rafter locations are laid out on the rafter plates first, and the locations are then transferred to the ridge by matching the ridge against a rafter plate.

The rafter-plate locations on the ridge-end common rafters in an equal-pitch hip roof measure half the span (or the run of a main-roof common rafter) away from the building corners. These locations, plus the rafter-plate locations of the rafters lying between the ridge-end common rafters, can be transferred to the ridge by matching the ridge against the rafter plates.

The locations of addition ridges and valley rafters can be determined as indicated in Fig. 39. In an equal-span situation (*1* and *2*, Fig. 39) the valley rafter locations on the main-roof ridge lie alongside the addition-ridge location. In *1*, Fig. 39 the distance between the end of the main roof ridge and the addition-ridge location is equal to distance *A* plus distance *B*, distance *B* being half the span of the addition. In *2*, Fig. 39 the distance between the line length end of the main-roof ridge and the addition-ridge location is the same as distance *A*—in both cases the line length of the addition plus the length of the addition side-wall rafter plate.

An unequal-span situation is shown in *3*, Fig. 39. If framing is by the long-and-short valley rafter method, the distance from the end of the main-roof ridge to the upper end of the longer valley rafter is equal to distance *A* plus distance *B*, distance *B* being half the span of the main roof. The location of the inboard end of the shorter valley rafter on the longer valley rafter can be determined as follows.

First calculate the unit length of the longer valley rafter, or obtain it from the unit-length rafter tables. Let us suppose that the common-rafter unit rise is 8; in that case the unit length of a valley rafter is 18.76.

The total run of the longer valley rafter between the point where the shorter rafter ties in and the rafter plate is the hypotenuse of a right triangle with its other sides equal to half the span of the addition. Suppose the addition is 20' wide; then the total run in question is the square root of $(10^2 + 10^2)$, or 14.14'.

You know that the valley rafter is 18.76 units long for every 16.97 units of run. The length of rafter for 14.14' of run must therefore be the value of x in the proportional equation 16.97:18.76 :: 14.14:x, or 15.63'. The location mark for the inboard

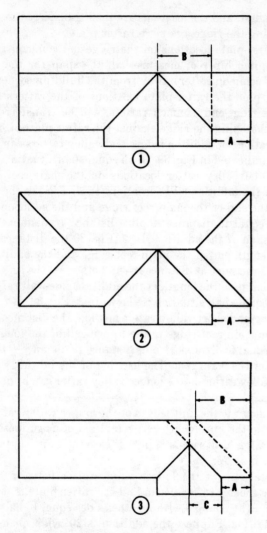

**Fig. 39.** Intersection ridge and valley rafter
location layout.

end of the shorter valley rafter on the longer valley rafter, then,
will be 15.63', or 15' 7 9/16" from the heel plumb-cut line on the

longer valley rafter. The length of the addition ridge will be equal to half the span of the addition, plus the length of the addition side-wall rafter plate, minus a shortening allowance equal to half the 45° thickness of the longer valley rafter.

If framing is by the suspended-ridge method, the distance between the suspension point on the main-roof ridge and the end of the main-roof ridge is equal to distance *A* plus distance *C*; distance *C* is half the span of the addition. The distance between the point where the inboard ends of the valley rafters (both short in this method of framing) tie into the addition ridge and the outboard end of the ridge is equal to half the span of the addition plus the length of the addition side-wall rafter plate. The length of the addition ridge is equal to half of the span of the main roof plus the length of the addition side-wall rafter plate.

## COLLAR TIE

Gable or double-pitch roof rafters are often reinforced by horizontal members called *collar ties* (Fig. 40). In a finished attic the ties may also function as ceiling joists.

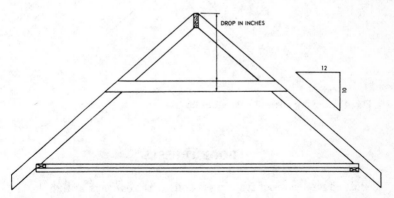

**Fig. 40.** Calculation for a collar tie.

To find the line length of a collar tie, divide the amount of drop of the tie in inches by the unit of rise of the common rafter. This will equal one half the length of the tie in feet. Double the result for actual length. The formula is: drop in inches × 2 over unit of rise equals the length in feet.

The length of the collar tie depends on whether the drop is measured to the top edge or bottom edge of the collar tie (Fig. 40). The tie must fit the slope of the roof. To obtain this angle use the framing square. Hold unit of run and unit of rise of the common rafter. Mark and cut on unit of run side (Fig. 41).

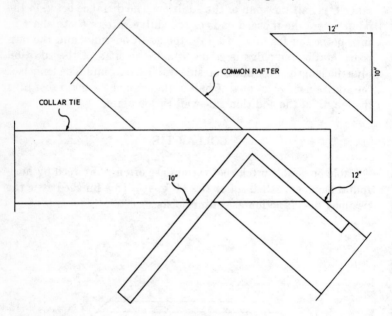

**Fig. 41.** Laying out end cut on a collar tie.

## ROOF TRUSSES

Much modern roof framing is done with *roof trusses* like the one shown in Fig. 42. The principal parts of a truss are the *upper chord* (consisting of the rafters), the *lower chord* (corresponding to a ceiling joist), and various diagonal and/or vertical bracing and connecting members, which are known collectively as the *web members*.

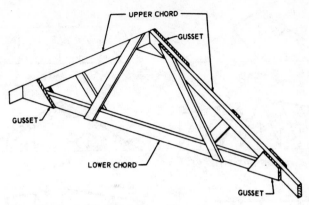

**Fig. 42.** Typical lightweight roof truss.

The truss shown in Fig. 42 is joined at the corners with plywood *gussets*. Other methods of corner joining are metal gussets or various types of notched joints, reinforced with bolts. Construction information on trusses is usually given in detail drawings. (*See* Fig. 43 for various types of trusses used.)

## ROOF FRAMING ERECTION

Roof framing should be done from a scaffold with planking not less than four feet below the level of the main ridge. The usual type of roof scaffold consists of diagonally-braced two-legged horses, spaced about 10′ apart and extending the full length of the ridge.

If the building has an addition, as much as possible of the main roof is framed before the addition framing is started. Cripples and jack rafters are usually left out until after the headers, hip rafters, valley rafters, and ridges to which they will be framed have been installed.

For a gable roof the two pairs of gable-end rafters and the ridge are usually erected first. Two men, one at each end of the scaffold, hold the ridge in position while a third man sets the gable-end rafters in place and toenails them at the rafter plate with 8-penny nails, one to each side of a rafter. Each man on the scaffold then

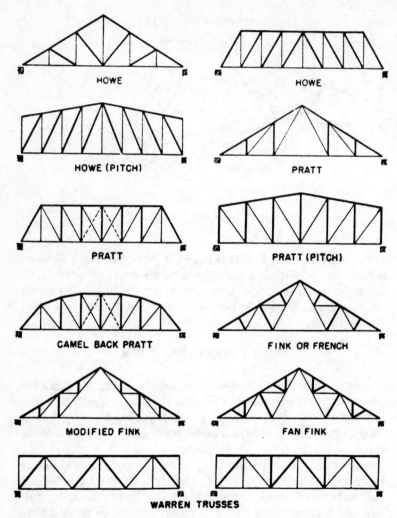

**Fig. 43.** Types of trusses.

end-nails the ridge to one of his rafters with two 10-penny nails driven through the ridge into the end of the rafter, and toenails the other rafter to the ridge and to the first rafter with two 10-penny nails, one on each side of the rafter. Temporary braces like

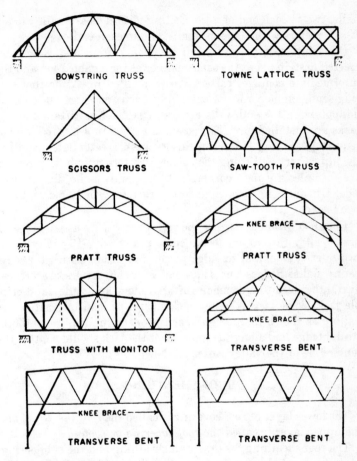

BOWSTRING TRUSS

TOWNE LATTICE TRUSS

SCISSORS TRUSS

SAW-TOOTH TRUSS

PRATT TRUSS

KNEE BRACE

PRATT TRUSS

TRUSS WITH MONITOR

KNEE BRACE

TRANSVERSE BENT

KNEE BRACE

TRANSVERSE BENT

TRANSVERSE BENT

**Fig. 43.** (continued).

those for a wall should be set up at the ridge ends to hold the rafters approximately plumb, after which the rafters between the end-rafters should be erected. The braces should then be released, and the pair of rafters at one end should be plumbed with a plumb line fastened to a stick extended from the end of the ridge. The braces should then be reset, and they should be left in place until enough sheathing has been installed to hold the rafters plumb. Collar ties, if any, are nailed to common rafters with 8-penny nails, two to each end of a tie. Ceiling-joist ends are nailed to adjacent rafters with 10-penny nails, two to each end.

On a hip roof the ridge-end common rafters and ridges are erected first, in about the same manner as for a gable roof, and the intermediate common rafters are then filled in. After that, the ridge-end common rafters extending from the ridge ends to the midpoints on the end walls are erected. The hip rafters and hip jacks are installed next. The common rafters in a hip roof do not require plumbing. If the hip rafters are correctly cut, installing the hip rafters will bring the common rafters plumb. Hip rafters are toenailed to plate corners with 16-penny nails, two to each side. Hip jacks are toenailed to hip rafters with 10-penny nails, two to each jack.

For an addition or dormer the valley rafters are usually erected first. Valley rafters are toenailed to plates with 16-penny nails, two to each side, and to ridge pieces and headers with three 10-penny nails. Ridges and ridge-end common rafters are erected next, other addition common rafters follow, and valley and cripple jacks come last. A valley jack should be held in position for nailing as shown in Fig. 44. When properly nailed, the end of a straightedge laid along the top edge of the jack should contact the center line of the valley rafter as shown.

## ROOF SHEATHING

The lower layer of roof covering is called the *roof sheathing* and the upper layer is called the *roof covering* or *roofing*.

The roof sheathing, like the wall sheathing and the subflooring, is a structural element and therefore a part of the framing. The roof covering or roofing is a part of the exterior finish. Roof sheathing, like wall sheathing and subflooring, may be laid either horizontally or diagonally. Horizontal sheathing may be either *closed* sheathing (laid with no spaces between courses) or *open* sheathing (laid with spaces between courses). (*See* Fig. 45.) Open sheathing is used for the most part only when the roof covering is to consist of wooden shingles. Closed sheathing is usually 8″ in width. It may consist of square-edged boards that may be dressed-and-matched or shiplap (*see* Fig. 46). Open sheathing usually

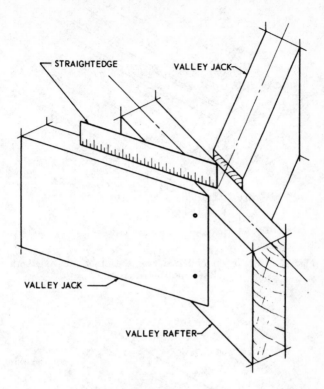

STRAIGHTEDGE

VALLEY JACK

VALLEY JACK

VALLEY RAFTER

**Fig. 44.** Correct position for nailing a valley jack rafter.

consists of $1 \times 3$ or $1 \times 4$ strips, with spacing O.C. equal to the specified exposure of shingles *to the weather*. An 18″ shingle which is lapped 12″ by the shingle above it is said to be laid six inches to the weather.

Sheathing should be nailed with two 8-penny nails to each rafter crossing. End joint requirements are the same as those previously described for wall sheathing. The sheathing ends should be sawed flush with the outer face of the end-wall sheathing, unless a projection of the roof sheathing over the end walls is called for. If such a projection is needed, projecting sheathing boards must be long enough to span at least three rafter spaces.

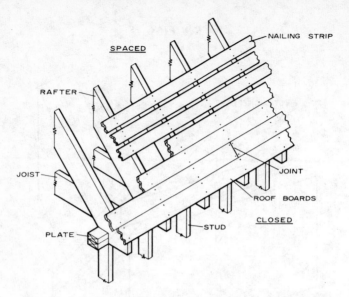

**Fig. 45.** Installation of board roof sheathing, showing both closed and spaced types.

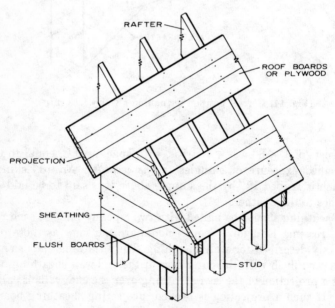

**Fig. 46.** Board roof sheathing at ends of gable.

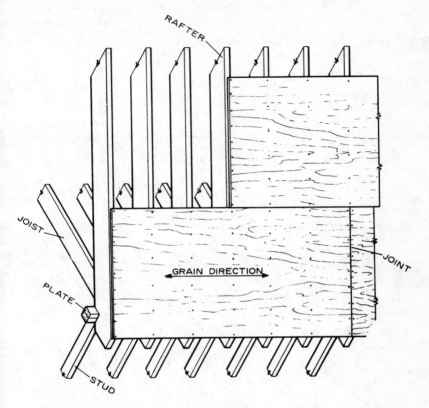

**Fig. 47.** Application of plywood roof sheathing.

Plywood, usually in 8′ × 4′ sheets laid horizontally, is frequently used for roof sheathing (*see* Fig. 47). Nailing requirements are the same as those previously described for 8′ × 4′ sheets of plywood wall sheathing. (*See* Chap. 17, Reroofing.)

## Section IV

# Exterior Projects

Reroofing—shingles, asphalt, coal-tar pitch, slate, and tile.

Exterior wood coverings—sidings and shingles.

Additions to the house—porches and garages.

Installing exterior frames, windows, and doors.

## CHAPTER 17

# Reroofing

Many roofing materials have withstood the test of time and proven satisfactory under given service conditions.

## TYPES OF ASPHALT-STRIP SHINGLES

The following two types of asphalt-strip shingles are used for reroofing buildings with pitched roofs. These shingles are applied directly over the existing roll roofings.

**Standard-weight shingles.** The shingles should be four-tab, 10″ by 36″ in size, intended for a 4″ maximum exposure. Weight per square (100 square feet) applied should be approximately 210 pounds. They are fastened with 1¼″ or 1½″ nails with heads having a minimum diameter of ⅜″. Zinc-coated nails are best.

**Thick-butt shingles.** Thick-butt shingles should be three-tab, 12″ by 36″ in size, intended for a 5″ maximum exposure. The entire surface of the shingles should be covered with mineral granules. The bottom part of each shingle, including the part intended to be exposed and a section at least 1″ above the cutout sections, should be thicker than the remainder of the shingle. Weight per square applied should be approximately 210 pounds. The shingles should be fastened with 1½ or 1¾″ nails with heads having a minimum diameter of ⅜″. Zinc-coated nails are best.

## PREPARATION OF ROOF DECKS

Assuming that the roof decks are covered with smooth or mineral-surfaced asphalt-prepared roofing and that the shingles will be applied directly over the existing roofing, proceed as follows.

1. Drive all loose and protruding nails in flush with the existing roll roofing.

2. Cut out all vertical and horizontal buckles or wrinkles in the existing roofing and nail down the edges with ¾″ or 1″ roofing nails so the entire roof deck is smooth (Fig. 1). (*See* Chap. 4, Methods of Fastening.)

**Fig. 1.** Flattening surface and nailing down roofing to be repaired.

3. Where shingles are applied over smooth-surfaced roofings or over mineral-surfaced roofing that does not match the shingles, apply an 18″ starting strip of mineral-surfaced roll roofing at the eaves. Use roofing surfaced with granules of the same type and color as the shingles. Before they are applied unroll the strips carefully and lay them on a smooth, flat surface until they lie perfectly flat. In applying starter strips, nail them at the top at about 18″ intervals so the lower edge, when bent down and nailed to the edge of the sheathing board, extends about ¾″ beyond the edge of the board to form a drip edge. Space nails in the edge of the sheathing board 6″ apart. A starter strip need not be used if the shingles are the same color as the existing roofing and the existing roofing is not buckled.

## APPLYING SHINGLES

**Standard-weight, four-tab, 10″ by 36″ shingles.** When applying these shingles proceed as follows.

Start the *first course* with a full shingle placed so one edge, which is cut off flush with the tab, is flush with the side of the roof. The bottoms of the tabs are placed flush with the eaves. Place nails about ¾″ above each cutout section (Fig. 2) and in the same relative position at each end of the shingle. Use two nails at every cutout. Nail at the center first, then above the cutout sections nearest the center, and finally at the ends. Nailing may start at one end and proceed regularly to the other. Complete the first course with full width shingles applied so the ends barely touch each other.

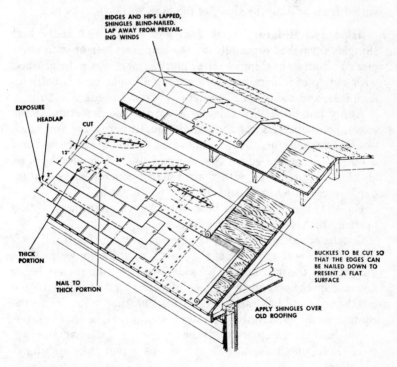

RIDGES AND HIPS LAPPED, SHINGLES BLIND-NAILED. LAP AWAY FROM PREVAILING WINDS

EXPOSURE

HEADLAP

CUT

12″

36″

THICK PORTION

NAIL TO THICK PORTION

BUCKLES TO BE CUT SO THAT THE EDGES CAN BE NAILED DOWN TO PRESENT A FLAT SURFACE

APPLY SHINGLES OVER OLD ROOFING

**Fig. 2.** Replacement of roofs.

Start the *second course* with a shingle from which half a tab has been cut. Place it so the bottoms of the tabs are flush with the tops of the cutout sections of the shingle in the first course. Complete this course with full-width shingles.

Start the *third course* with a shingle from which one tab has been cut; the fourth with one from which one and one-half tabs have been cut, and so on, until eventually a full shingle is used again.

**Thick-butt, three-tab shingles.** Follow the same method described for standard shingles. Always nail these shingles through the thick part about ¾″ above the cutout sections (Fig. 2). The importance of nailing through the thick part of asphalt shingles cannot be emphasized too strongly, because practically all difficulties experienced with asphalt shingles on buildings have resulted from nailing the shingles too high.

**Hips and Ridges.** Finish *hips and ridges* with individual shingles furnished especially by the manufacturer or with shingles cut from strip shingles. Hips and ridges may also be finished with a strip of mineral-surfaced roofing 9″ wide, bent equally on each side, and nailed on 2″ centers, ¾″ from the edges.

Apply individual hip shingles as on the roof, starting at the lowest point and bending the shingle equally across the hip. Place one nail on each side, about ¾″ above the section to be exposed and about ¾″ from the edge. The shingles used to finish the hips should be kept in line with the main roof courses. Expose standard-weight shingles 4″ and thick-butt shingles 5″.

Finish ridges the same as hips, always working in the direction opposite that of the prevailing winds.

Construct *valleys* from two layers of mineral-surfaced roll roofing surfaced with granules of the same type and color as the shingles. Apply the first layer, 18″ wide, with the mineral surfacing down. Lay the second layer the full width of the roll with the weather side up. Lay each sheet so it is smooth, conforming to the contour of the roof. Nail valley sheets at approximately 18″ intervals to hold them in place until the remainder of the roofing is applied. Follow manufacturers' instructions for cutting the shingles at valleys.

## ASPHALT-PREPARED ROLL ROOFINGS

**Mineral-surfaced roll roofing.** Mineral-surfaced, asphalt-prepared, two-ply roofing should consist of a layer of 15-pound asphalt-saturated felt and two plies of roll roofing, cemented together with hot asphalt. Cut roll roofing material into lengths of 18' or 20', stack free from wrinkles and buckles in protected piles, and maintain at a temperature of at least 50° F. For 24 hours before laying. First, cover the roof areas with a layer of 15-pound asphalt-saturated felt with all joints lapped 2", and nail as required to prevent blowing off during the application of roofing. Next, lay either plain unsurfaced roofing or mineral-surfaced roofing as a starter sheet. Lay this upside down, in dry condition, parallel to and at the eaves, and nail through tin or fiber discs on 12" staggered centers; that is, with one row of nails on 12" centers placed not more than 2" from the lower edge, and a second row on 12" centers staggered with respect to and about 8" above the first. Over the lower half of this sheet, apply a uniform coating of hot asphalt at 30 pounds per square (100 square feet) and place the first sheet of roll roofing in the asphalt. Cover the entire roof area. Lap each successive sheet in such a way as to obtain a two-ply roofing with a 2" headlap. Cement the lower or mineral-surfaced portion of each sheet with hot asphalt to the preceding sheet. Nail the edges through tin or fiber discs on 12" staggered centers. Use two rows of nails. Place the first row on 12" centers not more than 2" above the mineral surfacing, and the second row on 12" centers staggered with respect to the first and about 8" above the first. Perform the work in such a way that no fastenings or asphalt will show on the finished surface. Apply the asphalt immediately before unrolling the sheet of roofing. Do not apply the asphalt more than 3' ahead of the roll. Step the edge of each sheet into the asphalt so that all laps are securely sealed. Place the end laps 6" in width with the underlying edges nailed on 6" centers, asphalt-cement the overlying edges thereto and step down firmly. Place one ply of roofing at eaves and edges, turn down neatly, and secure it with a wood member nailed on an 8" center.

**Smooth-surfaced roll roofing.** Apply single-ply roll roofing for theater of operations construction horizontally with at least 4" side laps and 6″ end laps (Fig. 3). Nail the underlying edges of laps through tin or fiber discs on 6″ centers and cement overlying laps with hot asphalt or an approved cold-applied sealing compound. Step down firmly on the edges to provide proper adhesion. Double the roofing over the ridge, with at least 4″ laps. Turn roofing down neatly at eaves and edges and nail it in place on 6″ centers. Before laying the roll-roofing material, cut it into 18′ or 20′ lengths, stack them free of wrinkles and buckles in protected piles, and maintain them at a temperature of at least 50° F. for 24 hours.

## BUILT-UP ROOFS

Reroof buildings with roofs of relatively low pitch (less than two inches per foot) which were originally roofed with asphalt-prepared roll roofings with either *smooth-surfaced asphalt built-up roofing* or with *coal-tar-pitch built-up roofing*. Use smooth-surfaced asphalt built-up roofing to reroof buildings with original smooth-surfaced roll roofing. Mobilization-type buildings with roofs of relatively low pitch (usually one-half inch per foot), originally roofed with wide-selvage mineral-surfaced roll roofing, should be reroofed with asphalt built-up roofing, or with coal-tar-pitch built-up roofing. If the roof is nearly flat, so that water collects and stands, the latter type of roofing is best. Asphalt roofs may be smooth or mineral-surfaced. Coal-tar-pitch roofs *must* be mineral-surfaced.

**Asphalt built-up roofs.** Prepare the roof deck by driving in all loose and protruding nails and cutting out all buckles and wrinkles. Then apply a three-ply, smooth-surfaced, asphalt built-up roof as follows.

1. Lay one layer of 15-pound, asphalt-saturated felt over the entire surface. Lap each sheet 3″ horizontally and vertically and nail the laps on 12″ centers. Also nail through the center of each sheet on 12″ centers staggered with respect to the nails at the horizontal laps. Use nails long enough to penetrate into the sheathing at least ¾″. They should be driven through tin or hard fiber discs.

2. Mop the entire surface with a uniform coating of hot asphalt,

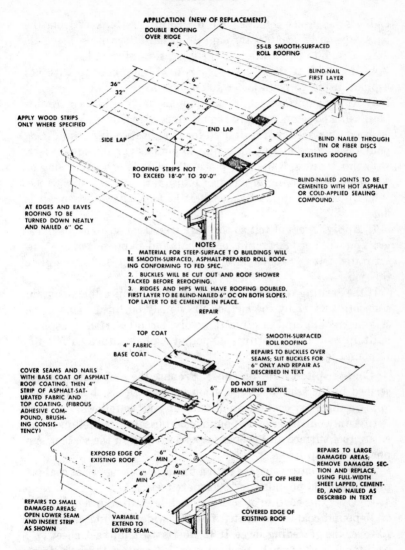

**Fig. 3.** Smooth surface roll roofing.

using 25 pounds per 100 square feet.

3. Over this coating of asphalt, lay two additional layers of 15-pound, 36″ asphalt-saturated felt, lapping each sheet 10″. Lap the

ends of the sheets not less than 6″. Nail these felts 1″ from the back edge on 12″ centers through tin or hard fiber discs. Use nails long enough to penetrate into the wood sheathing at least ¾″.

4. Mop each of these sheets the full width of the lap with hot asphalt, using 25 pounds per 100 square feet.

5. Apply a uniform mopping of hot asphalt over the entire surface, using 80 pounds per 100 square feet of roof surface. If a slag or gravel-surfaced roof is desired for mobilization-type buildings, pour the surface coating on, using 45 pounds per 100 square feet. Into this coating, while hot, place 300 pounds of roofing slag or 400 pounds of roofing gravel per 100 square feet of roof surface.

6. Do not heat asphalt above 400° F. Lay felt while asphalt is hot.

7. Apply layers of felt so they are free from wrinkles or buckles. You will need 80 pounds of asphalt and 45 pounds of asphalt-saturated felt per 100 square feet of roofing surface to complete this job.

If the existing roofing is so rough that it is impossible to obtain a smooth surface by the method previously outlined, remove the original roofing and apply a three-ply, smooth-surfaced, asphalt built-up roof, but substitute 30-pound asphalt-saturated felt for 15-pound felt.

**Coal-tar-pitch built-up roofs.** Prepare the roof surface as described in the section, Preparation of Roof Decks, 1 and 2, and apply a three-ply coal-tar-pitch built-up roof as follows.

1. Apply one layer of 15-pound, coal-tar-saturated felt over the entire roof surface and prepare it as described in the section, Asphalt Built-Up Roofs, 1.

2. Mop the entire surface with a uniform coating of hot coal-tar pitch, using 30 pounds per 100 square feet.

3. Over this coating of coal-tar pitch lay two additional layers of 15-pound coal-tar-saturated felt 36″ wide, lapping each sheet 19″ over the preceding sheet. If 32″ felt is used, lap each sheet 17″. Nail the felt 1″ from the back edge on 12″ centers through tin or hard fiber discs. Use nails long enough to penetrate into the wood sheathing at least ¾″. Lap the ends of the sheets at least 6″.

4. Mop each of these sheets the full width of the lap with hot coal-tar pitch, using 25 pounds per 100 square feet.

5. Apply over the entire surface a uniform pouring of hot coal-tar pitch, using 55 pounds per 100 square feet. While the pitch is hot, place over it 300 pounds of roofing slag or 400 pounds of roofing gravel per 100 square feet.

6. Materials required per 100 square feet of roof surface are:

| | |
|---|---|
| Coal-tar pitch | 110 pounds |
| Coal-tar-saturated felt | 45 pounds |
| Roofing slag | 300 pounds |
| or | |
| Roofing gravel | 400 pounds |

7. Do not heat the coal-tar pitch above 375° F. and lay felt while it is still hot.

8. Apply the layers of felt so they are free from wrinkles or buckles.

## SLATE ROOFS

Very old slate roofs sometimes fall apart due to failure of the nails used to fasten the slates. In such cases, remove and replace the entire roof, including the felt underlay materials. Remove or drive in any protruding nails. Make every effort to obtain a smooth, even deck similar to the original one. Apply 30-pound asphalt-saturated felt horizontally over the entire roof deck. Lap the sheets not less than 3″ and turn them up on vertical surfaces not less than 6″ and over ridges and hips not less than 12″. Secure the sheets along laps and exposed edges with large-head roofing nails spaced about 6″.

Relay all original slates that are in good condition. Replace defective slates with new slates of the same size, matching the original as nearly as possible in color and texture.

Recommended slate sizes for large new buildings are 20″ or 22″ long; for small new buildings, 16″ or 18″ long. Use slates of uniform length in random widths, and punches for a head lap of not less than 3″.

Lay roof slates with a 3″ head lap and fasten each slate with two large-head slating nails. Drive the slating nails so their heads just touch the slate. Do not drive the nails "home." The opposite is true of wood shingles; therefore, workers accustomed to laying wood shingles must nail slate carefully. Bed all slates on each side of hips and ridges within 1' of the top and along gable rakes within 1' of the edge in an approved elastic cement. Match slate courses on dormer roofs with those on the main roof. Lay slate with open valleys.

## TILE ROOFS

**Preparation.** Before reroofing with tiles, restore the roof deck as nearly as possible to the original condition by replacing defective boards and applying asphalt-saturated felt (30-pound type) or prepared roofing. Lap the sheets not less than 3"; turn them up on vertical surfaces not less than 12". Secure the sheets along laps and exposed edges with large-head roofing nails spaced about 6".

**Roof tiles.** Tiles must be free from fire cracks or other defects that will impair the durability, appearance, or weather tightness of the finished roof. Special shapes are provided for eaves starters, hips, ridges, top fixtures, gable rakes, and finials. Special shapes for field tile at hips and valleys may be factory-molded before burning, or may be job-cut from whole tile and rubbed down to clean, sharp lines.

## CEMENT-ASBESTOS ROOFS

Before reroofing with cement-asbestos shingles, restore the roof deck as nearly as possible to its original condition by replacing defective boards and applying new 30-pound asphalt-saturated felt or prepared roofing. Lay this covering in horizontal courses. Lap the sheets not less than 3"; turn them up on vertical surfaces not less than 6" and over ridges and hips not less than 12". Secure the sheets along laps and exposed edges with large-head roofing nails spaced about 6".

**Laying cement-asbestos shingles.** Relay all cement-asbestos shingles that are in good condition. Replace defective shingles with new shingles of the same size and matching the originals as nearly as possible in color and texture.

Lay each shingle with a 2" head lap and secure it with two

large-head slating nails. Drive the nails so their heads just touch the shingles. Do not drive the nails "home" as in laying wood shingles. Bed all shingles on each side of hips and ridges within 1' of the top and along gable rakes within 1' of the edge in an approved elastic slater's cement. Project the shingles 1" over the rear edges of gutters. Lay shingles with 1" head lap on sides of dormers. Match the shingle courses on dormer roofs with those on the main roof. Lay shingles with open valleys.

## WOOD SHINGLES

When old roofing is removed, proceed as follows.

1. Restore the roof deck as nearly as possible to its original condition by replacing all rotted boards and pulling out or driving down all protruding nails.

2. Install flashings and apply new shingles.

**Applying new wood shingles.** Apply new wood shingles directly over weathered wood-shingle roofs, if the existing shingle roofs can be made smooth and can be nailed properly. *Reroof* over existing wood shingles as follows.

1. Nail down or cut off curled and warped shingles, nail loose shingles securely, and remove or drive down protruding nails.

2. Cut off the old first-course shingles at the eaves just below the butts of the second course and replace them with a 1" by 3" or a 1" by 4" strip nailed flush with the eaves line.

3. Cut back the shingles at the gable ends about 3" and replace them with a 1" by 2", 1" by 3", or 1" by 4" strip nailed flush with the gable end.

4. Remove weathered shingles at the ridge and replace them with a strip of beveled siding, thin edge down, to provide a solid base for nailing the ridge shingles. Treat hips the same as ridges.

5. Fill open valleys with wooden strips level with the old shingle surface, or with a narrow strip placed across the "V" of the valley to act as a support for new flashings.

6. Inspect flashings carefully, including valley flashings. Replace terne and galvanized flashings. Reuse old flashings if they are in good condition.

7. Use the following nails in applying shingles over an existing

roof—5d box or special overroofing nails, 14-gage, 1¾″ long for 16″ and 18″ shingles; 6d, 13-gage, 2″ long for 24″ shingles. One square of roofing (100 square feet) will need about 3½ pounds of nails.

8. Apply new shingles as recommended by the manufacturer. (*See* Chap. 16, Roofing.)

*CHAPTER 18*

# Exterior Wood Coverings

Because siding and other types of coverings used for exterior walls have an important influence on the appearance as well as on the maintenance of the house, a careful selection of the pattern should be made. The homeowner now has a choice of many wood and wood-base materials which may be used to cover exterior walls. Masonry, veneers, metal or plastic siding, and other nonwood materials are additional choices. *Wood siding* can be obtained in many different patterns and can be finished naturally, stained, or painted. Wood shingles, plywood, wood siding, or paneling, fiberboard, and hardboard are some of the types used as exterior coverings. Many prefinished sidings are available, and the coatings and films applied to several types of base materials presumably eliminate the need of refinishing for many years.

## WOOD SIDING

One of the materials most characteristic of the exteriors of American houses is *wood siding*. The essential properties required for siding are good painting characteristics, easy working qualities, and freedom from warp. Such properties are present to a *high degree* in the cedars, eastern white pine, sugar pine, western white pine, cypress, and redwood; to a *good degree* in western hemlock, ponderosa pine, the spruces, and yellow poplar; and to a *fair degree* in Douglas fir, western larch, and southern pine.

Material used for exterior siding which is to be painted should preferably be of a high grade and free from knots, pitch pockets, and waney edges. Vertical grain and mixed grain (both vertical and flat) are available in some species such as redwood and western red cedar.

The moisture content at the time of application should be that which it would attain in service. This would be approximately 10 to 12 percent except in the dry southwestern states where the moisture content should average about 8 to 9 per cent. To minimize seasonal movement due to changes in moisture content, vertical-grain (edge-grain) siding is preferred. While this is not as important for a stained finish, the use of edge-grain siding for a paint finish will result in longer paint life. A three-minute dip in a water-repellent preservative before siding is installed will not only result in longer paint life but also will resist moisture entry and decay. Some manufacturers supply siding with this treatment. Freshly cut ends should be brush-treated on the job.

### HORIZONTAL SIDINGS

Some wood-siding patterns are used only horizontally and others only vertically. Some may be used in either manner if adequate nailing areas are provided. Following are descriptions of each of the general types.

### BEVEL SIDING

Plain bevel siding can be obtained in sizes from ½" by 4" to ½" by 8" and also in sizes of ¾" by 8" and ¾" by 10" (Fig. 1). "Anzac" siding (Fig. 1) is ¾" by 12" in size. Usually the finished width of bevel siding is about ½" less than the size listed. One side of bevel siding has a smooth planed surface, while the other has a rough resawn surface. For a stained finish, the rough or sawn side is exposed because wood stain is most successful and longer lasting on rough wood surfaces.

### DOLLY VARDEN SIDING

*Dolly Varden siding* is similar to true bevel siding except that shiplap edges are used, resulting in a constant exposure distance (Fig. 1). Because it lies flat against the studs, it is sometimes used for garages and similar buildings without sheathing. Diagonal bracing is then needed to provide racking resistance to the wall.

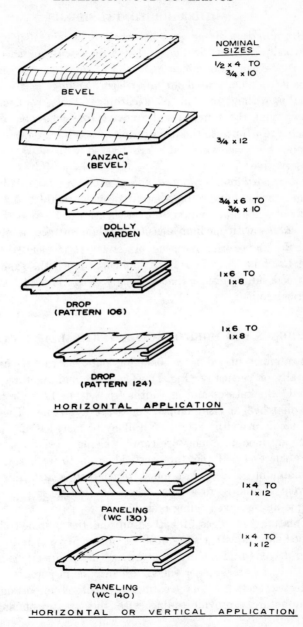

**Fig. 1.** Wood siding types.

## OTHER HORIZONTAL SIDINGS

Regular *drop sidings* can be obtained in several patterns, two of which are shown in Fig. 1. This siding, with matched or ship-lap edges, can be obtained in 1″ and 6″ and 1″ by 8″ sizes. This type is commonly used for lower-cost dwellings and for garages, usually without benefit of sheathing. Tests conducted have shown that the tongued-and-grooved (matched) patterns have greater resistance to the penetration of wind-driven rain than the shiplap patterns when both are treated with a water-repellent preservative.

*Fiberboard and hardboard sidings* are also available in various forms. Some have a backing to provide rigidity and strength while others are used directly over sheathing. Plywood horizontal lap siding, with medium density overlaid surface, is also available as an exterior covering material. It is usually ⅜″ thick and 12″ and 16″ wide. It is applied in much the same manner as wood siding, except that a shingle wedge is used behind each vertical joint.

## SIDINGS FOR HORIZONTAL OR VERTICAL APPLICATIONS

A number of siding or paneling patterns can be used horizontally or vertically (Fig. 1). These are manufactured in nominal 1″ thicknesses and in widths from 4″ to 12″. Both dressed and matched and shiplapped edges are available. The narrow-and medium-width patterns will likely be more satisfactory when there are moderate moisture-content changes. Wide patterns are more successful if they are vertical grain to keep shrinkage to a minimum. The correct moisture content is also important to prevent shrinkage to a point where the tongue is exposed when tongue-and-grooved siding is wide.

Treating the edges of both drop and the matched and ship-lapped sidings with water-repellent preservative usually prevents wind-driven rain from penetrating the joints if exposed to weather. In areas under wide overhangs, or in porches and other protected sections, this treatment is not as important. Some manufacturers provide siding with this treatment applied at the factory.

#### SIDINGS FOR VERTICAL APPLICATION

A method of siding application, popular for some architectural styles, utilizes rough sawn boards and battens applied vertically. These boards can be arranged in various ways: (a) board and batten, (b) batten and board, (c) board and board (Fig. 2). As in the vertical application of most siding materials, nominal 1″ sheathing boards or plywood sheathing ⅝″ or ¾″ thick should

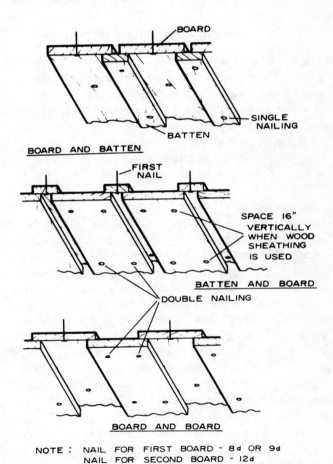

Fig. 2. Vertical board siding.

be used for nailing surfaces. When other types of sheathing materials or thinner plywood are used, nailing blocks between studs commonly provide the nailing areas. Nailers of 1″ by 4″, laid horizontally and spaced from 16″ to 24″ apart vertically, can be used over nonwood sheathing. Special or thicker casing is sometimes required around doors and window frames when this procedure is used. It is good practice to use a building paper over the sheathing before applying the vertical siding.

## SIDING WITH SHEET MATERIALS

A number of sheet materials are now available for use as siding. These include plywood in a variety of face treatments and species, paper-overlaid plywood, and hardboard. Plywood or paper-overlaid plywood is sometimes used without sheathing and is known as panel siding, with ⅜″ often considered the minimum thickness for such use for 16″ stud spacing. However, from the standpoint of stiffness and strength, better performance is usually obtained by using ½″ or ⅝″ thickness.

These 4′ by 8′ and longer sheets must be applied vertically with intermediate and perimeter nailing to provide the desired rigidity. Most other methods of applying sheet materials require some type of sheathing beneath. When horizontal joints are necessary, they should be protected by a simple flashing.

An exterior-grade plywood should always be used for siding and can be obtained in such surfaces as grooved, brushed, and saw-textured. These surfaces are usually finished with some type of stain. If shiplap or matched edges are not provided, some method of providing a waterproof joint should be used. This often consists of caulking and a batten at each joint and a batten at each stud if closer spacing is desired for appearance. An edge treatment of water-repellent preservative will also aid in reducing moisture penetration. Allow 1/16″ edge and end spacing when installing plywood in sheet form.

*Exterior grade particle board* might also be considered for panel siding. Normally ⅝″ thickness is required for 16″ stud spacing and ¾″ for 24″ stud spacing.

*Paper-overlaid plywood* has many of the advantages of plywood with the addition of providing a very satisfactory base for paint. A medium-density, overlaid plywood is most commonly used.

*Hardboard sheets* used for siding are applied the same way as plywood—by using battens at vertical points and at intermediate studs. Medium-density fiberboards might also be used in some areas as exterior coverings over certain types of sheathing.

Many of these sheet materials resist the passage of water vapor. When they are used, it is important that a good vapor barrier, well installed, be employed on the warm side of the insulated walls. (*See* Chap. **31**, Thermal Insulation, Vapor Barriers, and Sound Insulation.)

## WOOD SHINGLES AND SHAKES

*Wood shingles* and *shakes* are desirable for sidewalls in many styles of houses. In Cape Cod or Colonial houses, shingles may be painted or stained. For ranch or contemporary designs, wide exposures of shingles or shakes often add a desired effect. They are easily stained and, therefore, provide a finish which is long lasting on those species commonly used for shingles.

### GRADES AND SPECIES

Western red cedar is perhaps the most available species, although northern white cedar, bald cypress, and redwood are also satisfactory. The heartwood of these species has a natural decay resistance which is desirable if shingles are to remain unpainted or unstained.

Western red cedar shingles can be obtained in three grades. The first grade (No. 1) is all heartwood, edge grain, and knot free. It is primarily intended for roofs but is desirable in double-course sidewall application where much of the face is exposed.

Second-grade shingles (No. 2) are often used in single-course application for sidewalls, since only three-fourths of the shingle length is blemish free. A 1″ width of sapwood and mixed vertical and flat grain are permissible.

The third-grade shingle (No. 3) is clear for 6″ from the butt. Flat grain is acceptable, as are greater widths of sapwood. Third-grade shingles are likely to be somewhat thinner than the first and second grades. They are used for secondary buildings and sometimes as the undercourse in double-course application.

A lower grade than the third grade, known as under-coursing shingle, is used only as the under and completely covered course in double-course sidewall application.

## SHINGLE SIZES

*Wood shingles* are available in three standard lengths—16″, 18″, and 24″. The 16″ length is perhaps the most popular, having five butt thicknesses per 2″ when green (designated as 5⁄2). These shingles are packed in bundles with 20 courses on each side. Four bundles will cover 100 square feet of wall or roof with an exposure of 5″. The 18″ and the 24″ length shingles have thicker butts, five in 2¼″ for the 18″ shingles and four in 2″ for the 24″ lengths.

*Shakes* are usually available in several types, the most popular being the split and resawn. The sawed face is used as the back face. The butt thickness of each shake ranges between ¾″ and 1½″. They are usually packed in bundles (20 sq. ft.), five bundles to the square.

## OTHER EXTERIOR FINISH

*Nonwood* materials, such as asbestos cement siding and shingles, metal sidings, and the like are available and are used in some types of architectural design. Stucco or a cement plaster finish, preferably over a wire mesh base, is most often seen in the southwest and the west coast areas. Masonry veneers may be used effectively with wood siding in various finishes to enhance the beauty of both materials.

Some homeowners favor an exterior covering which requires a minimum of maintenance. While some of the nonwood materials are chosen for this reason, developments by the paint industry are providing comparable long-life coatings for wood-base materials. Plastic films on wood siding or plywood are also promising, so that little or no refinishing is indicated for the life of the house.

## INSTALLATION OF SIDING

One of the important factors in successful performance of

various siding materials is the type of fasteners used. Nails are the most common of these, and it is poor economy to use them sparingly. Corrosion-resistant nails, galvanized or made of aluminum, stainless steel, or similar metals may cost more, but their use will insure spot-free siding under adverse conditions.

Two types of nails are commonly used with siding, the finishing nail having a small head and the siding nail having a moderate size flathead. The *small head finishing nail* is set (driven with a nail set) about $\frac{1}{16}''$ below the face of the siding, and the hole is filled with putty after the prime coat of paint is applied. The *flathead siding nail* is commonly used and driven flush with the face of the siding. The head is later covered with paint.

Ordinary steel wire nails tend to rust in a short time and cause a disfiguring stain on the face of the siding. In some cases, the small-head nails will show rust spots through the putty and the paint. Noncorrosive nails that will not cause rust are available.

Siding to be *natural finished* with a water-repellent preservative or stain should be fastened with stainless steel or aluminum nails. In some types of prefinished sidings, nails with color-matched heads are supplied.

In recent years, nails with modified shanks have become quite popular. These nails include the *annularly* threaded shank nail and the *helically* threaded shank nail. Both have greater withdrawal resistance than the smooth shank nail and, for this reason, a shorter nail is often used.

Exposed nails in siding should be driven just flush with the surface of the wood. Overdriving may not only show the hammer mark but may also cause objectionable splitting and crushing of the wood. In sidings with prefinished surfaces or overlays, the nails should be driven so as not to damage the finished surface.

### BEVEL SIDING

The minimum lap for *bevel siding* should not be less than 1''. The average exposure distance is usually determined by the distance from the underside of the window sill to the top of the drip cap (Fig. 3). From the standpoint of weather resistance

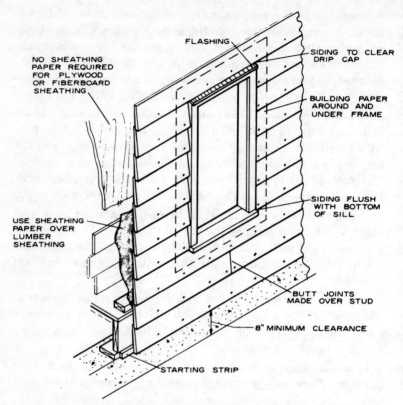

FLASHING

SIDING TO CLEAR DRIP CAP

NO SHEATHING PAPER REQUIRED FOR PLYWOOD OR FIBERBOARD SHEATHING

BUILDING PAPER AROUND AND UNDER FRAME

USE SHEATHING PAPER OVER LUMBER SHEATHING

SIDING FLUSH WITH BOTTOM OF SILL

BUTT JOINTS MADE OVER STUD

8" MINIMUM CLEARANCE

STARTING STRIP

**Fig. 3.** Installation of bevel siding.

and appearance, the butt edge of the first course of siding above the window should coincide with the top of the window drip cap. In many one-story houses with an overhang, this course of siding is often replaced with a frieze board. It is also desirable that the bottom of a siding course be flush with the underside of the window sill. This may not always be possible because of varying window heights and the types of windows that might be used in a house.

One procedure used to determine the siding exposure width so that it is about equal both above and below the window sill is as follows:

Divide the overall height of the window frame by the approximate recommended exposure distance for the siding used (4 for

6" wide siding, 6 for 8" siding, 8 for 10" siding, and 10 for 12" siding). This will result in the number of courses between the top and bottom of the window. *For example,* the overall height of the window from top of the drip cap to the bottom of the sill is 61". If 12" siding is used, the number of courses would be $61/10 = 6.1$ or six courses. To obtain the exact exposure distance, divide 61 by 6 and the result would be $10\frac{1}{6}$". The next step is to determine the exposure distance from the bottom of the sill to just below the top of the foundation wall. If this is 31", three courses at $10\frac{1}{3}$" each should be used. Therefore, the exposure distance above and below the window would be almost the same (Fig. 3).

When this procedure is not satisfactory because of big differences in the two areas, it is preferable to use an equal exposure distance for the entire wall height and notch the siding at the window sill. The fit should be tight to prevent moisture entry.

Siding may be installed starting with the bottom course. It is normally blocked out with a starting strip the same thickness as the top of the siding board (Fig. 3). Each succeeding course overlaps the upper edge of the lower course. Siding should be nailed to each stud or on 16" centers. When plywood or wood sheathing or spaced wood nailing strips are used over nonwood sheathing, sevenpenny or eightpenny nails ($2\frac{1}{4}$" and $2\frac{1}{2}$" long) may be used for $\frac{3}{4}$" thick siding. If gypsum or fiberboard sheathing is used, the tenpenny nail is used to penetrate into the stud. For $\frac{1}{2}$" thick siding, nails may be $\frac{1}{4}$" shorter than those used for $\frac{3}{4}$" siding.

The nails should be located far enough up from the butt to miss the top of the lower siding course (Fig. 4). This clearance distance is usually $\frac{1}{8}$". This allows for slight movement of the siding due to moisture changes without causing splitting. Such an allowance is especially required for the wider sidings of 8" to 12" wide.

It is good practice to avoid butt joints whenever possible. Use the longer sections of siding under windows and other long stretches and utilize the shorter lengths for areas between windows and doors. If unavoidable, butt joints should be made over a stud and staggered between courses as much as practical (Fig. 3).

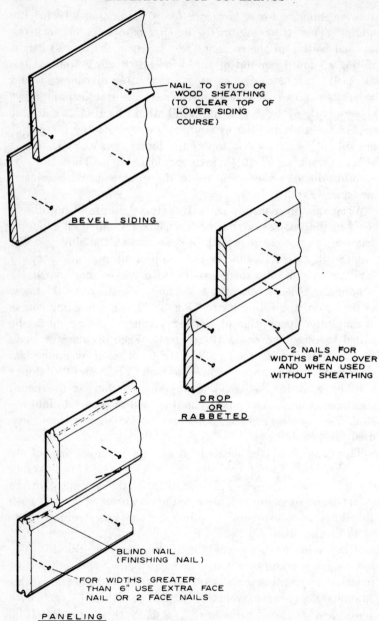

**Fig. 4.** Nailing of siding.

Siding should be *square cut* to provide a good joint at window and door casings and at butt joints. Open joints permit moisture to enter, often leading to paint deterioration. It is good practice to brush or dip the freshly cut ends of the siding in a water-repellent preservative before boards are nailed in place. Using a small finger-actuated oil can to apply the water-repellent preservative at end and butt joints after siding is in place is also helpful.

## DROP AND SIMILAR SIDINGS

*Drop siding* is installed much the same way as lap siding except for spacing and nailing. Drop, Dolly Varden, and similar sidings have a constant exposure distance. This face width is normally $5\frac{1}{4}''$ for 1" by 6" siding and $7\frac{1}{4}''$ for 1" by 8" siding. Normally, one or two eightpenny nails or ninepenny nails should be used at each stud crossing depending on the width (Fig. 4). The length of the nail depends on the type of sheathing used, but penetration into the stud or through the wood backing should be at least $1\frac{1}{2}''$.

Horizontally applied matched paneling in narrow widths should be blind nailed at the tongue with a corrosion-resistant finishing nail (Fig. 4). For widths greater than 6", an additional nail should be used as shown in the illustration.

Other materials such as plywood, hardboard, or medium-density fiberboard, which are used horizontally in widths up to 12", should be applied in the same manner as lap or drop siding, depending on the pattern. Prepackaged siding should be applied according to the manufacturers' directions.

## VERTICAL SIDINGS

Vertically applied matched and similar sidings having inter-lapping joints are nailed in the same manner as when applied horizontally. However, they should be nailed to blocking used between studs or to wood or plywood sheathing. Blocking is spaced from 16" to 24" apart. With plywood or nominal 1" board sheathing, nails should be spaced on 16" centers.

When the various combinations of boards and battens are used, they should also be nailed to blocking spaced from 16" to 24" apart between studs, or closer for wood sheathing. The first boards or battens should be fastened with one eightpenny nail or ninepenny nail at each blocking, to provide at least $1\frac{1}{2}''$ penetration. For wide underboards, two nails spaced about $2''$ apart may be used rather than the single row along the center (Fig. 2). The second or top boards or battens should be nailed with twelvepenny nails. Nails of the top board or batten should always miss the underboards and not be nailed through them (Fig. 2). In such applications, double nails should be spaced closely to prevent splitting if the board shrinks. It is also good practice to use a sheathing paper, such as 15-pound asphalt felt, under vertical siding.

## PLYWOOD AND OTHER SHEET SIDING

Exterior-grade plywood, paper-overlaid plywood, and similar sheet materials used for siding are usually applied vertically. When used over sheathing, plywood should be at least $\frac{1}{4}''$ thick, although $\frac{5}{16}''$ and $\frac{3}{8}''$ will normally provide a more even surface. Hardboard should be $\frac{1}{4}''$ thick and materials such as medium-density fiberboard should be $\frac{1}{2}''$.

All nailing should be over studs and total effective penetration into wood should be at least $1\frac{1}{2}''$. *For example*, $\frac{3}{8}''$ plywood siding over $\frac{3}{4}''$ wood sheathing would require about a seven-penny nail, which is $2\frac{1}{4}''$ long. This would result in a $1\frac{1}{8}''$ penetration into the stud, but a total effective penetration of $1\frac{7}{8}''$ into the wood.

Plywood should be nailed at $6''$ intervals around the perimeter and $12''$ at intermediate members. Hardboard siding should be nailed at $4''$ and $8''$ intervals. All types of sheet material should have a joint caulked with mastic unless the joints are of the interlapping or matched type or battens are installed. A strip of 15-pound asphalt felt under uncalked joints is good practice.

## CORNER TREATMENT

The method of finishing wood siding or other materials at exterior corners is often influenced by the overall design of the house. A mitered corner effect on horizontal siding or the using of corner boards are perhaps the most common methods of treatment.

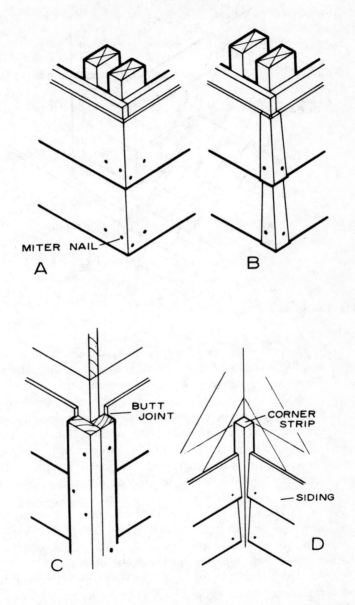

**Fig. 5.** Siding details. *A*, miter corner. *B*, metal corners. *C*, corner boards. *D*, siding return at roof.

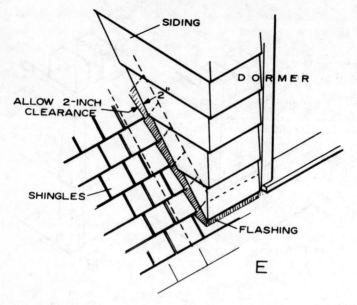

**Fig. 5** *(continued)*. *E*, interior corner.

*Mitering corners* (*A*, Fig. 5) of bevel and similar sidings, unless carefully done to prevent openings, is not always satisfactory. To maintain a good joint, it is necessary that the joint fit tightly the full depth of the miter. It is also good practice to treat the ends with a water-repellent preservative prior to nailing.

*Metal corners* (*B*, Fig. 5) are perhaps more commonly used than the mitered corner and they give a mitered effect. They are easily placed over each corner as the siding is installed. The metal corners should fit tightly without openings and should be nailed on each side to the sheathing or corner stud beneath. If made of galvanized iron, they should be cleaned with a mild acid wash and primed with a metal primer before the house is painted to prevent early peeling of the paint. Weathering of the metal will also prepare it for the prime paint coat.

*Corner boards* of various types and sizes may be used for horizontal siding of all types (*C*, Fig. 5). They also provide a satisfactory termination for plywood and similar sheet materials. Vertical applications of matched paneling or of boards and battens are terminated by lapping one side and nailing into the edge of this member, as well as to the nailing members beneath. Corner boards are usually $1\frac{1}{8}''$ or $1\frac{3}{8}''$ material and for a distinctive appearance may be quite narrow. Plain outside casing commonly used for window and door frames can be adapted for corner boards.

Prefinished shingle or shake exteriors sometimes are used with color-matched metal corners. They can also be lapped over the adjacent corner shingle, alternating each course. This is called *lacing*. This type of corner treatment usually requires that some kind of flashing be used beneath.

*Interior corners* (*E*, Fig. 5) are butted against a square corner board of nominal $1\frac{1}{4}''$ or $1\frac{3}{8}''$ size, depending on the thickness of the siding.

When siding returns against a roof surface, such as at a dormer, there should be a clearance of about $2''$ (*D*, Fig. 5). Siding cut tight against the shingles retains moisture after rains and usually results in paint peeling. Shingle flashing extending well up on the dormer wall will provide the necessary resistance to entry of wind-driven rain. Be sure to use a water-repellent preservative on the ends of the siding at the roof line.

## MATERIAL TRANSITION

At times, the materials used in the gable ends and in the walls below differ in form and application. The details of construction used at the juncture of the two materials should be such that good drainage is assured. *For example,* if vertical boards and battens are used at the gable end and horizontal siding below, a drip cap or similar molding might be used (Fig. 6). Flashing should be used over and above the drip cap so that moisture will clear the gable material.

Another method of material transition might also be used. By extending the plate and studs of the gable end out from the wall a short distance, or by the use of furring strips, the gable siding will project beyond the wall siding and provide good drainage (Fig. 7).

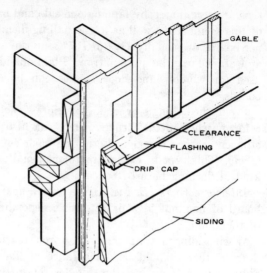

**Fig. 6.** Gable-end finish (material transition).

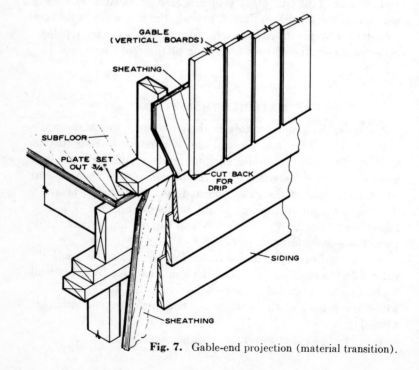

**Fig. 7.** Gable-end projection (material transition).

## INSTALLATION OF WOOD SHINGLES AND SHAKES

*Wood shingles* and *shakes* are applied in a single- or double-course pattern. They may be used over wood or plywood sheathing. If sheathing is ⅜″ plywood, use threaded nails. For non-wood sheathing, 1″ by 3″ or 1″ by 4″ wood nailing strips are used as a base. In the single-course method, one course is simply laid over the other as lap siding is applied. The shingles can be second grade because only one-half or less of the butt portion is exposed (Fig. 8). Shingles should not be soaked before application but should usually be laid up with about ⅛″ to ¼″ space between adjacent shingles to allow for expansion during rainy weather. When a *siding effect* is desired, shingles should be laid up so that they are only lightly in contact. Prestained or treated shingles provide the best results for this method.

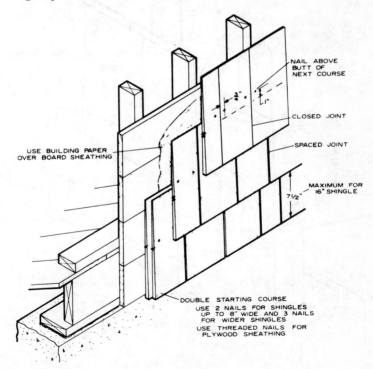

**Fig. 8.** Single coursing of sidewalls (wood shingles-shakes).

In a double-course method, the undercourse is applied over the wall and the top course nailed directly over a $\frac{1}{4}''$ to $\frac{1}{2}''$ projection of the butt (Fig. 9). The first course should be nailed only enough to hold it in place while the outer course is being applied. The first shingles can be of a lower quality, such as third grade or the undercourse grade. The top course, because much of the shingle length is exposed, should be first-grade shingles.

Exposure distance for various-length shingles and shakes can be guided by those shown in Table 8.

As in roof shingles, joints should be *broken* so that the butt joints of the upper shingles are at least $1\frac{1}{2}''$ from the under shingle joints.

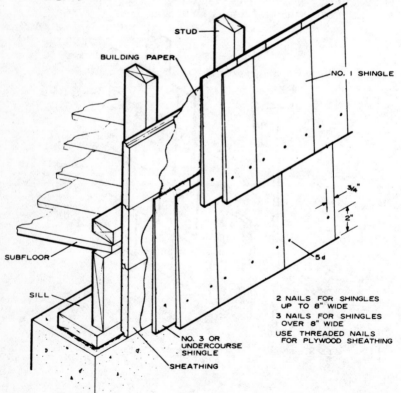

STUD

BUILDING PAPER

NO. 1 SHINGLE

$\frac{3}{4}''$

2"

SUBFLOOR

5 d

SILL

2 NAILS FOR SHINGLES UP TO 8" WIDE
3 NAILS FOR SHINGLES OVER 8" WIDE
USE THREADED NAILS FOR PLYWOOD SHEATHING

NO. 3 OR UNDERCOURSE SHINGLE

SHEATHING

**Fig. 9.** Double coursing of sidewalls (wood shingles-shakes).

TABLE 8

*Exposure distances for wood shingles and shakes on sidewalls*

| Material | Length | Maximum exposure | | |
| | | Single coursing | Double coursing | |
| | | | No. 1 grade | No. 2 grade |
| | *In.* | *In.* | *In.* | *In.* |
| Shingles | 16 | 7½ | 12 | 10 |
| | 18 | 8½ | 14 | 11 |
| | 24 | 11½ | 16 | 14 |
| Shakes (hand split and resawn) | 18 | 8½ | 14 | -------- |
| | 24 | 11½ | 20 | -------- |
| | 32 | 15 | ---------------- | |

Closed or open joints may be used in the application of shingles to sidewalls at the discretion of the worker (Fig. 8). Spacing of ¼″ to ⅜″ produces an individual effect, while close spacing produces a shadow line similar to bevel siding.

Shingles and shakes should be applied with rust-resistant nails long enough to penetrate into the wood backing strips or sheathing. In single coursing, a threepenny or fourpenny zinc-coated *shingle* nail is commonly used. In double coursing, where nails are exposed, a fivepenny zinc-coated nail with a small flat head is used for the top course and threepenny or fourpenny size for the undercourse. Be sure to use building paper over lumber sheathing.

Nails should be placed in from the edge of the shingle a distance of ¾″ (Fig. 8). Use two nails for each shingle up to 8″ wide and three nails for shingles over 8″. In single-course applications, nails should be placed 1″ above the butt line of the next higher course. In double coursing, the use of a piece of shiplap sheathing as a guide allows the outer course to extend ½″ below the undercourse, producing a shadow line (Fig. 9). Nails should be placed 2″ above the bottom of the shingle or shake. Rived or fluted processed shakes, usually factory stained, are available and have a distinct effect when laid with closely fitted edges in a double-course pattern.

## CHAPTER 19

# Porches and Garages

An attached porch or garage which is in keeping with the house design usually adds to its overall pleasing appearance. Therefore, any similar attachments to the house after it has been built should also be in keeping structurally and architecturally with the basic design. In such additions, the connections of the porch or garage to the main house should be by means of the framing members and roof sheathing. Rafters, ceiling joists, and studs should be securely attached by nailing to the house framing.

When *additions* are made to an existing house, the siding or other finish is removed so that framing members can be easily and correctly fastened to the house. In many instances, the siding can be cut with a skill saw to the outline of the addition and removed only where necessary. When concrete foundations, piers, or slabs are added, they should also be structurally correct. Footings should be of sufficient size, the bottoms located below the frostline, and the foundation wall anchored to the house foundation when possible.

## PORCHES

There are many types and designs of porches, some with roof slopes continuous with the roof of the house itself. Other porch roofs may have just enough pitch to provide drainage. The fundamental construction principles are somewhat alike no matter what type is built. Therefore, a general description—together with several construction details—can apply to several types.

Figure 1 shows the construction details of a typical flat-roofed porch with a concrete slab floor. An attached porch can be open or fully enclosed, or it can be constructed with a concrete slab floor (insulated or uninsulated). A porch can also be constructed using wood floor framing over a crawl space (Fig. 2). Most details of such a unit should comply with those previously outlined for various parts of the house itself.

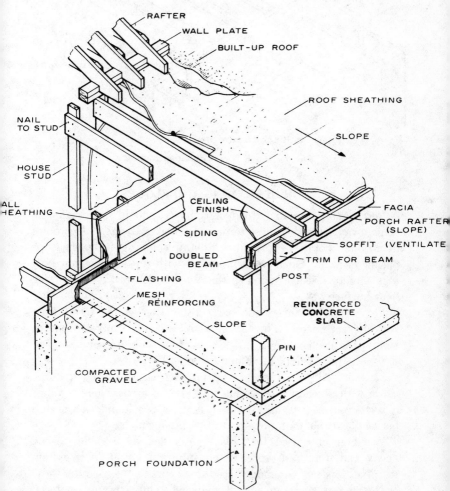

**Fig. 1.** Details of porch construction for concrete slab.

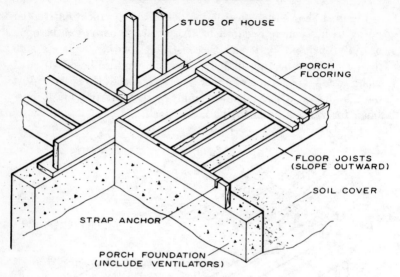

**Fig. 2.** Porch floor with wood framing.

## PORCH FRAMING AND FLOORS

*Porch floors,* whether wood or concrete, should have sufficient slope away from the house to provide good drainage. Weep holes or drains should be provided in any solid or fully sheathed perimeter wall. Open wood balusters with top and bottom railings should be constructed so that the bottom rail is free of the floor surface.

*Floor framing* for wood floor construction should be at least 18″ above the soil. The use of a soil cover of polyethylene or similar material under a partially open or a closed porch is good practice. (*See* Chap. 11, Floor Framing.)

Slats or grillwork used around an open crawl space should be made with a removable section for entry in areas where termites may be present. A fully enclosed crawl-space foundation should be vented or have an opening to the basement.

Wood species used for finish porch floor should have good decay and wear resistance, be nonsplintering, and be free from warping. Species commonly used are cypress, Douglas fir, western larch, southern pine, and redwood. Only treated material should be used where moisture conditions are severe.

## PORCH COLUMNS

Supports for enclosed porches usually consist of fully framed stud walls. The studs are doubled at openings and at corners. Because both interior and exterior finish coverings are used, the walls are constructed much like the walls of the house. In open or partially open porches, solid or built-up posts or columns are used. A more finished or cased column is often made up of doubled 2 by 4's which are covered with 1″ by 4″ casing on two opposite sides and 1″ by 6″ finish casing on the other sides (*A*, Fig. 3). Solid posts normally 4″ by 4″ in size are used mainly for open porches. An open railing may be used between posts.

A formal design of a large house entrance often includes the use of round built-up columns topped by *Doric* or *Ionic* capitals. These columns are factory made and ready for installation at the house site.

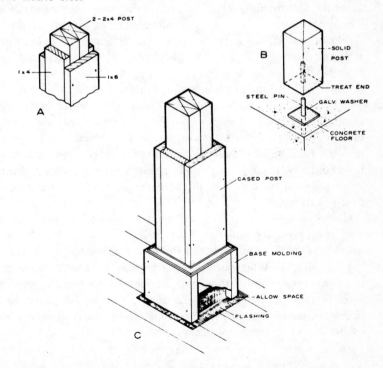

**Fig. 3.** Post details. *A*, cased post. *B*, pin anchor and spacer. *C*, flashing at base.

The base of posts or columns in open porches should be designed so that no pockets are formed to retain moisture and encourage decay. In single posts, a steel pin may be used to locate the post and a large galvanized washer or similar spacer used to keep the bottom of the post above the concrete or wood floor (*B*, Fig. 3). The bottom of the post should be treated to minimize moisture penetration. Often single posts of this type are made from a decay-resistant wood species. A cased post can be flashed under the base molding (*C*, Fig. 3). Post anchors which provide connections to the floor and to the post are available commercially, as are post caps.

## BALUSTRADE

A porch *balustrade* usually consists of one or two railings with *balusters* between them. They are designed for an open porch in order to provide protection and to improve the appearance. There are innumerable combinations and arrangements of them. A closed balustrade may be used with screens or combination windows above (*A*, Fig. 4). A balustrade with decorative railings may be used for an open porch (*B*, Fig. 4). This type can also be used with full-height removable screens.

All balustrade members that are exposed to water and snow should be designed to shed water. The top of the railing should be tapered and connections with balusters protected as much as possible (*A*, Fig. 5). Railings should not contact a concrete floor but should be blocked to provide a small space beneath. When wood must be in contact with the concrete, it should be treated to resist decay.

Connection of the railing with a post should be made in a way that prevents moisture from being trapped. One method provides a small space between the post and the end of the railing (*B*, Fig. 5). When the railing is treated with paint or water-repellent preservative, this type of connection should provide good service. Exposed members, such as posts, balusters, and railings, should be all-heartwood stock of decay-resistant or treated wood to minimize decay.

## GARAGES

*Garages* can be classified as attached, detached, basement, or

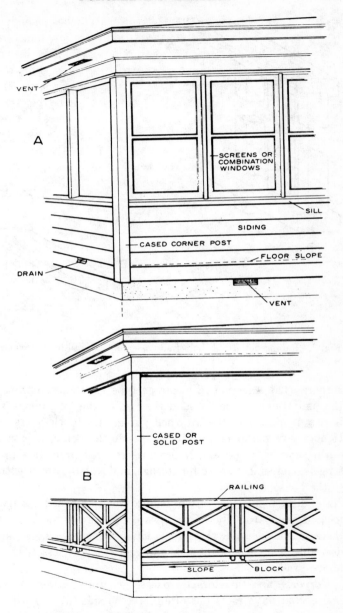

**Fig. 4.** Types of balustrades. *A,* closed. *B,* open.

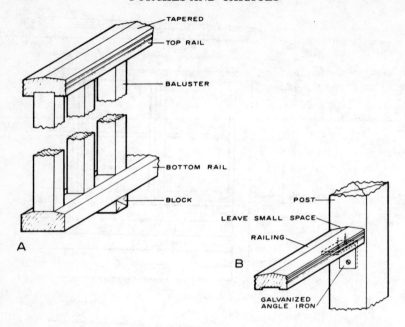

**Fig. 5.** Railing details. *A,* balustrade assembly. *B,* rail-to-post connection.

carport. The selection of a garage type is often determined by the limitations of the site and the size of the lot. Where space is not a limitation, the attached garage has much in its favor. It may give better architectural lines to the house, it is warmer during cold weather, and it provides covered protection to passengers, convenient space for storage, and a short, direct entrance to the house.

Building regulations often require that detached garages be located away from the house toward the rear of the lot. Where there is considerable slope to a lot, basement garages may be desirable, and generally such garages will cost less than those above grade.

*Carports* are car-storage spaces, generally attached to the house, that have roofs but often have no sidewalls. To improve the appearance and utility of this type of structure, storage cabinets are often used on a side and at the end of the carport.

## SIZE

It is a mistake to design the garage too small for convenient use. Cars vary in size from the small import models to the large foreign and domestic sedans. Many popular models are now up to 215″ long, and the larger and more expensive models are usually over 230″ (almost 20′ in length). Therefore, while the garage need not necessarily be designed to take all sizes with adequate room around the car, it is wise to provide a minimum distance of 21′ to 22′ between the inside face of the front and rear walls. If additional storage or work space is required at the back, a greater depth is required.

The inside width of a single garage should never be less than 11′; 13′ is much more satisfactory.

The minimum outside size for a single garage, therefore, would be 14′ by 22′. A double garage should be not less than 22′ by 22′ in outside dimensions to provide reasonable clearance and use. The addition of a shop or storage area would increase these minimum sizes.

For an attached garage, the foundation wall should extend below the frostline and about 8″ above the finish floor level. It should be not less than 6″ thick, but it is usually more because of the difficulty of trenching this width. The sill plate should be anchored to the foundation wall with anchor bolts spaced about 8′ apart, at least two bolts in each sill piece. Extra anchors may be required at the side of the main door. The framing of the sidewalls and roof and the application of the exterior covering material of an attached garage should be similar to that of the house.

The interior finish of the garage is often a matter of choice. The studs may be left exposed or covered with some type of sheet material or they may be plastered. Some building codes require that the wall between the house and the attached garage be made of fire-resistant material. Local building regulations and fire codes should be consulted before construction is begun.

If fill is required below the floor, it should preferably be sand or gravel well-compacted and tamped. If other types of soil fill are used, it should be wet down so that it will be well-compacted and can then be well-tamped. Time must be allowed before pouring. Unless these precautions are taken, the concrete floor will likely settle and crack.

The floor should be of concrete not less than 4″ thick and laid with a pitch of about 2″ from the back to the front of the garage. The use of wire reinforcing mesh is often advisable. The garage floor should be set about one inch above the drive or apron level. It is desirable at this point to have an expansion joint between the garage floor and the driveway or apron.

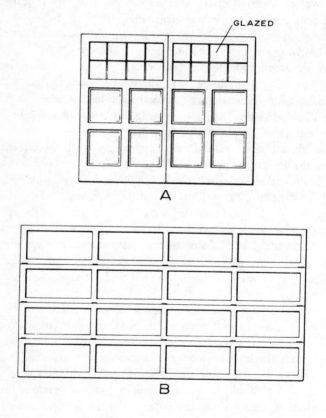

**Fig. 6.** Garage doors. *A,* one-section swing. *B,* sectional.

## GARAGE DOORS

The two overhead garage doors most commonly used are the sectional and the single-section swing types. The *swing door* (*A*, Fig. 6) is hung with side and overhead brackets and an overhead track and must be moved outward slightly at the bottom as it is opened. The *sectional-type door* (*B*, Fig. 6), in four or five horizontal hinged sections, has a similar track extending along the sides and under the ceiling framing, with a roller for the side of each section. It is opened by lifting and is adaptable to automatic electric opening with remote-control devices. The standard desirable size for a single door is 9′ in width by 6½′ or 7′ in height. Double doors are usually 16′ by 6½′ or 17′ in size.

Doors vary in design, but those most often used are the panel type with solid stiles and rails and panel fillers. A glazed panel section is often included. Clearance above the top of the door required for overhead doors is usually about 12″. However, low headroom brackets are available when such clearance is not possible.

The header beam over garage doors should be designed for the snow load which might be imposed on the roof above. In wide openings, this may be a steel I-beam or a built-up wood section. For spans of 8′ or 9′, two doubled 2 by 10's of high-grade Douglas fir or similar species are commonly used when only snow loads must be considered. If floor loads are also imposed on the header, a steel I-beam or wide-flange beam is usually selected.

## CHAPTER 20

# Exterior Frames, Windows, and Doors

Windows, doors, and their frames are millwork items that are usually fully assembled at the factory. Window units, *for example,* often have the sash fitted and weatherstripped, frame assembled, and exterior casing in place. Standard combination storms and screens or separate units can also be included. Door frames are normally assembled ready for use in the building. All such wood components are treated with a water-repellent preservative at the factory to provide protection before and after they are placed in the walls. (*See also* Chap. 26, Interior Doors, and Trim.)

Windows exist mainly to allow entry of light and air, but they may also be an important part of the architectural design. Some variation may occur, but normally in habitable rooms the glass area should be not less than 10 per cent of the floor area. Natural ventilation should be not less than 4 per cent of the floor area in a habitable room unless a complete air-conditioning system is used.

## TYPES OF WINDOWS

Windows are available in many types, each having advantages. The principal types are double-hung, casement, stationary, awning, and horizontal sliding. They may be made of wood or metal. Heat loss through metal frames and sash is much greater than through similar wood units. Glass blocks are sometimes used for admitting light in places where transparency or ventilation is not required.

Insulated glass, used both for stationary and movable sash,

consists of two or more sheets of spaced glass with hermetically sealed edges. This type has more resistance to heat loss than a single thickness and is often used without a storm sash.

Wood sash and door and window frames should be made from a clear grade of all-heartwood stock of a decay-resistant wood species or from wood which is given a preservative treatment. Species commonly used include ponderosa and other pines, the cedars, cypress, redwood, and the spruces.

Tables showing glass size, sash size, and rough opening size are available at lumber dealers, so that the wall openings can be framed accordingly.

### DOUBLE-HUNG WINDOWS

The *double-hung window* is perhaps the most familiar window type. It consists of an upper and lower sash that slide vertically in separate grooves in the side jambs or in full-width metal weatherstripping (Fig. 1). This type of window provides a maximum face opening for ventilation of one-half the total window area. Each sash is provided with springs, balances, or *compression weatherstripping* to hold it in place in any location. *For example*, compression weatherstripping prevents air infiltration, provides tension, and acts as a counterbalance. Several types allow the sash to be removed for easy painting or repair.

The *jambs* (sides and top of the frames) are made of nominal 1″ lumber; the width provides for use with dry wall or plastered interior finish. Sills are made from nominal 2″ lumber and sloped at about 3 in 12 for good drainage (D, Fig. 1). Sash are normally 1⅜″ thick and wood combination storm and screen windows are usually 1⅛″ thick.

*Sash* may be divided into a number of lights by small wood members called *muntins*. A ranch-type house may provide the best appearance with top and bottom sash divided into two horizontal lights. A colonial or Cape Cod house usually has each sash divided into six or eight lights. Some manufacturers provide preassembled dividers which snap in place over a single light, dividing it into six or eight lights. This simplifies painting and other maintenance.

*Assembled frames* are placed in the rough opening over strips

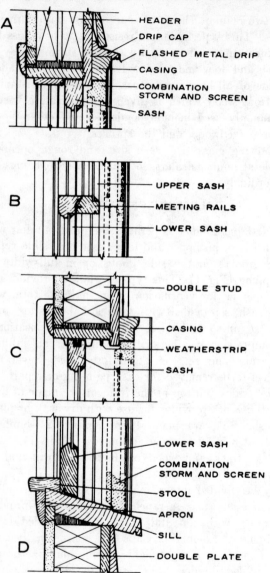

**Fig. 1.** Double-hung windows. Cross sections: *A,* head jamb. *B,* meeting rails. *C,* side jambs. *D,* sill.

of building paper put around the perimeter to minimize air infiltration. The frame is plumbed and nailed to side studs and header through the casings or the blind stops at the sides. Where nails are exposed, such as on the casing, use the corrosion-resistant type.

*Hardware* for double-hung windows includes the sash lifts that are fastened to the bottom rail, although they are sometimes eliminated by providing a finger groove in the rail. Other hardware consists of sash locks or fasteners located at the meeting rail. They not only lock the window, but also draw the sash together to provide a *windtight* fit.

Double-hung windows can be arranged as a single unit, doubled (or mullion) type, or in groups of three or more. One or two double-hung windows on each side of a large stationary insulated window are often used to effect a window wall. Such large openings must be framed with headers large enough to carry roofloads.

## CASEMENT WINDOWS

*Casement windows* consist of side-hinged sash, usually designed to swing outward (Fig. 2) because they can be made more weathertight than the in-swinging style. Screens are located inside these out-swinging windows, and winter protection is obtained with a storm sash or by using insulated glass in the sash. One advantage of the casement window over the double-hung type is that the entire window area can be opened for ventilation.

*Weatherstripping* is provided for the casement window, and units are usually received from the factory entirely assembled with hardware in place. Closing hardware consists of a rotary operator and sash lock. As in the double-hung units, the casement sash can be used in many ways—as a pair or in combinations of two or more pairs. Style variations are achieved by divided lights. Snap-in muntins provide a small, multiple-pane appearance for traditional styling.

*Metal sash* are sometimes used, but, because of low insulating value, should be installed carefully to prevent condensation and frosting on the interior surfaces during cold weather. A full storm window unit may be used to eliminate this problem in cold climates.

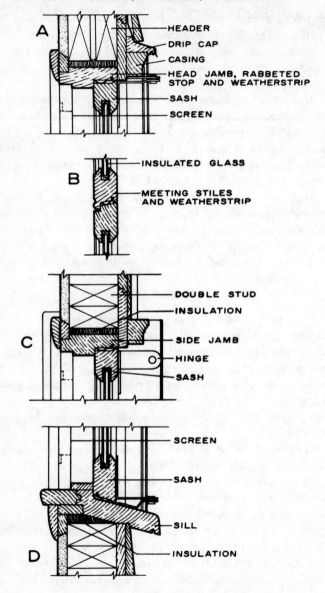

**Fig. 2.**  Out-swinging casement sash.  Cross sections:  *A*, head jamb.
*B*, meeting stiles.  *C*, side jambs.  *D*, sill.

*Stationary windows* used alone or in combination with double-hung or casement windows usually consist of a wood sash with a large single light of insulated glass. They are designed to provide light, as well as for attractive appearance, and are fastened permanently into the frame (Fig. 3). Because of their size (sometimes 6' to 8' wide) 1¾" thick sash is used to provide strength. The thickness is usually required because of the thickness of the insulating glass.

Other types of stationary windows may be used without a sash. The glass is set directly into rabbeted frame members and held in place with stops. As with all window sash units, back puttying and face puttying of the glass (with or without a stop) will assure moisture resistance.

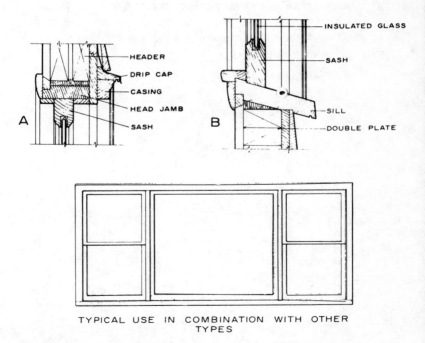

**Fig. 3.** Stationary window. Cross sections: *A*, head jamb. *B*, sill.

### AWNING WINDOWS

An *awning window unit* consists of a frame in which one or more operative sash are installed (Fig. 4). These units often are made up for a large window wall and consist of three or more units in width and height.

*Sash* of the awning type are made to swing outward at the bottom. A similar unit, called the *hopper type*, is one in which the top of the sash swings inward. Both types provide protection from rain when open.

*Jambs* are usually $1\frac{1}{16}''$ or more thick because they are rabbeted, while the sill is at least $1\frac{5}{16}''$ thick when two or more sash are used in a complete frame. Each sash may also be provided with an individual frame, so that any combination in width and height can be used. Awning or hopper window units may consist of a combination of one or more fixed sash with the remainder being the operable type. Operable sash are provided with hinges, pivots, and sash-supporting arms.

Weatherstripping and storm sash and screens are usually provided. The storm sash is eliminated when the windows are glazed with insulated glass.

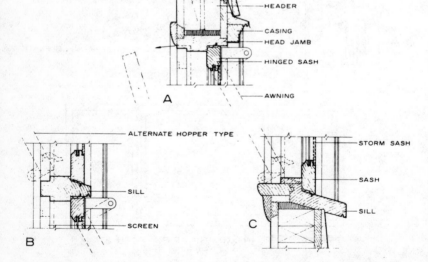

**Fig. 4.** Awning window. Cross sections: *A*, head jamb. *B*, horizontal mullion. *C*, sill.

## HORIZONTAL SLIDING WINDOW UNITS

*Horizontal sliding windows* appear similar to casement sash. However, the sash (in pairs) slide horizontally in separate tracks or guides located on the sill and head jamb. Multiple window openings consist of two or more single units and may be used when a window wall effect is desired. As in most modern window units of all types, weatherstripping, water-repellent preservative treatments, and sometimes hardware are included in these fully factory-assembled units.

## EXTERIOR DOORS AND FRAMES

*Exterior doors* are 1¾" thick and not less than 6' 8" high. The main entrance door is 3' wide and the side or rear service door 2' 8" wide.

The frames for these doors are made of 1⅛" or thicker material, so that rabbeting of side and head jambs provides stops for the main door (Fig. 5). The wood sill is often oak for wear resistance, but when softer species are used, a metal nosing and weatherstrips are included. As in many of the window units, the outside casings provide space for the 1⅛" combination or screen door.

The frame is nailed to studs and headers of the rough opening through the outside casing. The sill must rest firmly on the header or stringer joist of the floor framing, which commonly must be trimmed with a saw and hand ax or other means. After finish flooring is in place, a hardwood or metal threshold with a plastic weatherstop covers the joints between the floor and sill.

The exterior trim around the main entrance door can vary from a simple casing to a molded or plain pilaster with a decorative head casing. Decorative designs should always be in keeping with the architecture of the house. Many combinations of door and entry designs are used with contemporary houses, and manufacturers have millwork which is adaptable to most styles. If there is an entry hall, it is usually desirable to have glass included in the main door if no other light is provided.

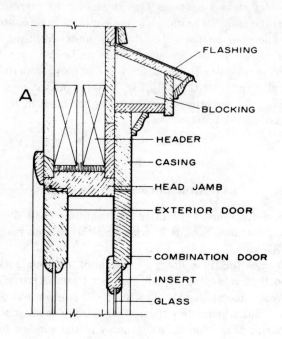

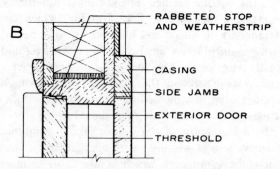

**Fig. 5.** Exterior door and frame. Exterior door and combination door (screen and storm). Cross sections: *A*, head jamb. *B*, side jamb.

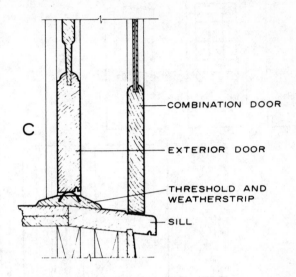

COMBINATION DOOR

EXTERIOR DOOR

THRESHOLD AND
WEATHERSTRIP

SILL

**Fig. 5** *(continued).* *C,* sill.

## TYPES OF EXTERIOR DOORS

Exterior doors and outside combination and storm doors can be obtained in a number of designs to fit the style of almost any house. Doors in the traditional pattern are usually the *panel type* (*A,* Fig. 6). They consist of *stiles* (solid vertical members), *rails* (solid cross members), and *filler panels* in a number of designs. Glazed upper panels are combined with raised wood or plywood lower panels.

*Exterior flush doors* should be of the solid-core type rather than hollow-core to minimize warping during the heating season. (Warping is caused by a difference in moisture content on the exposed and unexposed faces.) Flush doors consist of thin plywood faces over a framework of wood with a wood-block or particle-board core. Many combinations of designs can be obtained, ranging from plain flush doors to others with a variety of panels and glazed openings (*B,* Fig. 6).

*Wood combination doors* (storm and screen) are available in

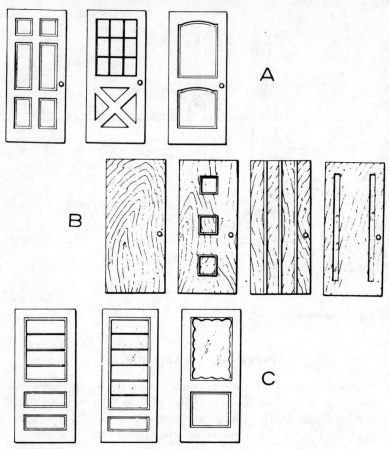

**Fig. 6.** Exterior doors. *A*, traditional panel. *B*, flush. *C*, combination.

several styles (*C*, Fig. 6). Panels which include screen and storm inserts are normally located in the upper portion of the door. Some types can be obtained with self-storing features, similar to window combination units. Heat loss through metal combination doors is greater than through similar-type wood doors.

Weatherstripping of the 1¾″ thick exterior door will reduce both air infiltration and frosting of the glass on the storm door during cold weather.

## Section V

# Interior Projects

Construction of stairs—stringers, carriages, and treads.

Basement rooms—floors, walls, and ceilings.

Interior wall and ceiling coverings—plaster, wood, plaster board, plywood, and fiberboard.

Installing the finish floor, the final wearing surface of a floor.

Installation of door frames and doors.

## CHAPTER 21

# Construction of Stairs

Stairways in houses should be designed and constructed to afford safety and adequate headroom for the occupants as well as space for the passage of furniture. The two types of stairs commonly used in houses are (a) the finished main stairs leading to the second floor or split-level floors and (b) the basement or service stairs leading to the basement or to the garage area. The main stairs are designed to provide ascent and descent and may be made a feature of the interior design. The service stairs to the basement areas are usually somewhat steeper and are constructed of less-expensive materials, although safety and convenience should be the prime factors in their design.

Most *finish* and *service stairs* are constructed in place. The *main stairs* are assembled with prefabricated parts, which include housed stringers, treads, and risers. *Basement stairs* may be made simply of 2″ by 12″ carriages and plank treads. In split-level design or a midfloor outside entry, stairways are often completely finished with plastered walls, handrails, and appropriate moldings.

Wood species appropriate for main stairway components include oak, birch, maple, and similar hardwoods. Treads and risers for the basement or service stairways may be of Douglas fir, southern pine, and similar species. A hardwood tread with a softwood or lower-grade hardwood riser may be combined to provide greater resistance to wear.

## TYPES OF STAIRWAYS

Three general types of stairway runs commonly used in house construction are the *straight run* (*A*, Fig. 1), the *long L* (*B*, Fig. 1), and the *narrow U* (*A*, Fig. 2). Another type is similar to the long *L* except that *winders* or *pie shaped* treads (*B*, Fig. 2) are substituted for the landing. This type of stairs is *not* desirable and should be avoided whenever possible because it is obviously not as convenient or as safe as the long *L*. It is used where the stair run is not sufficient for the more conventional stairway containing a landing. In such instances, the winders should be adjusted to replace the landings so that the width of the tread, 18″ from the narrow end, will not be less than the tread width on the straight run (*A*, Fig. 3). Therefore, if the standard tread is 10″ wide, the winder tread should be at least 10″ wide at the 18″ line.

Another basic rule in stair layout concerns the landing at the top of the stairs when the door opens into the stairway, such as on a stair to the basement. This landing, as well as middle landings, should not be less than 2′ 6″ long (*B*, Fig. 3).

Sufficient headroom in a stairway is a primary requisite. For main stairways, clear vertical distance should not be less than 6′ 8″ (*A*, Fig. 4). Basement or service stairs should provide not less than a 6′ 4″ clearance.

The minimum tread width and riser height must also be considered. For *closed stairs*, a 1″ tread width and an 8¼″ riser height should be considered a minimum even for basement stairways (*B*, Fig. 4). Risers with less height are always more desirable. The nosing projection should be at least 1⅛″, but if the projection is too much greater, the stairs will be awkward and difficult to climb.

## RATIO OF RISER TO TREAD

There is a definite relation between the height of a riser and the width of a tread, and all stairs should be laid out to conform to well-established rules governing these relations. If the combination of run and rise is too great, there is undue strain on the leg muscles and on the heart of the climber. If the combination

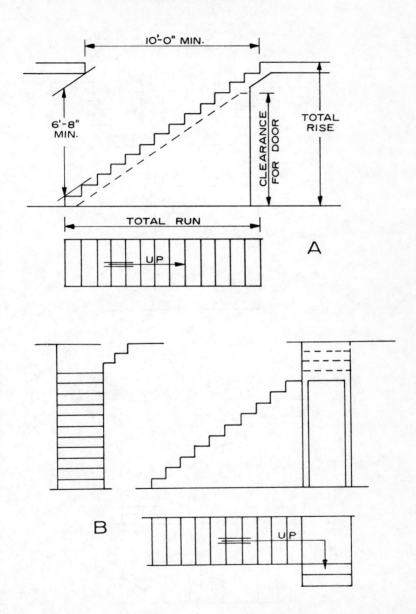

**Fig. 1.** Common types of stair runs. *A*, straight. *B*, long "L".

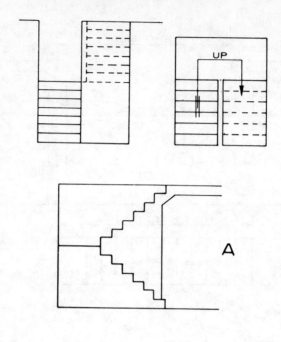

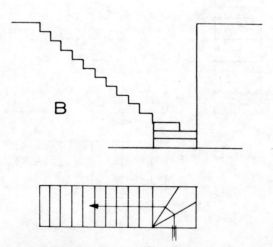

**Fig. 2.** Space-saving stairs. *A*, narrow "U". *B*, winder.

of run and rise is too small, his or her foot may kick the riser at each step and an attempt to shorten stride may be tiring. Experience has proved that a riser 7½″ to 7¾″ high with appropriate tread width combines both safety and comfort.

A rule of thumb which sets forth a good relation between the height of the riser and the width of the tread is as follows.

The tread width multiplied by the riser height in inches should equal to 72 to 75. The stairs shown in *B*, Fig. 4 would conform to this rule (9 times 8¼″ = 74¼″). If the tread is 10″, the riser should be 7½″, which is more desirable for common stairways. Another rule sometimes used: the tread width plus twice the riser height should equal about 25.

These desirable riser heights should be used to determine the number of steps between floors. *For example,* fourteen risers are commonly used for main stairs between the first and second floors. The 8′ ceiling height of the first floor plus the upper story floor joists, subfloor, and finish floor result in a floor-to-floor

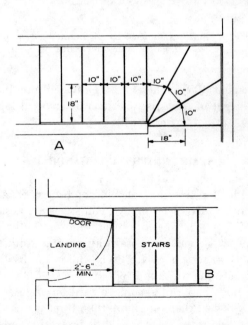

**Fig. 3.** Stair layout. *A*, winder treads. *B*, landings.

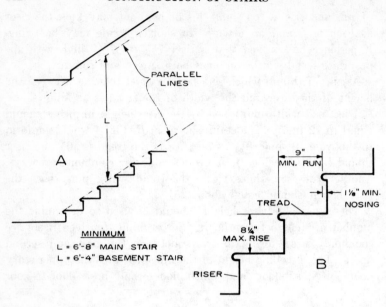

**Fig. 4.** Stairway dimensions. *A*, minimum headroom.
*B*, closed stair dimensions.

height of about 105″. Therefore, 14 divided into 105 is exactly
7½″, the height of each riser. Fifteen risers used for this height
would result in a 7″ riser height.

## STAIR WIDTHS AND HANDRAILS

The width of main stairs should not be less than 2′ 8″ clear
of the handrail. However, many main stairs are designed with a
distance of 3′ 6″ between the centerline of the enclosing sidewalls. This will result in a stairway with a width of about 3′.
Split-level entrance stairs are even wider; for basement stairs,
the minimum clear width is 2′ 6″.

A continuous handrail should be used on at least one side of
the stairway when there are more than three risers. When stairs
are open on two sides, there should be protective railings on each
side.

## FRAMING FOR STAIRS

Openings in the floor for stairways, fireplaces, and chimneys are framed out during construction of the floor. (*See* Chap. 11, Figs. 9 and 11.) The long dimension of stairway openings may be either parallel or at right angles to the joists. However, it is much easier to frame a stairway opening when its length is parallel to the joists. For *basement stairways,* the rough openings may be about 9' 6" long by 32" wide (two joist spaces). Openings in the second floor for the *main stair* are usually a minimum of 10' long. Widths may be 3' or more. Depending on the short header required for one or both ends, the opening is usually framed as shown in *A,* Fig. 5 when joists parallel the length of the opening. Nailing should conform to that shown in Chap. 11, Figs. 9 and 11.

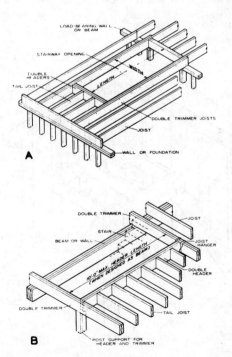

**Fig. 5.**   Framing for stairs.  *A,* length of opening parallel to joists.
*B,* length of opening perpendicular to joists.

When the length of the stair opening is perpendicular to the length of the joists, a long doubled header is required (*B*, Fig. 5). A header under these conditions without a supporting wall beneath is usually limited to a 10′ length. A load-bearing wall under all or part of this opening simplifies the framing immensely, as the joists will then bear on the top plate of the wall rather than be supported at the header by joist hangers or other means. Nailing should conform to that shown in Chap. 11, Figs. 9 and 11.

The framing for an L-shaped stairway is usually supported in the basement by a post at the corner of the opening or by a load-bearing wall beneath. When a similar stair leads from the first to the second floor, the landing can be framed out (Fig. 6). The platform frame is nailed into the enclosing stud walls and provides a nailing area for the subfloor as well as a support for the stair carriages.

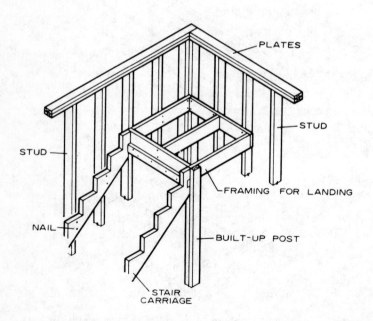

**Fig. 6.** Framing for stair landing.

## STAIRWAY DETAILS

### BASEMENT STAIRS

*Stair carriages* which carry the treads and support the loads on the stair are made in two ways. Rough stair carriages commonly used for basement stairs are made from 2″ by 12″ planks. The effective depth below the tread and riser notches must be at least 3½″ (A, Fig. 7). Such carriages are usually placed only at each side of the stairs. However, an intermediate carriage is required at the center of the stairs when the treads are 1½₆″ thick and the stairs wider than 2′ 6″. Three carriages are also required when treads are 1⅝″ thick and stairs are wider than 3′. The carriages are fastened to the joist header at the top of the stairway or rest on a supporting ledger nailed to the header (B, Fig. 7).

*Firestops* should be used at the top and bottom of all stairs as shown at A, Fig. 7.

Perhaps the simplest system is one in which carriages are not cut out for the treads and risers. Rather, cleats are nailed to the side of the unnotched carriage and the treads nailed to them. This design may not be as desirable as the notched carriage system when walls are present. Carriages may also be supported by walls located below them.

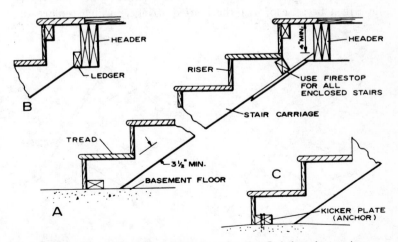

**Fig. 7.** Basement stairs. *A*, carriage details. *B*, ledger for carriage. *C*, kicker plate.

The bottom of the stair carriages may rest and be anchored to the basement floor. A better method is to use an anchored 2" by 4" or 2" by 6" treated *kicker plate* (*C*, Fig. 7).

*Basement stair treads* can consist of simple 1½" thick plank treads without risers. From the standpoint of appearance and maintenance, the use of 1⅛" finished tread material and nominal 1" boards for risers is usually justified. Use finishing nails to fasten them to the plank carriages.

A *fully enclosed stairway* might be used from the main floor to the attic. It combines the rough notched carriage with a finish stringer along each side (*A*, Fig. 8). The finish stringer is fastened to the wall, before carriages are fastened. Treads and risers are cut to fit snugly between the stringers and are fastened to the rough carriage with finishing nails (*A*, Fig. 8). This may be varied by nailing the rough carriage directly to the wall and by notching the finished stringer to fit (*B*, Fig. 8). The treads and risers are installed as previously described.

## MAIN STAIRWAY

An *open* main stairway with its railing and balusters ending in a *newel* post can be very decorative and pleasing in the traditional house interior. It can also be translated to a contemporary stairway design and again result in a pleasing feature.

The main stairway differs from the other types previously described because of (a) the housed stringers which replace the

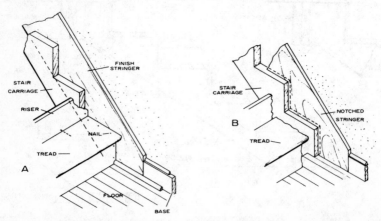

**Fig. 8.** Enclosed stairway details. *A*, with full stringer. *B*, with notched stringer.

rough plank carriage; (b) the routed and grooved treads and risers; (c) the decorative railing and balusters in open stairways; and (d) the wood species, most of which can be given a natural finish.

The supporting member of the finished main stairway is the housed stringer (*A*, Fig. 9). One is used on each side of the stairway and fastened to the plastered or finished walls. They are routed to fit both the tread and the riser. The stair is assembled by means of hardwood wedges which are spread with glue and driven under the ends of the treads and in back of the risers. Assembly is usually done from under and the rear side of the stairway. In addition, nails are used to fasten the riser to the tread between the ends of the step (*B*, Fig. 9). When treads and risers are wedged and glued into housed stringers, the maxi-

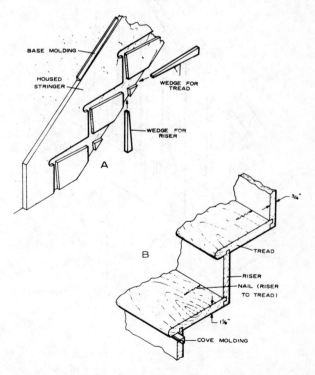

**Fig. 9.** Main stair detail. *A*, with housed stringer. *B*, with combination of treads and risers.

mum allowable width is usually 3′ 6″. For wider stairs, a notched carriage is used between the housed stringers.

When stairs are open on one side, a railing and balusters should be used. The balusters may be fastened to the end of the treads which have a finished return (Fig. 10). The balusters are also fastened to a railing which is terminated at a newel post. Balusters may be turned to form doweled ends, which fit into drilled holes in the treads and the railing. A stringer and appropriate moldings are used to complete the stairway trim.

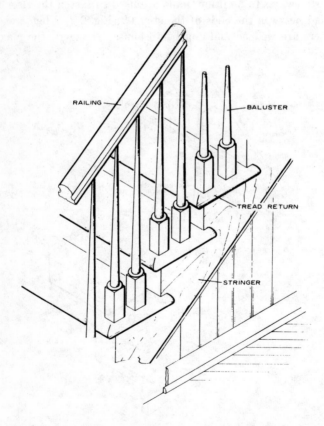

RAILING

BALUSTER

TREAD RETURN

STRINGER

**Fig. 10.** Details of open main stairway.

## ATTIC FOLDING STAIRS

Where attics are used primarily for storage and where space for a fixed stairway is not available, *hinged* or *folding* stairs are often used and may be purchased ready to install. They operate through an opening in the ceiling of a hall and swing up into the attic space, out of the way when not in use. Where such stairs are to be installed, the attic floor joists should be designed for limited floor loading. One common size of folding stairs requires only a 26" by 54" rough opening. These openings should be framed out as described for normal stair openings.

## EXTERIOR STAIRS

Proportioning of risers and treads in laying out *porch steps* or *approaches to terraces* should be as carefully considered as the design of interior stairways. Similar riser-to-tread ratios can be used. The riser used in principal exterior steps should be between 6" and 7" in height. The need for a good support or foundation for outside steps is often overlooked. Where wood steps are used, the bottom step should be concrete or supported by treated wood members. Where the steps are located over backfill or disturbed ground, the foundation should be carried down to undisturbed ground.

## CHAPTER 22

# Basement Rooms

Many houses are now designed so that one or more of the rooms in lower floors are constructed on a concrete slab. In multilevel houses, this area may include a family room, a spare bedroom, or a study. Furthermore, it is sometimes necessary to provide a room in the basement of an existing house. Therefore, in a new house or in remodeling the basement of an existing one, several factors should be considered, including insulation, waterproofing, and vapor resistance.

## FLOORS

In the construction of a new building having basement rooms, provision should be made for reduction of heat loss and for prevention of ground moisture movement. Perimeter insulation reduces heat loss and a vapor barrier under a concrete slab will prevent problems caused by a concrete floor damp from ground moisture (Fig. 1). Providing these essential details is somewhat more difficult in existing construction than in new construction.

The installation of a vapor barrier over an existing unprotected concrete slab is normally required when the floor is at or below the outside ground level and some type of finish floor is used. Flooring manufacturers recommend that preparation of the slab for wood-strip flooring consist of the following steps:

1. Mop or spread a coating of tar or asphalt mastic followed by an asphalt felt paper.
2. Lay short lengths of 2″ by 4″ screeds in a coating of tar or

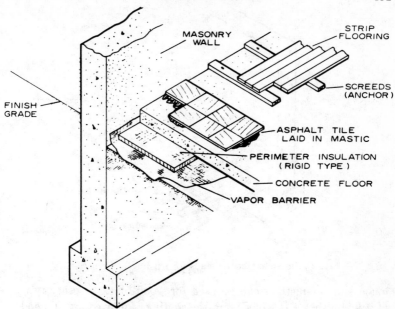

MASONRY WALL

STRIP FLOORING

FINISH GRADE

SCREEDS (ANCHOR)

ASPHALT TILE LAID IN MASTIC

PERIMETER INSULATION (RIGID TYPE)

CONCRETE FLOOR

VAPOR BARRIER

**Fig. 1.** Basement floor details for new construction.

asphalt, spacing the rows about 12" apart, starting at one wall and ending at the opposite wall.

3. Place insulation around the perimeter, between screeds, where the outside ground level is near the basement floor elevation.

4. Install wood-strip flooring across the wood screeds.

This procedure can be varied somewhat by placing a conventional vapor barrier of good quality directly over the slab. Two-by four-inch furring strips spaced 12" to 16" apart are then anchored to the slab with concrete nails or with other types of commercial anchors. Some leveling of the 2 by 4's might be required. Strip flooring is then nailed to the furring strips after perimeter insulation is placed (Fig. 2). If a wood-block flooring is desired under these conditions, a plywood subfloor may be used over the furring strips. Plywood, ½" or ⅝" thick, is normally used if the edges are unblocked and furring strips are spaced 16" or more apart.

When insulation is not required around the perimeter because of the height of the outside grade above the basement floor, a

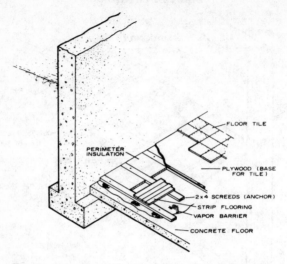

**Fig. 2.** Basement floor details for existing construction.

much simpler method can be used for wood-block or other type of tile finish. An asphalt mastic coating, followed by a good vapor barrier, serves as a base for the tile. An adhesive recommended by the flooring manufacturer is then used over the vapor barrier, after which the wood tile is applied. It is important that a smooth, vapor-tight base be provided for the tile.

It is likely that such floor construction should be used only under favorable conditions where drain tile is placed at the outside footings and soil conditions are favorable. When the slab or walls of an existing house are inclined to be damp, it is often difficult to insure a dry basement. Under such conditions, it is often advisable to use resilient tile or a similar finish over some type of stable base such as plywood. This construction is to be preceded by installation of vapor barriers and protective coatings.

## WALLS

The use of an *interior finish* over masonry basement walls is usually desirable for habitable rooms. Furthermore, if the outside wall is partially exposed, it is advisable to use *insulation* between the wall and the inside finish. *Waterproofing* the wall is important if there is any possibility of moisture entry. It can be done by applying one of the many waterproof coatings available to the inner surface of the masonry.

After the wall has been waterproofed, furring strips are commonly used to prepare the wall for interior finish. A 2″ by 2″ bottom plate is anchored to the floor at the junction of the wall and the floor. A 2″ by 2″ or larger top plate is fastened to the bottom of the joists, to the joist blocks, or anchored to the wall (Fig. 3). Studs or furring strips, 2″ by 2″ or larger in size, are then placed between the top and the bottom plates, anchoring them at the center when necessary with concrete nails or similar fasteners (Fig. 3). Electrical outlets and conduit should be installed and insulation with vapor barrier placed between the furring strips. The interior finish of gypsum board, fiberboard, plywood, or other material is then installed. *Furring strips* are commonly spaced 16″ on center, but this depends on the type and thickness of the interior finish.

*Foamed plastic insulation* is sometimes used on masonry walls without furring. It is important that the inner face of the wall be smooth and level without protrusions when this method is used. After the wall has been waterproofed, ribbons of adhesive are applied to the wall and sheets of foam insulation installed (Fig.

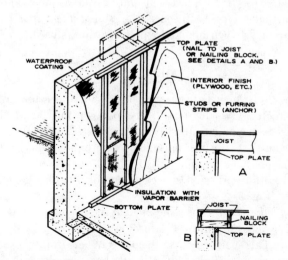

**Fig. 3.** Basement wall finish with furring strips.

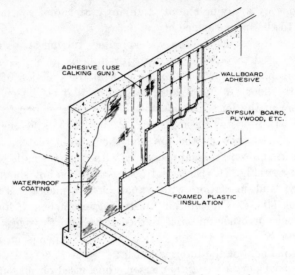

**Fig. 4.**  Basement wall finish without furring strips.

4). Dry wall adhesive is then applied and the gypsum board, plywood, or other finish pressed into place. Manufacturers' recommendations on adhesives and methods of installation should be followed. Most foam plastic insulations have some vapor resistance in themselves, so the need for a separate vapor barrier is not as great as when blanket-type insulation is used.

### CEILINGS

Some type of finish is usually desirable for the ceiling of the basement room. Gypsum board, plywood, or fiberboard sheets may be used and nailed directly to the joists. Acoustic ceiling tile and similar materials normally require additional nailing areas. This may be supplied by 1″ by 2″ or 1″ by 3″ strips nailed across the joists and spaced to conform to the size of the ceiling tile (Fig. 5).

A *suspended ceiling*, consisting of light metal angles hung from the ceiling joists, may also be desirable. Tiles are then dropped into place. This will decrease sound transfer from the rooms above. *Be sure* to install ceiling lights, heat supply and return ducts, or other utilities before the finish is applied.

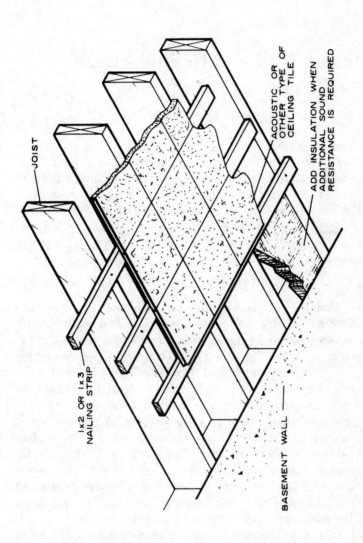

**Fig. 5.** Installation of ceiling tile.

JOIST

1x2 OR 1x3 NAILING STRIP

ACOUSTIC OR OTHER TYPE OF CEILING TILE

ADD INSULATION WHEN ADDITIONAL SOUND RESISTANCE IS REQUIRED

BASEMENT WALL

## CHAPTER 23

# Interior Wall and Ceiling Finish

*Interior finish* is the material used to cover the interior framed areas or structures of walls and ceilings. It should be prefinished or serve as a base for paint or other finishes including wallpaper. Because of moisture conditions, finishes in the bath and the kitchen areas should have more rigid requirements. Several types of interior finishes are used in the modern home: (a) lath and plaster, (b) wood paneling, fiberboard, or plywood, and (c) gypsum wallboard.

## TYPES OF FINISHES

Though lath and plaster finish is widely used in home construction, use of dry wall materials has been increasing. Dry wall is often selected because there is usually a time saving in the work. A plaster finish, being a wet material, requires drying time before other interior work can be started; dry wall finish does not. A gypsum dry wall demands a moderately low moisture content of the framing members in order to prevent *nail pops*. This happens when frame members dry out to moisture equilibrium, causing the nailhead to form small *humps* on the surface of the board. Furthermore, stud alignment is more important for single-layer gypsum finish in order to prevent a wavy, uneven appearance. Therefore, there are advantages to both plaster and gypsum dry wall finishes, and each should be considered along with the initial cost and future maintenance involved.

A plaster finish requires some type of base upon which to be applied. *Rock lath* is the most common such base. *Fiberboard lath* is also used; and *wood lath*, common many years ago, is permitted in some areas. *Metal lath* or similar mesh forms are normally used only in bathrooms and as reinforcement. They provide a rigid base for plaster finish but usually cost more than other materials. Some of the rigid foam insulations cemented to masonry walls also serve as plaster bases.

There are many types of dry wall finishes. One of the most widely used is gypsum board in 4′ by 8′ sheets and in lengths up to 16′, used for horizontal application. Plywood, hardboard, fiberboard, particle board, wood paneling, and similar types, many in prefinished form, are also used.

## LATH AND PLASTER

### PLASTER BASE

A plaster finish requires some type of base upon which to be applied. The base must have bonding qualities so that plaster adheres to, or is keyed to, the base which has been fastened to the framing members.

One of the most common types of plaster base that may be used on sidewalls or ceilings is *gypsum lath* which is 16″ by 48″ and is applied horizontally across the framing members. It has paper faces with a gypsum filler. For stud or joist spacing of 16″ on center, ⅜″ thickness is used. For 24″ on-center spacing, ½″ thickness is required. This material can be obtained with a foil back that serves as a vapor barrier. If the foil faces an air space, it also has reflective insulating value. Gypsum lath may be obtained with perforations, which, by improving the bond, would lengthen the time the plaster would remain intact when exposed to fire. Some city building codes require such perforation.

*Insulating fiberboard* lath, ½″ in thickness and 16″ by 48″ in size, is also used as a plaster base. It has greater insulating value than the gypsum lath, but horizontal joints must usually be reinforced with metal clips.

*Metal lath* in various forms such as diamond mesh, flat rib, and wire lath is another type of plaster base. It is 27″ by 96″ in size and is galvanized or painted to resist rusting.

### INSTALLATION OF PLASTER BASE

*Gypsum lath* should be applied horizontally with joints broken

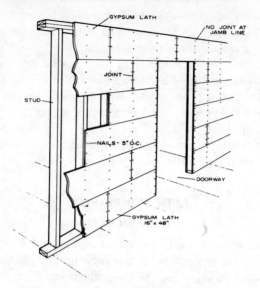

**Fig. 1.**  Application of gypsum lath.

(Fig. 1). Vertical joints should be made over the center of studs or joists and nailed with 12-gage or 13-gage gypsum lathing nails 1½″ long and with a ⅜″ flat head. Nails should be spaced 5″ on center, or four nails for the 16″ height, and used at each stud or joist crossing. Some manufacturers specify the ring-shank nails with a slightly greater spacing. Lath joints over heads of openings should not occur at the jamb lines (Fig. 1).

*Insulating lath* should be installed in much the same manner as gypsum lath, except that slightly longer blued nails should be used. A special waterproof facing is provided on one type of gypsum board for use as a ceramic tile base when the tile is applied with an adhesive.

*Metal lath* is often used as a plaster base around tub recesses and other bath and kitchen areas (Fig. 2). It is also used when a ceramic tile is applied over a plastic base. It must be backed with water-resistant sheathing paper over the framing. The metal lath is applied horizontally over the waterproof backing with side and end joints lapped. It is nailed with No. 11 and No. 12 roofing nails. These are long enough to provide about 1½″ penetration into the framing member or blocking.

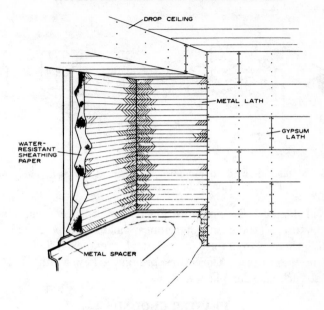

**Fig. 2.** Application of metal lath.

## PLASTER REINFORCING

Because some drying usually takes place in wood framing members after a house is completed, some shrinkage can be expected. This may cause plaster cracks to develop around openings and in corners. To minimize, if not eliminate, this cracking, use expanded metal lath in key positions over the plaster-base material as reinforcement. Strips of expanded metal lath may be used over window and door openings (*A*, Fig. 3). A strip about 10″ by 20″ is placed diagonally across each upper corner of the opening and tacked into place.

Metal lath should also be used under flush ceiling beams to prevent plaster cracks (*B*, Fig. 3). On wood drop beams extending below the ceiling line, the metal lath is applied with self-furring nails to provide space for keying of the plaster.

*Corner beads* of expanded metal lath or of perforated metal should be installed on all exterior corners (Fig. 4). They should be applied plumb and level. The bead acts as a leveling edge when walls are plastered and reinforces the corner against me-

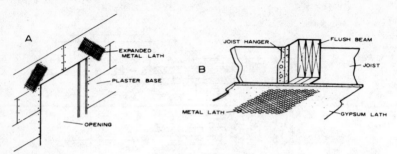

**Fig. 3.** Metal lath used to minimize cracking. *A,* at door and window openings. *B,* under flush beams.

chanical damage. To minimize plaster cracks, inside corners at the juncture of walls and of ceilings should also be reinforced. Metal lath or wire fabric *(cornerites)* are tacked lightly into place in these areas. Cornerites provide a key width of 2″ to 2½″ at each side for plaster.

## PLASTER GROUNDS

*Plaster grounds* are strips of wood used as guides or strike-off edges when plastering and are located around window and door openings and at the base of the walls. Grounds around interior door openings are often full-width pieces nailed to the sides over the studs and to the underside of the header (*A,* Fig. 5). They are 5¼″ in width, which coincides with standard jamb widths for interior walls with a plaster finish, and they are removed after plaster has dried. Narrow-strip grounds might also be used around these interior openings (*B,* Fig. 5).

In window and exterior door openings, the frames are normally in place before plaster is applied. Therefore, the inside edges of the side and head jamb can serve as grounds. The edge of the window sill might also be used as a ground, or a narrow ⅞″ thick ground strip is nailed to the edge of the 2″ by 4″ sill. Narrow ⅞″ by 1″ grounds might also be used around window and door openings (*C,* Fig. 5). These are normally left in place and are covered by casing.

A similar narrow ground or screed is used at the bottom of the wall in controlling thickness of the gypsum plaster and providing an even surface for the baseboard and molding (*A,* Fig.

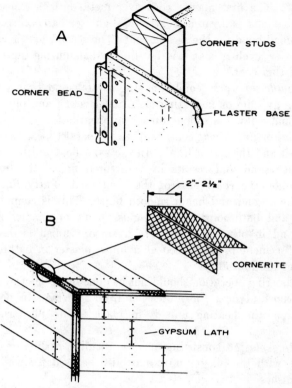

**Fig. 4.** Reinforcing of plaster at corners. *A,* outside. *B,* inside.

5). These strips are also left in place after plaster has been applied.

## PLASTER MATERIALS

Plaster for interior finishing is made from combinations of sand, lime, or prepared plaster and water. Waterproof-finish wall materials are available and should be used in bathrooms, especially in showers or tub recesses when tile is not used, and sometimes in the kitchen wainscot.

## METHOD OF APPLICATION

*Plaster* should be applied in three-coat or two-coat double-up work. The minimum thickness over ⅜″ gypsum lath should be about ½″. The first plaster coat over metal lath is called the scratch coat and is scratched, after a slight set has occurred, to insure a good bond for the second coat. The second coat is called the brown or leveling coat, and leveling is done during the application of this coat.

The *double-up work*, combining the scratch and brown coat, is used on gypsum or insulating lath, and leveling and plumbing of walls and ceilings are done during application.

The *final* or *finish coat* consists of two general types: the *sand float* finish and the *putty* finish. In the sand float finish, lime is mixed with sand and results in a textured finish, the texture depending on the coarseness of the sand used. Putty finish is used without sand and has a smooth finish. This is common in kitchens and bathrooms where a gloss paint or enamel finish is used and in other rooms where a smooth finish is desired. "Keene's" cement is often used as a finish plaster in bathrooms because of its durability.

The plastering operation should not be done in freezing weather without constant heat for protection from freezing. In normal construction, the heating unit is in place before plastering is started.

*Insulating plaster*, consisting of a vermiculite, perlite, or other aggregate with the plaster mix, may also be used for wall and ceiling finishes.

### DRY WALL FINISH

*Dry wall* finish is a material that requires little, if any, water for application. Dry wall finish includes gypsum board, plywood, fiberboard, or similar sheet material, as well as wood paneling in various thicknesses and forms.

The use of thin sheet materials such as gypsum board or plywood requires that studs and ceiling joists have good alignment to provide a smooth, even surface. Wood sheathing will often correct misaligned studs on exterior walls. A *strong back* provides for aligning of ceiling joists of unfinished attics (*A*, Fig. 6) and can be used at the center of the span when ceiling joists are uneven.

See Table **9** for thicknesses of wood materials commonly used for interior covering.

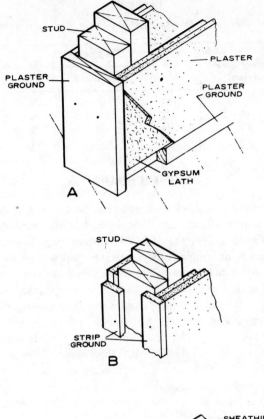

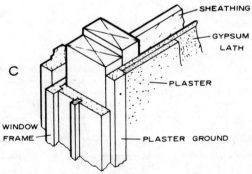

**Fig. 5.** Plaster grounds. *A*, at doorway and floor. *B*, strip ground at doorway. *C*, ground at window.

## TABLE 9

*Maximum thicknesses for plywood, fiberboard, and wood paneling*

| Framing spaced (inches) | Thickness | | |
|---|---|---|---|
| | Plywood | Fiberboard | Paneling |
| | *In.* | *In.* | *In.* |
| 16 | ¼ | ½ | ⅜ |
| 20 | ⅜ | ¾ | ½ |
| 24 | ⅜ | ¾ | ⅚ |

## GYPSUM BOARD

*Gypsum board* is a sheet material composed of a gypsum filler faced with paper. Sheets are 4′ wide and 8′ in length but can be obtained in lengths up to 16′. The edges along the length are usually tapered, although some types are tapered on all edges. This allows for a filled and taped joint. This material may also be obtained with a foil back which serves as a vapor barrier on exterior walls. It is also available with vinyl or other prefinished surfaces. In new construction, ½″ thickness is recommended for single-layer application. In laminated two-ply applications, two ⅜″ thick sheets are used. The ⅜″ thickness, while considered minimum for 16″ stud spacing in single-layer applications, is specified for repair and remodeling work.

Table 10 lists maximum member spacing for the various thicknesses of gypsum board.

## TABLE 10

*Gypsum board thickness (single layer)*

| Installed long direction of sheet | Minimum thickness | Maximum spacing of supports (on center) | |
|---|---|---|---|
| | | Walls | Ceilings |
| | *In.* | *In.* | *In.* |
| Parallel to | ⅜ | 16 | |
| framing members | ½ | 24 | 16 |
| | ⅝ | 24 | 16 |
| | ⅜ | 16 | 16 |
| Right angles to | ½ | 24 | 24 |
| framing members | ⅝ | 24 | 24 |

When the single-layer procedure is used, the 4′ wide gypsum sheets are applied vertically or horizontally on the walls after the ceiling has been covered. Vertical application covers three stud spaces when studs are spaced 16″ on center and two when spacing is 24″. Edges should be centered on studs, and only moderate contact should be made between edges of the sheet.

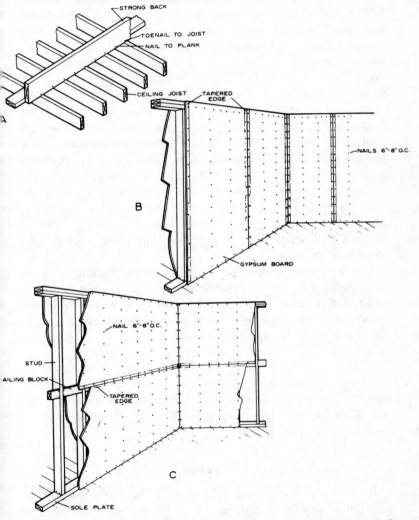

**Fig. 6.** Application of gypsum board finish. *A*, strong back. *B*, vertical application. *C*, horizontal application.

Fivepenny cooler-type nails (1⅝″ long) should be used with ½″ gypsum, and fourpenny (1⅜″ long) with the ⅜″ thick material. Ring-shanked nails, about ⅛″ shorter, can also be used. Some manufacturers recommend the use of special screws to reduce *bulging* of the surface (*nail pops* caused by drying out of the frame members). If moisture content of the framing members is less than 15 percent when gypsum board is applied, *nail pops* will be greatly reduced. It is good practice, when framing members have a high moisture content to allow them to approach moisture equilibrium before application of the gypsum board. Nails should be spaced 6″ to 8″ for sidewalls and 5″ to 7″ for ceiling application (*B*, Fig. 6). Minimum edge distance is ⅜″.

The *horizontal* method of application is best adapted to rooms in which full-length sheets can be used since it minimizes the number of vertical joints. Where joints are necessary, they should be made at windows or doors. Nail spacing is the same as that used in vertical application. When studs are spaced 16″ on center, horizontal nailing blocks between studs are normally not required when stud spacing is not greater than 16″ on center and gypsum board is ⅜″ or thicker. When spacing is greater, or an impact-resistant joint is required, nailing blocks may be used (*C*, Fig. 6).

Another method of gypsum board application (laminated two-ply) includes an undercourse of ⅜″ material applied vertically and nailed in place. The finish ⅜″ sheet is applied horizontally, usually in room-size lengths, with an adhesive. This adhesive is either applied in ribbons or is spread with a notched trowel. *Be sure* to follow the manufacturer's recommendations.

*Nails* in the finish gypsum wallboard should be driven with the heads slightly below the surface. The crowned head of the hammer will form a small dimple in the wallboard (*A*, Fig. 7). A nail set should *not* be used, and care should be taken to avoid breaking the paper face.

## TAPING

Joint cement *spackle* is used to apply the tape over the tapered edge joints and to smooth and level the surface. It comes in powder form and is mixed with water to a soft putty consistency so that it can be easily spread with a trowel or putty knife. It can also be obtained in premixed form.

The procedure for taping (*B*, Fig. 7) is as follows:

1. Use a wide spackling knife (5″) and spread the cement in the tapered edges, starting at the top of the wall.

2. Press the tape into the recess with the putty knife until the joint cement is forced through the perforations.

3. Cover the tape with additional cement, feathering the outer edges.

4. Allow to dry, sand the joint light, and then apply the second coat, feathering the edges. A steel trowel is sometimes used in applying the second coat. For good results, a third coat may be

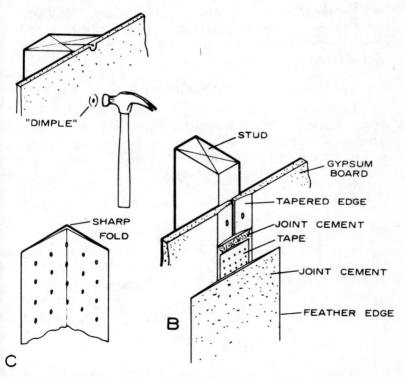

**Fig. 7.** Finishing gypsum dry wall. *A*, nail set with crowned hammer. *B*, cementing and taping joint. *C*, taping at inside corners.

applied, feathering beyond the second coat.

5. After the joint cement is dry, sand smooth with an electric hand vibrating sander.

6. For hiding hammer indentations, fill with joint cement and sand smooth when dry. Repeat with the second coat when necessary.

Interior corners may be treated with tape. Fold the tape down the center to a right angle (*C*, Fig. 7) and (1) apply cement at the corner, (2) press the tape in place, and (3) finish the corner with joint cement. Sand smooth when dry and apply a second coat.

The interior corners between walls and ceilings may also be concealed with some type of molding (*D*, Fig. 7). When moldings are used, taping this joint is not necessary. Wallboard corner beads at exterior corners will prevent damage to the gypsum board. They are fastened in place and covered with the joint cement.

## PLYWOOD

*Prefinished plywood* is available in a number of species, and its use should not be overlooked for accent walls or to cover entire room wall areas. Plywood for interior covering may be used in 4' by 8' and longer sheets. They may be applied ver-

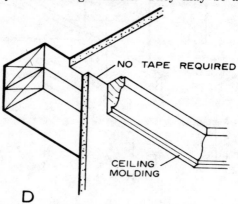

**Fig. 7.** *(continued)*. *D*, alternate finish at ceiling.

tically or horizontally, but with solid backing at all edges. For 16" frame member spacing, ¼" thickness is considered minimum. For 20" or 24" spacing, ⅜" plywood is the minimum thickness. Casing or finishing nails 1¼" to 1½" long are used. Space them 8" apart on the walls and 6" apart on the ceilings. Edge nailing distance should be not less than ⅜". Allow ¹⁄₃₂" end and edge distance between sheets when installing. Most wood or wood-base panel materials should be exposed to the conditions of the room before installation. Place them around the heated room for at least 24 hours.

Adhesives may also be used to fasten prefinished plywood and other sheet materials to wall studs. These panel adhesives usually eliminate the need for more than two guide nails for each sheet. Application usually conforms to the following procedure: (a) position the sheet and fasten it with two nails for guides at the top or side, (b) remove plywood and spread contact or similar adhesive on the framing members, (c) press the plywood in place for full contact using the nails for positioning, (d) pull the plywood away from the studs and allow adhesive to set, and (e) press plywood against the framing members and tap lightly with a rubber mallet for full contact. Manufacturers of adhesives supply full instructions for application of sheet materials.

## HARDBOARD AND FIBERBOARD

*Hardboard* and *fiberboard* are applied the same way as plywood. *Hardboard* must be at least ¼" when used over open framing spaced 16" on center. Rigid backing of some type is required for ⅛" hardboard.

*Fiberboard* in tongued-and-grooved plank or sheet form must be ½" thick when frame members are spaced 16" on center and ¾" when 24" spacing is used as previously described. The casing or finishing nails must be slightly longer than those used for plywood or hardboard, and spacing is about the same. Fiberboard is also used in the ceiling as acoustic tile and may be nailed to strips fastened to ceiling joists. It is also installed in 12" by 12" or larger tile forms on wood or metal hangers which are hung from the ceiling joists. This is called a *suspended ceiling*.

## WOOD PANELING

Various types and patterns of woods are available for application on walls to obtain desired decorative effects. For informal treatment, knotty pine, white-pocket Douglas fir, sound wormy chestnut, and pecky cypress, finished natural or stained and varnished, may be used to cover one or more sides of a room. *Wood paneling* should be thoroughly seasoned to a moisture content near the average it reaches in service. In most areas it is about 8 percent. Allow the material to reach this condition by placing it around the wall of the heated room. Boards may be applied horizontally or vertically, but the same general methods of application should pertain to each. The following may be used as a guide in the application of matched wood paneling:

1. Apply over a vapor barrier and insulation when application

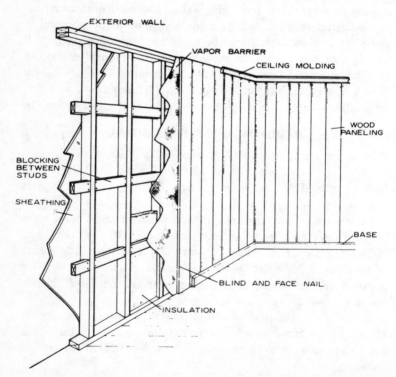

**Fig. 8.** Blocking between studs for vertical wood paneling.

is on the exterior wall framing or blocking (Fig. 8).

2. Boards should not be wider than 8″ except when a long tongue or matched edges are used.

3. Thickness should be at least ⅜″ for 16″ spacing of frame members, ½″ for 20″ spacing, and ⅝″ for 24″ spacing.

4. Maximum spacing of supports for nailing should be 24″ on center (blocking for vertical applications).

5. Nails should be fivepenny or sixpenny casing or finishing nails.

Use two nails for boards 6″ or less wide and three nails for 8″ and wider boards. One nail can be blind-nailed in matched paneling.

Wood paneling in the form of *small plywood squares* can also be used for an interior wall covering (Fig. 9). When these squares are used over framing and a vapor barrier, blocking should be so located that each edge has full bearing. Each edge should be fastened with casing or finish nails. When two sides are tongued-and-grooved, one edge (tongued side) may be blind-nailed. When paneling (16″ by 48″ or larger) crosses studs, it should also be nailed at each intermediate bearing. Matched (tongued-and-grooved) sides should be used when no horizontal blocking is provided or paneling is not used over a solid backing.

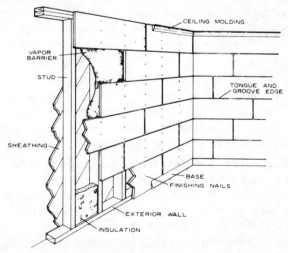

**Fig. 9.**   Application of tongued-and-grooved paneling over studs.

## CHAPTER 24

# Window and Door Screens, and Hood or Canopy

## WINDOW SCREENS

Screen sash is usually ¾″ stock, but for large windows and doors 1⅛″ material frequently is used, or ¾″ lumber is braced with a horizontal member. (*See* Chap. 5, Lumber.)

**Construction.** Window-screen sash is usually 1¾″ or 2¼″ wide. Screen may be attached by stapling or tacking. Cut screen about 1″ wider and longer than the opening; cover the edges with molding; then rabbet the inside edges about ⅜″ by ½″, attach the screen in the rabbet, and nail ⅜″ by ½″ molding flush with face of sash. Figure 1 illustrates the construction of screen sashes using mesh wire cloth.

**Joints.** Window sashes may be made with open mortise, four tenons, with rails tenoned into stiles; with half-lap corners; or with butt joints or corrugated fasteners. In either of the first two cases, the joints may be nailed or glued. (*See* Chap. 6, Woodworking Joints and Splices, and Chap. 4, Methods of Fastening.)

**Attaching screen material.** When attaching screen material, start at one end and tack or staple it with copper staples, holding the material tightly. Then hand-stretch the screen along the side, working toward the other end, and attach, making sure that the weave is parallel to the ends and sides. Tack the sides and apply the molding. Copper staples should be used for bronze or copper screen, and cadmium staples for aluminum screens.

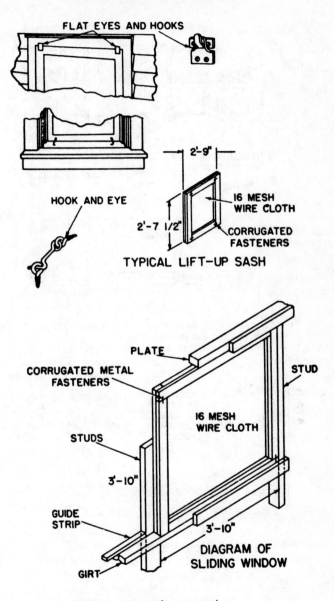

**Fig. 1.** Window screen sash construction.

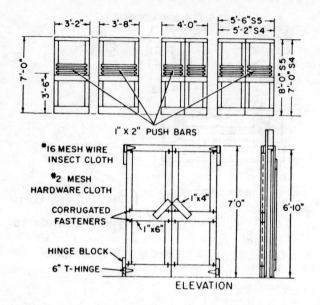

ELEVATION

NOTE: COVER EXTERIOR FACE OF ALL EXTERIOR DOORS WITH FELT AND LATH.
LAP STILES AND RAILS TO AVOID THRU JOINTS

BATTEN DOOR & SCREEN DOOR

**Fig. 2.** Door screen construction.

## DOOR SCREENS

*Door screens* are made as shown in Fig. 2. Two separate frames are made of 1 by 4 material for the sides and top and of 1 by 6 material for the bottom and middle pieces. The first frame is made of two side pieces the full length of the door; the crosspieces are the width of the door less the width of the two side pieces. This frame is put together with corrugated metal fasteners, then the screen wire is applied. The second frame is made with the crosspiece the full width of the door. The side pieces are cut to correspond with the distance between the crosspieces. The second frame is placed over the first frame and nailed securely. For push-and-pull plates, two short braces 1″ by 4″ are nailed to the side opposite the hinge side.

## HOOD OR CANOPY

The hood or canopy is used mostly in tropical climates, but is also used in other parts of the country. It protects the screened opening at the ends of the buildings. It is framed to the end walls with short rafters that are nailed to the building with knee braces, as shown in Fig. 3. The rafters are nailed to the wall, the bottom edge flush with the bottom of the end plate. The rafters and braces are 2 by 4's nailed with 8- or 10-penny nails. The sheathing is of the same material as the roof sheathing and is covered with roll roofing. The hood should extend about 2½′ or 3′ from the building.

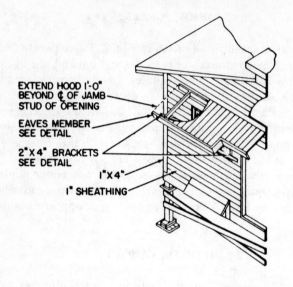

EXTEND HOOD 1'-0"
BEYOND ₵ OF JAMB
STUD OF OPENING

EAVES MEMBER
SEE DETAIL

2" X 4" BRACKETS
SEE DETAIL

1" X 4"

1" SHEATHING

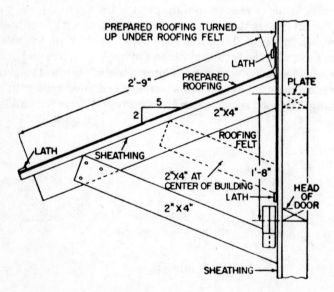

PREPARED ROOFING TURNED
UP UNDER ROOFING FELT

LATH

2'-9"     PREPARED
          ROOFING

PLATE

5
2          2" X 4"

LATH     SHEATHING     ROOFING
                       FELT

2" X 4" AT
CENTER OF BUILDING
LATH

1'-8"

HEAD
OF
DOOR

2" X 4"

SHEATHING

**Fig. 3.** Hood or canopy.

## CHAPTER 25

# Floor Coverings

The term *finish flooring* refers to the material used as the final wearing surface that is applied to a floor. Perhaps in its simplest form it might be paint over a concrete floor slab. Any one of the many resilient tile floorings applied directly to the concrete slab would likely be an improvement from the standpoint of maintenance but not necessarily from the standpoint of comfort.

## FLOORING MATERIALS

Numerous flooring materials are available and may be used over a variety of floors. Each has a property that adapts it to a particular usage. Of the practical properties, durability and maintenance ease are the most important. The initial cost, comfort, and beauty or appearance must also be considered.

There is a wide selection of wood materials that are used for flooring. Hardwoods and softwoods are available as *strip flooring* in a variety of widths and thicknesses and as random-width planks and block flooring. Other materials include linoleum, asphalt, rubber, cork, vinyl, and other materials in tile or sheet forms. Tile flooring is also available in a particle board which is manufactured with small wood particles combined with resin and fabricated under high pressure. Ceramic tile and carpeting are used in many areas nowadays. Plastic floor coverings used over concrete or stable wood subfloors are another variation in the types of finishes available.

## WOOD-STRIP FLOORING

*Softwood finish flooring* costs less than most hardwood species and is often used to good advantage in bedroom and closet areas where traffic is light. It might also be selected to fit the interior decor. It is less dense than the hardwoods, less wear resistant, and shows surface abrasions more readily. Softwoods most commonly used for flooring are southern pine, Douglas fir, redwood, and western hemlock.

Softwood flooring has tongued-and-grooved edges and may be hollow-backed or grooved. Some types are also end-matched. Vertical-grain flooring generally has better wearing qualities than flat-grain flooring under hard usage. Table 11 lists the grades and description of softwood strip.

The *hardwoods* commonly used for flooring are red oak, white oak, beech, birch, maple, and pecan. (*See* Table 11.) Manufacturers supply both prefinished and unfinished flooring.

The most widely used pattern is a $25/32''$ by $2\frac{1}{4}''$ strip flooring. These strips are laid lengthwise in a room and normally at right angles to the floor joists. Some type of subfloor of diagonal boards or plywood is normally used under the finish floor. This type of strip flooring is *tongued-and-grooved* and *end-matched* (Fig. 1). Strips are of random length and vary from 2' to 16'' or more. End-matched strip flooring in $25/32''$ thickness is generally hollow-backed (*A*, Fig. 1). The face is slightly wider than the bottom so that tight joints result when flooring is laid. The tongue fits tightly into the groove to prevent movement and floor *squeaks*. These details are designed to provide beautiful finished floors that require a minimum of maintenance.

Another matched pattern is available in $3/8''$ by $2''$ size (*B*, Fig. 1). This is used for remodeling work or when subfloor is edge-blocked or thick enough to provide very little deflection under loads.

*Square-edged strip flooring* (*C*, Fig. 1) is used occasionally. It is $3/8''$ by $2''$ in size and is laid up over a substantial subfloor; face nailing is required.

*Wood-block flooring* (Fig. 2) is made in a number of patterns. Blocks may vary in size from 4'' by 4'' to 9'' by 9'' and larger. Its thickness varies by type from $25/32''$ for laminated blocking

TABLE 11

*Grade and description of strip flooring of several species and grain orientation*

| Species | Grain orientation | Size: Thickness | Size: Width | First grade | Second grade | Third grade |
|---|---|---|---|---|---|---|
| | | *In.* | *In.* | | | |
| | | | SOFTWOODS | | | |
| Douglas-fir and hemlock | Edge grain | 25/32 | 2 3/8–5 3/16 | B and Better | C | D |
| | Flat grain | 25/32 | 2 3/8–5 3/16 | C and Better | D | ---------- |
| Southern pine | Edge grain and Flat grain | 5/16–1 5/16 | 1 3/4–5 7/16 | B and Better | C and Better | D (and No. 2) |
| | | | HARDWOODS | | | |
| Oak | Edge grain | 25/32 | 1 1/2–3 1/4 | Clear | Select | ---------- |
| | Flat grain | 3/8 | 1 1/2, 2 | Clear | Select | No. 1 Common |
| | | 1/2 | 1 1/2, 2 | | | |
| Beech, birch, maple, and pecan[1] | | 25/32 | 1 1/2–3 1/4 | First grade | Second grade | ---------- |
| | | 3/8 | 1 1/2, 2 | | | |
| | | 1/2 | 1 1/2, 2 | | | |

[1] Special grades are available in which uniformity of color is a requirement.

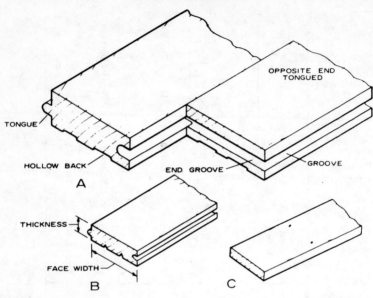

**Fig. 1.** Types of strip flooring. *A*, side- and end-matched (25⁄32″). *B*, thin flooring strips (matched). *C*, thin flooring strips (square-edged).

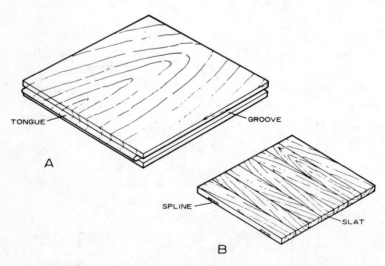

**Fig. 2.** Wood-block flooring. *A*, tongued-and-grooved. *B*, square-edged (splined).

or plywood block tile (*A*, Fig. 2) to ⅛″ stabilized veneer. Solid wood tile is often made up of narrow strips of wood splined or keyed together in a number of ways. Edges of the thicker tile are tongued-and-grooved, but thinner sections of wood are usually square-edged (*B*, Fig. 2). Plywood blocks may be ⅜″ and thicker and are usually tongued-and-grooved. Many block floors are factory finished and require only waxing after installation. While stabilized veneer squares are still in the development stage, it is likely that research will produce a low-cost wood tile which can even compete with some of the cheaper nonwood resilient tile now available.

## INSTALLATION OF WOOD-STRIP FLOORING

Flooring should be laid after plastering or other interior wall and ceiling finish is completed and dried out, when windows and exterior doors are in place, and when most of the interior trim, except base, casing, and jambs, are applied so that it may not be damaged by wetting or by construction activity.

*Board subfloors* should be clean, level, and covered with a deadening felt or heavy building paper. This felt or paper will stop a certain amount of dust, will deaden sound, and where a crawl space is used will increase the warmth of the floor by preventing air infiltration. To provide nailing into the joists wherever possible, location of the joists should be chalklined on the paper as a guide. *Plywood subfloor* does not normally require building paper.

*Strip flooring* should normally be laid crosswise to the floor joists (*A*, Fig. 3). In conventionally designed houses, the floor joists span the width of the building over a center-supporting beam or wall. Hence, the finish flooring of the entire floor area of a rectangular house will be laid in the same direction. Flooring with *L*- or *T*-shaped plans will usually have a direction change at the wings, depending on joist direction. As joists usually span the short way in a living room, the flooring will be laid lengthwise to the room. This is desirable for the sake of appearance and will also reduce shrinkage and swelling effects on the flooring during seasonal changes.

Flooring should be delivered only during dry weather and stored in the warmest and driest place available in the house.

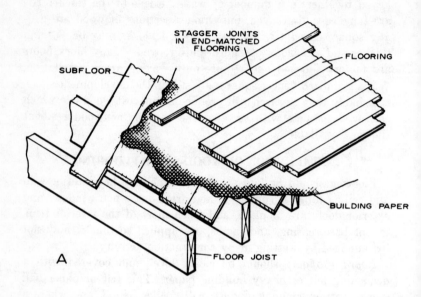

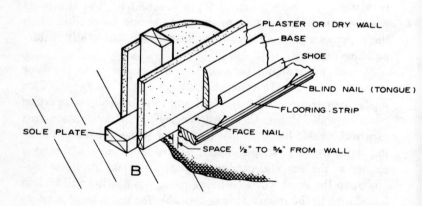

**Fig. 3.** Application of strip flooring. *A,* general application. *B,* starting strip.

The recommended average moisture content for flooring at the time of installation varies somewhat in different sections of the United States. Moisture absorbed after delivery to the site of the house will cause open joints between flooring strips to appear after several months of the heating season.

*Floor squeaks* are usually caused by the movement of one board against another. Such movement may occur because (a) floor joists are too light, causing excessive deflection, (b) sleepers over concrete slabs are not held down tightly, (c) tongues are loose fitting, or (d) nailing is poor. Adequate nailing is an important means of minimizing squeaks; another is to apply the finish floors only after the joists have dried to 12 per cent moisture content or less. A much better job results when it is possible to nail the finish floor through the subfloor into the joists than if the finish floor is nailed *only* to the subfloor.

Various types of nails are used in nailing different thicknesses of flooring. For $25/32''$ flooring, use eightpenny flooring nails; for $1/2''$ use sixpenny; and for $3/8''$ use fourpenny casing nails. These types of flooring are blind-nailed. For thinner square-edged flooring, use a $1\frac{1}{2}''$ flooring brad and face nail every seven inches with two nails, one near each edge of the strip, into the subfloor.

The ring shank and screw shank type of nails have been developed in recent years for nailing of flooring. When using these nails, be sure to check with the floor manufacturer's recommendations as to size and diameter for specific uses. Flooring brads are also available with blunted points to prevent splitting of the tongue.

Figure *B*, 3 shows the method of nailing the first strip of flooring placed $1/2''$ to $5/8''$ away from the wall. The space is to allow for expansion of the flooring when moisture content increases. The nail is driven straight down through the board at the groove edge. The nails should be driven into the joist and near enough to the edge so that they will be covered by the base or shoe molding. The first strip of flooring can also be nailed through the tongue. Figure *A*, 4 shows in detail how nails should be driven into the tongue of the flooring at an angle of 45° to 50°. The nail should not be driven quite flush in order to prevent damaging the edge by the hammerhead (*B*, Fig. 4). The nail

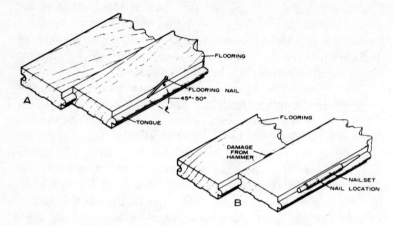

**Fig. 4.** Nailing of flooring. *A,* nail angle. *B,* setting of nail.

can be set with the end of a large-size nail set or by laying the
nail set flatwise against the flooring (*B,* Fig. 4). Nailing devices
using standard flooring or special nails are often used by flooring contractors. One blow of the hammer on the plunger drives
and sets the nail.

To prevent splitting the flooring, it is sometimes desirable to
predrill through the tongue, especially at the ends of the strip.
For the second course of flooring from the wall, select pieces so
that the butt joints will be well separated from those in the first
course. Under normal conditions each board should be driven up
tightly. Crooked pieces may require wedging to force them into
alinement or may be cut and used at the ends of the course or
in closets. In completing the flooring, a ½″ to ⅝″ space is provided between the wall and the last flooring strip. Because of
the closeness of the wall, this strip is usually face-nailed so that
the base or shoe covers the set nailheads.

## INSTALLATION OF WOOD FLOORING OVER CONCRETE SLABS

The most desirable properties in a vapor barrier to be used
under a concrete slab are: (a) good vapor transmission rating
(less than 0.5 perimeter); (b) resistance to damage by moisture
and rot; and (c) ability to withstand normal usage during pouring operations.

The vapor barrier is placed under a slab during construction. An alternate method must be used when the concrete is already in place. (*See* Chap. 22, Fig. 2.)

Another method of preparing a base for wood flooring when there is no vapor barrier under the slab is shown in Fig. 5. To resist decay, treated 1″ by 4″ furring strips are anchored to the existing slab, shimming when necessary to provide a level base. Strips should be spaced no more than 16″ on center. A good waterproof or water-vapor-resistant coating on the concrete before the treated strips are applied is usually recommended to aid in reducing moisture movement. A vapor barrier, such as a 4-mil polyethylene or similar membrane, is then laid over the anchored 1″ by 4″ wood strips and a second set of 1 by 4's nailed to the first. Use 1½″ long nails spaced 12″ to 16″ apart in a staggered pattern. The moisture content of these second members should be about the same as that of the strip flooring to be applied (6 to 11 per cent). Strip flooring can then be installed as previously described in this chapter.

When other types of finish floor, such as a resilient tile, are used, plywood is placed over the 1 by 4's as a base.

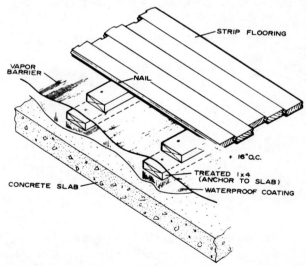

**Fig. 5.** Base for wood flooring on concrete slab (without an underlying vapor barrier).

## WOOD AND PARTICLE BOARD TILE FLOORING

*Wood* and *particle board tile* are applied with adhesive on a plywood or similar base. The exception is $25/32''$ wood-block floor, which has tongues on two edges and grooves on the other two edges. If the base is wood, these tiles are commonly nailed through the tongue into the subfloor. However, wood block may be applied on concrete slabs with an adhesive. *Wood-block flooring* is installed by changing the grain direction of alternate blocks. This minimizes the effects of shrinking and swelling of the wood.

One type of wood-floor tile is made up of a number of narrow slats to form 4″ by 4″ and larger squares. Four or more of these squares with alternating grain direction form a block. Slats, squares, and blocks are held together with an easily removed membrane. Adhesive is spread on the concrete slab or underlayment with a notched trowel and the blocks installed immediately. The membrane is then removed and the blocks tamped in place for full adhesive contact. Be sure to follow the manufacturer's recommendations for the adhesive and method of application.

*Plywood squares* with tongued-and-grooved edges are another form of wood tile. Installation is much the same as for the wood tile previously described. Usually tile of this type is factory finished.

A wood-base product used for finish floors is *particle board tile*. It is commonly 9″ by 9″ by ⅜″ in size with tongued-and-grooved edges. The back face is often marked with small saw kerfs to stabilize the tile and provide a better key for the adhesive. Manufacturer's directions as to the type of adhesive and method of installation are usually very complete. Some manufacturers even include instructions on the preparation of the base upon which the tile is to be laid. This tile should not be used over concrete.

## BASE FOR RESILIENT FLOORS

Resilient floors should *not* be installed directly over a board or plank subfloor. Underlayment grade of wood-based panels

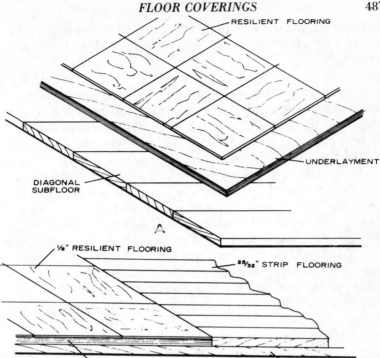

RESILIENT FLOORING

UNDERLAYMENT

DIAGONAL
SUBFLOOR

A

⅛" RESILIENT FLOORING

²⁵⁄₃₂" STRIP FLOORING

⅝" UNDERLAYMENT   B   SUBFLOOR

**Fig. 6.** Base for wood flooring on concrete slab (without an underlying
vapor barrier).

such as plywood, particle board, and hardboard is widely used
for suspended floor applications (*A*, Fig. 6).

Plywood or particle board panels 4' by 8' and in a range of
thicknesses from ⅜" to ¾" are generally selected for use in new
construction. Sheets of untempered hardboard, plywood, or particle board 4' by 4' or larger and ¼" or ⅜" in thickness are used
in remodeling work because of the floor thicknesses involved.
The underlayment grade of particle board is a standard product
and is available from many producers. Manufacturer's instructions should be followed in the care and use of the product. Plywood underlayment is also a standard product and is available
in interior types, exterior types, and interior types with an exterior glueline. The underlayment grade provides for a sanded
panel with a C-plugged or better face play and a C-ply or better

immediately under the face. This construction resists damage to the floor surface from concentrated loads such as chair legs and the like.

Generally, underlayment panels are separate and installed over structurally adequate subfloors. Combination subfloor underlayment panels of plywood construction find increasing usage. Panels for this dual use generally have tongued-and-grooved or blocked edges and C-plugged or better faces to provide a smooth, even surface for the resilient floor covering.

The method of installing plywood combination subfloor and underlayment has been covered in Chap. 21, section on Subfloor—Plywood. Underlayment should be laid up as described with $\frac{1}{32}''$ edge and end spacing. Sand smooth to provide a level base for the resilient flooring. To prevent nails from showing on the surface of the tile, joists and subfloor should have a moisture content near the average value they reach in service.

The thickness of the underlayment will vary somewhat depending on the floors in adjoining rooms. The installation of tile in a kitchen area, *for example*, is usually made over a $\frac{5}{8}''$ underlayment when finish floors in the adjoining living or dining areas are $\frac{25}{32}''$ strip flooring ($B$, Fig. 6). When thinner wood floors are used in adjoining rooms, adjustments are made in the thickness of the underlayment.

Concrete for resilient floors should be prepared with a good vapor barrier installed somewhere between the soil and the finish floor, preferably just under the slab. Concrete should be leveled carefully when a resilient floor is to be used directly on the slab; this will minimize dips and waves.

Tile should not be laid on a concrete slab until the slab has completely dried. One method which may be used to determine if the slab is dry is to place a small square of polyethylene or other low-perm material on the slab overnight. If the underside is dry in the morning, the slab is usually considered dry enough for the installation of the tile.

## CARPETING

Carpeting of a home from living room to kitchen and bath is becoming more popular as new carpeting materials are developed. The cost, however, may be considerably higher than a finished wood floor, and the life of the carpeting before replacement would be much less than that of the wood floor. Many wise homeowners or builders will specify *oak floors* even though they expect to carpet some areas. The resale value of the home is then retained even if the carpeting is removed. However, the advantage of carpeting in sound-absorption and impact-resistant materials should be considered. This is particularly important in multifloor apartments where impact noise reduction is an extremely important phase of construction. If carpeting is to be used, subfloor can consist of 5/8" (minimum) tongued-and-grooved plywood (over 16" joist spacing). Top face of the plywood should be C-plugged grade or better. Mastic adhesives are also being used to advantage in applying plywood to floor joists. Plywood, particle board, or other underlayments are also used for a carpet base when installed over subfloor.

## CHAPTER 26

# Interior Doors and Trim

Doors, both exterior and interior, are classified as batten, panel, and flush (Fig. 1).

## JOB-BUILT DOORS

The *batten door* is the most commonly used door and most easily constructed type of job-built door. It can be made in several ways, one of the simplest consisting of diagonal boards nailed together as two layers, each layer at right angles to the other. This type of door frequently is used as the core for metal-sheathed fire doors. Another type of batten door is made up of vertical boards tongued and grooved or shiplapped and held rigid by two to four cross-pieces—ledgers—that may or may not be diagonally braced. If two additional pieces forming the sides of the door and corresponding to the ledgers are used, these are known as the frames. (*See* Chap. 5, Lumber, and Chap. 20, Exterior Frames, Windows, and Doors.)

**Construction.** In hasty construction, the carpenter makes a batten door from several 2 by 6 boards with ledgers and braces as shown in Fig. 1. The ledgers are nailed with their edge 6″ from the ends of the door boards. A diagonal is placed between the ledgers, beginning at the top-ledger end opposite the hinge side of the door and running to the lower ledger diagonally across the door. If it is an outside door, roofing felt is used to cover the boards on the weather side. The ledgers are nailed over the felt. Wooden laths are nailed around the edges and across the middle of the door to hold the roofing felt in place. In hanging these doors, ¼ of an inch clearance should be left around the door to take care of expansion.

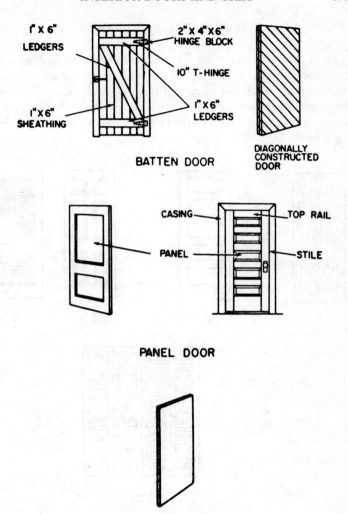

**Fig. 1.** Types of doors.

T-strap hinges are fastened to the ledgers of the door and to the hinge blocks on the door casing or post (Fig. 1).

## INTERIOR MILL-BUILT DOORS

The two general *interior* type of doors are the *panel* and the *flush doors* (Fig. 2). *Louvered doors* (Fig. 2) are also popular and are used as hinged or as sliding doors. Any hinged interior door should not open or swing in the direction of a natural entry or into hallways or blank walls, or be obstructed by other swinging doors.

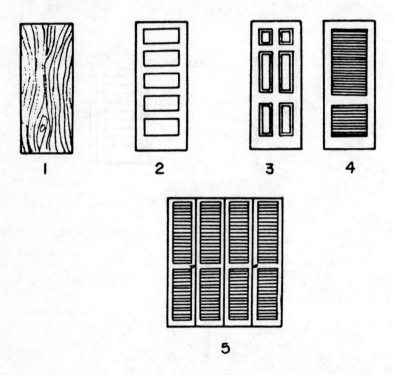

**Fig. 2.** Interior doors. (1) Flush, (2) panel (five cross), (3) panel (Colonial), (4) louvered, (5) folding (louvered).

## INTERIOR DOOR FRAMES

Inside door frames, like outside frames, are constructed in several ways. In most hasty construction, the type shown in Fig. 3 is used. The interior type is constructed like the outside type except that no casing is used on inside door frames. Hinge blocks are nailed to the inside wall finish, where the hinges are to be placed, to provide a nailing surface for the hinge flush with the door. Figure 3 shows the elevation of a single inside door. Both the outside and inside door frames may be modified to suit a climatic condition.

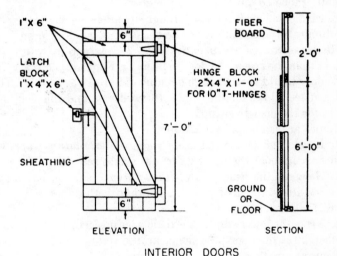

**Fig. 3.** Single inside door.

## DOOR JAMBS

*Door jambs* (Fig. 4) are the linings of the framing of door openings. Casings and stops are nailed to the door jambs and the door is hung from them. Inside jambs are made of ¾" stock and outside jambs of 1⅜" stock. The width of the stock will vary in accordance with the thickness of the walls. Inside jambs are built up with ⅜" by 1⅜" stops nailed to the jamb, while outside jambs are usually rabbeted out to receive the door.

Regardless of how carefully rough openings are made, be sure to plumb the jambs and level the heads when jambs are set.

Rough openings are usually made 2½" larger in width and height than the size of the door to be hung. For example, a 2'8" by 6'8" door would need a rough opening of 2'10½" by 6'10½". This extra space allows for the jambs, the wedging, and the clearance space for the door to swing.

Jambs are made and set as follows.

1. Level the floor across the opening to determine any variation in floor heights at the point where the jambs rest on the floor.

2. Now cut the head jamb with both ends square, having allowed width of the door plus the depth of both dados and a full 3/16" for door clearance.

3. From the lower edge of the dado, measure a distance equal to the height of the door plus the clearance wanted under it. Mark and cut square.

4. On the opposite jamb do the same, only make additions or subtractions for the variation in the floor, if any.

5. Now nail the jambs and jamb heads together with 8-penny common nails through the dado into the head jamb.

6. Set the jambs into the opening and place small blocks under each jamb on the subfloor just as thick as the finish floor will be. This is to allow the finish floor to go under.

7. Plumb the jambs and level the jamb head.

8. Wedge the sides with shingles between the jambs and the studs, to align, and then nail securely in place.

9. Take care not to wedge the jamb unevenly.

10. Use a straightedge five or six feet long inside the jambs to help prevent uneven wedging.

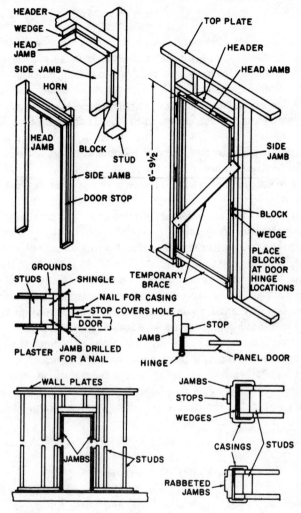

**Fig. 4.** Door jamb and door trim.

11. Check jambs and head carefully, because jambs placed out of plumb will have a tendency to swing the door open or shut, depending on the direction in which the jamb is out of plumb.

## DOOR TRIM

*Door trim* material is nailed onto the jambs to provide a finish between the jambs and the plastered wall. It is frequently called "casing" (Fig. 4). Sizes vary from ½″ to ¾″ in thickness, and from 2½″ to 6″ in width. Most trim has a concave back, to fit over uneven plaster. In mitered work, care must be taken to make all joints clean, square, neat, and well fitted. (If the trim is to be mitered at the top corners, a miter box, miter square, hammer nail set, and block plane will be needed.) Door openings are cased up in the following manner.

1. Leave a margin of ¼″ from the edge of the jamb to the casing all around.

2. Cut one of the side casings square and even at the bottom, with the bottom of the jamb.

3. Cut the top or mitered end next, allowing ¼″ extra length for the margin at the top.

4. Nail the casing onto the jamb and even with the ¼″ margin line, starting at the top and working toward the bottom.

5. Use 4-penny finish nails along the jamb side and 6-penny or 8-penny case nails along the outer edge of the casings.

6. The nails along the outer edge will need to be long enough to go through the casing and plaster and into the studs.

7. Set all nailheads about ⅛″ below the surface of the wood with a nail set.

8. Now apply the casing for the other side and then the head casing.

## FITTING A DOOR

If a number of doors are to be fitted and hung, a *door jack* like the one shown in Fig. 5 should be constructed to hold doors upright for the planing of edges and the installation of *hardware* (hinges, locks, knobs, and other metal fittings on a door or window).

*Note:* The edge of the door can be beveled to prevent binding and to give a tighter fit.

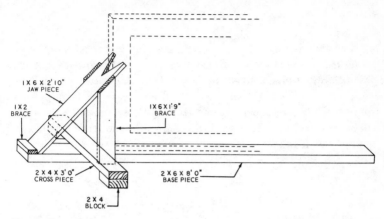

**Fig. 5.** Door jacks.

The first step in fitting a door is to determine from the floor plan which stile is the hinge stile and which the lock stile, and to mark both the stiles and the corresponding jambs accordingly. Next, carefully measure the height of the finished opening *on both side jambs* and the width of the opening *at both top and bottom.* The finished opening should be perfectly rectangular, but *it may not be.* Your job now is to fit the door accurately to the opening, regardless of its shape.

A well-fitted door, when hung, should conform to the shape of the finished opening, less a clearance allowance of 1/16″ at the sides and on top. For an interior door without sill or threshold there should be a bottom clearance above the finished floor of from ⅜″ to ½″. This clearance is required to ensure that the door will swing clear of carpeting. If the carpeting is to be extra-thick, the bottom clearance will have to be greater than ½″. For a door with a sill and no threshold, the bottom clearance should be 1/16″ above the threshold. The sill and threshold, if any, should be set in place before the door is hung.

Lay off the measured dimensions of the finished opening, less allowances, on the door. Check the door jambs for trueness, and if you find any irregularities transfer them to the door lines. Place the door in the jack and plane the edges to the lines, setting the door in the opening frequently to check the fit.

## HANGING A DOOR

There are various types of side hinges, but you most likely will use *loose-pin butt mortise hinges* like the one shown in Fig. 6. A loose-pin butt hinge consists of two rectangular *leaves* pivoted on a pin named a *loose pin* because it can be removed by simple extraction. The hinge is called a *mortise* hinge because the leaves are mortised into gains cut in the hinge stile of the door and the hinge jamb of the door frame.

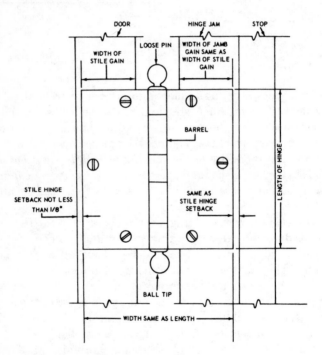

**Fig. 6.** Loose-pin butt mortise hinge.

The first step in *hanging a door* is to lay out the locations of the hinges on the hinge stile and the hinge. Set the door in the frame and force the hinge stile against the hinge jamb with the wedge (*A*, Fig. 7). Then insert a 4-penny finish nail between the top rail and the head jamb, and force the top rail up against the nail with the wedge (*B*, Fig. 7). Since a 4-penny finish nail has a diameter of 1/16″ (which is the standard top clearance for a door), the door is now at the correct height.

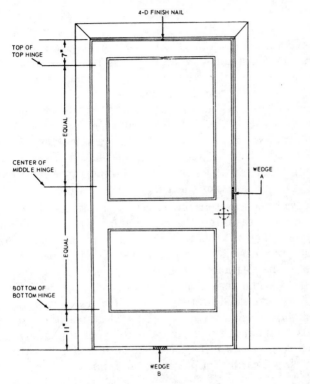

**Fig. 7.** Laying out hinge locations on a door.

Exterior doors usually have three hinges; interior doors, as a rule, have only two. The vertical distance between the top of the door and the top of the top hinge, and between the top of the finish floor and the bottom of the bottom hinge, may be specified. If not, the distances customarily used are those shown in Fig. 7. The middle hinge, if there is one, is usually located midway between the other two.

The size of a loose-pin butt mortise hinge is designated by the length (height) and by the combined width of the leaves in inches (height is always given first). The width varies with the requirements of setback, clearance, door thickness, and so on, and is calculated individually for each door. Doors 1⅛″ to 1⅜″ thick and up to 32″ wide take 3½″ hinges. Doors 1⅛″ to 1⅜″ thick and from 32″ to 37″ wide take 4″ hinges. Doors more than 1⅜″ but not more than 1⅞″ thick and up to 32″ wide take 4½″ hinges; if more than 32″ but not more than 37″ wide, they take 5″ hinges; if from 37″ to 43″ wide they take 5″ *extra heavy* hinges. Doors thicker than 1⅞″ and up to 43″ wide take 6″ extra heavy hinges.

Place the door in the door jack and lay off the outlines of the gains on the edge of the hinge stile, using a hinge leaf as a marker. The *stile hinge setback* (Fig. 6) should be not less than ⅛″ and is usually made about ¼″. Lay out gains of exactly the same size on the hinge jamb, and then chisel out the gains to a depth exactly equal to the thickness of a leaf.

Separate the leaves on the hinges by extracting the loose pins, and screw the leaves into the gains, taking care to ensure that the loose pin will be up when the door is hung in place. Hang the door in place, insert the loose pins, and check the clearances at the side jambs. If the clearance along the hinge jamb is too large (more than 1/16″) and that along the lock jamb too small (less than 1/16″), remove the door, remove the hinge leaves from the gains, and slightly deepen the gains. If the clearance along the hinge jamb is too small and that along the lock jamb too large, the gains are too deep. This can be corrected by shimming up the leaves with strips of cardboard placed in the gains.

## LOCK INSTALLATION

Since types of door locks differ, follow the installation instructions that come with lock sets. After placing hinges in position, mark off the position of the lock (Fig. 8) on the lock stile, about 36″ from the floor level. Hold the case of the mortise lock on the face of the lock stile and mark off, with a sharp knife, the area to be removed from the edge of the stile that is to house the entire case. Next, mark off the position of the doorknob hub and the po-

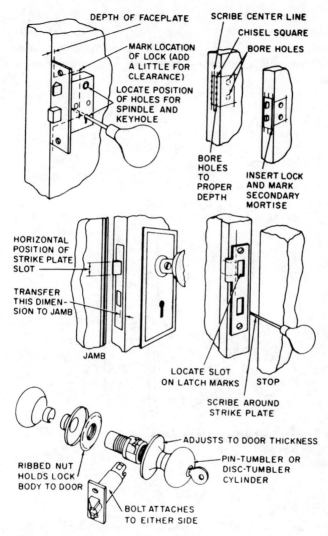

**Fig. 8.** Installation of lock.

sition of the key. Then mark off the position of the strike plate on the jamb. Bore out the wood to house the lock and strike chisel and mortises, clean, and then install the lock set. The strike plate should be flush or slightly below the face of the door jamb (Fig. 9).

Use the template that is usually supplied with a cylinder lock. Place the template on the face of the door (at proper height and alignment with layout lines), and mark the center of holes to be drilled (Fig. 10).

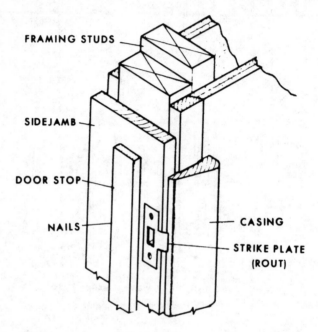

**Fig. 9.** Installation of strike plate.

## INTERIOR TRIM

The casing around the doors and windows, the baseboard with its base mold and shoe mold, the picture mold, chair rail, cornice mold, and panel mold are the various trim members used in finishing the interior of a building.

Various types of wood can be used for interior trim, such as birch, oak, mahogany, walnut, white and yellow pine, or other

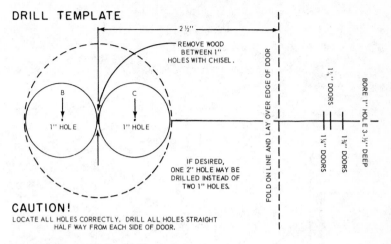

**Fig. 10.** One type of template.

available woods. A close-grain wood should be used when the trim is to be painted. However, harder woods free from pitch will provide a better paint surface.

## BASEBOARDS

A trim member called a *baseboard* is usually installed on the line along which the walls join the floors. Baseboard is nailed to the studs with two 6-penny finish nails at each stud crossing. The first step in installing baseboard, therefore, is to locate all the studs in the wall and mark the locations on the floor with light pencil marks.

Baseboard is miter-joined at outside corners and butt-joined at inside corners. Where baseboards cannot be miter-joined or butt-joined at corners, they should be capped. Since the walls at corner baseboard locations may not be perfectly vertical, inside and outside corners should be joined as follows.

To butt-join a piece of baseboard to another piece already in place at an inside corner, set the piece to be joined in position on the floor, bring the end against or near the face of the other piece, and take off the line of the face with a scriber as shown in Fig. 11.

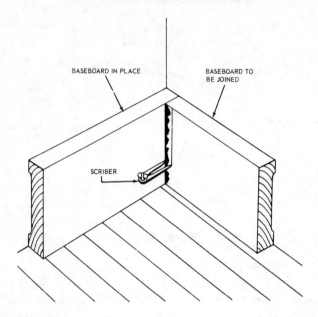

**Fig. 11.** Butt-joining baseboard at an inside corner.

Use the same procedure when butting ends of baseboard against the side casings of doors.

For miter-joining at an outside corner, proceed as shown in Fig. 12. First set a *marker piece* of baseboard across the wall corner, as shown in the left-hand view, and mark the floor along the edge of the piece. Then set the piece to be mitered in place, and mark the point where the wall corner intersects the top edge and the point where the mark on the floor intersects the bottom edge. Lay 45° lines across the edge from these points (for a 90° corner), connect these lines with a line across the face, and miter to the lines as indicated.

The line along which the baseboard joins the floor is usually covered by a strip of quarter-round molding called a *shoe* molding. The shoe molding should be nailed to the floor, as shown in Fig. 13, and not to the baseboard. If it is nailed to the baseboard and the floor should happen to settle, a space will appear between the bottom of the shoe molding and the floor surface.

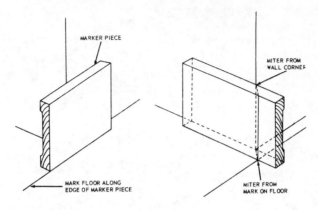

**Fig. 12.** Miter-joining baseboard at an outside corner.

The upper edges of baseboards are sometimes trimmed with a strip of molding called a *base cap*.

## MISCELLANEOUS TRIM MEMBERS

The *picture mold* is usually placed against the wall near the ceiling; however, you may at times prefer to lower it to 12″ or 16″ below the ceiling. *Cornice mold* is usually a large cove mold fitted and nailed against both the wall and ceiling. The cornice mold of a room is sometimes ornamental and made up of several members. The *chair rail* may be placed at various heights on the wall, usually around 48″ up from the floor. The chair rail can be used to fasten fixtures. The *panel mold* is used to divide wall spaces into panels; this mold may be used horizontally or vertically. *Shelf cleats* make removal of shelves easier and they are very convenient for closets.

*Casings* and *stops* for doors and windows as well as *stools* and *aprons* usually come in rough lengths. When this happens, it is a good plan to assort, select, and place the various members at each opening. When they come in random lengths, cut them to the rough lengths and then assort them. Most base members and other moldings come in random lengths. Remember that the longest

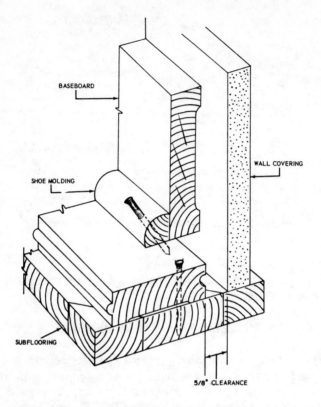

**Fig. 13.** Blind-nailing starter strip of wood finish flooring.

pieces should be reserved for the longest distances to be trimmed, to avoid unsightly patching and piecing of trim.

# Paints and Painting

Equipment; preparing the surface for paint; methods of application; deterioration of paint; safe painting procedures; the application of wood preservatives.

## CHAPTER 27

# Fundamental Purposes of Painting, Paints, and Equipment

To employ paint materials and painting man-hours effectively and economically, the fundamental purposes of painting must be borne in mind. The importance of each of these purposes depends on the particular surface that is to be painted.

## PREVENTIVE MAINTENANCE

The primary purpose of painting is protection. This is provided initially with new construction and maintained by a sound and progressive preventive maintenance program.

Resistance to moisture from rain, snow, ice, and condensation constitutes perhaps the greatest single protective characteristic of paint. Moisture causes wood to swell, warp, and rot. Interior wall finishes of buildings are ruined by neglect of exterior surfaces. Porous masonry is attacked and destroyed by moisture. Paint films must therefore be as impervious to moisture as possible in order to provide a protective waterproof film over the surface to which they are applied. Paint also acts as a protective film against attack by acids, alkalies, or marine organisms.

## HABITABILITY

Scientific tests have proved that, correctly used, painted color on interior surfaces has a soothing effect on the nervous system. A room painted in pastel tints is more pleasant to live in than a room painted a brilliant red or orange. It can be readily seen that the function of paint extends further than merely material protection.

Painting is used as a sanitary measure. A smooth, washable, painted surface that can be cleaned easily helps produce a cleaner and healthier environment. A painted room is usually a more wholesome place to live in than one that is unpainted.

Another purpose of paint is the reflection of light. Used in the interior, light-colored paints reflect and distribute both natural and artificial light, and thus help secure maximum efficiency from the lighting system.

## PAINTS

The term *paint* is broadly applied to any mixture designed to be spread on a surface in liquid form and to "dry" to a thin, permanent surface coating. By general custom, however, the term paint is often restricted to materials containing pigments and designed to obscure the underlying substrata. *Oil paint* consists of pigments dispersed in a drying oil—usually linseed oil. *Enamels* are paints designed to resist scrubbing and washings. (Enamels are obtainable in flat, semigloss and gloss.)

*Varnish* is distinguished from paint by the fact that it contains little or no pigment and is not designed to obscure the surface to which it is applied. *Oil* varnishes are usually a combination of drying oil with a synthetic resin. When the resin is glyceryl phthalate, the varnish is referred to as an *alkyd varnish. Spirit varnishes* are made by dissolving a resin, usually *shellac*, in alcohol.

*Lacquers,* which may be clear or pigmented, consist of a cellulose derivative, commonly nitrocellulose, dissolved in a suitable solvent.

Paints that are applied to bare wood or metal surfaces to form undercoats for subsequent coats are called *primers.* The most common primers for metal surfaces contain anticorrosive pigments, such as *red lead, zinc dust,* or *zinc chromate.* Primers for wood are usually specially formulated to adhere to the wood and to form a good surface for top coats. Paints designed to resist weather and sunlight are called *exterior* or *outside* paints; paints not primarily so designed are called *interior* or *inside* paints. Paints that dry to a dull finish are called *flat* paints; paints that dry to a shiny finish are called *gloss* paints; paints with an intermediate surface are called *eggshell* or *semigloss* paints.

Paints are composed of various ingredients. Among these are pigment, nonvolatile vehicle or binder, and solvent or thinner.

**Pigments.** *Pigments* are insoluble solids divided finely enough to remain suspended in the vehicle for a considerable time after thorough stirring or shaking. There are several types of pigments.

*Opaque* pigments give the paint its hiding or covering capacity, and contribute other properties as well. The most common opaque pigments are *white lead, zinc oxide,* and *titanium dioxide.*

*Color* pigments give the paint its color. They may be inorganic, such as *chrome green, chrome yellow,* or *iron oxide,* or *organic,* such as *toluidine red* or *phthalocyanine blue.*

*Transparent* or *extender* pigments contribute bulk and also control the application properties, durability, and resistance to abrasion of the coating.

*Miscellaneous* pigments are used for a variety of special purposes. Metallic zinc dust is used to prevent corrosion; luminous pigments are used for safety markings on signs; aluminum is used as a heat-resistant pigment.

**Vehicles.** The *vehicle* or *binder* of paint is the material that holds the pigment together and also adheres to the surface. In general, the durability of the paint is determined by the resistance of the binder to the exposure conditions.

Formerly linseed oil was the most common binder, and it is still used in certain paints. It has, however, largely been superseded by various synthetic resins. *Alkyd* resins are the most common. These are made by the reaction of glyceryl phthalate and an oil, and may be made with almost any properties desired. Common synthetic resins, which may be used themselves or mixed with oil, include *phenolics, vinyls, epoxies, urethanes, polyesters, chlorinated rubber,* and others. Each has its own advantages and disadvantages. It is particularly important in the newer materials that the manufacturer's instructions be explicitly followed.

Certain synthetic materials, called *latexes,* are dispersed in water. Paints made from these are useful because they can be applied to damp surfaces, and tools and spills may be cleaned up easily with water. They have extremely high alkali resistance, and many have excellent durability. They are particularly useful for plaster and masonry surfaces. There are many different chemicals involved in latexes, but the commonest are *styrene-butadiene* (or "synthetic rubber"), *polyvinyl acetate* ("Pva" or "vinyl"), and *acrylic*. All are very similar in their performance.

Other common binders are *portland cement* (in a dry-powder form to be mixed with water) and *bituminous material* (usually asphalt or coal tar).

**Solvents.** The only purpose of a *solvent* is to adjust the consistency of the material so that it may be applied readily to the surface. The solvent then evaporates, contributing nothing further to the film. For this reason the cheapest *suitable* solvent should be used. The solvents most used are *mineral spirits* and *naptha*. *Turpentine* is sometimes used, but contributes little that other solvents do not, and costs much more. Many synthetic resins require a special solvent, and it is *important that the correct one be used,* otherwise the paint may be entirely spoiled. Cement paints usually use water as a solvent.

## STORAGE OF MATERIALS AND EQUIPMENT

*Paints,* except cement-water paints, are usually provided ready-mixed in 1-gallon, 5-gallon, and 55-gallon containers. Large quantities of paint in 1-gallon and 5-gallon containers should be stored in enclosures with fireproof walls; small quantities should be stored in properly constructed storage cabinets. Metal cabinets should be used if available; if not, cabinets should be constructed of asbestos-cement board not less than 5/32″ thick. Bottoms and sides should be double thickness, with a 1½″ air space between the boards. Doors should also be of double thickness, with raised sills 2″ above the bottoms of the cabinets. Doors should be provided with suitable locks and should be kept closed and locked whenever paint is not being taken from or stored in the cabinet.

All mixed paint must be stored in nearly filled, tightly sealed containers to prevent skinning over, the loss by evaporation of volatile materials, and to reduce the danger of fire.

Paint in storage should be arranged so that the oldest paint of each type is the first available. If old paint must be used with new paint, the entire lot should be blended to ensure uniform gloss and color.

Your *equipment* may include either a paint spray outfit of 5-gallon capacity or a lightweight, portable, 1-quart capacity sprayer, driven either by air or electricity. The equipment may also include a paint mixer of the type used with a portable electric or pneumatic drill, and respirators of the chemical-cartridge or mechanical-filter type. The number and types of brushes available also will vary. You will have to use your own judgment as to the number of brushes to be kept available.

Before new paint brushes are used they should be rinsed with thinner. This tightens the bristles and also removes those which are loose. Brushes should not be soaked in water to tighten the bristles as this will cause the metal ferrule to rust or split due to the swelling of the wooden handle. Brushes that are to be reused the following day should be marked for white, light colors, or dark colors. Excess paint should be removed with thinner and the brushes suspended by the handle with the bristles immersed in thinner or linseed oil to just below the bottom of the ferrule. The weight of the brush must not rest on the bristles as that will cause them to become distorted. Brushes that are not to be reused immediately should be carefully cleaned with thinner of the type recommended by the manufacturer, washed thoroughly with soap and water, then rinsed. A protective cover and preservative should be applied when appropriate. They should be stored suspended from racks or laid flat.

To clean a frozen brush, soak it in a solvent-type, nonflammable paint and varnish remover, squeeze and scrape the softened paint out of the bristles, and then clean the brush with thinner as previously described.

## BRUSHES

*Brushes,* like any other tool, must be of first quality and maintained in perfect working condition at all times. Brushes are identified first by the type of bristle used. Brushes are made with either natural, synthetic, or mixed bristles. *Chinese hog bristles* represent the finest of the natural bristles because of their length, durability, and resiliency. Hog bristle has one unique characteristic in that the bristle end forms out like a tree branch. This "flagging" permits more paint to be carried on the brush and leaves finer brush marks that flow together more readily on the applied coating, resulting in a smoother finish. *Horsehair bristles* are used in cheap brushes and are a very unsatisfactory substitute. The ends do not flag, the bristles quickly become limp, they hold far less paint and do not spread it as well. Brush marks left in the applied coating tend to be coarse and do not level out as smoothly. Some brushes contain a mixture of hog bristle and horsehair, and their quality depends upon the percentage of each type used. Animal hair is utilized in very fine brushes for special purposes. *Badger* hair, for example, produces a particularly good varnish brush. *Squirrel* and *sable* are ideal for striping, lining, lettering, and free-hand art. Of the synthetics, *nylon* is by far the most common. By artificially "exploding" the ends and kinking the fibers, manufacturers have increased the paint-load nylon can carry, and have reduced the coarseness of brush marks. Nylon is almost always superior to horsehair. The very fact that nylon is a synthetic makes it unsuitable for applying lacquer, shellac, many creosote products, and some other coatings that would soften or dissolve the bristles. Because water does not cause any appreciable swelling of nylon bristles, they are especially recommended for use with latex paints. Brushes are further identified by types; that is, the variety of shapes and sizes as are required for specific painting jobs. Types can be classified as follows. (*See* Fig. 1.)

*Wall brushes* (Fig. 2) are flat, square-edged brushes ranging in widths from 3" to 6" and used for painting large, continuous surfaces, either interior or exterior.

*Sash and trim brushes* (Fig. 3) are available in four shapes: flat square-edged, flat angle-edged, round, and oval. These brushes range in width from 1½" to 3" or diameters of ½" to 2" and are used for painting window frames, sashes, narrow boards, as well as interior and exterior trim surfaces. For fine-line painting, the edge of the brush is often chisel-shaped to make precise edging easier to accomplish.

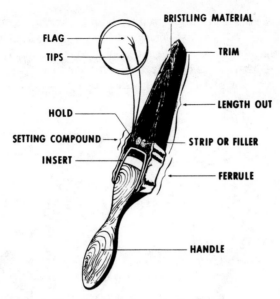

**Fig. 1.** Nomenclature of a typical paint brush.

**Fig. 2.** Flat wall brush.

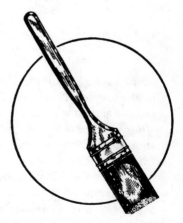

**Fig. 3.** Flat sash and trim brush.

The *oval sash* or *trimming brush* (Fig. 4) is available vulcanized in rubber, in numbered sizes from 1 to 10. They are made of

Chinese bristles and can be used for both paint and varnish.

*Enameling and varnish brushes* (Fig. 5) are available in flat square-edged or chisel-edged shapes, in widths from 2″ to 3″. The select, fine bristles are comparatively shorter in length, allowing relatively high-viscosity gloss finishes to lay down in a smooth, even film.

**Fig. 4.** Oval sash or trimming brush.

**Fig. 5.** Oval varnish brush.

*Oval varnish brushes* (Fig. 6) are excellent brushes made of Chinese bristles. They are oval in shape with open centers, and are available in many sizes, which are designated from 1/0 to 10/0.

*Dutch calcimine brushes* (Fig. 7) are used for calcimining rough plaster or stucco. They are made of gray Russian bristle, with the bristles set in knots and vulcanized in a solid rubber block so they will not pull out. A good general size is 6″ in width, with the length of the bristle not exceeding 5″.

*Flat calcimine brushes* (Fig. 8) are made of stiff Russian hard bristle. The Russian variety of bristle is heavier in texture than the Chinese and is preferable for painting smooth plastered walls with calcimine and should not be used for any other purpose. These brushes are made of either gray or yellow bristle, available in 6″, 7″, and 8″ widths. The 7″ width is the popular all-around

**Fig. 6.** Flat woodwork or varnish brush.

**Fig. 7.** Dutch calcimine brush.

**Fig. 8.** Flat calcimine brush.

**Fig. 9.** Whitewash brush.

size, with bristles 5¼″ in length.

*Whitewash brushes* (Fig. 9) are made of gray and yellow Russian bristles, set in cement and leather-bound. Available in various sizes, the 9″ width is the size generally used for applying whitewash and exterior cold-water paints.

*Flat duster brushes* (Fig. 10) are used for the removal of dust before painting. They clean spots and corners where a cloth will not do an efficient job. There are many types of duster brushes, but the flat variety is more practical. They are made of various kinds of bristles and horsehair, and the better types are vulcanized in rubber. It is an inexpensive brush and should be used for dusting *only*. Available in one size, 4½″ wide.

*Radiator brushes* (Fig. 11) are made with long handles and a flat, thin structure for painting between radiator coils and other unreachable places. They are made of black Chinese bristle from 1″ to 2½″ in width.

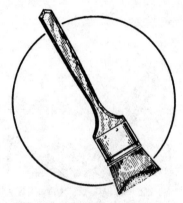

**Fig. 10.** Flat duster brush.          **Fig. 11.** Radiator brush.

*Flat artists' brushes* (Fig. 12) are made of black or white Chinese bristle, cement-set and metal-bound. They are designed for painting fine lines and for decorating. Available in widths ranging from ¼″ to 2″.

*Stippling brushes* (Fig. 13) are used to pound or stipple paint that has previously been applied to a smooth plaster wall, so as to give it a stipple effect. They are usually made of stiff gray Russian bristle.

*Waxing brushes* (Fig. 14) are used for finishing after wax has been applied to floors. They are equipped with felt protectors, to

Fig. 12. Flat artist's brush.

**Fig. 13.** Stippling brushes.

prevent scarring or marring baseboards, and are made of tampico and fiber, stapled into a solid block 7½″–9¼″. Available in 15- and 25-pound sizes.

The *roof-paint brush* shown in Fig. 15, *A* is made of gray Russian bristle, double-nailed and leather-bound, and is used for painting shingles. The brush shown at *C* is attached to a long handle and is used in the same manner as a broom for painting large roof surfaces. The roof-painting brush shown at *B* is made of poorer quality Russian bristle mixed with a percentage of horsehair. It is less expensive than the type previously described but is adequate for painting smaller metal roofs and for applying tar. It is available in two-, three-, and four-knot sizes with bristles about 3½″ in length.

*Flat color brushes* (Fig. 16) are made of pure squirrel hair, usually called camel's hair, cement-set and bound in brass. Available in ½″ sizes ranging from 1″ to 3″ in width.

*Flowing brushes* (Fig. 17) are usually made of a mixture of badger hair and French bristle with an outer layer of pure badger hair, although various other mixtures of hair and bristle are sometimes used. The type shown in Fig. 17 is the one most generally used in applying color varnish and finishing coats on automobiles and boats.

**Fig. 14.** Waxing brush.

**Fig. 15.** Roof-painting brushes.

**Fig. 16.** Flat color brush.

**Fig. 17.** Flowing brush.

A *stencil brush* (Fig. 18) is a stiff, stubby brush used for stenciling. It is made of tampico or fiber and set in vulcanized rubber.

**Fig. 18.** Stencil brush.

**Fig. 19.** Twirling brush to remove loose bristles.

## CARE OF BRUSHES

To remove short or loose bristles before using, twirl the brush by rolling the handle between the palms and against the extended fingers of the hand (Fig. 19).

Before using varnish brushes, rinse them in thinner to remove dust. To keep brushes in good condition never suspend or soak them in water. In addition to making the bristles soft and flabby, water will swell the divider or handle of the brush and will cause the brush to spread out, like a mop, sometimes breaking the ferrule.

Never let a brush rest for any length of time on the ends of the bristles. It will put a kink in them and will ruin the brush.

To keep brushes in good condition when in use, suspend them in the proper thinner with the bristle a short distance from the bottom of the can or paint pot. To suspend a brush properly, drill a ⅛″ hole through its handle at the proper point so that a stiff wire passing through it and resting upon the upper edge of the can or paint pot will suspend it at the desired height. Several brushes can be hung on the same wire (Fig. 20).

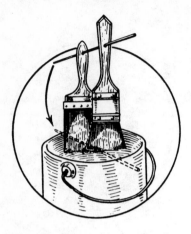

**Fig. 21.** Wrap brushes separately in oiled paper.

**Fig. 20.** Supporting brushes in thinner.

## STORING BRUSHES

Brushes used in oil paint, varnish, or enamel should be thoroughly washed out in thinner. Use plenty of thinner and then pour the used thinner into a bottle. The color will settle to the bottom and the clear thinner can again be used for cleaning brushes or thinning paint. Follow this cleaning by washing the bristles with hand soap and warm water. Get the suds well into the base of the brush, and rinse. Repeat this until no color comes out. Comb bristles straight, shake out all excess water, and lay brush flat. When it is thoroughly dry, wrap it in paper to keep the bristles clean and in shape (Fig. 21).

Other brushes should be treated in the same manner, using for the first cleaning the proper thinner as previously recommended.

Do not attempt to clean old brushes with strong soap powders or other detergents, lye, or strong cleaners.

Never leave a brush in benzine or benzine substitutes. The brush will become full of hardened specks of paint or varnish which can never be removed.

Never put a brush on a hot radiator to dry. It will take the life out of the bristles and ruin the brush.

## ROLLERS

A *paint roller* (Fig. 22) consists of a cylindrical sleeve or cover that slips onto a rotating cage to which a handle is attached. The cover may be 1½″ to 2¼″ inside diameter, and usually 3″, 4″, 7″ or 9″ in length. Special rollers are available in lengths from 1½″ to 18″. Proper roller application depends on the selection of the specific fabric and the thickness of fabric (nap length) based on the type of paint used and the smoothness or roughness of the surface to be painted. Special rollers are used for painting pipes, fences, and hard to reach areas. (*See* Figs. 23 and 24.) The fabrics generally used for rollers are lamb's wool, mohair, dynel, dacron, and rayon.

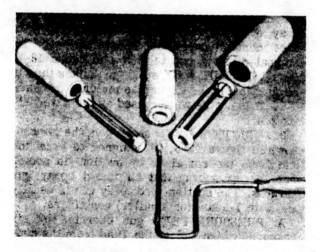

**Fig. 22.** Parts of a roller.

*Lamb's wool* (pelt) is the most solvent-resistant type of material used and is available in nap lengths up to 1¼″. It is recommended for synthetic finishes for application on semismooth and rough surfaces. It mats badly in water, and is not recommended for water paints.

*Mohair* is made primarily of Angora hair. It also is solvent-re-

**Fig. 24.** Fence roller.

**Fig. 23.** Pipe roller.

sistant and is supplied in 3/16″ and ¼″ nap length. It is recommended for synthetic enamels and for use on smooth surfaces. It can be used with water paints also.

*Dynel* is a modified acrylic fiber that has excellent resistance to water. It is best used for application of conventional water paints and solvent paints, except those that contain strong solvents, such as ketones. It is available in all nap lengths from ¼″ to 1¼″.

*Dacron* is a synthetic fiber that is somewhat softer than dynel. It is best suited for exterior oil or latex paints. It is available in nap lengths from 5/16″ to ½″.

*Rayon* fabric is not recommended because of the poor results generally obtained from its use. Furthermore, rayon mats badly in water. Table 12 can be used as a guide for choosing the proper roller cover.

Immediately after use, rollers should be cleaned with the type of thinner recommended for the paint in which the roller was

TABLE 12
*Roller selection guide*

| *Type of Paint* | *Smooth (1)* | *Semi-smooth (2)* | *Rough (3)* |
|---|---|---|---|
| | | ***Type of Surface*** | |
| Aluminum | C | A | A |
| Enamel or Semigloss (Alkyd) | A or B | A | |
| Enamel undercoat | A or B | A | |
| Epoxy coatings | B or D | D | D |
| Exterior House Paint: | | | |
| Latex for wood | C | A | |
| Latex for masonry | A | A | A |
| Oil or alkyd—wood | C | A | |
| Oil or alkyd—masonry | A | A | A |
| Floor enamel—all types | A or B | A | |
| Interior Wall paint: | | | |
| Alkyd or oil | A | A or D | A |
| Latex | A | A | A |
| Masonry sealer | B | A or D | A or D |
| Metal primers | A | A or D | |
| Varnish—all types | A or B | | |
| *Roller Cover Key** | | *Nap Length* (inches) | |
| A—Dynel (modified acrylic) | $\frac{1}{4}$–$\frac{3}{8}$ | $\frac{3}{8}$–$\frac{3}{4}$ | 1–1$\frac{1}{4}$ |
| B—Mohair | $\frac{3}{16}$–$\frac{1}{4}$ | | |
| C—Dacron polyester | $\frac{1}{4}$–$\frac{3}{8}$ | $\frac{1}{2}$ | |
| D—Lambswool pelt | $\frac{1}{4}$–$\frac{3}{8}$ | $\frac{1}{2}$–$\frac{3}{4}$ | 1–1$\frac{1}{4}$ |

(1) Smooth Surface: hardboard, smooth metal, smooth plaster, drywall, etc.

(2) Semi-smooth Surface: sand finished plaster and drywall, light stucco, blasted metal, semi-smooth masonry.

(3) Rough Surface: concrete or cinder block, brick, heavy stucco, wire fence.

* Comprehensive product standards do not exist in the Paint Roller Industry. Roller covers vary significantly in performance between manufacturers and most manufacturers have more than one quality level in the same generic class. This table is based on field experience with first line products of one manufacturer.

used. After cleaning with thinner, the roller should be thoroughly washed in soap and water, rinsed in clear water, and dried.

## SPRAY GUNS

A *spray gun* is a precision tool that mixes air under pressure with paint, breaks it up into spray, and ejects it out in a controlled pattern.

There are several types to choose from. Spray guns come either with a container attached to the gun or with the gun connected to a separate container by means of hoses. There are bleeder or nonbleeder, external- or internal-mix, and pressure-, gravity-, or suction-feed guns.

The *bleeder* type of gun is one in which air is allowed to leak—or bleed—from some part of the gun in order to prevent air pressure from building up in the air hose. In this type of gun the trigger controls the fluid only. It is generally used with small air compressing outfits that have no pressure control on the air line.

The *nonbleeder* gun is equipped with an air valve that shuts off the air when the trigger is released. It is used with compressing outfits having a pressure-controlling device.

An *external-mix* gun is one that mixes air and paint outside and in front of the gun's air cap. This type of gun can do a wide variety of work and has the power to throw a very fine spray, even of heavy material. It also permits exact control over the spray pattern. An external-mix air cap is shown in Fig. 25.

An *internal-mix* spray gun mixes the air and fluid inside the air cap as illustrated in Fig. 26. It is not as widely used as the external-mix gun.

In a *suction-feed* spray gun, the air cap, shown in Fig. 27, is designed to draw the fluid from the container by suction, in somewhat the same way that an insect spray gun operates. The suction-feed spray gun is usually used with one-quart (or smaller) containers.

A *pressure-feed* gun operates by air pressure, which forces the fluid from the container into the gun. This is the type (Fig. 28) used for large-scale painting.

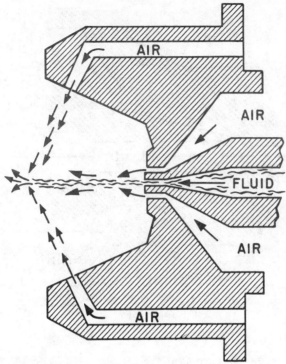

**Fig. 25.** An external-mix air cap.

## PARTS OF THE SPRAY GUN

The two main assemblies of the spray gun are the gun body assembly and the spray head assembly. Each of these assemblies is a collection of small parts, all of which are designed to do specific jobs.

The principal parts of the gun body assembly are shown in Fig. 29. The *air valve* controls the supply of air and is operated by the *trigger*. The *spreader adjustment valve* regulates the amount of air that is supplied to the spreader horn holes of the *air cap*, thus varying the paint pattern. It is fitted with a dial that can be set to give the pattern desired. The *fluid needle adjustment* controls the

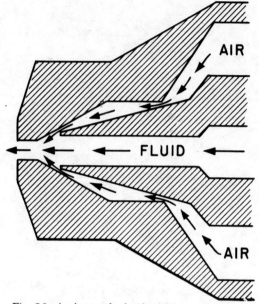

**Fig. 26.** An internal-mix air cap.

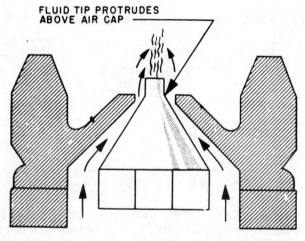

**Fig. 27.** A suction-feed air cap.

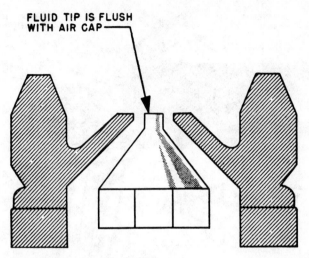

**Fig. 28.** A pressure-feed air cap.

amount of spray material that passes through the gun. The *spray head locking bolt* locks the gun body and the removable spray head together.

Most guns are now fitted with a removable *spray head assembly*. This type has many advantages. It can be cleaned more easily, it permits quick change of the head when you want to use a new color or material, and, if it is damaged, a new head can be put on the old gun body.

The principal parts of the spray head assembly are the *air cap*, the *fluid tip, fluid needles,* and *spray head barrel* (Fig. 30). The fluid tip regulates the flow of the spray material into the air stream. The tip encloses the end of the fluid needle. The spray head barrel is the housing that encloses the head mechanism.

## LUBRICATION OF THE SPRAY GUN

Your spray gun also needs lubrication. The fluid needle packing should be removed occasionally and softened with oil. The fluid needle spring should be coated with grease or petrolatum.

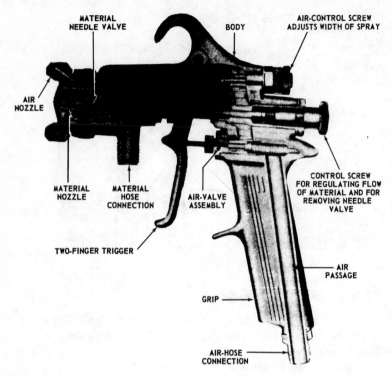

**Fig. 29.** Cross section of a spray gun.

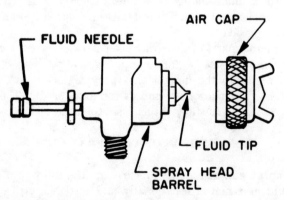

**Fig. 30.** Principal parts of the spray head.

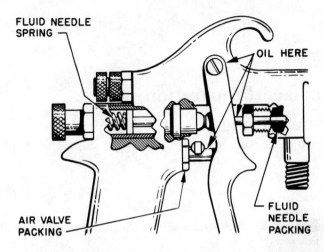

**Fig. 31.** Lubrication points of a spray gun.

Figure 31 shows where these parts are and also the oil holes in which you occasionally should put a few drops of light oil.

(*See* Chap. 28, Surface Preparation for Painting; Chap. 29, Mixing and Conditioning Paint, Methods of Applying Paint, and Colors; and Chap. 30, Deterioration of Paint, Painting Safety, and Wood Preservatives.)

*CHAPTER 28*

# Surface Preparation for Painting

*Surface preparation* consists of (1) thorough cleaning of the surface and (2) such mechanical or chemical pretreatment as may be necessary.

## PLASTER AND WALLBOARD

Whenever possible, new plaster should be aged at least two months before painting. Prior to painting, fill all holes and cracks with *spackling compound* and *patching plaster*. Cut out the material along the crack or hole in inverted V-shape. To avoid excessive absorption of water from the patching material, wet the edges and bottom of the crack or hole before applying the material. Fill the opening to within ¼″ of the surface and allow the material partially to set before you bring the level up flush with the surface. After the material has thoroughly set, smooth it up with fine sandpaper. Allow at least 72 hours for setting before painting. Plaster and wallboard should be primed.

## WOOD

Prior to painting, a *wood surface* should be closely inspected for loose boards, defective lumber, protruding nailheads, or any other defects or irregularities. Loose boards should be nailed tight, defective lumber should be replaced, and all nailheads should be countersunk.

A dirty wood surface is cleaned for painting by sweeping, dusting, and washing with solvent or soap and water. When washing wood, take care to avoid excessive wetting, which tends to raise the grain. Wash a small area at a time, and rinse and dry immediately.

Wood that is to be given a *natural* finish (meaning wood that will not be concealed by an opaque surface coating) may require *bleaching* to a uniform and/or light color. Bleaching is done by applying a solution of one pound of *oxalic acid* to one gallon of hot water. More than one application may be required. After the solution has dried, smooth the surface with fine sandpaper.

Rough wood surfaces must be sanded smooth for painting. Mechanical *sanders* of various types are used for large areas. Hand-sanding of small areas is done by wrapping the sandpaper around a rubber, wood, or metal *sanding block*. For a very rough surface start with a coarse paper, about No. 2 or 2½; follow up with a No. ½, No. 1, or No. 1½; finish with about a No. 2/0 grit. For fine work, such as furniture work, finish with a still finer grit.

Sap or resin in wood will stain through a coat, or even several coats, of paint. Remove sap or resin by scraping and/or sanding. Knots in resinous wood should be treated with *knot sealer.*

## PAINT REMOVERS

*Paint* and *varnish removers* generally are used for small areas. Solvent-type removers or solvent mixtures are selected according to the type and condition of the old finish as well as the nature of the substrate. Removers are available as flammable or non-flammable types; also liquid or semi-paste in consistency. While most paint removers require scraping or steel wool to physically remove the softened paint, types are available that allow the loosened finish to be flushed off with steam or hot water. Many of the flammable and non-flammable removers contain paraffin wax to retard evaporation. It is absolutely essential that this residue be removed from the surface prior to painting in order to prevent loss of adhesion of the applied coating. In such instances, follow the manufacturer's label directions or use mineral spirits to remove any wax residue. As a safety precaution, it should be noted that while non-flammable removers eliminate fire hazards, they are toxic to a degree (as are all removers). Proper ventilation must be provided whenever they are used.

## CONDITIONERS, SEALERS, AND FILLERS

*Conditioners* are often applied on masonry to seal a chalky surface in order to improve adhesion of water-based topcoats. *Sealers* are used on wood to prevent resin exudation or bleeding. *Fillers* are used to produce a smooth finish on open-grain wood and rough masonry. (*See* Table 13, Treatment of Various Substrates.)

Latex (water-thinned) paints do not adhere well to chalky masonry surfaces. To overcome this problem, an oil-based conditioner is applied to the chalky substrate before the latex paint is applied. The entire surface should be vigorously wire brushed by hand or power tools, then dusted to remove all loose particles and chalk residue. The conditioner is then brushed on freely to assure effective penetration and allowed to dry. This surface conditioner is not intended for use as a finish coat.

*Sealers* are used on bare wood to prevent resin exudation (bleeding) through applied paint coatings. Freshly exuded resin, while still soft, may be scraped off with a putty knife and the affected area solvent-cleaned with alcohol. Hardened resin may be removed by scraping or sanding. Since the sealer is not intended for use as a priming coat, it should be used only when necessary, and applied only over the affected area. When previous paint on pine lumber has become discolored over knots, the sealer should be applied over the old paint before the new paint is applied.

*Fillers* are used on porous wood, concrete, and masonry to fill the pores in order to provide a smoother finish coat.

*Wood fillers* are used on open-grained hardwoods. In general, those hardwoods with pores larger than those in birch should be filled. (*See* Table 14, Characteristics of Wood.)

When filling is necessary, it is done after any staining operation. Stain should be allowed to dry for 24 hours before filler is applied. If staining is not warranted, natural (uncolored) filler is applied directly to the bare wood. The filler may be colored with some of the stain in order to accentuate the grain pattern of the wood. To apply, first thin the filler with mineral spirits to a

TABLE 13

*Treatment of various substrates*

| | Wood | Metal | | Concrete | Plaster |
| --- | --- | --- | --- | --- | --- |
| | | Steel | Other | Masonry | Wallboard |
| **Mechanical** | | | | | |
| Hand Cleaning | S | S | S | S | S |
| Power Tool Cleaning | S* | S | … | S | … |
| Flame Cleaning | … | S | … | … | … |
| Blast Cleaning: | | | | | |
|   Brush-Off | … | S | S | S | … |
|   All Other | … | S | … | … | … |
| **Chemical and Solvent** | | | | | |
| Solvent Cleaning | S | S | S | … | … |
| Alkali Cleaning | … | S | … | S | … |
| Steam Cleaning | … | S | … | S | … |
| Acid Cleaning | … | S | … | S | … |
| Pickling | … | S | … | … | … |
| **Pretreatments** | | | | | |
| Hot Phosphate | … | S | … | … | … |
| Cold Phosphate | … | S | … | … | … |
| Wash Primers | … | S | S | … | … |
| **Conditioners, Sealers and Fillers** | | | | | |
| Conditioners | … | … | … | S | … |
| Sealers | S | … | … | … | … |
| Fillers | S | … | … | S | … |

S—Satisfactory for use as indicated
*—Sanding only

TABLE 14
*Characteristics of wood*

| Name of Wood | Soft Closed | Open | Hard Closed | Notes on Finishing |
|---|---|---|---|---|
| Ash | | X | | Requires filler. |
| Alder | X | | | Stains well. |
| Aspen | | | X | Paints well. |
| Basswood | | | X | Paints well. |
| Beech | | | X | Paints poorly; varnishes well. |
| Birch | | | X | Paints and varnishes well. |
| Cedar | X | | | Paints and varnishes well. |
| Cherry | | | X | Varnishes well. |
| Chestnut | | X | | Requires filler; paints poorly. |
| Cottonwood | | | X | Paints well. |
| Cypress | | | X | Paints and varnishes well. |
| Elm | | X | | Requires filler; paints poorly. |
| Fir | X | | | Paints poorly. |
| Gum | | | X | Varnishes well. |
| Hemlock | X | | | Paints fairly well. |
| Hickory | | X | | Requires filler. |
| Mahogany | | X | | Requires filler. |
| Maple | | | X | Varnishes well. |
| Oak | | X | | Requires filler. |
| Pine | X | | | Variable depending on grain. |
| Teak | | X | | Requires filler. |
| Walnut | | X | | Requires filler. |
| Redwood | X | | | Paints well. |

Note: Any type finish may be applied unless otherwise specified.

creamy consistency, then liberally brush it across the grain, followed by light brushing along the grain. Allow to stand five to ten minutes until most of the thinner has evaporated, at which time the finish will have lost its glossy appearance. Before it has a chance to set and harden, wipe the filler off *across* the grain using burlap or other coarse cloth, rubbing the filler into the pores of the wood while removing the excess. Finish by stroking along the grain with clean rags. It is essential that all excess filler be removed. Knowing when to start wiping is important; wiping too soon will pull the filler out of the pores, while allowing the filler to set too long will make it very difficult to wipe off. A simple test for dryness consists of rubbing a finger across the surface. If a ball is formed, it is time to wipe. If the filler slips under the pressure of the finger, it is still too wet for wiping. Allow the filler to dry for 24 hours before applying finish coats.

*Masonry fillers* are applied by brush to bare and previously prepared (all loose, powdery, flaking material removed) rough concrete, concrete block, stucco or other masonry surfaces, both new and old. The purpose is to fill the open pores by brushing the filler into the surface to produce a fairly smooth finish. If the voids on the surface are large, it is preferable to apply two coats of filler, rather than one heavy coat, in order to avoid mud-cracking. Allow one to two hours drying time between coats. Allow the final coat to dry for 24 hours before painting.

## WEATHER AND TEMPERATURE

Oil-painting and water-painting should not be done in temperatures above 95° or below 45°. Varnishing, shellacking, lacquering, and enameling should not be done in temperatures below 65° or above 95°. No painting except water-painting should be done on a damp surface, or on one which is exposed to hot sunlight.

(*See* Chap. 27, Fundamental Purposes of Painting; Chap. 29, Mixing and Conditioning Paint, Methods of Applying Paint, and Color; and Chap. 30, Deterioration of Paint, Painting Safety, and Wood Preservatives.)

## CHAPTER 29

# Mixing and Conditioning Paint, Methods of Applying Paint, and Colors

Most paints used are *ready-mixed,* meaning that most paints have the ingredients already mixed together in the proper proportions. When *oil paints* are left in storage for a long while, however, the pigments settle to the bottom and must again be mixed into the vehicle before the paint is used. This procedure is what is meant by the term "mixing" as used in this chapter.

## MIXING TECHNIQUES

Whenever possible, mix paint with a mechanical *agitator,* which mixes paint by rapidly shaking the container. In the absence of an agitator, use a strong, smooth, clean wood or metal paddle. If the pigment has settled in a cake, pour the vehicle off into another container and break up the pigment with the paddle. Then pour the vehicle back in, a little at a time, while continuing to work in the pigment. Then *box* the paint by pouring it back and forth from one container to the other. Continue boxing until the pigment and vehicle form a smooth mixture of uniform consistency and color.

A newly-opened can of *ready-mixed paint* is usually of the proper consistency for application. Eventually, however, the paint will thicken as the volatile portion of the thinner evaporates from the open can. When this happens, enough of the appropriate thinner must be added to bring the paint back to working consistency.

The same applies to the drier. When the paint takes longer than it should to dry, the drier has evaporated below the required level, and more drier should be added. Great care must be taken against adding too much drier, however. Paint containing to much drier will dry too rapidly on the surface, which may cause *wrinkling.*

*Oil paint* should be stirred frequently during use to keep the pigment from settling to the bottom. *Varnish* and *shellac,* however, should not be stirred or agitated. *Enamel* should be mixed with a hand-paddle, not with a shake-type mechanical agitator. A shake-type agitator whips air into enamel, causing it to bubble or froth. Bubbled or frothed enamel must be allowed to stand six to eight hours before it can be used.

## CONDITIONING PAINT

When a partially filled can of oil paint is placed in storage, the surface of the paint should be covered with a 1/16" layer of the appropriate thinner and the can should be covered as tightly as possible. The layer of thinner will prevent the paint from skinning over, and the tight cover on the can will prevent the thinner from evaporating.

To remove lumps, pieces of skin, or foreign materials from paint, strain the paint through a sieve made of fine wire mesh, silk, or cheesecloth. All paint used in spray guns must be thoroughly strained.

## METHODS OF APPLYING PAINT

The most common methods of applying paint are by brush, roller, and spray. Of the three used, *brushing* is the slowest method, *rolling* is much faster, and *spraying* is usually the fastest of all. The choice of method is based on many factors such as environment, type of substrate, type of coating to be applied, appearance of finish desired, and the skill of the worker involved in the operation.

The general surroundings may prohibit the use of *spray application* because of possible fire hazards or potential damage from overspray. Typical of these are parking lots and open storage areas. Adjacent areas not to be coated must be masked when spraying is performed. This results in loss of time and, if extensive, may offset the advantage of the rapidity of spraying operations.

*Roller coating* is most efficient on large flat surfaces. Corners, edges, and odd shapes, however, must be brushed. Spraying also is most suitable for large surfaces, except that it can also be used for round or irregular shapes. *Brushing* is ideal for small surfaces or for cutting in corners and edges. Dip and flow coat methods are suitable for volume production painting of small items in the shop.

Rapid-drying, lacquer-type products such as vinyls should be sprayed. Application to such products by brush or roller may be extremely difficult, especially in warm weather or outdoors on breezy days.

Coatings applied by brush may leave brush marks in the dried film. Rolling leaves a stippled effect, while spraying yields the smoothest finish, if done properly. (*See* Chap. 27, Fundamental Purpose of Painting, Paints, and Equipment.)

## BRUSH AND PAINT APPLICATION

Select the type of brush and paint pot needed for the job. The best type of paint pot for brush painting is a 1-gallon paint can from which the lip around the top has been removed. (The lid of the can is fitted to the lip around the top.) You can cut this lip off with a cold chisel. If you leave the lip on the pot, it will fill up with paint as you scrape the brush, and this paint will be continually streaking down the outside of the pot and dripping off.

Dip the brush to only one-third the length of the bristles, and scrape the surplus paint off the lower face of the brush, so there will be no drip as you transfer the brush from the pot to the work.

To apply paint by brush, proceed as follows.

For complete coverage, first "lay on," then "lay off." Laying on means applying the paint first in long, horizontal strokes. Laying off means crossing your first strokes by working up and down. (*See* Fig. 1.)

By using the laying on and laying off method and crossing your

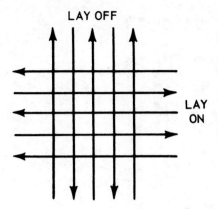

**Fig. 1.** Laying on and laying off.

strokes, the paint is distributed evenly over the surface, the surface is completely covered, and a minimum amount of paint is used. A good rule is to "lay on" the paint the shortest distance across the area and "lay off" the longest distance. When painting walls, or any vertical surface, "lay on" in horizontal strokes, "lay off" vertically.

Always paint the ceiling first and work from the far corner. By working the ceiling first, you can keep the wall free of drippings by wiping up as you go along.

When painting ceiling surfaces, you will find that paint coats on the ceiling should normally be "lay on" for the shortest ceiling distance and "lay off" for the longest ceiling distance.

To avoid brush marks when finishing up a square, use strokes directed toward the last square finished, gradually lifting the brush near the end of the stroke while the brush is still in motion. Every time the brush touches the painted surface of the start of a stroke, it leaves a mark. For this reason, never finish a square by brushing toward the unpainted area, but always end up by brushing back toward the area already painted.

When painting pipes and stanchions and narrow straps, beams, and angles, lay the paint on diagonally as shown in Fig. 2. Lay off along the long dimension.

Always carry a rag for wiping dripped or smeared paint.

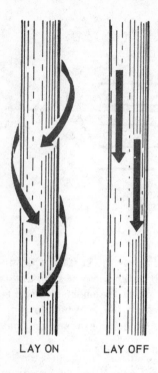

LAY ON   LAY OFF   **Fig. 2.** Painting pipes and stanchions.

## ROLLER METHOD

Pour the premixed paint into the tray to about half the depth of the tray. Immerse the roller completely and remove any excess paint. As an alternative to using the tray, place a specially designed galvanized wire screen into a five gallon can of the paint. This screen attaches to the can and remains at the correct angle for loading and spreading paint on the roller. (*See* Figs. 3 and 4.) The first load of paint on a roller should be worked out on newspaper to remove entrapped air from the roller cover. It is then ready for application. As the roller is passed over a surface, thousands of tiny fibers continually compress and expand, metering out the coating and wetting the surface. This is in sharp contrast to other application methods that depend upon the skill and technique of the painter. The uniformity of application by roller is less suscep-

**Fig. 3.** Roller and tray.

**Fig. 4.** Roller and wire screen attachment to can.

tible to variance in painting ability than other methods. Basic rules must still be followed. Always trim around ceilings, moldings, and the like before rolling the major wall or ceiling surfaces. Then roll as close as possible to maintain the same texture. Trimming is usually done with a 3″ wall brush. Always roll paint onto the surface working from the dry area into the just-painted area. Never roll completely in the same or one direction. Do not roll too fast and avoid spinning the roller at the end of the strike. Always feather out final strokes to pick up any excess paint on the surface. This is accomplished by rolling the final stroke out with minimal pressure.

## SPRAY METHOD

Complete instructions for the care, maintenance, and operation of a spray gun are contained in the manufacturer's literature, and these instructions should be carefully followed. Only a few of the major spray-painting techniques follow.

### SPRAY GUN ADJUSTMENT

The first essential is the correct adjustment of the *air control* and *material control* screws in order to produce the type of spray best suited to the nature of the work. The air control screw adjusts the width and the density of the spray. Turning the screw clockwise concentrates the material into a round, denser spray; turning it counterclockwise widens the material into a fan-shaped, more diffuse spray. As the spray is widened, the flow of material must be increased; if it is not, the spray will reduce itself to a fog. Turning the material control screw clockwise increases the flow of material; turning it counterclockwise decreases the flow. The most desirable character of spray (from round and solid to fan-shaped and diffuse) depends upon the character of the surface and the type of material being sprayed. Experience and experiment are the only guides here. Practice spraying should be done on waste material, using different practice adjustments, until a spray is obtained that covers uniformly and adequately.

## OPERATIONAL DEFECTS OF THE SPRAY GUN

Uneven distribution of the spray pattern is caused by clogging of one or more of the air outlets or by incorrect adjustment of the air and/or material controls.

*Spitting* is the alternate discharge of paint and air. Common causes of spitting are drying of the packing around the material control needle-valve, looseness of the material nozzle, and dirt in the material nozzle-seat. To remedy dry packing, back off the material control needle-valve and place two drops of machine oil on the packing. To remedy looseness of the material nozzle and dirt on the nozzle-seat, remove the nozzle, clean the nozzle and seat with thinner, and screw the nozzle tightly back into place.

*Air leakage* from the front of the gun is usually caused by improper seating of the air valve in the *air valve assembly* shown in Chap. 27, Fig. 29. Improper seating may be caused by foreign matter on the valve or seat, by wear on or damage to the valve or seat, by a broken valve spring, or by sticking of the valve stem caused by lack of lubrication.

*Paint leakage* from the front of the gun is usually caused by improper seating of the material needle valve. Improper seating may be caused by damage to the valve stem or tip, by foreign matter on the tip or seat, or by a broken valve spring.

## SPRAY-GUN STROKE

Figure 5 shows the correct method of stroking with a spray gun. Hold the gun 6″ to 8″ from the surface to be painted, keep the axis of the spray perpendicular to the surface, and take strokes back and forth in horizontal lines. Pull the trigger just after you start a stroke, to avoid applying too much paint at the starting and stopping points.

Figure 6 shows right and wrong methods of spraying an outside corner. If you use the wrong method, a good deal of paint will be wasted into the air.

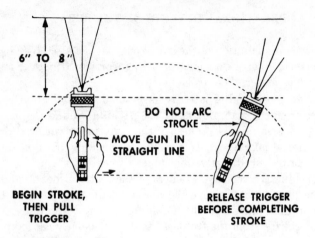

**Fig. 5.** Correct method of stroking with a spray gun.

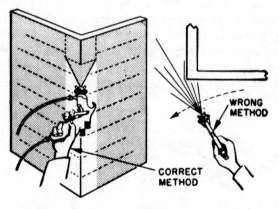

**Fig. 6.** Correct and wrong methods of spraying an outside corner.

## AVERAGE COVERAGE OF PAINT

The area a gallon of paint will cover varies considerably with the nature of the surface, the character of the paint, and the method of application. Table 15 is intended only to give you a

TABLE 15
*Average paint coverage*

| Type of Surface | Area in Square Feet per Gallon | | |
|---|---|---|---|
| | Primer or First Coat | Second Coat | Third Coat |
| **Exterior** | | | |
| Wood Siding and Trim | | | |
| Flat Oil | 300 | 350 | 400 |
| Shingle Stain | 80 | 125 | |
| Concrete Masonry Unit | | | |
| Cement Base | 100 | 150 | 200 |
| Latex | 150 | 200 | 250 |
| **Interior** | | | |
| Plaster | | | |
| Flat Oil | 300 | 350 | 400 |
| Gloss Oil | 300 | 350 | 400 |
| Latex | 300 | 350 | 400 |
| Concrete Masonry Unit | | | |
| Cement Base | 100 | 150 | 200 |
| Latex | 150 | 200 | 250 |

rough estimate of the average coverage per gallon for brush painting.

Spray painting allows greater per-gallon coverage, as you can tell from this comparison:

1. Enamel—400 square feet by brush
2. Enamel—425 square feet by spray
3. Flat—400 square feet by brush
4. Flat—430 square feet by spray

## COLORS

The mixing and use of colored paints to produce a desired color scheme or harmony is technical in nature and difficult to do well. Much could be written about color, but unless a person works with them and gains experience, he or she will never fully understand how to use the different colored paints.

## MIXING

As you know, there are three primary colors—red, blue, and yellow. These are the only true colors and are the basis for all other shades, tints, and hues, which are derived by mixing any combination of these colors in various proportions. Figure 7 illustrates a color triangle with one primary color at each of its points.

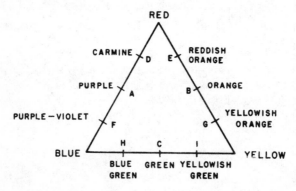

**Fig. 7.** A color triangle.

The lettering in the triangle indicates the hues that will result when these colors are intermixed, as follows.

Equal proportions of red and blue produce a purple.

Equal proportions of red and yellow produce an orange.

Equal parts of blue and yellow produce a green.

Three parts of red to one part of blue will make a carmine.

Three parts of red to one of yellow will result in a reddish-orange.

Three parts of blue to one of red will produce a purple-violet.

Three parts of yellow to one of red will produce a yellowish-orange.

Three parts of blue to one of yellow will result in a blue-green.

Three parts of yellow to one of blue will produce a yellowish-green.

Many other hues can be produced by varying the proportions of the primary colors. Hues are known as chromatic colors, while black, white, and the gray series are known as the achromatic (neutral) colors. The gray series can be produced by mixing black and white in different proportions.

## TINTING

*Tinting* is the process of mixing a colored pigment with a vehicle, such as linseed oil, turpentine, or varnish, and then blending this combination with a base paint to produce the desired shade or tint.

Some of the most commonly used tinting pigments are lampblack, raw sienna, Venetian red or vermilion, ultramarine, and the chrome yellow group. Any of these pigments when mixed with white will result in a lighter tint of the same color. When one of these pigments (excepting lampblack) is mixed with a little black and then added to white, it will result in a darker shade of the same color as the pigment.

When tinting oil paints, the pigment is mixed with linseed oil to thin it to the consistency of canned milk. If an enamel paint is to be tinted, the pigment is mixed with varnish or linseed oil to the same consistency as is used for oil paints. After the tint is thoroughly mixed, it should be strained to remove any remaining lumps of pigments. If this is not done, dark streaks will appear in the tinted paint when it is applied to a surface.

The tint should be added a little at a time to the material being tinted and the mixture spread on a test board so that its color may be compared to the color of the surface being matched. There are differences in the tinting strength of the various brands of tinting colors and between the colors of one brand. For example, Prussian blue is stronger in tinting strength than other blue tint colors, chrome yellow is stronger than raw sienna or yellow ochre, and vermilion is much stronger than Venetian red. This refers only to their ability to tint or color white paint. However, this does not mean that a satisfactory tinting job cannot be done by using any of the tinting pigments, provided the proper amount of tinting material is blended with the base.

The following points are good ones to remember when tinting.

Colors always appear darker in the mixing can than on a surface.

Artificial light causes colors to appear darker than they are in daylight.

All colors dry to a lighter shade than they appear before being applied to a surface. Paints should be mixed to a slightly darker shade than the color being matched.

The eyes easily become saturated with a color and the colors may seem to fade or change. To assure accuracy when you are mixing colors, it is a good policy to look away from the work for a few minutes and rest your eyes.

(*See* Chap. 28, Surface Preparation for Painting, and Chap. 30, Deterioration of Paint, Painting Safety, and Wood Preservatives.)

## CHAPTER 30

# Deterioration of Paint, Painting Safety, and Wood Preservatives

Repainting at the proper time avoids the problems resulting from painting either too soon or too late. Painting before it is necessary is uneconomical and eventually results in a heavy film buildup leading to abnormal *deterioration* of the paint system.

A paint that reaches the end of useful life *prematurely* is said to have *failed*. The following sections describe the more common types of paint failures, the reasons for such failures, and methods of prevention and/or cure.

## CHALKING

*Chalking* is the result of weathering of the paint at the surface of the coating. The vehicle is broken down by sunlight and other destructive influences, leaving behind loose powdery pigment that can easily be rubbed off with the finger. (*See* Fig. 1.) Chalking takes place more rapidly with softer paints such as those based on linseed oil. Chalking is most rapid in areas exposed to large amounts of sunshine. For example, in the northern hemisphere chalking will be most rapid on the south side of a building. On the other hand, little chalking will take place in areas protected from sunshine and rain, such as under eaves or overhangs. Controlled chalking can be an asset, especially in white paints, since it is a self-cleaning process and helps to keep the surface clean and white. Furthermore, by gradually wearing away it reduces the

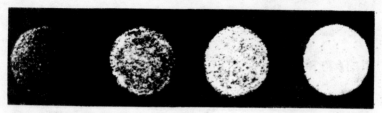

**Fig. 1.** Degrees of chalk.

thickness of the coating, thus allowing continuous repainting without making the coating too thick for satisfactory service. Chalked paints are also generally easier to repaint since the underlying paint is in good condition and generally little surface preparation is required. This is not the case when water-thinned paints are to be applied. Their adhesion to chalky surfaces is poor.

## ALLIGATORING

*Alligatoring* describes a pattern in a coating that looks like the hide of an alligator (Fig. 2). It is caused by uneven expansion and contraction of a relative undercoat. Alligatoring can be caused by (1) applying an enamel over an oil primer, (2) painting over bituminous paint, asphalt, pitch or shellac, or (3) painting over grease or wax.

## PEELING

*Peeling* (Fig. 3) results from inadequate bonding of the top coat with the undercoat or the underlying surface. It is nearly always caused by inadequate surface preparation. A top coat will peel if it is applied to a wet surface, a dirty surface, an oily or waxy surface, or a glossy surface. All glossy surfaces must be sanded before painting.

## BLISTERING

*Blistering* (Fig. 4) is caused by the development of gas or liquid pressure under the paint. The root cause of most blistering, other than that caused by excessive heat, is inadequate ventilation

**Fig. 2.** Alligatoring.

**Fig. 3.** Peeling.

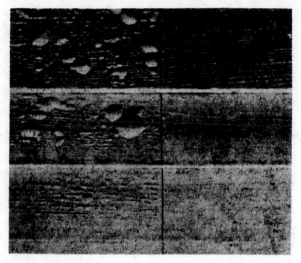

**Fig. 4.** Blistering.

plus some structural defect that allows moisture to accumulate under the paint. Before repainting, the cause of the blistering must be determined and corrected. Blisters should be scraped off, the paint edges around them should be feathered off with sandpaper, and the bare places primed before the blistered area is repainted.

## CHECKING AND CRACKING

*Checking* and *cracking* describe breaks in the paint film that are formed as the paint becomes hard and brittle. Temperature changes cause the substrate and overlying paint to expand and contract. As the paint becomes hard, it gradually loses its ability to expand without breaking to some extent. *Checking* is described as tiny breaks that take place only in the upper coat or coats of the paint film without penetrating to the substrate. The pattern is usually similar to a crowsfoot (Fig. 5). *Cracking* describes larger and longer breaks that extend through to the substrate (Fig. 6). Both are a result of stresses in the paint film that exceed the

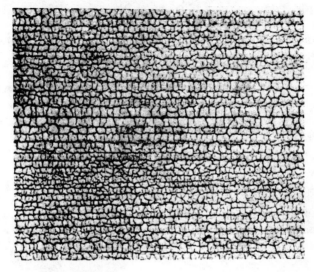

**Fig. 5.** Severe checking.

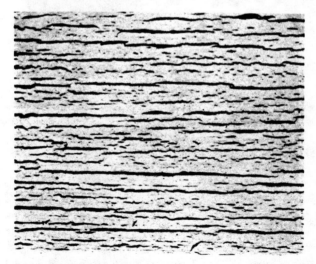

**Fig. 6.** Severe cracking.

strength of the coating. Whereas checking arises from stresses within the paint film, cracking is caused by stresses between the film and the substrate. Cracking will generally take place to a greater extent on wood than on other substrates because of its grain. When wood expands, it expands more across the grain than along the grain. Therefore, the stress in the coating is greatest across the grain, causing cracks to form parallel to the grain of the wood. Checking and cracking are aggravated by excessively thick coatings because of their reduced elasticity.

## CRAWLING

*Crawling* occurs when the new coating fails to wet and form a continuous film over the preceding coat. Examples are applying latex paints over high gloss enamel or applying paints on concrete or masonry treated with a silicone water repellant. (*See* Fig. 7.)

**Fig. 7.** Crawling.

## INADEQUATE GLOSS

Sometimes a gloss paint fails to attain the normal amount of gloss. This may be caused by (1) inadequate surface preparation, (2) application over an undercoat that is not thoroughly dry, or (3) application in cold or foggy weather.

## PROLONGED TACKINESS

A coat of paint is dry when it ceases to be *tacky*, or slightly sticky to the touch, and prolonged tackiness indicates excessively slow drying. This may be caused by (1) insufficient drier in the paint, (2) a low-quality vehicle in the paint, (3) applying the paint too thickly, (4) painting over an undercoat that is not thoroughly dry, (5) painting over a waxy, oily, or greasy surface, or (6) painting in damp, wet, or foggy weather.

## WRINKLING

When paint is applied too thickly, especially in cold weather, the surface of the coat dries to a skin over a layer of undried paint underneath. This usually causes *wrinkling* like that shown in Fig. 8. To avoid wrinkling when you are brush painting or roller painting, be sure to brush or roll each coat of paint out as thin as possible. To avoid wrinkling when spray painting, be careful to keep the gun in constant motion over the surface whenever you have the trigger down.

## PAINTING SAFETY

The frequent necessity of having to use toxic and flammable materials, pressurized equipment, ladders, scaffolding, and rigging always presents a potential hazard. Hazards may also be inherent in the very nature of the environment, or caused through ignorance or carelessness of the worker. It is, therefore, extremely important to be aware of all potential hazards, since continuous and automatic precautionary measures will minimize the problem and improve efficiency.

Painting hazards can be broadly divided into three major categories, as follows:

**Fig. 8.** Wrinkling.

1. Hazards involved in the use of scaffolds, ladders, and rigging equipment.
2. Fire hazards from flammable materials in paints.
3. Health hazards from toxic (poisonous) materials in paints.

## EQUIPMENT HAZARDS

The following basic procedures in setting up and use of equipment are imperative to assure safety standards and maximum protection of workers.

## LADDERS

Store wood ladders in warm, dry areas protected from the weather and the ground.

Protect wood ladders with clear coatings only, so that cracks, splinters or other defects will be readily visible.

Inspect all ladders frequently for loose or bent parts, cracks, breaks, or splinters.

All straight and extension ladders must have safety shoes. These should be of insulating material for metal ladders. (*See* Fig. 9.)

**Fig. 9.** Ladder safety shoes.

Do not use portable ladders greater in length than can be readily carried and placed. Never splice ladders to form a longer ladder.

Pretest all ladders and scaffolding before use by placing horizontally with blocks under ends and "bouncing" in the center or walking along ladder or scaffold.

Extension ladders should have a minimum overlap of 15 per cent for each section (Fig. 10).

Do not use stepladders over 12' high. Never use one as a straight ladder. Never stand on the top platform.

Place ladders so that the horizontal distance from the top support to foot is at least one-quarter of the working length. Be sure that the ladder is securely in place. Rope off all doorways in front of the ladder and place warning signs.

Use hand lines to raise or lower tools and materials. Do not overreach when working on ladders. Move the ladder instead.

Never use metal ladders in areas where contact with electric power lines is possible.

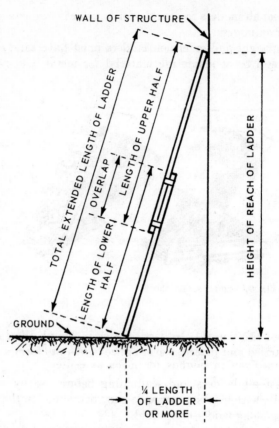

WALL OF STRUCTURE

TOTAL EXTENDED LENGTH OF LADDER

OVERLAP

LENGTH OF UPPER HALF

LENGTH OF LOWER HALF

HEIGHT OF REACH OF LADDER

GROUND

¼ LENGTH OF LADDER OR MORE

**Fig. 10.** Ladder stability.

## SCAFFOLDING

Inspect all parts before use. Reject metal parts damaged by corrosion and wood parts with defects such as checks, splits, unsound knots, and decay.

Provide adequate sills or underpinnings when erecting on filled or soft ground. Be sure that scaffolds are plumb and level. Compensate for unevenness of the ground by blocking or using adjusting screws.

Anchor scaffolds to the wall about every 28' in length and 18' in height. Do not force braces to fit. Use horizontal diagonal bracing at bottom and at every 30' in height.

Lumber should be straight grained. All nails should be driven full length and not subject to direct pull.

Provide guard railings regardless of height on the full length of the scaffold and also on the ends.

Erect scaffolding so that ladders are lined up from top to bottom. Always use ladders when climbing scaffolding.

Tubular pole scaffolds should be made of 2" O.D. galvanized steel tubing or other corrosion resistant metal of equal strength. They should be erected or dismantled by experienced workers only.

Planking should have at least a 2' overlap. Secure well to wood scaffolding. Platforms should be made of planking of uniform thickness laid close together. They must overlap and be fastened at supports. They must not extend over the edge without being properly supported. An unsupported plank is a deadly trap. Do not use planking for other purposes; paint them only at the ends to identify them. Nominal sizes of planking should be determined from Table 16, Safe Center Loads for Scaffold Plank. Values are given in pounds for loads at center and allow for weight of planking.

Test scaffolds and extensive planking (extended to working length) by raising them 1' off the ground and loading them with weights at least four times the anticipated working load.

### TABLE 16
*Safe center loads for scaffold plank*

| Span feet | 2 x 8* | 2 x 10* | 2 x 12* | 3 x 8* | 3 x 10* | 3 x 12* |
|---|---|---|---|---|---|---|
| 6 | 200 | 255 | 310 | 525 | 665 | 805 |
| 8 | 150 | 190 | 230 | 390 | 500 | 605 |
| 10 | 120 | 155 | 185 | 315 | 400 | 485 |
| 12 | 100 | 130 | 155 | 265 | 335 | 405 |
| 14 | — | 110 | 135 | 225 | 285 | 346 |
| 16 | — | — | 115 | 195 | 250 | 305 |

Above values are for planks supported at the ends, wide side of plank face up, and with loads concentrated at the center of the span. For loads uniformly distributed on the wide surface throughout the length, the safe loads may be twice those given in the table. Loads given are net and do not include the weight of the plank. If select structural coast region Douglas fir, merchantable structural longleaf southern pine, or dense structural square edge sound southern pine are used, above loads may be increased 25 percent.

* Dressed sizes of planks, reading left to right, are: 1⅝ x 7½, 1⅝ x 9½, 1⅝ x 11½, 2⅝ x 7½, 2⅝ x 9½, 2⅝ x 11½, respectively.

## SWING SCAFFOLDS, SWING STAGES, BOSUN CHAIRS

Always read instructions on the proper use and maintenance of the equipment. Follow prescribed load capacities.

Stages should be at least 27″ wide and supplied with guard rails (not rope).

Only experienced workers should erect or operate stages. Check ropes and blocks before use by suspending stages 1′ off the ground and loading at least four times the anticipated work load. Before locating on the job site, check for nearby electric power lines.

Power stages should have free-fall safety devices with hand controls in case of power failure.

## FIRE HAZARDS

Certain general rules regarding fire and explosion hazards apply to all situations. All paint materials should have complete label instructions that stipulate the potential fire hazards and precautions to be taken. Painters must be continuously advised and reminded of the fire hazards that exist under the particular conditions of each job, so that they will be aware of the dangers involved and insure that the necessary precautions are taken and maintained. Fire fighting equipment of the proper type must always be readily available where a potential fire hazard exists. Electric wiring and equipment installed or used in the paint storage room and spray room must conform to the applicable requirements of the National Electrical Code. The following precautions against fire should be carefully observed by all paint-handling workers.

Prohibit smoking anywhere that paint is either stored, prepared for use, or applied.

Provide for adequate ventilation in all of these areas.

Perform recurrent spray operations on portable items, such as signs, in an approved spray booth equipped with adequate ventilation, a water-wash system of fume removal, and explosion-proof electrical equipment.

Wet down spray booth surfaces before cleaning them.

Use rubber feet on metal ladders, and be certain when working in hazardous areas to use rubber soled shoes.

Use non-sparking scrapers and brushes to clean metal surfaces where fire hazards are present.

Wet down paint sweepings, rags, and waste with water and store in closed metal containers until disposed of in an approved manner. Do not burn in heaters or furnaces.

Extinguish all pilot lights on water heaters, furnaces, and other open flame equipment on all floors of the structure being painted. Be sure to turn the gas valve off.

When painting in confined areas near machinery or electrical equipment, open all switches and tag them to prevent their being turned on inadvertently.

Be sure that all mixers, pumps, motors, and lights used in painting area or spray room are explosion-proof and electrically grounded.

Use pails of sand (never sawdust) near dispensing pumps and spigots to absorb any spillage or overflow.

During painting operations keep fire extinguisher(s) nearby. Be sure that they are of the proper type. (*See* Table 17, Use the Proper Fire Extinguisher.)

Check ventilation and temperature regularly when working in confined areas.

Keep all work areas clear of obstructions.

Clean up before, during, and after painting operations. Dispose of sweepings and waste.

## HEALTH HAZARDS

A variety of ingredients used in the manufacture of paint materials are injurious to the human body in varying degrees. While the body can withstand nominal quantities of most of these poisons for relatively short periods of time, continuous or overexposure to them may have harmful effects. Furthermore, continued exposure to some may cause the body to become sensitized so that subsequent contact, even in small amounts, can cause an aggravated reaction. To this extent, these materials are a very definite threat to the normally healthy individual and a serious danger to

TABLE 17
*Use the proper fire extinguisher*

**Three Classes of Fires**

| Choose from these 5 basic types of extinguishers | CLASS A FIRES<br>Paper, wood, cloth, excelsior, rubbish, etc., where quenching and cooling effect of water is required. | CLASS B FIRES<br>Burning liquids (gasoline oil, paints, cooking fats, etc.) where smothering action is required. | CLASS C FIRES<br>Fires in live electrical equipment (motors, switches, appliances, etc.) where a non-conducting extinguishing agent is required. |
|---|---|---|---|
| CARBON DIOXIDE ........ | Small surface fires only. | **YES**<br>**Excellent**<br>Carbon dioxide leaves no residue, does not affect equipment or foodstuffs. | **YES**<br>**Excellent**<br>Carbon doxide is a non-conductor, leaves no residue, will not damage equipment. |
| DRY CHEMICAL .......... | Small surface fires only. | **YES**<br>**Excellent**<br>Chemical absorbs heat and releases smothering gas on fire; chemical shields operator from heat. | **YES**<br>**Excellent**<br>Chemical is a non-conductor; fog of dry chemical shields operator from heat. |
| WATER ................. | **YES**<br>**Excellent**<br>Water saturates material and prevents rekindling. | **NO**<br>Water will spread fire, not put it out. | **NO**<br>Water, a conductor, should not be used on live electrical equipment. |
| FOAM ................... | **YES**<br>**Excellent**<br>Foam has both smothering and wetting action. | **YES**<br>**Excellent**<br>Smothering blanket does not dissipate, floats on top of most spilled liquids. | **NO**<br>Foam is a conductor and should never be used on live electrical equipment. |
| VAPORIZING LIQUID ..... | Small surface fires only. | **YES**<br>Releases heavy smothering gas on fire. | **YES**<br>Liquid is a non-conductor and will not damage equipment. |

persons with chronic illnesses or disorders. These materials are divided into two major groups—toxic materials and skin-irritating materials.

Nevertheless, health hazards can easily be avoided by a commonsense approach of avoiding unnecessary contact with hazardous materials and by strict adherence to established safety measures.

The following rules should always be strictly observed.

Toxic or dermatitic materials must be properly identified and kept tightly sealed when not in use.

Check at regular intervals to ensure that the equipment is in a safe and proper operating condition.

Be sure that ventilation is adequate in all painting areas. Provide artificial ventilation where natural ventilation is inadequate. Use air respirators if necessary.

Spray all portable items within exhaust ventilated booths especially designed for that purpose.

Wear goggles and the proper type of respirator when spraying, blast cleaning, or performing any operation where an abnormal amount of vapor, mist, or dust is formed.

When handling dermatitic materials, use protective creams (or preferably gloves) and wear appropriate clothing.

Avoid touching any part of the body, especially the face, when handling dermatitic materials. Wash hands and face thoroughly before eating and at the end of each job.

## WOOD PRESERVATIVES

Damage to houses and other structures by termites, wood bores, and fungi is needless waste.

The capacity of any wood to resist dry rot, termites, and decay can be greatly increased by impregnating the wood with a general-purpose wood preservative or fungicide. Prescribed preservatives are listed in Table 18, Recommended Preservatives and Retentions for Ties, Lumber, Piles, Poles, and Posts (Federal Specification TT-W-571), and in Table 19, Minimum Retentions of Water-Borne Preservatives Recommended in Federal Specifications TT-W-571.

Different woods have different capacities for absorbing preservatives or other liquids, and in any given wood the sapwood is much more absorbent than the heartwood. Hardwoods are, in general, less absorbent than softwoods. Naturally, the extent to which the preservative affords protection increases directly with the distance to which it penetrates below the surface of the wood. The best penetration is obtained by a pressure process that requires equipment you will not have available. Nonpressure methods of applying preservatives are by dipping and by ordinary surface application with a brush or spray gun.

Figure 11 shows how you can improvise long tanks for the dipping process. Absorption is rapid at first, much slower later. A

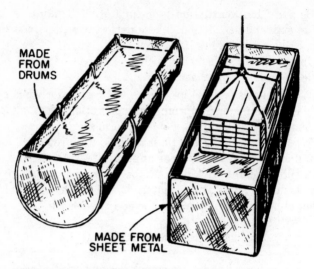

**Fig. 11.** Improvised tanks for dip-treating lumber.

rule of thumb is that in three minutes wood will have absorbed half the total amount of preservative it will absorb in two hours. However, the extent of the penetration obtained will depend upon the type of wood, its moisture content, and the length of time it remains immersed.

Surface application by brush or spray is, from the standpoint of a desire for maximum penetration, the least satisfactory method of treating wood. However, it is more or less unavoidable in the case of any wood that is already installed as well as for treated wood that has been cut or drilled to expose the untreated interior.

Pentachlorophenol and creosote coal tar are likely to be the only preservatives used by builders. The type of treatment or preservative depends on the severity of exposure and the desired life of the end product. Types and uses of wood preservatives are shown in Tables 18 and 19.

Safety precautions in the use of preservatives are as follows.

Avoid undue skin contact.

Avoid touching the face or rubbing the eyes when handling

TABLE 18

Recommended preservatives and retentions for ties, lumber, piles, poles, and posts (Federal Specification TT-W-571)

| Product | Minimum net retention of—(Pounds per cubic foot) | | | | |
|---|---|---|---|---|---|
| | Coal-tar creosote (TT-W-556) | Creosote-coal tar solution (TT-W-566) | Creosote-petroleum solution (TT-W-568) | Pentachlorophenol, 5 percent in petroleum (TT-W-570) | Copper naphthenate (0.75 percent copper metal) in petroleum (AWPA P8) |
| Ties (crossties, switch ties, and bridge ties) .......... | 8 | 8 | 9 | | |
| Lumber, and structural timbers: | | | | | |
| For use in coastal waters: | | | | | |
| Douglas fir (coast type) lumber and timbers. | 14 | 14 | | | |
| Southern yellow pine lumber and timbers | 20 | 20 | | | |
| For use in fresh water, in contact with ground or for important structural members not in contact with ground or water. | 10 | 10 | 12 | 10 | 10 |
| For other use not in contact with ground or water. | 6 | 6 | 7 | 6 | 6 |
| Piles: | | | | | |
| For use in coastal waters: | | | | | |
| Douglas fir (coast type). ... | 17 | 17 | | | |
| Southern yellow pine ..... | 20 | 20 | | | |
| For land or fresh water use .. | 12 | 12 | 14 | 12 | |
| Poles (utility and building) ..... | 8, 10 | 6 | ...... | 8, 10 | 8, 10 |
| Posts (round, fence) ......... | 6 | 6 | 7 | 6 | 6 |

TABLE 19

*Minimum retentions of water-borne preservatives recommended in Federal Specifications TT-W-571*

| Preservative | Minimum retentions for uses | | Federal Specification covering preservatives |
|---|---|---|---|
| | Not in contact with ground or in water | Involving occasional exposure to rainwater or continually to ground in areas of low rainfall | |
| | Pounds per cubic foot | Pounds per cubic foot | |
| Acid copper chromate............ | 0.5 | 1.00 | TT-W-546 |
| Ammoniacal copper arsenite ..... | .3 | .5 | TT-W-549 |
| Chromated copper arsenate ...... | .35 | .75 | TT-W-550 |
| Chromated zinc arsenate (including copperized form)............. | .5 | 1.00 | TT-W-538 |
| Chromated zinc chloride......... | .75 | 1.00 | TT-W-551 |
| Copperized chromated zinc chloride ... | .75 | 1.00 | TT-W-562 |
| Fluor-chrome-arsenate-phenol..... | .35 | .50 | TT-W-535 |

pretreated material.

Avoid inhalation of toxic material.

The application of preservative is very hazardous; apply only in a properly ventilated space and use approved respirators.

Wash with soap and water after contact.

(*See* Chap. 27, Fundamental Purposes of Painting, Paints, and Equipment; Chap. 28, Surface Preparation for Painting; Chap. 29, Mixing and Conditioning Paint, Methods of Applying Paint, and Colors.)

# Home Improvements

Insulation, vapor barriers, and sound control; ventilation; termites and decay prevention.

## CHAPTER 31

# Thermal Insulation, Vapor Barriers, and Sound Absorption

Most materials used in houses have some insulating value. Even air spaces between studs resist the passage of heat. When these stud spaces are filled or partially filled with a material high in resistance to heat transmission, namely thermal insulation, the stud space has many times the insulating value of the air alone.

The inflow of heat through outside walls and roofs in hot weather or its outflow during cold weather have important effects upon (a) the comfort of the occupants of a house and (b) the cost of providing either heating or cooling to maintain temperatures at acceptable limits for occupancy. During cold weather, high resistance to heat flow also means a saving in fuel. While the wood in the walls provides good insulation, commercial insulating materials are usually incorporated into exposed walls, ceilings, and floors to increase the resistance to heat passage. The use of insulation in warmer climates is justified with air conditioning, not only because of reduced operating costs but also because units of smaller capacity are required. Therefore, whether from the standpoint of thermal insulation alone in cold climates or whether for the benefit of reducing cooling costs, the use of 2″ or more of insulation in the walls can certainly be justified.

## CLASSES OF INSULATING MATERIALS

*Commercial insulation* is manufactured in a variety of forms and types, each with advantages for specific uses. Materials commonly used for insulation may be grouped in the following classes: (1) flexible insulation (blanket and batt); (2) loose fill insulation; (3) reflective insulation; (4) rigid insulation (structural and nonstructural); and (5) miscellaneous types.

The thermal properties of most building materials are known, and the rate of heat flow or coefficient of transmission for most combinations of construction can be calculated. This coefficient, or *U-value*, is a measure of heat transmission between air on the warm side and air on the cold side of the construction unit. The insulating value of the wall will vary with different types of construction, with materials used in construction, and with different types and thickness of insulation. Comparisons of U-values may be made and used to evaluate different combinations of materials and insulation based on overall heat loss, potential fuel savings, influence on comfort, and installation costs.

Air spaces add to the total resistance of a wall section to heat transmission; but an empty air space is not as effective as one filled with an insulating material. Great importance is frequently given to dead air spaces in speaking of a wall section. Actually, the air is never dead in cells where there are differences in temperature on opposite sides of the space since the difference causes convection currents.

## FLEXIBLE INSULATING MATERIALS

*Flexible insulation* is manufactured in two types, *blanket* and *batt*. *Blanket insulation* (*A*, Fig. 1) is furnished in rolls or packages in widths suited to 16″ and 24″ stud and joist spacing. Usual thicknesses are 1½″, 2″, and 3″. The body of the blanket is made of felted mats of mineral or vegetable fibers, such as rock or glass wool, wood fiber, and cotton. Organic insulations are treated to make them resistant to fire, decay, insects, and vermin. Most blanket insulation is covered with paper or other sheet material with tabs on the sides for fastening to studs or joists. One covering sheet serves as a vapor barrier to resist movement of water vapor and should always face the warm side of the wall. Aluminum foil or asphalt or plastic laminated paper are commonly used as barrier materials. *Batt insulation* (*B*,

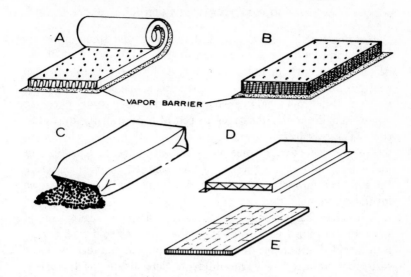

**Fig. 1.** Types of insulation.

Fig. 1) is also made of fibrous material preformed to thicknesses of 4″ and 6″ for 16″ and 24″ joist spacing. It is supplied with or without a vapor barrier. (*See* section on Vapor Barriers, in this chapter.) One friction type of fibrous glass batt is supplied without a covering and is designed to remain in place without the normal fastening methods.

## LOOSE FILL INSULATION

*Loose fill insulation* (*C*, Fig. 1) is usually composed of materials used in bulk form, supplied in bags or bales, and placed by pouring, blowing, or packing by hand. This includes rock or glass wool, wood fibers, shredded redwood bark, cork, wood-pulp products, vermiculite, sawdust, and shavings. *Fill insulation* is suited for use between first-floor ceiling joists in unheated attics. It is also used in sidewalls of existing houses that were not insulated during construction. Where no vapor barrier was installed during construction, suitable paint coatings, as described later in this chapter, should be used for vapor barriers when blown insulation is added to an existing house.

## REFLECTIVE INSULATION

Most materials reflect some radiant heat, and some materials have this property to a very high degree. Materials high in reflective properties include aluminum foil, sheet metal with tin coating, and paper products coated with a reflective oxide composition. Such materials can be used in enclosed stud spaces, in attics, and in similar locations to retard heat transfer by radiation. These *reflective insulations* are effective *only* when used where the reflective surface faces an air space at least ¾″ or more deep. Where a reflective surface contacts another material, the reflective properties are lost and the material has little or no insulating value.

Reflective insulations are equally effective regardless of whether the reflective surface faces the warm or cold side. There is a decided difference in the equivalent conductance and the resistance to heat flow. The difference depends on (a) the orientation of the reflecting material and the dead air space, (b) the direction of heat flow (horizontal, up, or down), and (c) the mean summer or winter temperatures. Each possibility requires separate consideration. Reflective insulation is perhaps more effective in preventing summer heat flow through ceilings and walls. It should likely be considered more for use in the southern United States than in the northern.

Reflective insulation of the foil type is sometimes applied to blankets and to the stud surface side of gypsum lath. Metal foil suitably mounted on some supporting base makes an excellent vapor barrier. The type of reflective insulation shown in *D*, Fig. 1, includes reflective surfaces and air spaces between the outer sheets.

### RIGID INSULATION

*Rigid insulation* is usually a *fiberboard material* manufactured in sheet and other forms (*E*, Fig. 1). The most common types are made from processed wood, sugarcane, or other vegetable products. Structural insulating boards, in densities ranging from 15 pounds to 31 pounds per cubic foot, are fabricated in such forms as building boards, roof decking, sheathing, and wallboard. While they have moderately good insulating properties, their primary purpose is structural.

*Roof insulation* is nonstructural and serves mainly to provide thermal resistance to heat flow in roofs. It is called *slab* or *block* insulation and is manufactured in rigid units ½″ to 3″ thick and usually 2′ by 4′ in size.

In house construction, perhaps the most common forms of rigid insulation are sheathing and decorative coverings in sheets or in tile squares. *Sheathing board* is made in thicknesses of ½″ and $^{25}/_{32}$″. It is coated or impregnated with an asphalt compound to provide water resistance. *Sheets* are made in 2′ by 8′ size for horizontal application and 4′ by 8′ or longer for vertical application.

## MISCELLANEOUS INSULATION

Some insulations do not fit in the classifications previously described, such as insulation blankets made up of multiple layers of corrugated paper. Other types, such as lightweight vermiculite and perlite aggregates, are sometimes used in plaster as a means of reducing heat transmission.

Other materials are foamed-in-place insulations, which include sprayed and plastic foam types. Sprayed insulation is usually inorganic fibrous material blown against a clean surface which has been primed with an adhesive coating. It is often left exposed for acoustical as well as insulating properties.

Expanded *polystyrene* and *urethane* plastic foams may be molded or foamed-in-place. Urethane insulation may also be applied by spraying. Polystyrene and urethane in board form can be obtained in thicknesses from ½″ to 2″.

*See* Table **20** for thermal conductivity values of some insulating materials. These are expressed as "k" values or heat conductivity and are defined as the amount of heat, in British thermal units, that will pass in one hour through one square foot of material one inch thick per 1°F temperature difference between faces of the material. *For example,* "k" represents heat loss; the lower this numerical value, the better the insulating qualities.

Insulation is also rated on its resistance or "R" value, which is merely another expression of the insulating value. The "R" value is usually expressed as the total resistance of the wall or of a thick insulating blanket or batt, whereas "k" is the rating per inch of thickness. *For example,* a "k" value of one inch of insulation is 0.25. Then the resistance, "R" is $\frac{1}{0.25}$ or 4.0. For 3 inches of this insulation, the total "R" is three times 4.0, or 12.0.

TABLE 20

*Thermal conductivity values of some insulating materials*

| Insulation group | | "k" range (conductivity) |
|---|---|---|
| General | Specific type | |
| Flexible | | 0.25 — 0.27 |
| Fill | Standard materials | .28 — .30 |
| | Vermiculite | .45 — .48 |
| Reflective (2 sides) | | (1) |
| Rigid | Insulating fiberboard | .35 — .36 |
| | Sheathing fiberboard | .42 — .55 |
| Foam | Polystyrene | .25 — .29 |
| | Urethane | .15 — .17 |
| Wood | Low density | .60 — .65 |

[1] Insulating value is equal to slightly more than 1 inch of flexible insulation. (Resistance, "R" = 4.3)

The "U" value is the overall heat loss value of all materials in the wall. The lower this value, the better the insulating value. Specific insulating values for various materials are also available. For comparison with Table 20, the "U" value of the window glass is:

| *Glass* | *U value* |
|---|---|
| Single | 1.13 |
| Double | |
| Insulated, with ¼" air space | .61 |
| Storm sash over single glazed window | .53 |

## WHERE TO INSULATE

To reduce heat loss from the house during the cold weather in most climates, all walls, ceilings, roofs, and floors that separate the heated spaces from the unheated spaces should be insulated. Insulation should be placed on all outside walls and in the ceiling (*A*, Fig. 2). In houses involving unheated crawl spaces, it should be placed between the floor joists or around the wall perimeter. If a flexible type of insulation (blanket or batt) is used, it should be well supported between joists by slats and a galvanized wire mesh or by a rigid board with the vapor barrier installed toward the subflooring. Press-fit or friction insulations fit tightly between joists and require only a small amount of support to hold them in place. Reflective insulation is often used for crawl spaces, but only one dead air space should be assumed in calculating heat loss when the crawl space is ventilated. A ground cover of roll roofing or plastic film such as polyethylene should be placed on the soil of crawl spaces to decrease the moisture content of the space as well as of the wood members.

In one and one-half story houses, insulation should be placed along all walls, floors, and ceilings that are adjacent to unheated areas (*B*, Fig. 2). These include stairways, dwarf (knee) walls, and dormers. Provisions should be made for ventilation of the unheated areas.

Where attic space is unheated and a stairway is included, insulation should be used around the stairway as well as in the first-floor ceiling (*C*, Fig. 2). The door leading to the attic should be weatherstripped to prevent heat loss. Walls adjoining an unheated garage or porch should also be insulated.

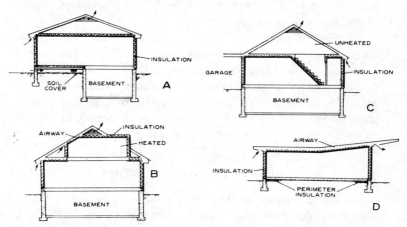

**Fig. 2.** Placement of insulation. *A*, in walls, floor, and ceiling. *B*, in one and one-half story house. *C*, at attic door. *D*, in flat roof.

In houses with flat or low-pitched roofs (*D,* Fig. 2), insulation should be used in the ceiling area with sufficient space allowed above for clear unobstructed ventilation between the joists. Insulation should be used along the perimeter of houses built on slabs. A vapor barrier should be included under the slab.

In the summer, outside surfaces exposed to the direct rays of the sun may attain temperatures of 50°F or more above shade temperatures and will tend to transfer this heat toward the inside of the house. Insulation in the walls and in attic areas retards the flow of heat and consequently less heat is transferred through such areas resulting in improved summer comfort conditions.

Where air-conditioning systems are used, insulation should be placed in all exposed ceilings and walls in the same manner as insulating against cold weather heat loss. Shading of glass against direct rays of the sun and the use of insulated glass will aid in reducing the air-conditioning load.

Ventilation of attic and roof spaces is an important adjunct to insulation. Without ventilation, an attic space may become very hot and hold the heat for many hours. (*See* Chap. 32, Ventilation.) More heat will be transmitted through the ceiling when the attic temperature is 150°F than when it is 100° to 120°F. Ventilation methods suggested for protection against cold weather condensation apply equally well to protection against excessive hot weather roof temperatures.

The use of storm windows or insulated glass will greatly reduce heat loss. Almost twice as much heat loss occurs through a single glass as through a window glazed with insulated glass or protected by a storm sash. Furthermore, double glass will normally prevent surface condensation and frost forming on inner glass surfaces in winter. When excessive condensation persists, paint failures or even decay of the sash rail or other parts can occur.

## HOW TO INSTALL INSULATION

Blanket insulation or batt insulation with a vapor barrier should be placed between framing members so that the tabs of the barrier lap the edge of the studs as well as the top and bottom plates. This method assures a minimum amount of vapor loss as compared to the loss occurring when tabs are stapled to the sides of the studs. To protect the head and soleplate as well as the headers over openings, it is good practice to use narrow strips of vapor-barrier material along the top and bottom of the wall (*A*, Fig. 3). Ordinarily, these areas are not covered too well by the barrier on the blanket or batt. A hand stapler is commonly used to fasten the insulation and the barriers in place.

For insulation without a barrier (press-fit or friction-type), a plastic film vapor barrier such as 4-mil polyethylene is commonly used to envelop the entire exposed wall and ceiling (*B*, Fig. 3). It covers the openings as well as window and door headers and edge studs. This system is one of the best from

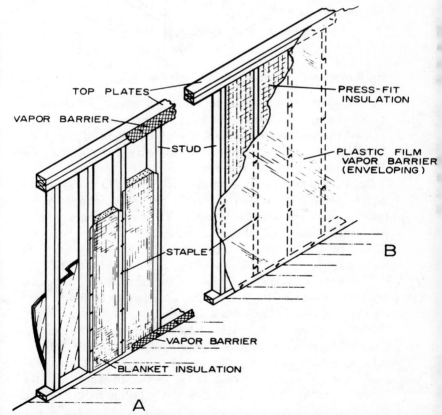

**Fig. 3.** Application of insulation. *A*, wall section with blanket type. *B*, wall section with "press-fit" insulation.

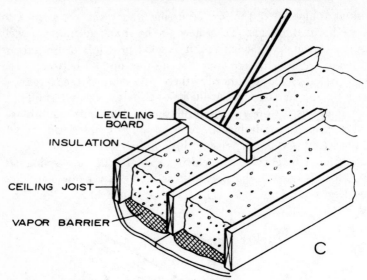

**Fig. 3** *(continued)*. *C*, ceiling with full insulation.

the standpoint of resistance to vapor movement. Furthermore, it does not have the installation inconveniences encountered when tabs of the insulation are stapled over the edges of the studs. After the dry wall is installed or plastering is completed, the film is trimmed around the window and door openings.

*Reflective insulation*, in a single sheet form with two reflective surfaces, should be placed to divide the space formed by the framing members into two approximately equal spaces. Some reflective insulations include air spaces and are furnished with nailing tabs. This type is fastened to the studs to provide at least a ¾″ space on each side of the reflective surfaces.

*Fill insulation* is commonly used in ceiling areas and is poured or blown into place (*C*, Fig. 3). A vapor barrier should be used on the warm side (the bottom, in case of ceiling joists) before insulation is placed. A leveling board, as shown in the illustration, will give a constant insulation thickness. Thick *batt insulation* is also used in ceiling areas. Batt and fill insulation might also be combined to obtain the desired thickness with the vapor barrier against the back face of the ceiling finish. Ceiling insulation six or more inches thick greatly reduces heat loss in the winter and also provides summertime protection.

## PRECAUTIONS IN INSULATING

Areas over door and window frames and along side and head jambs also require insulation. Because these areas are filled with small sections of insulation, a vapor barrier must be used around the opening as well as over the header above the openings (*A*, Fig. 4). Enveloping the entire wall eliminates the need for this type of vapor-barrier installation.

In one and one-half and two-story houses and in basements, the area at the joist header at outside walls should be insulated and protected with a vapor barrier (*B*, Fig. 4).

Insulation should be placed behind electrical outlet boxes and other utility connections in exposed walls to minimize condensation on cold surfaces.

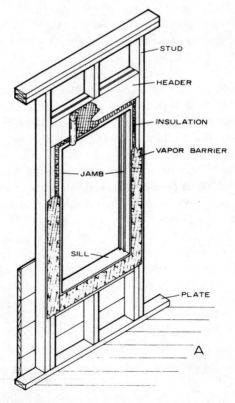

**Fig. 4.** Precautions in insulating. *A,* around openings.

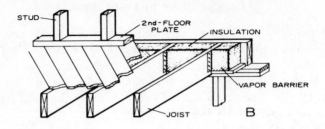

**Fig. 4** *(continued).* **B,** joist space in outside walls.

### VAPOR BARRIERS

Some discussion of vapor barriers has been included in previous sections of this chapter because vapor barriers are usually a part of flexible insulation. *A,* Figure 5 illustrates water vapor from inside the house moved out through the wall. When the vapor met outside cold air, moisture condensed and froze. As the outside temperatures rose in the spring and summer, ice melted, and the moisture was free to move through the siding and destroy the paint coating. *B,* Figure 5, shows that the vapor barrier (on the warm side of the wall) has prevented moisture from getting into the walls.

Most building materials are permeable to water vapor. This presents problems because considerable water vapor is generated in a house from cooking, dishwashing, laundering, bathing, humidifiers, and other sources. In cold climates during cold

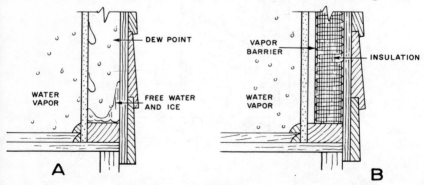

**Fig. 5.**

weather, this vapor may pass through wall and ceiling materials and condense in the wall or attic space; therefore, in severe cases it may damage the exterior paint and interior finish or even result in decay in structural members. For protection, a material highly resistive to vapor transmission, called a *vapor barrier*, should be used on the warm side of a wall or below the insulation in an attic space.

Among the effective vapor-barrier materials are asphalt laminated papers, aluminum foil, and plastic films. Most blanket and batt insulations are provided with a vapor barrier on one side, some of them with paper-backed aluminum foil. Foil-backed gypsum lath or gypsum boards are also available and serve as excellent vapor barriers.

The perm (a measure of water-vapor movement through a material) values of vapor barriers vary, but ordinarily it is good practice to use those which have values less than $\frac{1}{4}$ (0.25) perm. Although a value of $\frac{1}{2}$ perm is considered adequate, aging reduces the effectiveness of some materials.

Some types of flexible blanket and batt insulation have a barrier material on one side. Such flexible insulations should be attached with the tabs at their sides fastened on the inside (narrow) edges of the studs, and the blanket should be cut long enough so that the cover sheet can lap over the face of the sole-plate at the bottom and over the plate at the top of the stud space. When a positive seal is desired, wall-height rolls of plastic film vapor barriers should be applied over studs, plates, and window and door headers. This system (called enveloping) is used over insulation having no vapor barrier or to insure excellent protection when used over any type of insulation. The barrier should be fitted tightly around outlet boxes and sealed if necessary. A ribbon of sealing compound around an outlet or switch box will minimize vapor loss at this area. Cold air returns in outside walls should consist of metal ducts to prevent vapor loss and subsequent paint problems.

Paint coatings on plaster may be very effective as vapor barriers if materials are properly chosen and applied. They *do not* offer protection during the period of construction, and moisture may cause paint blisters on exterior paint before the interior paint can be applied. This is most likely to happen in houses that are constructed during periods when outdoor temperatures are 25°F or more below inside temperatures. Paint coatings cannot be considered a substitute for the membrane types of vapor barriers, but they do provide some protection for houses where other types of vapor barriers were not installed during construction.

Of the various types of paint, one coat of *aluminum primer* followed by two decorative coats of *flat wall* or *lead* and *oil* paint is quite effective. For rough plaster or for houses in very cold climates, two coats of aluminum primer may be necessary. A primer and sealer of the pigmented type, followed by decorative finish coats or two coats of rubber-base paint, are also effective in retarding vapor transmission.

Because no type of vapor barrier can be considered 100 per cent resistive and some vapor leakage into the wall may be expected, the flow of vapor to the outside should not be impeded by materials of relatively high vapor resistance on the cold side of the vapor barrier. *For example*, sheathing paper should be of a type that is waterproof but not highly vapor resistant. This also applies to *permanent* outer coverings or siding. In such cases, the vapor barrier should have an equally low perm value. This will reduce the danger of condensation on cold surfaces within the wall.

## SOUND INSULATION

Development of the *quiet* home or the need for incorporating sound insulation in a new house is becoming more and more important. In the past, the reduction of sound transfer between rooms was more important in apartments, hotels, and motels than in private homes. House designs now often incorporate a family room or *active* living room as well as *quiet* living room. It is usually desirable in such designs to isolate these rooms from the remainder of the house. *Sound insulation* between the bedroom area and the living area is usually desirable, as is isolation of the bathrooms. Isolation from outdoor sounds is also often advisable. Therefore, sound control has become a vital part of house design and construction and will be even more important in the coming years.

## HOW SOUND TRAVELS

How does sound travel? How is it transferred through a wall or floor? Airborne noises inside a house, such as loud conversation or a barking dog, create sound waves which radiate outward from the source through the air until they strike a wall, floor, or ceiling. These surfaces are set in vibration by the fluctuating pressure of the sound wave in the air. Because the wall vibrates, it conducts sound to the other side in varying degrees, depending on the wall construction.

The resistance of a building element, such as a wall, to the passage of airborne sound is rated by its *Sound Transmission Class* (STC). Therefore, the higher the number, the better the sound barrier. The approximate effectiveness of walls with varying STC numbers is shown in the following table.

| *STC No.* | *Effectiveness* |
|---|---|
| 25 | Normal speech can be understood quite easily |
| 35 | Loud speech audible but not intelligible |
| 45 | Must strain to hear loud speech |
| 48 | Some loud speech barely audible |
| 50 | Loud speech not audible |

Sound travels readily through the air and also through some materials. When airborne sound strikes a conventional wall, the studs act as sound conductors unless they are separated in some way from the covering material. Electrical switches or convenience outlets placed back-to-back in a wall readily pass sound. Faulty construction, such as poorly fitted doors, often allows sound to travel through. Therefore, good construction practices are important in providing sound-resistant walls.

Thick walls of dense materials such as masonry can stop sound. But in the wood frame house, an interior masonry wall results in increased costs and structural problems created by heavy walls. To provide a satisfactory sound-resistant wall economically has been a problem. At one time, sound-resistant frame construction for the home involved significant additional costs because it usually meant double walls or suspended ceilings. A relatively simple system has been developed using sound-deadening insulating board in conjunction with a gypsum board outer covering. This provides good sound transmission resistance suitable for use in the home with only slight additional cost. A number of combinations are possible with this system, providing different STC ratings.

## WALL CONSTRUCTION

As the STC table shows, a wall providing sufficient resistance to airborne sound transfer more than likely has an STC rating of 45 or greater. Therefore, in construction of such a wall between the rooms of a house, its cost as related to the STC rating should be considered. As shown in Fig. 6, details *A*, with gypsum wallboard, and *B*, with plastered wall, are commonly used for partition walls. However, the hypothetical rating of 45 cannot be obtained in this construction. An 8″ concrete block wall (*C*, Fig. 6) has the minimum rating, but this construction is not always practical in a wood frame house.

Good STC ratings can be obtained in a wood frame wall by using a combination of materials for *D* and *E*, Fig. 6. One-half-inch sound-deadening board nailed to the studs, followed by a lamination of ½″ gypsum wallboard, will provide an STC value

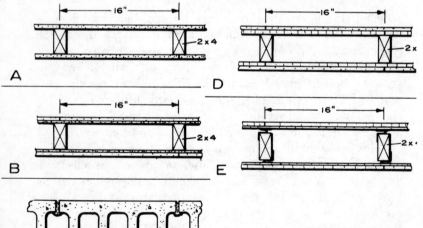

**Fig. 6.**  Sound insulation of single walls.

of 46 at a relatively low cost. A slightly better rating can be obtained by using ⅝″ gypsum wallboard rather than ½″. A very satisfactory STC rating of 52 can be obtained by using resilient clips to fasten gypsum backed boards to the studs, followed by adhesive laminated ½″ fiberboard (*E*, Fig. 6). This method further isolates the wall covering from the framing.

A similar isolation system consists of resilient channels nailed horizontally to 2″ by 4″ studs spaced 16″ on center. Channels are spaced 24″ apart vertically and ⅝″ gypsum wallboard is screwed to the channels. An STC rating of 47 is therefore obtained at a moderately low cost.

The use of a double wall, which may consist of a 2 by 6 or wider plate and staggered 2″ by 4″ studs, is sometimes desirable. One-half-inch gypsum wallboard on each side of this wall (*A*, Fig. 7) results in an STC value of 45. However, two layers

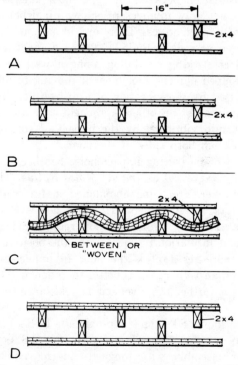

**Fig. 7.** Sound insulation of double walls.

of ⅝" gypsum wallboard add little, if any, additional sound-transfer resistance (*B*, Fig. 7). When 1½" blanket insulation is added to this construction (*C*, Fig. 7), the STC rating increases to **49**. This insulation may be installed as shown in the illustration or placed between studs on one wall. A single wall with 3½" of insulation will show a marked improvement over an open stud space and is low in cost.

The use of ½" sound-deadening board and a lamination of gypsum wallboard in the double wall will result in an STC rating of 50 (*D*, Fig. 7). The addition of blanket insulation to this combination will likely provide an even higher value, perhaps 53 or 54.

### FLOOR-CEILING CONSTRUCTION

Sound insulation between an upper floor and the ceiling of a lower floor not only involves resistance of airborne sounds but also that of impact noises. Therefore, impact noise control must be considered as well as the STC value. Impact noise is caused by an object striking or sliding along a wall or floor surface, such as dropped objects, footsteps, or moving furniture. It may also be caused by the vibration of a dishwasher, bathtub, food-disposal apparatus, or other equipment. In all instances, the floor is set into vibration by the impact or contact and sound is radiated from both sides of the floor.

A method of measuring impact noise has been developed and is commonly expressed as *Impact Noise Ratings* (INR). (INR ratings, however, are being abandoned in favor of *Impact Insulation Class* (IIC) ratings. IIC is a new system utilized in the Federal Housing Administration recommended criteria for impact sound insulation.) The greater the positive value of the INR, the more resistant is the floor to impact-noise transfer. *For example,* an INR of −2 is better than one of −17, and one of +5 INR is a further improvement in resistance to impact-noise transfer.

Figure 8 shows STC and approximate INR (db) values for several types of floor constructions. *A*, Figure 8, perhaps a minimum floor assembly with tongued-and-grooved floor and ⅜" gypsum board ceiling, has an STC value of 30 and an approx-

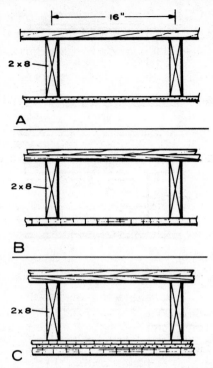

**Fig. 8.**  Relative impact and sound transfer in floor-ceiling combinations
(2″ by 8″ joists).

imate INR value of $-18$. This is improved somewhat by construction shown in $B$, Fig. 8, and still further by the combination of materials in $C$, Fig. 8.

The value of isolating the ceiling joists from a gypsum lath and plaster ceiling by means of spring clips is illustrated in $A$, Fig. 9. An STC value of 52 and an approximate INR value of $-2$ result.

Foam rubber padding and carpeting improve both the STC and the INR values. The STC value increases from 31 to 45 and the approximate INR from $-17$ to $-5$ ($B$ and $C$, Fig. 9). This can likely be further improved by using an isolated ceiling finish with spring clips. The use of sound-deadening board and a lamination of gypsum board for the ceiling would also improve resistance to sound transfer.

An economical construction similar to (but an improvement

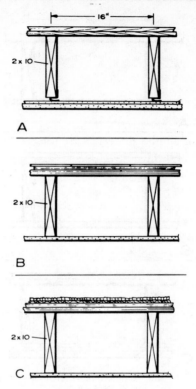

**Fig. 9.**  Relative impact and sound transfer in floor-ceiling combinations (2″ by 10″ joists).

over) *C*, Fig. 9, with an STC value of **48** and an approximate INR of +18, consists of the following: (a) a pad and carpet over ⅝″ tongued-and-grooved plywood underlayment, (b) 3″ fiberglass insulating batts between joists, (c) resilient channels spaced 24″ apart, across the bottom of the joists, and (d) ⅝″ gypsum board screwed to the bottom of the channels and finished with taped joints.

The use of separate floor joists with staggered ceiling joists below provides reasonable values but adds a good deal to construction costs. Separate joists with insulation between and a soundboard between subfloor and finish provide an STC rating of 53 and an approximate INR value of −3.

## SOUND ABSORPTION

Design of the *quiet* house can incorporate another system of sound insulation, namely, *sound absorption*. Sound-absorbing materials can minimize the amount of noise by stopping the reflection of sound back into a room. Sound-absorbing materials do not necessarily have resistance to airborne sounds. Perhaps the most commonly used sound-absorbing material is *acoustic tile*. Wood fiber or similar materials are used in the manufacture of the tile, which is usually processed to provide some fire resistance and designed with numerous tiny sound traps on the tile surfaces. These may consist of tiny drilled or punched holes, fissured surfaces, or a combination of both.

Acoustic tile is most often used in the ceiling and areas where it is not subjected to excessive mechanical damage, such as above a wall wainscoting. It is normally manufactured in sizes from 12″ by 12″ to 12″ by 48″. Thicknesses vary from ½″ to ¾″, and the tile is usually factory finished ready for application. Paint or other finishes which fill or cover the tiny holes or fissures for trapping sound will greatly reduce its efficiency.

Acoustic tile may be applied to existing ceilings or any smooth surface with a mastic adhesive designed specifically for this purpose or to furring strips nailed to the underside of the ceiling joists. Nailing or stapling tile is the normal application method in this system. It is also used with a mechanical suspension system involving small "H," "Z," or "T" members. Manufacturers' recommendations should be followed in application and finishing.

## CHAPTER 32

# Ventilation

―――――――:――――――――――

Condensation of moisture vapor may occur in attic spaces and under flat roofs during cold weather. Even where vapor barriers are used, some vapor will probably work into these spaces around pipes and other inadequately protected areas and some through the vapor barrier itself. Although the amount might be unimportant if equally distributed, it may be sufficiently concentrated in some cold spot to cause damage. While wood shingle and wood shake roofs do not resist vapor movement, such roofings as asphalt shingles and built-up roofs are highly resistant. The most practical method of removing the moisture is by adequately ventilating the roof spaces.

A warm attic that is inadequately ventilated and insulated may cause formation of *ice dams* at the cornice. During cold weather after a heavy snowfall, heat causes the snow next to the roof to melt. (*See* **Chaps. 16 and 17.**) Water running down the roof freezes on the colder surface of the cornice, often forming an ice dam at the gutter which may cause water to back up at the eaves and into the wall and ceiling. Similar dams often form in roof valleys. Ventilation, therefore, provides part of the answer to the problems. With a well-insulated ceiling and adequate ventilation, attic temperatures are low and melting of snow over the attic space will be greatly reduced.

In hot weather, ventilation of attic and roof spaces offers an effective means of removing hot air, thereby lowering the temperature in these spaces. Insulation should be used between ceiling joists below the attic or roof space to further retard heat flow into the rooms below and materially improve comfort conditions.

It is common practice to install louvered openings in the end walls of gable roofs for ventilation. Air movement through such openings depends primarily on wind direction and velocity. No appreciable movement can be expected when there is no wind or unless one or more openings face the wind. More positive air movement can be obtained by providing openings in the soffit areas of the roof overhang in addition to openings at the gable ends or ridge. Hip roof houses are best ventilated by inlet ventilators in the soffit area and by outlet ventilators along the ridge. The differences in temperature between the attic and the outside will then create an air movement independent of the wind, also a more positive movement when there is wind.

Where there is a crawl space under the house or the porch, ventilation is necessary to remove moisture vapor rising from the soil. Such vapor may otherwise condense on the wood below the floor and facilitate decay. A permanent vapor barrier on the soil of the crawl space greatly reduces the amount of ventilating area required.

Tight construction (including storm windows and storm doors) and the use of humidifiers have created potential moisture problems which must be resolved through planning of adequate ventilation as well as through the proper use of vapor barriers. Blocking of ventilating areas, *for example*, must be avoided since such practices will prevent ventilation of attic spaces. Inadequate ventilation will often lead to moisture problems which, to correct, can result in unnecessary costs.

## AREA OF VENTILATORS

Types of ventilators and minimum recommended sizes have been generally established for various types of roofs. The minimum net area for attic- or roof-space ventilators is based on the projected ceiling area of the rooms below (Fig. 1). The ratio of ventilator openings as shown in Fig. 1 are net areas, and the actual area must be increased to allow for any restrictions such as louvers and wire cloth or screen. The screen area should be double the specified net area as shown in Figs. 1, 2, and 3.

To obtain extra area of screen without adding to the area of

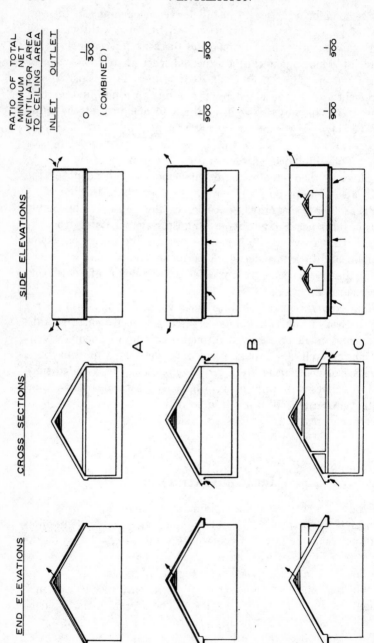

**Fig. 1.** Ventilating areas of gable roofs.

the vent, use a frame of required size to hold the screen away from the ventilator opening. Use as coarse a screen as conditions permit, not smaller than No. 16, since lint and dirt tend to clog fine mesh screens. Screens should be installed in such a way that paint brushes will not easily contact the screen and close the mesh with paint.

### GABLE ROOFS

Louvered openings are generally provided in the end walls of *gable roofs* and should be as close to the ridge as possible (*A*, Fig. 1). The net area for the openings should be 1/300 of the ceiling area (*A*, Fig. 1). *For example,* where the ceiling area equals 1,200 square feet, the minimum total net area of the ventilators should be 4 square feet.

As previously explained, more positive air movement can be obtained if additional openings are provided in the soffit area. The minimum ventilation areas for this method are shown in *B*, Fig. 1.

Where there are rooms in the attic with sloping ceilings under the roof, the insulation should follow the roof slope and be so placed that there is a free opening of at least 1½″ between the roof boards and insulation for air movement (*C*, Fig. 1).

### HIP ROOFS

*Hip roofs* should have air-inlet openings in the soffit area of the eaves and outlet openings at or near the peak. For minimum net areas of openings see *A*, Fig. 2. The most efficient type of inlet opening is the continuous slot, which should provide a free opening of not less than ¾″. The air-outlet opening near the peak can be a globe-type metal ventilator or several smaller roof ventilators located near the ridge. They can be located below the peak on the rear slope of the roof so that they will not be visible from the front of the house. Gabled extensions of a hip-roof house are sometimes used to provide efficient outlet ventilators (*B*, Fig. 2).

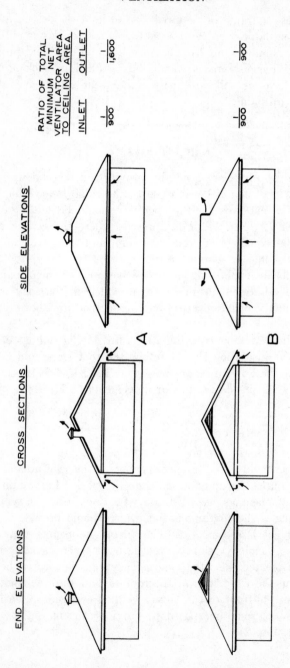

**Fig. 2.** Ventilating areas of hip roofs.

## FLAT ROOFS

A greater ratio of ventilating area is required in some types of *flat roofs* than in pitched roofs because the air movement is less positive and is dependent upon wind. It is important that there be a clear open space above the ceiling insulation and below the roof sheathing for free air movement from inlet to outlet openings. Solid blocking should *not* be used for bridging or for bracing over bearing partitions if its use prevents the air circulation.

Perhaps the most common type of flat or low-pitched roof is one in which the rafters extend beyond the wall, forming an overhang (*A*, Fig. 3). When soffits are used, this area can contain the combined inlet-outlet ventilators, preferably a continuous slot. When single ventilators are used, they should be distributed evenly along the overhang.

A parapet-type wall and flat roof combination may be constructed with the ceiling joists separate from the roof joists or combined. When members are separate the space between can be used for an airway (*B*, Fig. 3). Inlet and outlet vents are then located as shown in the illustration, or a series of outlet stack vents can be used along the center line of the roof in combination with the inlet vents. When ceiling joists and flat rafters are served by one member in parapet construction, vents may be located as shown in *C*, Fig. 3. Wall-inlet ventilators combined with center stack outlet vents might also be used in this type of roof.

## TYPES AND LOCATION OF OUTLET VENTILATORS

Various styles of gable-end ventilators are available ready for installation. Many are made with metal louvers and frames, while others may be made of wood to fit the house design more closely. However, the most important factors are to have sufficient net ventilating area and to locate ventilators as close to the ridge as possible without affecting house appearance.

One of the types commonly used fits the slope of the roof and is located near the ridge (*A*, Fig. 4). It can be made of wood or metal; in metal it is often adjustable to conform to the roof slope. A wood ventilator of this type is enclosed in a frame and

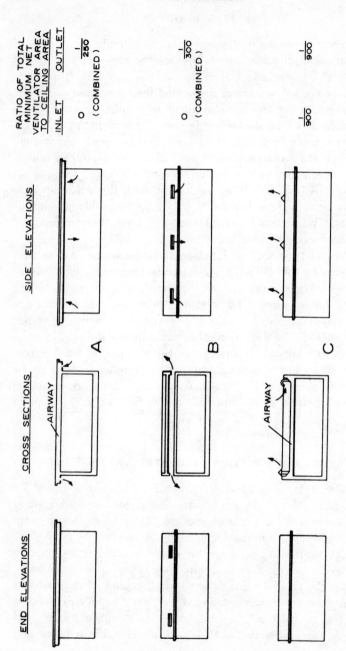

**Fig. 3.** Ventilating area of flat roofs.

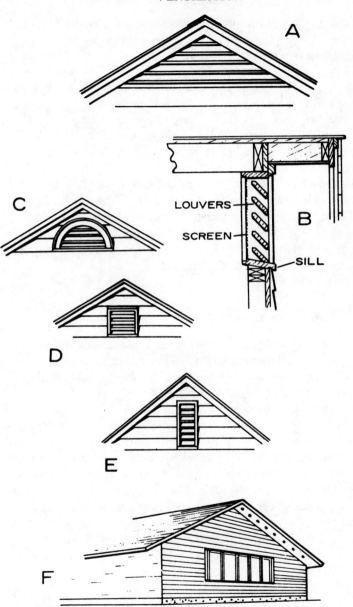

**Fig. 4.** Outlet ventilators. *A*, triangular. *B*, typical cross section. *C*, half-circle. *D*, square. *E*, vertical. *F*, soffit.

placed in the rough opening much as a window frame (*B*, Fig.
4). Other forms of gable-end ventilators which might be used
are shown in *C*, *D*, and *E*, Fig. 4.

A system of attic ventilation which can be used on houses with
a wide roof overhang at the gable end consists of a series of
small vents or a continuous slot located on the underside of the
soffit areas (*F*, Fig. 4). Several large openings located near the
ridge might also be used. This system is especially desirable on
low-pitched roofs where standard wall ventilators may not be
suitable.

It is important that the roof framing at the wall line does not
block off ventilation areas to the attic area. This might be accomplished by the use of a *ladder* frame extension. A flat nailing block used at the wall line will provide airways into the
attic. This can also be adapted to narrower rake sections by providing ventilating areas to the attic.

## TYPES AND LOCATION OF INLET VENTILATORS

Small, well-distributed ventilators or a continuous slot in the
soffit provide inlet ventilation. These small louvered and
screened vents can be obtained in most local lumberyards or
hardware stores and are simple to install.

Only small sections need to be cut out of the soffit and can be
sawed out before the soffit is applied. It is more desirable to use
a number of smaller well-distributed ventilators than several
large ones (*A*, Fig. 5). Any blocking which might be required
between rafters at the wall line should be installed in order to
provide an airway into the attic area.

A continuous screened slot, which is often desirable, should be
located near the outer edge of the soffit near the facia (*B*, Fig.
5). Locating the slot in this area will minimize the chance of
snow entering. This type may also be used on the extension of
flat roofs.

## CRAWL-SPACE VENTILATION AND SOIL COVER

The crawl space below the floor of a basementless house and

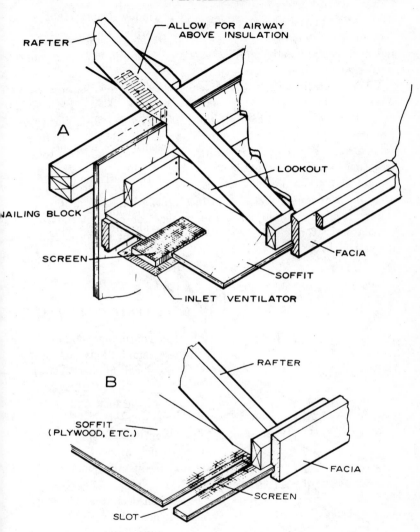

**Fig. 5.** Inlet ventilators. *A,* small insert ventilator. *B,* slot ventilator.

under porches should be ventilated and protected from ground moisture by the use of a *soil cover* (Fig. 6). The soil cover should be a vapor barrier with a perm value of less than 1.0. This includes such barrier materials as plastic films, roll roofing, and asphalt laminated paper. Such protection will minimize the effect of ground moisture on the wood framing members. High moisture content and humidity encourage staining and decay of untreated members.

Where there is a partial basement open to a crawl-space area, no wall vents are required if there is some type of operable window. The use of a soil cover in the crawl space is still important. For crawl spaces with no basement area, provide at least four foundation wall vents near corners of the building. The total free (net) area of the ventilators should be equal to 1/160 of the ground area when no soil cover is used. Therefore, for a ground area of 1,200 square feet, a total net ventilating area of about 8 square feet is required, or 2 square feet for each of the four ventilators. More smaller ventilators having the same net ratio are satisfactory.

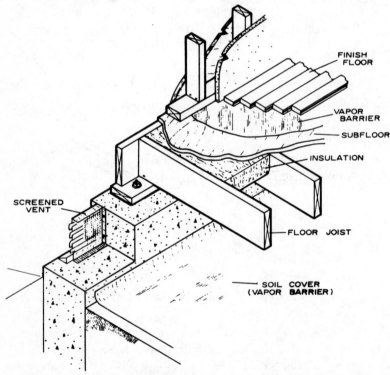

**Fig. 6.** Crawl-space ventilator and soil cover.

When a vapor-barrier ground cover is used, the required ventilating area is greatly reduced. The net ventilating area required with a ground cover is 1/1600 of the ground area, or for the 1,200-square-foot house, an area of 0.75 square foot. This should be divided between two small ventilators located on opposite sides of the crawl space. Vents should be covered (Fig. 6) with a corrosion-resistant screen of No. 8 mesh.

The use of a ground cover is normally recommended under all conditions. It not only protects wood framing members from ground moisture but also allows the use of small, inconspicuous ventilators.

## CHAPTER 33

# Protection Against Decay
# and Termites

Wood and wood products in construction use are susceptible to decay if kept wet for long periods under temperature conditions favorable to the growth of decay organisms. Most of the wood used in a house is not subjected to such conditions. There are places where water can work into the structure, but such places can be protected. Protection is accomplished by methods of design and construction, by use of suitable materials, and in some cases by using treated material.

Wood is also subject to attack by *termites* and some other *insects*. Termites can be grouped into two main classes—*subterranean* and *dry-wood*. Subterranean termites are important in the northernmost states where serious damage is confined to scattered, localized areas of infestation. (*See* Fig. 1.) Buildings may be fully protected against subterranean termites by incorporating comparatively inexpensive protection measures during construction. The Formosan subterranean termite has recently been discovered in several locations in the south. It is a serious pest because the colonies contain large numbers of the worker caste that cause damage rapidly. Though presently in localized areas, they could become more widespread. Controls are similar to those for other subterranean species. Dry-wood termites are found principally in Florida, southern California, and the Gulf Coast states. They are more difficult to control, but their damage is less serious than that caused by subterranean termites. Wood has proved itself through the years to be desirable and satisfactory as a building material. Damage from decay and termites has been small in

**Fig. 1.** The northern limit of damage in the United States by subterranean termites, line *A;* by dry-wood or by nonsubterranean termites, line *B.*

proportion to the total value of wood in residential structures, but it has been a troublesome problem to many homeowners. With changes in building design features and use of new building materials, it becomes pertinent to restate the basic safeguards to protect buildings against both decay and termites.

## DECAY

*Wood decay* is caused by certain fungi that can utilize wood for food. These fungi, like the higher plants, require air, warmth, food, and moisture for growth. Early stages of decay caused by these fungi may be accompanied by a discoloration of the wood. Paint also may become discolored where the underlying wood is rotting. Advanced decay is easily recognized because the wood has then undergone definite changes in properties and appearance. In advanced stages of building decay, the affected wood generally is brown and crumbly, and sometimes may be comparatively white and spongy. These changes may not be apparent on the surface, but the loss of sound wood inside often is reflected by sunken areas on the surface or by a "hollow" sound when the wood is tapped with a hammer. Where the surrounding atmosphere is very damp, the decay fungus may grow out on the surface, appearing as white or brownish growths in patches or strands or in special cases as vine-like structures.

*Fungi* grow most rapidly at temperatures of about 70° to 85° F. Elevated temperatures such as those used in kiln-drying of lumber kill fungi, but low temperatures, even far below zero, merely cause them to remain dormant.

Moisture requirements of fungi are within definite limitations. Wood-destroying fungi will not become established in dry wood. A moisture content of 20 per cent (which can be determined with an electrical moisture meter) is safe. Moisture contents greater than this are practically never reached in wood sheltered against rain and protected, if necessary, against wetting by condensation or fog. Decay can be permanently arrested by simply taking measures to dry out the infected wood and to keep it dry. Brown crumbly decay, in the dry condition, is sometimes called "dry rot," but this is a misnomer. Such wood must necessarily be damp if rotting is to occur.

The presence of mold or stain fungi should serve as a warning that conditions are or have been suitable for decay fungi. Heavily molded or stained lumber, therefore, should be examined for evidence of decay. Furthermore, such discolored wood is not entirely satisfactory for exterior millwork because it has greater capacity for water absorption than bright wood.

The natural decay resistance of all common native species of wood lies in the heartwood. When untreated, the sapwood of all species has low resistance to decay and usually has a short life under decay-producing conditions. Of the species of wood commonly used in house construction, the heartwood of bald cypress, redwood, and the cedars is classified as being highest in decay resistance. All-heartwood, quality lumber is becoming more and more difficult to obtain, however, as increasing amounts of timber are cut from the smaller trees of second-growth stands. In general, when substantial decay resistance is needed in load-bearing members that are difficult and expensive to replace, appropriate preservative-treated wood is recommended.

## SUBTERRANEAN TERMITES

*Subterranean termites* are the most destructive of the insects that infest wood in houses. The chance of infestation is great enough to justify preventive measures in the design and construction of buildings in areas where termites are common. Several types of copper barrier and deflector shielding that can be installed during construction are shown in Figs. 2, 3, and 4.

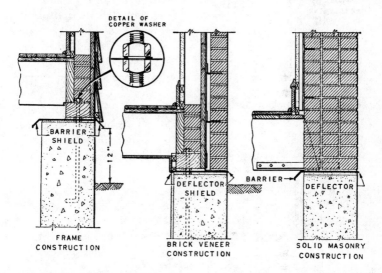

**Fig. 2.** Typical foundation wall's termite protection.

Subterranean termites are common throughout the southern two-thirds of the United States, except in mountainous and extremely dry areas.

One of the requirements for subterranean-termite life is the moisture available in the soil. These termites become most numerous in moist, warm soil containing an abundant supply of food in the form of wood or other cellulosic material. In their search for additional food (wood), they build earthlike shelter tubes over foundation walls or in cracks in the walls, or on pipes or supports leading from the soil to the house. These flattened tubes are from

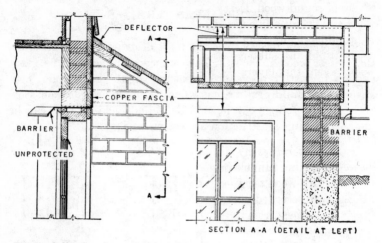

**Fig. 3.** Cellar hatchway termite protection.

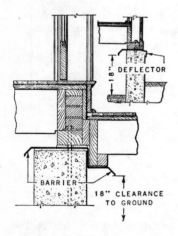

**Fig. 4.** Porch termite protection.

¼″ to ½″ or more in width and serve to protect termites in their travels between food and shelter.

Since subterranean termites eat the interior of the wood, they may cause much damage before they are discovered. They honeycomb the wood with definite tunnels that are separated by thin layers of sound wood. Decay fungi, on the other hand, soften the wood and eventually cause it to shrink, crack, and crumble without producing anything like these continuous tunnels. When both decay fungi and subterranean termites are present in the same wood, even the layers between the termite tunnels will be softened.

## DRY-WOOD TERMITES

*Dry-wood termites* fly directly to and bore into the wood, instead of building tunnels from the ground as do the subterranean termites. Dry-wood termites are common in the tropics, and damage has been recorded in the United States in a narrow strip along the Atlantic coast from Cape Henry, Va., to the Florida Keys, and westward along the coast of the Gulf of Mexico to the Pacific coast as far as northern California. Serious damage has been noted in southern California and in localities around Tampa, Miami, and Key West, Fla. Infestations may be found in structural timber and other woodwork in buildings, and also in furniture, particularly where the surface is not adequately protected by paint or other finishes.

Dry-wood termites cut across the grain of the wood and excavate broad pockets, or chambers, connected by tunnels about the diameter of the termite's body. They destroy both springwood and the usually harder summerwood, whereas subterranean termites principally attack springwood. Dry-wood termites remain hidden in the wood and are seldom seen, except when they make dispersal flights.

## SAFEGUARDS AGAINST DECAY

Except for special cases of wetting by condensation or fog, a dry piece of wood, when placed off the ground under a tight roof with wide overhang, will stay dry and never decay. This principle of "umbrella protection," when applied to houses of proper design and construction, is a good precaution. The use of dry lumber in designs that will keep the wood dry is the simplest way to avoid decay in buildings.

Untreated wood should *not* come in contact with the soil. It is desirable that the foundation walls have a clearance of at least 8″ above the exterior finish grade, and that the floor construction have a clearance of 18″ or more from the bottom of the joists to the ground in basementless spaces. The foundation should be accessible at all points for inspection. Porches that prevent access should be isolated from the soil by concrete or from the building proper by metal barriers or aprons (Fig. 5).

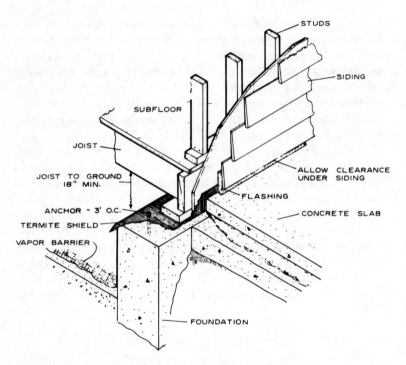

**Fig. 5.** Metal shield used to protect wood or porch slab.

Steps and stair carriages, posts, wallplates, and sills should be insulated from the ground with concrete or masonry. Sill plates and other wood in contact with concrete near the ground should be protected by a moistureproof membrane, such as a heavy roll roofing or 6-mil polyethylene. Girder and joist openings in masonry walls should be big enough to assure an air space around the ends of these members.

## DESIGN DETAILS

Surfaces such as steps, porches, door and window frames, roofs, and other protections should be sloped to promote runoff of water. (*See* Chap. 19, Porches and Garages.) Noncorrosive flashing should be used around chimneys, windows, doors, or other places where water might seep in. Roofs with considerable overhang give added protection to the siding and other parts of the house. Gutters and downspouts should be placed and maintained to divert away from the buildings. Porch columns and screen rails should be shimmed above the floor to allow quick drying, or posts should slightly overhang raised concrete bases. (*See* Chap. 19.)

Exterior steps, rails, and porch floors exposed to rain need protection from decay, particularly in warm, damp parts of the country. Pressure treatment of the wood provides a high degree of protection against decay and termite attack. Where the likelihood of decay is relatively small or where pressure-treated wood is not readily obtainable, on-the-job application of water-repellent preservatives by dipping or soaking has been found to be worthwhile. The wood should be dry, cut to final dimensions, and then dipped or soaked in the preservative solution. Soaking is the best of these nonpressure methods, and the ends of the boards should be soaked for a minimum of three minutes. It is important to protect the end grain of wood at joints, for this area absorbs water easily and is the most common infection point. The edges of porch flooring should be coated with thick white lead or other durable coating as it is laid.

Leaking pipes should be remedied immediately to prevent damage to the house, as well as to guard against possible decay.

## GREEN OR PARTIALLY SEASONED LUMBER

Construction lumber that is green or partially seasoned may be infected with one or more of the staining, molding, or decay fungi and should be avoided. Such wood may contribute to serious decay in both the substructure and exterior parts of buildings. If wet lumber must be used, or if wetting occurs during construction, the wood should not be fully enclosed or painted until thoroughly dried. (*See* Chap. 5, Lumber.)

## WATER VAPOR FROM THE SOIL

Crawl spaces of houses built on poorly-drained sites may be subjected to high humidity. During the winter when the sills and outer joists are cold, moisture condenses on them and, in time, the wood absorbs so much moisture that it is susceptible to attack by fungi. Unless this moisture dries out before temperatures favorable for fungus growth are reached, considerable decay may result. However, this decay may progress so slowly that no weakening of the wood becomes apparent for a few years. Placing a layer of 45-pound or heavier roll roofing or a 6-mil sheet of polyethylene over the soil to keep the vapor from getting into the crawl space would prevent such decay. This might be recommended for all sites where, during the cold months, the soil is wet enough to be compressed in the hand.

If the floor is uninsulated, there is an advantage in closing the foundation vents during the coldest months from the standpoint of fuel savings. However, unless the crawl space is used as a heat-plenum chamber, insulation is usually located between floor joists. The vents could then remain open. Crawl-space vents can be very small when soil covers are used—only 10 per cent of the area required without covers. (*See* Chap. 32, Ventilation.)

## WATER VAPOR FROM HOUSEHOLD ACTIVITIES

*Water vapor* is also given off during cooking, washing, and other household activities. This vapor can pass through walls and ceilings during very cold weather and condense on sheathing, studs, and rafters, causing condensation problems. A vapor barrier of an approved type is needed on the warm side of the walls. (*See* Chap. 31, Thermal Insulation, Vapor Barriers, and Sound Absorption, section on Vapor Barriers.) It is also important that the attic space be ventilated. (*See* Chap. 32, Ventilation.)

## WATER SUPPLIED BY THE FUNGUS ITSELF

In the warmer coastal areas principally, some sub-structure decay is caused by a fungus that provides its own needed moisture by conducting it through a vine-like structure from moist ground to the wood. The total damage caused by this water-conducting fungus is not large, but in individual instances it tends to be unusually severe. Preventive and remedial measures depend on getting the soil dry and avoiding untreated wood "bridges" such as posts between ground and sills or beams.

## SAFEGUARDS AGAINST TERMITES

The best time to provide protection against termites is during the planning and construction of the building. The first requirement is to remove all woody debris like stumps and discarded form boards from the soil at the building site before and after construction. Steps should also be taken to keep the soil under the house as dry as possible.

Next, the foundation should be made impervious to subterranean termites to prevent them from crawling up through hidden cracks to the wood in the building above. Properly reinforced concrete makes the best foundation, but unit-construction walls or piers capped with at least 4" of reinforced concrete are also satisfactory. No wood member of the structural part of the house should be in contact with the soil.

The best protection against subterranean termites is to treat the soil near the foundation or under an entire slab foundation. The effective soil treatments are water emulsions of aldrin (0.5 per cent), chlordane (1.0 per cent), dieldrin (0.5 per cent), and heptachlor (0.5 percent). The rate of application is four gallons per 10 linear feet at the edge and along expansion joints of slabs or along a foundation. For brick or hollow-block foundations, the rate is four gallons per 10 linear feet for each foot of depth to the footing. One to 1½ gallons of emulsion per 10 square feet of surface area is recommended for overall treatment before pouring concrete slab foundations. Any wood used in secondary appendages, such as wall extensions, decorative fences, and gates, should be pressure-treated with a good preservative.

In regions where dry-wood termites occur, the following measures should be taken to prevent damage.

All lumber, particularly secondhand material, should be carefully inspected before use. If infected, discard the piece.

All doors, windows (especially attic windows), and other ventilation openings should be screened with metal wire, not less than 20 meshes to the inch.

Preservative treatment can be used to prevent attack in construction timber and lumber.

Several coats of house paint will provide considerable protection to exterior woodwork in buildings. All cracks, crevices, and joints between exterior wood members should be filled with a mastic calking or plastic wood before painting.

The heartwood of foundation-grade redwood, particularly when painted, is more resistant to attack then most other native commercial species.

Pesticides used improperly can be injurious to man, animals, and plants. Follow manufacturer's directions and heed all precautions on the labels.

Store pesticides in original containers—out of reach of children and pets—and away from foodstuffs.

Apply pesticides selectively and carefully. Do not apply a pesticide when there is danger of drift to other areas. Avoid prolonged inhalation of a pesticide spray or dust. When applying a pesticide it is advisable that you be fully clothed.

After handling a pesticide do not eat, drink, or smoke until you have washed. If a pesticide is swallowed or gets in the eyes, follow the first aid treatment given on the label and get prompt medical attention. If the pesticide is spilled on your skin or clothing, remove clothing immediately and wash skin thoroughly.

Dispose of empty pesticide containers by wrapping them in several layers of newspaper and placing them in your trash can.

It is difficult to remove all traces of a herbicide (weed killer) from equipment. Therefore, to prevent injury to desirable plants do not use the same equipment for insecticides and fungicides that you use for herbicides.

*Note:* Registrations of pesticides are under constant review by the U.S. Department of Agriculture. Use only pesticides that bear the USDA registration number and carry directions for home and garden use.

(*See* Chap. 30, Deterioration of Paint, Painting Safety, and Wood Preservatives.)

## APPENDIX 1

# Glossary of Terms

**Adhesive.** A substance capable of holding materials together by surface attachment. It is a general term and includes cements, mucilage, and paste, as well as glue.

**Air-dried lumber.** Lumber that has been piled in yards or sheds for any length of time.

**Airway.** A space between roof insulation and roof boards for movement of air.

**Alligatoring.** Coarse checked pattern characterized by slippage of the new paint coating over the old coating to the extent that the old coating can be seen through the fissures.

**American lumber standards.** American lumber standards embody provisions for softwood lumber dealing with recognized classifications, nomenclature, basic grades, sizes, description, measurements, tally, shipping provisions, grade marking, and inspection of lumber. The primary purpose of these standards is to serve as a guide or basic example in the preparation or revision of the grading rules of the various lumber manufacturers' associations. A purchaser must make use of association rules as the basic standards are not in themselves commercial rules.

**Anchor bolts.** Bolts to secure a wooden sill plate to concrete or masonry floor or wall.

**Apron.** The flat member of the inside trim of a window placed against the wall immediately beneath the stool.

**Areaway.** An open subsurface space adjacent to a building used to admit light or air or as a means of access to a basement.

**Asphalt.** Most native asphalt is a residue from evaporated petroleum. It is insoluble in water but soluble in gasoline and melts when heated. Used widely in building for waterproofing roof coverings of many types, exterior wall coverings, flooring tile, and the like.

**Astragal.** A molding attached to one of a pair of swinging doors against which the other door strikes.

**Attic ventilators.** In houses, screened openings provided to ventilate an attic space. They are located in the soffit area as inlet ventilators and in the gable end or along the ridge as outlet ventilators. They can also consist of power-driven fans used as an exhaust system. (*See also* Louver.)

619

**Backband.** A simple molding sometimes used around the outer edge of plain rectangular casing as a decorative feature.

**Backfill.** The replacement of excavated earth into a trench around and against a basement foundation.

**Backing.** The bevel on the top edge of a hip rafter that allows the roofing board to fit the top of the rafter without leaving a triangular space between it and the lower side of the roof covering.

**Balloon frame.** The lightest and most economical form of construction, in which the studding and corner posts are set up in continuous lengths from first-floor line or sill to roof plate.

**Balusters.** Usually small vertical members in a railing used between a top rail and the stair treads or a bottom rail.

**Balustrade.** A railing made up of balusters, top rail, and sometimes bottom rail, used on the edge of stairs, balconies, and porches.

**Band.** A low, flat molding.

**Barge board.** A decorative board covering the projecting rafter (fly rafter) of the gable end. At the cornice, this member is a facia board.

**Base.** The bottom of a column; the finish of a room at the junction of the walls and floor.

**Baseboard.** A board placed against the wall around a room next to the floor to finish properly between floor and plaster.

**Base molding.** Molding used to trim the upper edge of interior baseboard.

**Base shoe.** Molding used next to the floor on interior baseboard. Sometimes called a carpet strip.

**Batten.** Narrow strips of wood used to cover joints or as decorative vertical members over plywood or wide boards.

**Batter board.** One of a pair of horizontal boards nailed to posts set at the corners of an excavation and used to indicate the desired level; also as a fastening for stretched strings to indicate outlines of foundation walls.

**Batter pile.** Pile driven at an angle to brace a structure against lateral thrust.

**Bay window.** Any window space projecting outward from the walls of a building, either square or polygonal in plan.

**Beam.** A structural member transversely supporting a load.

**Bearing partition.** A partition that supports any vertical load in addition to its own weight.

**Bearing wall.** A wall that supports any vertical load in addition to its own weight.

**Bed molding.** A molding in an angle, as between the over-hanging cornice, or eaves, of a building and the sidewalls.

**Belt course.** A horizontal board across or around a building, usually made of a flat member and a molding.

**Bevel board (pitch board).** A board used in framing a roof or stairway to lay out bevels.

**Blind-nailing.** Nailing in such a way that the nailheads are not visible on the face of the work. Usually the nails are placed at the tongue of matched boards.

**Blind stop.** A rectangle molding, usually ¾ inch by 1⅝ inches or more in width, used in the assembly of a window frame. Serves as a stop for storm and screen or combination windows and to resist air infiltration.

**Blue stain.** A bluish or grayish discoloration of the sapwood caused by the growth of certain moldlike fungi on the surface and in the interior of a piece, made possible by the same conditions that favor the growth of other fungi.

**Board.** Lumber less than two inches thick.

**Board foot.** The equivalent of a board one foot square and one inch thick.

**Boarding in.** The process of nailing boards on the outside studding of a house.

**Bodied linseed oil.** Linseed oil that has been thickened in viscosity by suitable processing with heat or chemicals. Bodied oils are obtainable in a great range in viscosity from a little greater than that of raw oil to just short of a jellied condition.

**Boiled linseed oil.** Linseed oil in which enough lead, manganese, or cobalt salts have been incorporated to make the oil harden more rapidly when spread in thin coatings.

**Bolster.** A short horizontal timber or steel beam on top of a column to support and decrease the span of beams or girders.

**Boston ridge.** A method of applying asphalt or wood shingles at the ridge or at the hips of a roof as a finish.

**Brace.** An inclined piece of framing lumber applied to wall or floor to stiffen the structure. Often used on walls as temporary bracing until framing has been completed.

**Bracket.** A projecting support for a shelf or other structure.

**Break joints.** Joints arranged so that they do not come directly under or over the joints of adjoining pieces, as in shingling, siding, and the like.

**Brick veneer.** A facing of brick laid against and fastened to sheathing of a frame wall or tile wall construction.

**Bridging.** Small wood or metal members that are inserted in a diagonal position between the floor joists at midspan to act both as tension and compression members for the purpose of bracing the joists and spreading the action of loads.

**Buck.** Often used in reference to rough-frame opening members. Door bucks used in reference to metal door frame.

**Building fiberboard.** A broad generic term inclusive of sheet materials of widely varying densities manufactured of refined or partially refined wood (or other vegetable) fibers. Bonding agents and other materials may be added to increase strength, resistance to moisture, fire, or decay, or to improve some other property.

**Building paper.** Cheap, thick paper used to insulate a building before the siding or roofing is put on; sometimes placed between double floors.

**Built-up member.** A single structural component made from several pieces fastened together.

**Built-up roof.** A roofing composed of three to five layers of asphalt felt laminated with coal tar, pitch, or asphalt. The top is finished with crushed slag or gravel. Generally used on flat or low-pitched roofs.

**Cant strip.** A triangular-shaped piece of lumber used at the junction of a flat deck and a wall to prevent cracking of the roofing which is applied over it.

**Cap.** The upper member of a column, pilaster, door cornice, molding, and the like.

**Carriages.** The supports or the steps and risers of a flight of stairs.

**Casement frames and sash.** Frames of wood or metal enclosing part or all of the sash, which may be opened by means of hinges affixed to the vertical edges.

**Casing.** Molding of various widths and thicknesses used to trim door and window openings at the jambs.

**Ceiling.** Narrow, matched boards; sheathing of the surfaces that inclose the upper side of a room.

**Center-hung sash.** A sash hung on its centers so that it swings on a horizontal axis.

**Chamfer.** A beveled surface cut upon the corner of a piece of wood.

**Checking.** Fissures that appear with age in many exterior paint coatings, at first superficial, but which in time may penetrate entirely through the coating.

**Checkrails.** Meeting rails, sufficiently thicker than the window, which fill the opening between the top and bottom sash made by the parting stop in the frame of double-hung windows. They are usually beveled.

**Checks.** Splits or cracks in a board, ordinarily caused by seasoning.

**Chord.** The principal member of a truss on either the top or bottom.

**Clamp.** A mechanical device used to hold two or more pieces together.

**Clapboards.** A special form of outside covering of a house; siding.

**Collar beam.** Nominal 1- or 2-inch-thick members connecting opposite roof rafters. They serve to stiffen the roof structure.

**Column.** A square, rectangular, or cylindrical support for roofs, ceilings, and so forth, composed of base, shaft, and capital.

**Combination doors or windows.** Combination doors or windows used over regular openings provide winter insulation and summer protection and often have self-storing or removable glass and screen inserts. This eliminates the need for handling a different unit each season.

**Combination frame.** A combination of the principal features of the full and balloon frames.

**Concrete plain.** Concrete either without reinforcement, or reinforced only for shrinkage or temperature changes.

**Condensation.** Beads or drops of water (and frequently frost in extremely cold weather) that accumulate on the inside of the exterior covering of a building when warm, moisture-laden air from the interior reaches a point where the temperature no longer permits the air to sustain the moisture it holds. Use of louvers or attic ventilators will reduce moisture condensation in attics. A vapor barrier under the gypsum lath or dry wall on exposed walls will reduce condensation in them.

**Conduit, electrical.** A pipe, usually metal, in which wire is installed.

**Construction, dry-wall.** A type of construction in which the interior wall finish is applied in a dry condition, generally in the form of sheet materials or wood paneling, as contrasted to plaster.

**Construction, frame.** A type of construction in which the structural parts are wood or depend upon a wood frame for support. In codes, if masonry veneer is applied to the exterior walls, the classification of this type of construction is usually unchanged.

**Coped joint.** (*See* Scribing.)

**Corbel out.** To build out one or more courses of brick or stone from the face of a wall, to form a support for timbers.

**Corner bead.** A strip of formed sheet metal, sometimes combined with a strip of metal lath, placed on corners before plastering to reinforce them. Also, a strip of wood finish three-quarters round or angular, placed over a plastered corner for protection.

**Corner boards.** Used as trim for the external corners of a house or other frame structure against which the ends of the siding are finished.

**Corner braces.** Diagonal braces at the corners of frame structures to stiffen and strengthen the wall.

**Cornerite.** Metal-mesh lath cut into strips and bent to a right angle. Used in interior corners of walls and ceilings on lath to prevent cracks in plastering.

**Cornice.** The molded projection that finishes the top of the wall of a building. Also the overhang of a pitched roof at the eave line, usually consisting of a fascia board, a soffit for a closed cornice, and appropriate moldings.

**Cornice return.** That portion of the cornice that returns on the gable end of a house.

**Counterflashings.** Strips of metal used to prevent water from entering the top edge of the vertical side of a roof flashing; they also allow expansion and contraction without danger of breaking the flashing.

**Cove molding.** A molding with a concave face used as trim or to finish interior corners.

**Crawl space.** A shallow space below the living quarters of a basementless house, normally enclosed by the foundation wall.

**Cricket.** A small drainage-diverting roof structure of single or double slope placed at the junction of larger surfaces that meet at an angle, such as above a chimney.

**Cross brace.** Bracing with two intersecting diagonals.

**Cross-bridging.** Diagonal bracing between adjacent floor joists, placed near the center of the joist span to prevent joists from twisting.

**Crown molding.** A molding used on cornice or wherever an interior angle is to be covered.

**Cut-in brace.** Nominal 2-inch-thick members, usually 2 by 4's, cut in between each stud diagonally. (*See also* Let-in brace.)

**d.** (*See* Penny.)

**Dado.** A rectangular groove across the width of a board or plank. In interior decoration, a special type of wall treatment.

**Deck paint.** An enamel with a high degree of resistance to mechanical wear, designed for use on such surfaces as porch floors.

**Dewpoint.** Temperature at which a vapor begins to deposit as a liquid. Applies especially to water in the atmosphere.

**Diagonal.** Inclined member of a truss or bracing system used for stiffening and wind bracing.

**Dimension.** (*See* Lumber dimension.)

**Direct nailing.** To nail perpendicular to the initial surface or to the junction of the pieces joined. Also termed *face nailing.*

**Doorjamb, interior.** The surrounding case into which and out of which a door closes and opens. It consists of two upright pieces, called side jambs, and a horizontal head jamb.

**Dormer.** An opening in a sloping roof, the framing of which projects out to form a vertical wall suitable for windows or other openings.

**Downspout.** A pipe, usually of metal, for carrying rainwater from roof gutters.

**Dressed and matched (tongued and grooved).** Boards or planks machined in such a manner that there is a groove on one edge and a corresponding tongue on the other.

**Drier paint.** Usually oil-soluble soaps of such metals as lead, manganese, or cobalt, which, in small proportions, hasten the oxidation and hardening (drying) of the drying oils in paints.

**Drip.** (a) A member of a cornice or other horizontal exterior-finish course that has a projection beyond the other parts for throwing off water. (b) A groove in the underside of a sill or drip cap causing water to drop off on the outer edge instead of drawing back and running down the face of the building.

**Drip cap.** A molding placed on the exterior top side of a door or window frame causing water to drip beyond the outside of the frame.

**Dry-wall.** Interior covering material, such as gypsum board or plywood, that is applied in large sheets or panels.

**Ducts.** In a house, usually round or rectangular metal pipes for distributing warm air from the heating plant to rooms, or air from a conditioning device or as cold air returns. Ducts are also made of asbestos and composition materials.

**Eaves.** The margin or lower part of a roof projecting over the wall.

**Equilibrium moisture content.** That moisture content of wood at which no expansion or contraction takes place (providing the relative humidity of air remains constant).

**Expansion joint.** A bituminous fiber strip used to separate blocks or units of concrete to prevent cracking due to expansion as a result of temperature changes. Also used on concrete slabs.

**Facia or fascia.** A flat board, band, or face, used sometimes by itself but usually in combination with moldings, often located at the outer face of the cornice.

**Fiber saturation.** Water filling only the wood substance in the lumber and not the cavities.

**Filler (wood).** A heavily pigmented preparation used for filling and leveling off the pores in open-pored woods.

**Fire-retardant chemical.** A chemical or preparation of chemicals used to reduce flammability or to retard spread of flame.

**Fire stop.** A solid, tight closure of a concealed space, placed to prevent the spread of fire and smoke through such a space. In a frame wall, this will usually consist of 2 by 4 cross-blocking between studs.

**Fishplate.** A wood or plywood piece used to fasten the ends of two members together at a butt joint with nails or bolts. Sometimes used at the junction of opposite rafters near the ridge line.

**Flashing.** Sheet metal or other material used in roof and wall construction to protect a building from water seepage.

**Flat paint.** An interior paint that contains a high proportion of pigment and dries to a flat or lusterless finish.

**Flush.** Adjacent surfaces even, or in same plane (with reference to two structural pieces).

**Fly rafters.** End rafters of the gable overhang supported by roof sheathing and lookouts.

**Footing.** A masonry section, usually concrete, in a rectangular form wider than the bottom of the foundation wall or pier it supports.

**Footing form.** A wooden or steel structure, placed around the footing, that will hold the concrete to the desired shape and size.

**Foundation.** The supporting portion of a structure below the first floor construction, or below grade, including the footings.

**Frame.** The surrounding or enclosing woodwork of windows, doors, and the like, and the timber skeleton of a building.

**Framing, balloon.** A system of framing a building in which all vertical structural elements of the bearing walls and partitions consist of single pieces extending from the top of the foundation sill plate in the roofplate and to which all floor joists are fastened.

**Framing, platform.** A system of framing a building in which floor joists of each story rest on the top plates of the story below or on the foundation sill for the first story, and the bearing walls and partitions rest on the subfloor of each story.

**Free water.** Water in excess of that held in the wood substance; also that held in the cavities between cells.

**Frieze.** In house construction, a horizontal member connecting the top of the siding with the soffit of the cornice.

**Fungi, wood.** Microscopic plants that live in damp wood and cause mold, stain, and decay.

**Fungicide.** A chemical that is poisonous to fungi.

**Fungus.** Microscopic plant growth feeding on wood and causing stain, mold, or rot.

**Furring.** Strips of wood or metal applied to a wall or other surface to even it and normally to serve as a fastening base for finish material.

**Gable.** In house construction, the portion of the roof above the eave line of a double-sloped roof.

**Gable end.** An end wall having a gable.

**Gage.** A tool used by carpenters to strike a line parallel to the edge of a board.

**Gain.** A mortise or notch cut to receive a hinge or other fitting.

**Gambrel.** A symmetrical roof with two different pitches or slopes on each side.

**Girder.** A large or principal beam of wood or steel used to support concentrated loads at isolated points along its length.

**Girt (ribband).** The horizontal member of the walls of a full or combination frame house which supports the floor joists or is flush with the top of the joists.

**Gloss (paint or enamel).** A paint or enamel that contains a relatively low proportion of pigment and dries to a sheen or luster.

**Gloss enamel.** A finishing material made of varnish and sufficient pigments to provide opacity and color, but little or no pigment of low opacity. Such an enamel forms a hard coating with maximum smoothness of surface and a high degree of gloss.

**Grade.** The horizontal ground level of a building or structure.

**Groove.** A long hollow channel cut by a tool, into which a piece fits or in which it works. Two special types of grooves are the *dado*, a rectangular groove cut across the full width of a piece, and the *housing*, a groove cut at any angle with the grain and part way across a piece.

**Grounds.** Guides used around openings and at the floorline to strike off plaster. They can consist of narrow strips of wood or of wide subjambs at interior doorways. They provide a level plaster line for installation of casing and other trim.

**Grout.** Mortar made of such consistency (by adding water) that it will just flow into the joints and cavities of the masonry and fill them solid.

**Gusset.** A flat wood, plywood, or similar type member used to provide a connection for intersection of wood members. Most commonly used at joints of wood trusses. They are fastened by nails, screws, bolts, or adhesives.

**Gutter or eave trough.** A shallow channel or conduit of metal or wood set below and along the eaves of a house to catch and carry off rainwater from the roof.

**Hanger.** Vertical-tension member supporting a load.

**Header.** (a) A beam placed perpendicular to joists and to which joists are nailed in framing for chimney, stairway, or other opening. (b) A wood lintel.

**Headroom.** The clear space between floor line and ceiling, as in a stairway.

**Hearth.** The inner or outer floor of a fireplace, usually made of brick, tile, or stone.

**Heartwood.** The wood extending from the pith to the sapwood, the cells of which no longer participate in the life processes of the tree.

**Heel of a rafter.** The end or foot that rests on the wall plate.

**Hip.** The external angle formed by the meeting of two sloping sides of a roof.

**Hip roof.** A roof that rises by inclined planes from all four sides of a building.

**I-beam.** A steel beam with a cross section resembling the letter *I*. It is used for long spans as basement beams or over wide wall openings, such as a double garage door, when wall and roof loads are imposed on the opening.

**Insulation board, rigid.** A structural building board made of coarse wood or cane fiber in ½- and 25/32-inch thicknesses. It can be obtained in various size sheets, in various densities, and with several treatments.

**Insulation, thermal.** Any material high in resistance to heat transmission that, when placed in the walls, ceiling, or floors of a structure, will reduce the rate of heat flow.

**Interior finish.** Material used to cover the interior framed areas, or materials of walls and ceilings.

**Jack rafter.** A rafter that spans the distance from the wallplate to a hip, or from valley to a ridge.

**Jamb.** The side and head lining of a doorway, window, or other opening.

**Joint.** The junction of two pieces of wood or veneer.

*Butt joint.* An end joint formed by abutting the squared ends of two pieces. Because of the inadequacy and variability in strength of butt joints when glued, they are not generally glued.

*Edge joint.* The place where two pieces of wood are joined together edge to edge, commonly by gluing. The joints may be made by gluing two squared edges as in a plain edge joint or by using machined joints of various kinds, such as tongued-and-grooved joints.

*End joint.* The place where two pieces of wood are joined together end to end, commonly by scarfing and gluing.

*Lap joint.* A joint made by placing one end partly over another and bonding the overlapped portions.

*Scarf joint.* An end joint formed by joining with glue the ends of two pieces that have been tapered or beveled to form sloping plane surfaces, usually to a featheredge, and with the same slope of the plane with respect to the length in both pieces.

*Starved joint.* A glue joint that is poorly bonded because an insufficient quantity of glue remained in the joint. Starved joints are caused by the use of excessive pressure or insufficient viscosity of the glue, or a combination of these, which results in the glue being forced out from between the surfaces to be joined.

**Joint-butt.** Squared ends or ends and edges adjoining each other.

*Dovetail.* Joint made by cutting pins the shape of dovetails which fit between dovetails on another piece.

*Drawboard.* A mortise-and-tenon joint with holes so bored that when a pin is driven through, the joint becomes tighter.

*Fished.* An end-butt splice strengthened by pieces nailed on the sides.

*Glue.* A joint held together with glue.

*Halved.* A joint made by cutting half the wood away from each piece so as to bring the sides flush.

*Housed.* A joint in which a piece is grooved to receive the piece that is to form the other part of the joint.

*Lap.* A joint of two pieces lapping over each other.

*Mortised.* A joint made by cutting a hole and fitting the other to it.

*Rub.* A glue joint made by carefully fitting the edges together, spreading glue between them, and rubbing the pieces back and forth until the pieces are well rubbed together.

*Scarfed.* A timber spliced by cutting various shapes of shoulders, or jogs, which fit each other.

**Joint cement.** A powder that is usually mixed with water and used for joint treatment in gypsum-wallboard finish. Often called "spackle."

**Joist.** One of a series of parallel beams, usually two inches in thickness, used to support floor and ceiling loads, and supported in turn by larger beams, girders, or bearing walls.

**Kerf.** The cut made by a saw.

**Kiln dried lumber.** Lumber that has been kiln dried often to a moisture content of 6 to 12 per cent. Common varieties of softwood lumber, such as framing lumber, are dried to a somewhat higher moisture content.

**Knee brace.** A corner brace, fastened at an angle from wall stud to rafter, stiffening a wood or steel frame to prevent angular movement.

**Landing.** A platform between flights of stairs or at the termination of a flight of stairs.

**Lath.** A building material of wood, gypsum, or insulating board that is fastened to the frame of a building to act as a plaster base.

**Lattice.** A framework of crossed wood or metal strips.

**Leader.** (*See* Downspout.)

**Ledger strip.** A strip of lumber nailed along the bottom of the side of a girder on which joists rest.

**Let-in brace.** Nominal one-inch-thick boards applied to notched studs diagonally.

**Level.** An instrument or tool used in testing for horizontal and vertical surfaces, and in determining differences of elevation.

**Light.** Space in a window sash for a single pane of glass. Also, a pane of glass.

**Lintel.** A horizontal structural member that supports the load over an opening such as a door or window.

**Lookout.** A short wood bracket or cantilever supporting an overhanging portion of a roof or the like, usually concealed from view.

**Louver.** An opening with a series of horizontal slats so arranged as to permit ventilation but to exclude rain, sunlight, or vision. (*See also* Attic ventilator.)

**Lumber.** The product of the saw and planing mill not further manufactured than by sawing, resawing, passing lengthwise through a standard planing machine, crosscutting to length, and matching.

*Boards.* Yard lumber less than two inches thick and one or more inches wide.

*Dimension.* Lumber from two inches to, but not including, five inches thick and two or more inches wide.

*Dressed size.* The dimensions of lumber after shrinking from the green dimension and being surfaced with a planing machine usually ⅜ or ½ inch less than the nominal or rough size.

*Factory and shop lumber.* Lumber intended to be cut up for use in further manufacture. It is graded on the basis of the percentage of the area that will produce a limited number of cuttings of a specified minimum size and quality.

*Matched lumber.* Lumber that is edge dressed and shaped to make a close tongued-and-grooved joint at the edges or ends when laid edge to edge or end to end.

*Nominal size.* As applied to timber or lumber, the rough-sawed commercial size by which it is known and sold in the market.

*Patterned lumber.* Lumber that is shaped to a pattern or to a molded form in addition to being dressed, matched, or shiplapped, or any combination of these workings.

*Rough lumber.* Lumber as it comes from the saw.

*Shiplapped lumber.* Lumber that is edge dressed to make a lapped joint.

*Shipping-dry lumber.* Lumber that is partially dried to prevent stain and mold in transit.

*Structural lumber.* Lumber that is two or more inches wide, intended for use where working stresses are required. The grading of structural lumber is based on the strength of the piece and the use of the entire piece.

*Surfaced lumber.* Lumber that is dressed by running it through a planer.

*Timbers.* Lumber five or more inches in least dimension. Timbers may be classified as beams, stringers, posts, caps, sills, girders, purlins, and the like.

*Timbers, round.* Timbers used in the original round form, such as poles, piling, posts, and mine timbers.

*Yard lumber.* Lumber of all sizes and patterns that is intended for general building purposes. The grading of yard lumber is based on the intended use of the particular grade, and is applied to each piece with reference to its size and length when graded without consideration to further manufacture.

**Mantel.** The shelf above a fireplace. Also used in referring to the decorative trim around a fireplace opening.

**Mastic.** A pasty material used as a cement (as for setting tile) or a protective coating (as for thermal insulation or waterproofing).

**Matching, or tonguing and grooving.** The method used in cutting the edges of a board to make a tongue on one edge and a groove on the other.

**Meeting rail.** The bottom rail of the upper sash of a double-hung window. Sometimes called the checkrail.

**Member.** A single piece in a structure, complete in itself.

**Metal lath.** Sheets of metal that are slit and drawn out to form openings. Used as a plaster base for walls and ceilings and as reinforcing over other forms of plaster base.

**Millwork.** Generally all building materials made of finished wood and manufactured in millwork plants and planing mills are included under the term "millwork." It includes such items as inside and outside doors, window and doorframes, blinds, porchwork, mantels, panelwork, stairways, moldings, and interior trim. It normally does not include flooring, ceiling, or siding.

**Miter joint.** The joint of two pieces at an angle that bisects the joining angle.

**Moisture content of wood.** Weight of the water contained in the wood, usually expressed as a percentage of the weight of the ovendry wood.

**Molding.** A wood strip having a curved or projecting surface used for decorative purposes.

*Molding base.* The molding on the top of a baseboard.

*Bed.* A molding used to cover the joint between the plancier and frieze (horizontal decorative band around the wall of a room); also used as a base molding upon heavy work, and sometimes as a member of a cornice.

*Lip.* A molding with a lip that overlaps the piece against which the back of the molding rests.

*Picture.* A molding shaped to form a support for picture hooks, often placed at some distance from the ceiling upon the wall to form the lower edge of the frieze.

*Rake.* The cornice upon the gable edge of a pitch roof, the members of which are made to fit those of the molding of the horizontal eaves.

**Mortise.** A slot cut into a board, plank, or timber, usually edgewise, to receive tenon of another board, plank, or timber to form a joint.

**Mullion.** A vertical bar or divider in the frame between windows, doors, or other openings.

**Muntin.** A small member that divides the glass or openings of sash or doors.

**Natural finish.** A transparent finish that does not seriously alter the original color or grain of the natural wood. Natural finishes are usually provided by sealers, oils, varnishes, water-repellent preservatives, and other similar materials.

**Newel.** A post to which the end of a stair railing or balustrade is fastened.

**Nonbearing wall.** A wall supporting no load other than its own weight.

**Nosing.** The projecting edge of a molding or drip. Usually applied to the projecting molding on the edge of a stair tread.

**Notch.** A crosswise rabbet at the end of a board.

**O. C. (on center).** The measurement of spacing for studs, rafters, joists, and the like in a building from the center of one member to the center of the next.

**O. G., or ogee.** A molding with a profile in the form of a letter $S$; having the outline of a reversed curve.

**Outrigger.** An extension of a rafter beyond the wall line. Usually a smaller member nailed to a larger rafter to form a cornice or roof overhang.

**Paint.** A combination of pigments with suitable thinners or oils to provide decorative and protective coatings.

**Panel.** In house construction, a thin flat piece of wood, plywood, or similar material, framed by stiles and rails as in a door or fitted into grooves of thicker material with molded edges for decorative wall treatment.

**Paper, building.** A general term for papers, felts, and similar sheet materials used in buildings without reference to their properties or uses.

**Paper, sheathing.** A building material, generally paper or felt, used in wall and roof construction as a protection against the passage of air and sometimes moisture.

**Parting stop or strip.** A small wood piece used in the side and head jambs of double-hung windows to separate the upper and lower sash.

**Partition.** A wall that subdivides spaces within any story of a building.

**Penny.** As applied to nails, it originally indicated the price per hundred. The term now serves as a measure of nail length and is abbreviated by the letter $d$.

**Perm.** A measure of water vapor movement through a material (grains per square foot per hour per inch of mercury difference in vapor pressure).

**Pigment.** A powdered solid in suitable degree of subdivision for use in paint or enamel.

**Pilaster.** A portion of a square column, usually set within or against a wall.

**Piles.** Long posts driven into the soil in swampy locations, or whenever it is difficult to secure a firm foundation, upon which the footing course of masonry or other timbers are laid.

**Piling.** Large timbers or poles driven into the ground or the bed of a stream to make a firm foundation.

**Pitch.** The incline slope of a roof or the ratio of the total rise to the total width of a house; for example, an 8-foot rise with a 24-foot width is a one-third pitch roof. Roof slope is expressed in the inches of rise per foot of run.

**Pitch board.** A board sawed to the exact shape formed by the stair tread, riser, and slope of the stairs and used to lay out the carriage and stringers.

**Pitch pocket.** An opening extending parallel to the annual rings of growth that usually contains, or has contained, either solid or liquid pitch.

**Pith.** The small, soft core at the original center of a tree around which wood formation takes place.

**Plan.** A horizontal geometrical section of a building, showing the walls, doors, windows, stairs, chimneys, columns, and so on.

**Plank.** A wide piece of sawed timber, usually 1½ to 4½ inches thick and 6 inches or more wide.

**Plaster grounds.** Strips of wood used as guides or strike-off edges around window and door openings and at base of walls.

**Plate cut.** The cut in a rafter that rests upon the plate; sometimes called the seat cut.

**Plough.** To cut a lengthwise groove in a board or plank.

**Plumb.** Exactly perpendicular; vertical.

**Ply.** A term to denote the number of thicknesses or layers of roofing felt, veneer in plywood, or layers in build-up materials, in any finished piece of such material.

**Plywood.** A crossbanded assembly made of layers of veneer or of veneer in combination with a lumber core or plies joined with an adhesive. Two types of plywood are recognized—namely (1) veneer plywood and (2) lumber-core plywood. The grain of adjoining plies is usually laid at right angles, and almost always an odd number of plies are used to obtain balanced construction.

*Molded plywood.* Plywood that is glued to the desired shape either between curved forms or more commonly by fluid pressure applied with flexible bags or blankets (bag molding) or other means.

*Postformed plywood.* The product formed by reshaping, by means of steaming or other plasticizing agent, flat plywood into a curved shape.

**Porch.** An ornamental entrance way.

**Pores.** Wood cells of comparatively large diameter that have open ends and are set one above the other to form continuous tubes. The openings of the vessels on the surface of a piece of wood are referred to as pores.

**Post.** A timber set on end to support a wall, girder, or other member of the structure.

**Preservative.** Any substance that, for a reasonable length of time, will prevent the action of wood-destroying fungi, borers of various kinds, and similar destructive agents when the wood has been properly coated or impregnated with it.

**Primer.** The first coat of paint in a paint job that consists of two or more coats; also the paint used for such a first coat.

**Pulley stile.** The member of a window frame that contains the pulleys and between which the edges of the sash slide.

**Purlin.** A timber supporting several rafters at one or more points, or the roof sheeting directly.

**Putty.** A type of cement usually made of whiting and boiled linseed oil, heated or kneaded to the consistency of dough, and used in sealing glass in sash, filling small holes and crevices in wood, and for similar purposes.

**Quarter round.** A small molding that has the cross section of a quarter circle.

**Rabbet.** A rectangular longitudinal groove cut in the corner edge of a board or plank.

**Rail.** Cross members of panel doors or of a sash. Also the upper and lower members of a balustrade or staircase extending from one vertical support, such as a post, to another.

**Rake.** Trim members that run parallel to the roof slope and form the finish between the wall and a gable roof extension.

**Raw linseed oil.** The crude product processed from flaxseed and usually without much subsequent treatment.

**Reflective insulation.** Sheet material with one or both surfaces of comparatively low heat emissivity, such as aluminum foil. When used in building construction the surfaces face air spaces, reducing the radiation across the air space.

**Reinforcing.** Steel rods or metal fabric placed in concrete slabs, beams, or columns to increase their strength.

**Relative humidity.** The amount of water vapor in the atmosphere, expressed as a percentage of the maximum quantity that could be present at a given temperature. (The actual amount of water vapor that can be held in space increases with the temperature.)

**Resorcinol glue.** A glue that is high in both wet and dry strength and resistant to high temperatures. It is used for gluing lumber or assembly joints that must withstand severe service conditions.

**Return.** The continuation of a molding or finish of any kind in a different direction.

**Ribband.** (*See* Ledgerboard.)

**Ribbon (Girt).** Normally a 1- by 4-inch board let into the studs horizontally to support ceiling or second-floor joists.

**Ridge.** The horizontal line at the junction of the top edges of two sloping roof surfaces.

**Ridge board.** The board placed on edge at the ridge of the roof into which the upper ends of the rafters are fastened.

**Ridge cut.** (*See* Plumb cut.)

**Rise.** The vertical distance through which anything rises, as the rise of a roof or stair.

**Riser.** Each of the vertical boards closing the spaces between the treads of stairways.

**Roll roofing.** Roofing material, composed of fiber and saturated with asphalt, that is supplied in 36-inch-wide rolls with 108 square feet of material. Weights are generally 45- to 90-pounds per roll.

**Roof sheathing.** The boards or sheet material fastened to the roof rafters on which the shingle or other roof covering is laid.

**Roofing.** The material put on a roof to make it wind resistant and waterproof.

**Rubber-emulsion paint.** Paint, the vehicle of which consists of rubber or synthetic rubber dispersed in fine droplets in water.

**Run.** In stairs, the net width of a step or the horizontal distance covered by a flight of stairs.

**Saddle.** Two sloping surfaces meeting in a horizontal ridge, used between the back side of a chimney, or other vertical surface, and a sloping roof.

**Saddle board.** The finish of the ridge on a pitch-roof house. Sometimes called comb board.

**Sand float finish.** Lime mixed with sand, resulting in a textured finish.

**Sapwood.** The outer zone of wood, next to the bark. In the living tree it contains some living cells (the heartwood contains none), as well as dead and dying cells. In most species, it is lighter colored than the heartwood. In all species, it is lacking in decay resistance.

**Sash.** A single light frame containing one or more panes of glass.

**Sash balance.** A device, usually operated by a spring or tensioned weather-stripping, designed to counterbalance double-hung window sash.

**Saturated felt.** A felt that is impregnated with tar or asphalt.

**Sawing, plain.** Lumber sawed regardless of the grain, the log simply squared and sawed to the desired thickness; sometimes called slash- or bastard-sawed.

**Scab.** A short piece of lumber used to splice, or to prevent movement of two pieces.

**Scaffold or staging.** A temporary structure or platform enabling workmen to reach high places.

**Scale.** A short measurement used as a proportionate part of a larger dimension; for example, the scale of a drawing is expressed as ¼ inch = 1 foot.

**Scantling.** Lumber with a cross-section ranging from 2- by 4-inches to 4- by 4-inches.

**Scotia.** A hollow molding used as a part of a cornice and often under the nosing of a stair tread.

**Scratch coat.** The first coat of plaster, which is scratched to form a bond for the second coat.

**Screed.** A small strip of wood, usually the thickness of the plaster coat, used as a guide for plastering.

**Scribing.** Fitting woodwork to an irregular surface. In moldings, cutting the end of one piece to fit the molded face of the other at an interior angle to replace a miter joint.

**Sealer.** A finishing material, either clear or pigmented, that is usually applied directly over uncoated wood for the purpose of sealing the surface.

**Seasoning.** Removing moisture from green wood in order to improve its serviceability.

**Seat cut or plate cut.** The cut at the bottom end of a rafter to allow it to fit upon the plate.

**Seat of a rafter.** The horizontal cut upon the bottom end of a rafter which rests upon the top of the plate.

**Semigloss paint or enamel.** A paint or enamel made with a slight insufficiency of nonvolatile vehicle so that its coating, when dry, has some luster but is not very glossy.

**Shake.** A thick handsplit shingle, resawed to form two shakes; usually edge-grained.

**Shakes.** Imperfections in timber occurring during growth caused by high winds or other adverse conditions of growth.

**Sheathing.** The structural covering, usually wood boards or plywood, used over studs or rafters of a structure. Structural building board is normally used only as wall sheathing.

**Sheathing paper.** (*See* Paper, sheathing.)

**Sheet metal work.** All components of a house employing sheet metal, such as flashing, gutters, and downspouts.

**Shellac.** A transparent coating made by dissolving *lac*, a resinous secretion of the lac bug (a scale insect that thrives in tropical countries, especially India), in alcohol.

**Shingles.** Roof covering of asphalt, asbestos, wood, tile, slate, or other material cut to stock lengths, widths, and thicknesses.

**Shingles, siding.** Various kinds of shingles, such as wood shingles or shakes and nonwood shingles, that are used over sheathing for exterior sidewall covering of a structure.

**Shiplap.** (*See* Lumber, shiplap.)

**Shutter.** Usually lightweight louvered or flush wood or non-wood frames in the form of doors located at each side of a window. Some are made to close over the window for protection; others are fastened to the wall as a decorative device.

**Siding.** The finish covering of the outside wall of a frame building, whether made of horizontal weatherboards, vertical boards with battens, shingles, or other material.

**Siding, bevel (lap siding).** Wedge-shaped boards used as horizontal siding in a lapped pattern. This siding varies in butt thickness from ½- to ¾-inch and in widths up to 12 inches. Normally used over some type of sheathing.

**Siding, Dolly Varden.** Beveled wood siding that is rabbeted on the bottom edge.

**Siding, drop.** Usually ¾-inch thick and 6 and 8 inches wide with tongue-and-groove or shiplap edges. Often used as siding without sheathing in secondary buildings.

**Sill.** The lowest member of the frame of a structure resting on the foundation and supporting the floor joists or the uprights of the wall. Also the member forming the lower side of an opening, as a door sill, window sill, and the like.

**Sill plate.** A horizontal member anchored to a masonry wall.

**Sizing.** Working material to the desired size; also a coating of glue, shellac, or other substance applied to a surface to prepare it for painting or other method of finish.

**Sleeper.** Usually a wood member embedded in concrete, as in a floor, that serves to support and to fasten subfloor or flooring.

**Soffit.** Usually the underside of an overhanging cornice.

**Soil cover (ground cover).** A light covering of plastic film, roll roofing, or similar material used over the soil in crawl spaces of buildings to minimize moisture permeation of the area.

**Sole plate.** Bottom horizontal member of a frame wall.

**Solid bridging.** A solid member placed between adjacent floor joists near the center of the span to prevent joists from twisting.

**Span.** The distance between structural supports such as walls, columns, piers, beams, girders, and trusses.

**Specifications.** The written or printed directions regarding the details of a building or other construction.

**Splice.** Joining of two similar members in a straight line.

**Square.** A unit of measure—100 square feet—usually applied to roofing material. Sidewall coverings are sometimes packed to cover 100 square feet and are sold on that basis.

**Stain, shingle.** A form of oil paint, very thin in consistency, intended for coloring wood with rough surfaces, such as shingles, without forming a coating of significant thickness or gloss.

**Stair carriage.** Supporting member to stair treads. Usually a 2-inch plank notched to receive the treads; sometimes called a "rough horse."

**Stair landing.** (*See* Landing.)

**Stair rise.** (*See* Rise.)

**Stairs, box.** Those built between walls, and usually with no support except the wall.

**Standing finish.** Term applied to the finish of the openings and the base, and all other finish work necessary for the inside.

**STC (Sound Transmission Class).** A measure of sound stoppage of ordinary noise.

**Stile.** An upright framing member in a panel door.

**Stool.** A flat molding fitted over the window sill between jambs and contacting the bottom rail of the lower sash.

**Storm sash or storm window.** An extra window usually placed on the outside of an existing one as additional protection against cold weather.

**Story.** That part of a building between any floor and the floor or roof next above.

**Strip flooring.** Wood flooring consisting of narrow, matched strips.

**String, or stringer.** A timber or other support for cross members in floors or ceilings. In stairs, the support on which the stair treads rest; also stringboard.

**Stucco.** A fine plaster used for interior decoration and fine work; also for rough outside wall coverings.

**Stud.** One of a series of slender wood or metal vertical structural members placed as supporting elements in walls and partitions.

**Subfloor.** Boards or plywood laid on joists over which a finish floor is to be laid.

**Suspended ceiling.** A ceiling system supported by hanging it from the overhead structural framing.

**Tail beam.** A relatively short beam or joist supported in a wall on one end and by a header at the other.

**Termite shield.** A shield, usually of a noncorrodible metal, placed in or on a foundation wall or other mass of masonry or around pipes to prevent passage of termites.

**Threshold.** A strip of wood or metal with beveled edges used over the finish floor and the sill of exterior doors.

**Tie beam (collar beam).** A beam so situated that it ties the principal rafters of a roof together and prevents them from thrusting the plate out of line.

**Timber.** Lumber with cross-section over four- by six-inches, such as posts, sills, and girders.

**Tin shingle.** A small piece of tin used in flashing and repairing a shingle roof.

**To the weather.** A term applied to the projecting of shingles or siding beyond the course above.

**Toenailing.** To drive a nail at a slant with the initial surface in order to permit it to penetrate into a second member.

**Tongued and grooved.** (*See* Dressed and matched.)

**Top plate.** Top horizontal member of a frame wall supporting ceiling joists, rafters, or other members.

**Tread.** The horizontal board in a stairway on which the foot is placed.

**Trim.** The finish materials in a building, such as moldings, applied around openings (window trim, door trim) or at the floor and ceiling of rooms (baseboard, cornice, and other moldings).

**Trimmer.** A beam or joist to which a header is nailed in framing for a chimney, stairway, or other opening.

**Truss.** A frame or jointed structure designed to act as a beam of long span, while each member is usually subjected to longitudinal stress only, either tension or compression.

**Turpentine.** A volatile oil used as thinner in paints and as a solvent in varnishes. Chemically, it is a mixture of terpenes.

**Undercoat.** A coating applied prior to the finishing or top coats of a paint job. It may be the first of two or the second of three coats. In some usage of the word it may become synonymous with priming coat.

**Underlayment.** A material placed under finish coverings, such as flooring or shingles, to provide a smooth, even surface for applying the finish.

**Valley.** The internal angle formed by the junction of two sloping sides of a roof.

**Vapor barrier.** Material used to retard the movement of water vapor into walls and prevent condensation in them. Usually considered as having a perm value of less than 1.0. Applied separately over the warm side of exposed walls or as a part of batt or blanket insulation.

**Varnish.** A thickened preparation of drying oil or drying oil and resin suitable for spreading on surfaces to form continuous, transparent coatings, or for mixing with pigments to make enamels.

**Vehicle.** The liquid portion of a finishing material; it consists of the binder (nonvolatile) and volatile thinners.

**Veneer.** A thin layer or sheet of wood cut on a veneer machine.

*Rotary-cut veneer.* Veneer cut in a lathe which rotates a log or bolt, chucked in the center, against a knife.

*Sawed veneer.* Veneer produced by sawing.

*Sliced veneer.* Veneer that is sliced off a log, bolt, or flitch with a knife.

**Vent.** A pipe or duct that allows flow of air as an inlet or outlet.

**Verge boards.** The boards that serve as the eaves finish on the gable end of a building.

**Vermiculite.** A mineral closely related to mica, with the property of expanding on heating to form lightweight material with insulation quality. Used as bulk insulation and also as aggregate in insulating and acoustical plaster and in insulating concrete floors.

**Vestibule.** An entrance to a house, usually enclosed.

**Volatile thinner.** A liquid that evaporates readily and is used to thin or reduce the consistency of finishes without altering the relative volumes of pigments and nonvolatile vehicles.

**Wainscoting.** Matched boarding or panel work covering the lower portion of a wall.

**Wale.** A horizontal beam.

**Wane.** Bark, or lack of wood from any cause, on edge or corner of a piece of wood.

**Wash.** The slant upon a sill, capping, and the like, to allow the water to run off easily.

**Water-repellent preservative.** A liquid designed to penetrate into wood and impart water repellency and a moderate preservative protection. It is used for millwork, such as sash and frames, and is usually applied by dipping.

**Water table.** The finish at the bottom of a house which carries water away from the foundation.

**Weatherstrip.** Narrow or jamb-width sections of thin metal or other material to prevent infiltration of air and moisture around windows and doors. Compression weather-stripping prevents air infiltration, provides tension, and acts as a counterbalance.

**Wind ("i" pronounced as in "kind").** A term used to describe the surface of a board when twisted (winding) or when resting upon two diagonally opposite corners, if laid upon a perfectly flat surface.

**Wood preservative.** (*See* Preservative.)

**Wood rays.** Strips of cells extending radially within a tree and varying in height from a few cells in some species to four inches or more in oak. The rays serve primarily to store food and to transport it horizontally in the tree.

**Wooden brick.** Piece of seasoned wood, made the size of a brick, and laid where it is necessary to provide a nailing space in masonry walls.

**Workability.** The degree of ease and smoothness of cut obtainable with hand or machine tools.

**Yard lumber.** (*See* Lumber.)

# Standard Lumber Abbreviations

The following standard lumber abbreviations are in common use in contracts and other documents arising in the transactions of purchase and sale of lumber.

AD—air-dried.
A. d. f.—after deducting freight.
A. l.—all lengths.
ALS—American lumber standards.
Av. or avg.—average.
Av. w.—average width.
Av. l.—average length.
A. w.—all widths.
B1S—beaded one side.
B2S—beaded two sides.
BBS—box bark strips.
B&B or B & Btr.—B and better.
B&S—beams and stringers.
Bd.—board.
Bd. ft.—board-foot (or board-feet); that is, an area of 1 square foot by 1 inch thick.
Bdl.—bundle.
Bdl. bk. s.—bundle bark strips.
Bev.—bevel.
B/L—bill of lading.
Bm.—board measure.
Btr.—better.
CB1S—center bead one side.
CB2S—center bead two sides.
CF—cost and freight.
CG2E—center groove two edges.
CIF—cost, insurance, and freight.
CIFE—cost, insurance, freight, and exchange.
Clg.—ceiling.
Clr.—clear.
CM—center matched; that is, the tongued-and-grooved joints are worked along the center of the edges of the piece.
Com.—common.
CS—calking seam.
Csg.—casing.

Ctg.—crating.

Cu. ft.—cubic foot or feet.

CV1S—center V one side.

CV2S—center V two sides.

DB. Clg.—double-beaded ceiling (E&CB1S).

DB. Part.—double-beaded partition (E&CB2S).

DET—Double end trimmed.

D&CM—dressed (1 or 2 sides) and center matched.

D&H—dressed and headed; that is, dressed 1 or 2 sides and worked to tongued-and-grooved joints on both the edge and the ends.

D&M—dressed and matched; that is, dressed 1 or 2 sides and tongued and grooved on the edges. The match may be center or standard.

D&SM—dressed (1 or 2 sides) and standard matched.

D2S&CM—dressed two sides and center matched.

D2S&M—dressed two sides and (center or standard) matched.

D2S&SM—dressed two sides and standard matched.

Dim.—dimension.

Dkg.—decking.

D/S or D/Sdg.—drop siding.

E—edge.

EB1S—edge bead one side.

EB2S—edge bead two sides.

E&CB1S—edge and center bead 1 side; surfaced 1 or 2 sides and with a longitudinal edge and center bead on a surfaced face.

E&CB2S—edge and center bead 2 sides; all 4 sides surfaced and with a longitudinal edge and center bead on the 2 faces.

ECM—ends center matched.

E&CV1S—edge and center V 1 side; surface 1 or 2 sides and with a longitudinal edge and center V-shaped groove on a surfaced face.

E&CV2S—edge and center V two sides.

EG—edge (vertical) grain.

EE—eased edges.

EM—end matched—either center or standard.

ESM—ends standard matched.

EV1S—edge V one side.

EV2S—edge V two sides.

Fac.—factory.

FAS—First and Seconds—a combined grade of the two upper grades of hardwoods.

FAS—free alongside (named vessel).

F. bk.—flat back.

FBM—foot or feet board measure.

Fcty.—factory (lumber).

FG—flat (slash) grain.

Flg.—flooring.

FOB—free on board (named point).

FOHC—free of heart center or centers.

F. o. k.—free of knots.

Frm.—framing.

Frt.—freight.

Ft.—foot or feet.   Also one accent (').

Feet b. m.—feet board measure.

Feet s. m.—feet surface measure.

GM—grade marked.

G/R or G/Rfg.—grooved roofing.

HB—hollow back.

Hdl.—handle (stock).
Hdwd.—hardwood.
H&M—hit and miss.
H or M—hit or miss.
Hrt.—heart.
Hrt. CC—heart cubical content.
Hrt. FA—heart facial area.
Hrt. G—heart girth.
Hrtwd.—heartwood.
1s&2s.—Ones and Twos—a combined grade of the hardwood grades of Firsts and Seconds.
In.—inch or inches.  Also two accent marks ('').
J&P—joists and planks.
KD—kiln-dried.
K. d.—knocked down.
Lbr.—lumber.
LCL—less than carload.
LFT or LIN. ft.—linear foot (or feet); that is 12 inches.
Lgr.—longer.
Lgth.—length.
Lin.—Linear.
Lng.—lining.
LR.—log run.
Lr. MCO—log run, mill culls out.
Lth.—lath.
M—thousand.
MBM—thousand (feet) board measure.
MC—moisture content.
MCO—mill culls out.
Merch.—merchantable.
M. l.—mixed lengths.
Mldg.—molding.
MR—mill run.
M. s. m.—thousand (feet) surface measure.
M. w.—mixed widths.
No.—number.
N1E—nosed one edge.
N2E—nosed two edges.
Og.—Ogee.
Ord.—order.
P.—planed.
Par.—paragraph.
Part.—partition.
Pat.—pattern.

Pc.—piece.
Pcs.—Pieces.
PE—plain end.
Pky.—pecky.
Pln.—plain, as plainsawed.
PO—purchase order.
P&T—post and timbers.
Qtd.—quartered—when referring to hardwoods.
Rdm.—random.
Reg.—regular.
Res.—resawed.
Rfg.—roofing.

Rfrs.—roofers.
Rgh.—rough.
Rip.—ripped.
R/L—random lengths.
Rnd.—round.
R. Sdg.—rustic siding.
R/W—random widths.
R/W&L—random widths and lengths.
S&E—surfaced 1 side and 1 edge.
S1E—surfaced one edge.
S2E—surfaced two edges.
S1S—surfaced one side.
S2S—surfaced two sides.
S1S1E—surfaced 1 side and 1 edge.
S2S1E—surfaced 2 sides and 1 edge.
S1S2E—surfaced 1 side and 2 edges.
S4S—surfaced four sides.
S4S&CS—surfaced four sides with a calking seam on each edge.
S&M—surfaced and matched; that is, surfaced 1 or 2 sides and tongued and grooved on the edges. The match may be center or standard.
S2S&SM—surfaced two sides and standard matched.
S2S&CM—surfaced two sides and center matched.
S2S&M—surfaced two sides and center or standard matched.
S2S&S/L—surfaced two sides and shiplapped.
Sap.—sapwood.
SB—standard bead.
Sd.—seasoned.
Sdg.—siding.
Sel.—select.
SE Sdg.—square-edge siding.
SE&S—square edge and sound.
S. f.—surface foot; that is, an area of 1 square foot.
Sftwd.—softwood.
Sh. D.—shipping dry.
Ship.—shiplap.
S. m.—surface measure.
SM—standard matched.
Smkd.—smoked (dried).
Smk. stnd.—smoke stained.
S. n. d.—sap no defect.
Snd.—sound.
Sq.—square.
Sqrs.—squares.
Std.—standard.
Stnd.—stained.
Stk.—stock.
SW—sound wormy.
T&G—tongued and grooved.
TB&S—top, bottom, and sides.
Tbrs.—timbers.
Thickness—4/4, 5/4, 6/4, 8/4, etc.=1 inch, 1¼ inches, 1½ inches, 2 inches, etc.
V1S—V 1 side; that is, a longitudinal V-shaped groove on 1 face of a piece of lumber.

V2S—V on 2 sides; that is, a longitudinal V-shaped groove on 2 faces of a piece of lumber.

VG—vertical grain.
W. a. l.—wider, all lengths.
Wth.—width.
Wdr.—wider.
Wt.—weight.

# Woodworking Symbols

## a. Architectural

Tile _____

Earth _____

Plaster _____

Sheet metal _____

Built-in cabinet _____

Outside door: Brick wall _____

                    Frame wall _____

Inside door: Frame wall _____

Brick _____

Firebrick _____

Concrete _____

Cast concrete block _____

Insulation: Loose fill _____

                  Board or quilts _____

Cut stone _____

Ashlar _____

Shingles (siding) _____

Wood, rough _____

Wood, finished _____

Cased or arched openings _____

Single casement window _____

Double-hung windows_____

Double casement window_____

### b. Plumbing.

Bathtubs:

    Corner_____

    Free standing_____

Floor drain_____

Shower drain_____

Hot-water tank_____

Grease trap_____

Hose bibb or sill cock____

Lavatories:

    Pedestal_____

    Wall-hung_____

    Corner_____

Toilets:

    Tank_____

    Flush valve_____

Urinals:

    Stall-type_____

    Wall-hung_____

Laundry trays_____

Built-in shower_____

Shower_____

Sinks:

    Single drain board.

    Double drain board.

### c. Electrical

Pull switch_____

Single-pole switch_____

Double-pole switch_____

Triple-pole switch_____

Buzzer_____

Floor outlet_____

Bell_____

Drop cord_____

Ceiling outlet_____

Wall bracket_____

Single convenience outlet _____

Double convenience outlet _____

Ceiling outlet, gas & electric _____

Motor_____

Light outlet with wiring and switches indicated_____

# The Metric System

## METRIC EQUIVALENTS OF FRACTIONS, INCHES, AND FEET

| Measurement in Inches | Millimeters | Centimeters | Measurement in Inches | Millimeters | Centimeters |
|---|---|---|---|---|---|
| 1/64 | .39688 | .039688 | 5/8 | 15.87500 | 1.587500 |
| 1/32 | .79375 | .079375 | 41/64 | 16.27188 | 1.627188 |
| 3/64 | 1.19063 | .119063 | 21/32 | 16.66875 | 1.666875 |
| 1/16 | 1.58750 | .158750 | 43/64 | 17.06563 | 1.706563 |
| 5/64 | 1.98438 | .198438 | 11/16 | 17.46250 | 1.746250 |
| 3/32 | 2.38125 | .238125 | 45/64 | 17.85938 | 1.785938 |
| 7/64 | 2.77813 | .277813 | 23/32 | 18.25625 | 1.825625 |
| 1/8 | 3.17500 | .317500 | 47/64 | 18.65313 | 1.865313 |
| 9/64 | 3.57188 | .356188 | 3/4 | 19.05000 | 1.905000 |
| 5/32 | 3.96870 | .396870 | 49/64 | 19.44688 | 1.944688 |
| 11/64 | 4.36563 | .436563 | 25/32 | 19.84375 | 1.984375 |
| 3/16 | 4.76250 | .476250 | 51/64 | 20.24063 | 2.024063 |
| 13/64 | 5.15938 | .515938 | 13/16 | 20.63750 | 2.063750 |
| 7/32 | 5.55625 | .555625 | 53/64 | 21.03438 | 2.103438 |
| 15/64 | 5.95313 | .595313 | 27/32 | 21.43125 | 2.143125 |
| 1/4 | 6.35000 | .635000 | 55/64 | 21.82810 | 2.182810 |
| 17/64 | 6.74688 | .674688 | 7/8 | 22.22500 | 2.222500 |
| 9/32 | 7.14375 | .714375 | 57/64 | 22.62188 | 2.262188 |
| 19/64 | 7.54063 | .754063 | 29/32 | 23.01875 | 2.301875 |
| 5/16 | 7.93750 | .793750 | 59/64 | 23.41563 | 2.341563 |
| 21/64 | 8.33438 | .833438 | 15/16 | 23.81250 | 2.381250 |
| 11/32 | 8.73125 | .873125 | 61/64 | 24.20930 | 2.420930 |
| 23/64 | 9.12813 | .912813 | 31/32 | 24.60625 | 2.460625 |
| 3/8 | 9.52500 | .952500 | 63/64 | 25.00313 | 2.500313 |
| 25/64 | 9.92188 | .992188 | 1 | 25.40000 | 2.540000 |
| 13/32 | 10.31875 | 1.031875 | 2 | 50.80000 | 5.080000 |
| 27/64 | 10.71563 | 1.071563 | 3 | 76.20000 | 7.620000 |
| 7/16 | 11.11250 | 1.111250 | 4 | 101.60000 | 10.160000 |
| 29/64 | 11.50938 | 1.150938 | 5 | 127.00000 | 12.700000 |
| 15/32 | 11.90625 | 1.190625 | 6 | 152.40000 | 15.240000 |
| 31/64 | 12.30313 | 1.230313 | 7 | 177.80000 | 17.780000 |
| 1/2 | 12.70000 | 1.270000 | 8 | 203.20000 | 20.320000 |
| 33/64 | 13.09688 | 1.309688 | 9 | 228.60000 | 22.860000 |
| 17/32 | 13.49375 | 1.349375 | 10 | 254.00000 | 25.400000 |
| 35/64 | 13.89063 | 1.389063 | 11 | 279.40000 | 27.940000 |
| 9/16 | 14.28750 | 1.428750 | 12 (1 ft.) | 304.80000 | 30.480000 |
| 37/64 | 14.68438 | 1.468438 | 24 (2 ft.) | 609.60000 | 60.960000 |
| 19/32 | 15.08125 | 1.508125 | 36 (3 ft. or 1 yd.) | 914.40000 | 91.440000 |
| 39/64 | 15.47813 | 1.547.813 | | | |

APPROXIMATE CONVERSION FACTORS FOR CHANGING

FROM CUSTOMARY UNITS TO METRIC UNITS.

| Symbol | When You Know | Multiply by | To Find | Symbol |
|--------|---------------|-------------|---------|--------|
| **LENGTH** | | | | |
| in | inches | 2.54 | centimeters | cm |
| ft | feet | 30 | centimeters | cm |
| yd | yards | 0.9 | meters | m |
| mi | miles | 1.6 | kilometers | km |
| **AREA** | | | | |
| $in^2$ | square inches | 6.5 | square centimeters | $cm^2$ |
| $ft^2$ | square feet | 0.09 | square meters | $m^2$ |
| $yd^2$ | square yards | 0.8 | square meters | $m^2$ |
| $mi^2$ | square miles | 2.6 | square kilometers | $km^2$ |
| | acres | 0.4 | hectares | ha |
| **MASS (weight)** | | | | |
| oz | ounces | 28 | grams | g |
| lb | pounds | 0.45 | kilograms | kg |
| | short tons (2000 lb) | 0.9 | tonnes | t |
| **VOLUME** | | | | |
| tsp | teaspoons | 5 | milliliters | ml |
| Tbsp | tablespoons | 15 | milliliters | ml |
| fl oz | fluid ounces | 30 | milliliters | ml |
| c | cups | 0.24 | liters | l |
| pt | pints | 0.47 | liters | l |
| qt | quarts | 0.95 | liters | l |
| gal | gallons | 3.8 | liters | l |
| $ft^3$ | cubic feet | 0.03 | cubic meters | $m^3$ |
| $yd^3$ | cubic yards | 0.76 | cubic meters | $m^3$ |
| **TEMPERATURE (exact)** | | | | |
| °F | Fahrenheit temperature | 5/9 (after subtracting 32) | Celsius temperature | °C |

APPROXIMATE CONVERSION FACTORS FOR CHANGING FROM
COMMONLY-USED METRIC UNITS TO CUSTOMARY UNITS.

| Symbol | When You Know | Multiply by | To Find | Symbol |
|--------|---------------|-------------|---------|--------|
| | | LENGTH | | |
| mm | millimeters | 0.04 | inches | in |
| cm | centimeters | 0.4 | inches | in |
| m | meters | 3.3 | feet | ft |
| m | meters | 1.1 | yards | yd |
| km | kilometers | 0.6 | miles | mi |
| | | AREA | | |
| $cm^2$ | square centimeters | 0.16 | square inches | $in^2$ |
| $m^2$ | square meters | 1.2 | square yards | $yd^2$ |
| $km^2$ | square kilometers | 0.4 | square miles | $mi^2$ |
| ha | hectares (10,000 $m^2$) | 2.5 | acres | |
| | | MASS (weight) | | |
| g | grams | 0.035 | ounces | oz |
| kg | kilograms | 2.2 | pounds | lb |
| t | tonnes (1000 kg) | 1.1 | short tons | |
| | | VOLUME | | |
| ml | milliliters | 0.03 | fluid ounces | fl oz |
| l | liters | 2.1 | pints | pt |
| l | liters | 1.06 | quarts | qt |
| l | liters | 0.26 | gallons | gal |
| $m^3$ | cubic meters | 35 | cubic feet | $ft^3$ |
| $m^3$ | cubic meters | 1.3 | cubic yards | $yd^3$ |
| | | TEMPERATURE (exact) | | |
| °C | Celsius temperature | 9/5 (then add 32) | Fahrenheit temperature | °F |

# Index